NEGMA!

20

Ken Akamatsu

TRANSLATED AND ADAPTED BY
Ikoi Hiroe

LETTERING AND RETOUCH BY
Steve Palmer

DEL REY

BALLANTINE BOOKS • NEW YORK

Negima! volume 20 is a work of fiction. Names, characters, places, and incidents are the products of the author's imagination or are used fictitiously. Any resemblance to actual events, locales, or persons, living or dead, is entirely coincidental.

A Del Rey Manga/Kodansha Trade Paperback Original

Published in the United States by Del Rey, an imprint of The Random House Publishing Group, a division of Random House, Inc., New York.

DEL REY is a registered trademark and the Del Rey colophon is a trademark of Random House, Inc.

Publication rights arranged through Kodansha Ltd.

First published in Japan in 2007 by Kodansha Ltd., Tokyo

ISBN 978-0-345-50527-9

Printed in the United States of America

www.delreymanga.com

9 8 7 6 5 4 3 2 1

Translator/adapter: Ikoi Hiroe
Lettering and retouch: Steve Palmer

Honorifics Explained

Throughout the Del Rey Manga books, you will find Japanese honorifics left intact in the translations. For those not familiar with how the Japanese use honorifics and, more important, how they differ from American honorifics, we present this brief overview.

Politeness has always been a critical facet of Japanese culture. Ever since the feudal era, when Japan was a highly stratified society, use of honorifics—which can be defined as polite speech that indicates relationship or status—has played an essential role in the Japanese language. When addressing someone in Japanese, an honorific usually takes the form of a suffix attached to one's name (example: "Asuna-san"), is used as a title at the end of one's name, or appears in place of the name itself (example: "Negi-sensei," or simply "Sensei!").

Honorifics can be expressions of respect or endearment. In the context of manga and anime, honorifics give insight into the nature of the relationship between characters. Many English translations leave out these important honorifics and therefore distort the feel of the original Japanese. Because Japanese honorifics contain nuances that English honorifics lack, it is our policy at Del Rey not to translate them. Here, instead, is a guide to some of the honorifics you may encounter in Del Rey Manga.

-*san*:   This is the most common honorific and is equivalent to Mr., Miss, Ms., or Mrs. It is the all-purpose honorific and can be used in any situation where politeness is required.

-*sama*:   This is one level higher than "-san" and is used to confer great respect.

-*dono*:   This comes from the word "tono," which means "lord." It is an even higher level than "-sama" and confers utmost respect.

-*kun*:   This suffix is used at the end of boys' names to express familiarity or endearment. It is also sometimes used by men among friends, or when addressing someone younger or of a lower station.

-chan: This is used to express endearment, mostly toward girls. It is also used for little boys, pets, and even among lovers. It gives a sense of childish cuteness.

Bōzu: This is an informal way to refer to a boy, similar to the English terms "kid" and "squirt."

Sempai/Senpai: This title suggests that the addressee is one's senior in a group or organization. It is most often used in a school setting, where underclassmen refer to their upperclassmen as "sempai." It can also be used in the workplace, such as when a newer employee addresses an employee who has seniority in the company.

Kohai: This is the opposite of "sempai" and is used toward underclassmen in school or newcomers in the workplace. It connotes that the addressee is of a lower station.

Sensei: Literally meaning "one who has come before," this title is used for teachers, doctors, or masters of any profession or art.

Anesan (or *nesan*): A generic term for a girl, usually older, that means sister.

Ojōsama: A way of referring to the daughter or sister of someone with high political or social status.

-[blank]: This is usually forgotten in these lists, but it is perhaps the most significant difference between Japanese and English. The lack of honorific means that the speaker has permission to address the person in a very intimate way. Usually, only family, spouses, or very close friends have this kind of permission. Known as *yobisute*, it can be gratifying when someone who has earned the intimacy starts to call one by one's name without an honorific. But when that intimacy hasn't been earned, it can be very insulting.

A Word from the Author

Negima! is finally heading into Volume 20. Starting with this volume, his childhood friend enters the picture... which shakes things up dramatically! We also get to see the results of the Negi Party's training!

And you can expect even more excitement in the *next* volume!

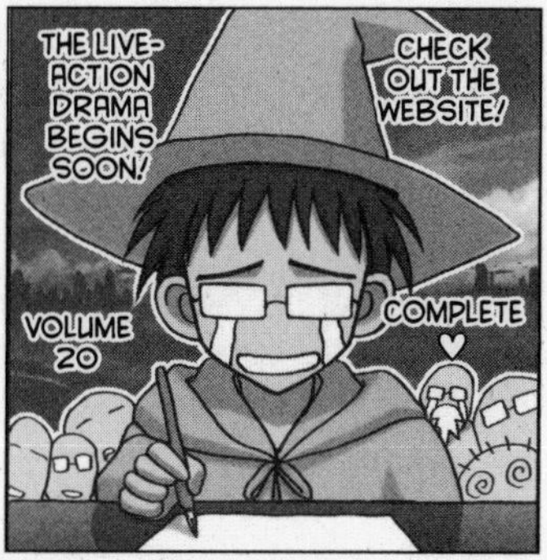
CHECK OUT THE WEBSITE!
THE LIVE-ACTION DRAMA BEGINS SOON!
COMPLETE ♥
VOLUME 20

The *Negima!* live-action TV series is making its debut! All heck will break loose as thirty-one girls compete to capture Negi's (played by an adorable thirteen-year-old girl) affection. And keep an eye out for Takamichi and Shizuna-Sensei! For more information, visit my website!

Ken Akamatsu's website
http://www.ailove.net

20

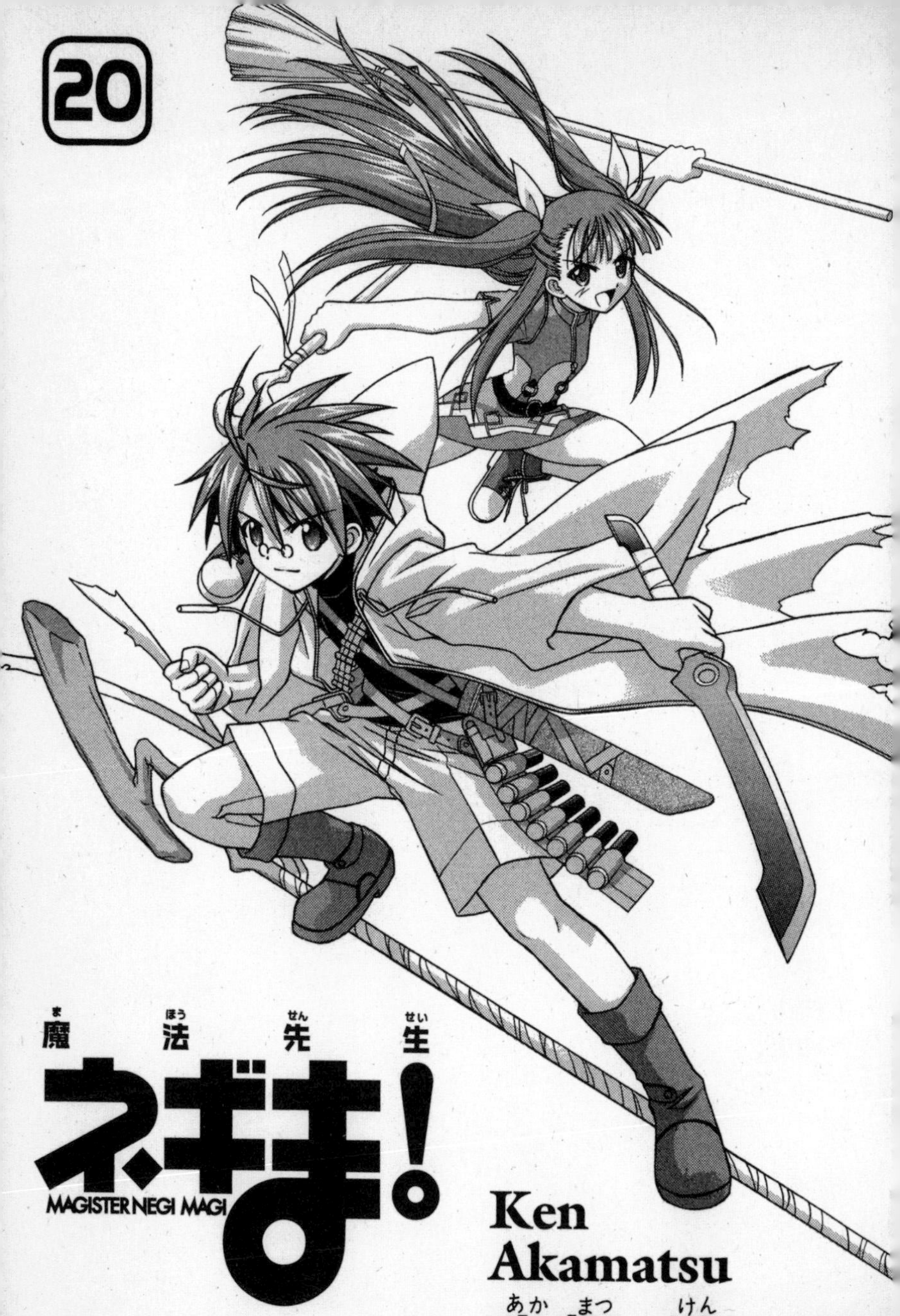

魔法先生ネギま!

MAGISTER NEGI MAGI

Ken Akamatsu

赤松 健

CONTENTS

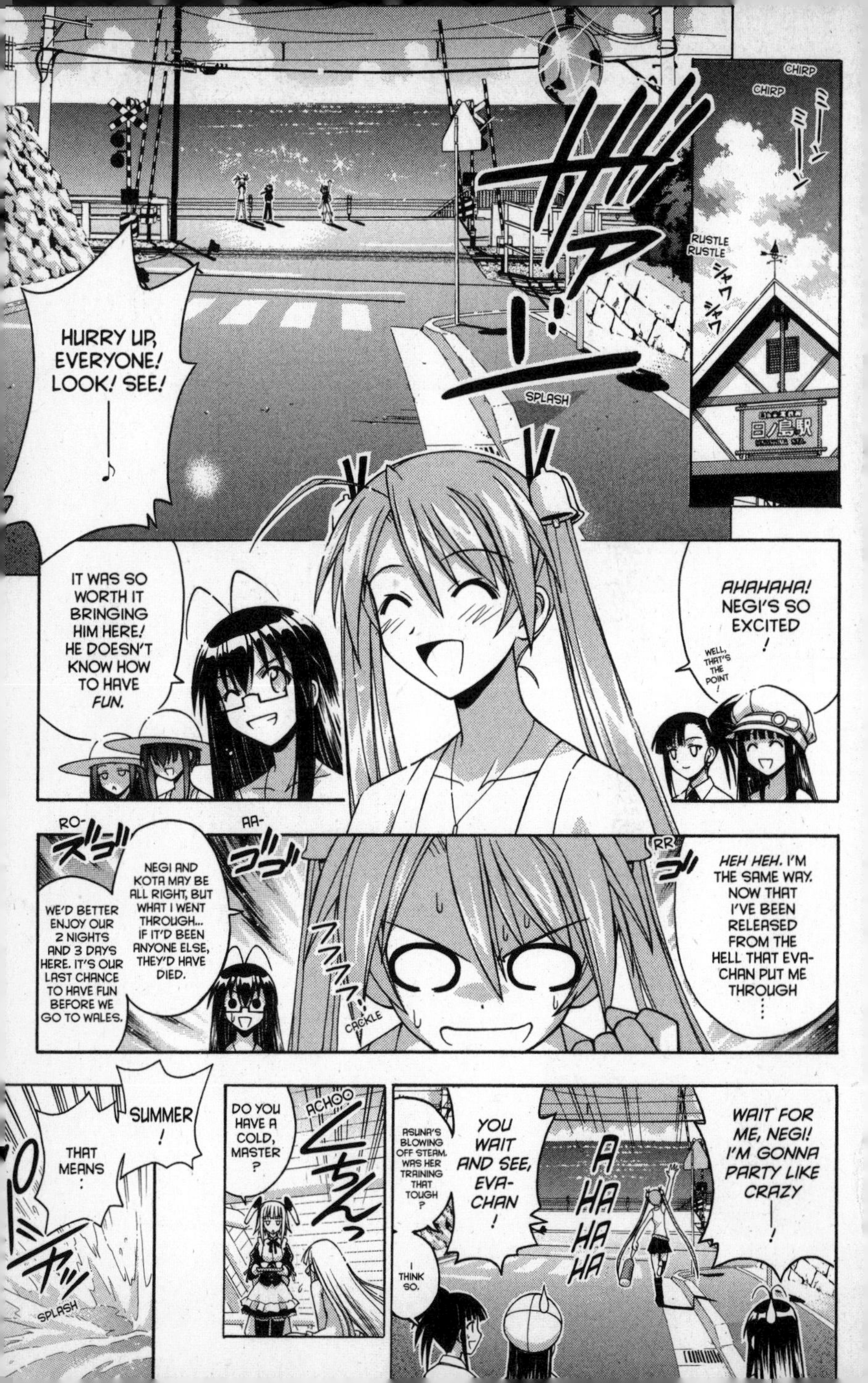
CHIRP
CHIRP
ミーン
ミーン
RUSTLE RUSTLE
シャワ シャワ
日ノ島駅
ザザァー
SPLASH
HURRY UP, EVERYONE! LOOK! SEE! ♪
AHAHAHA! NEGI'S SO EXCITED!
WELL, THAT'S THE POINT!
IT WAS SO WORTH IT BRINGING HIM HERE! HE DOESN'T KNOW HOW TO HAVE *FUN*.
RR
ゴ
HEH HEH. I'M THE SAME WAY. NOW THAT I'VE BEEN RELEASED FROM THE HELL THAT EVA-CHAN PUT ME THROUGH.....
AA-
ゴゴ
RO-
ズゴゴ
NEGI AND KOTA MAY BE ALL RIGHT, BUT WHAT I WENT THROUGH... IF IT'D BEEN ANYONE ELSE, THEY'D HAVE DIED.
WE'D BETTER ENJOY OUR 2 NIGHTS AND 3 DAYS HERE. IT'S OUR LAST CHANCE TO HAVE FUN BEFORE WE GO TO WALES.
ククク
CACKLE
WAIT FOR ME, NEGI! I'M GONNA PARTY LIKE CRAZY!
A HA HA HA HA
YOU WAIT AND SEE, EVA-CHAN!
ASUNA'S BLOWING OFF STEAM. WAS HER TRAINING THAT TOUGH?
I THINK SO.
ACHOO
くちんっ
DO YOU HAVE A COLD, MASTER?
SUMMER!
THAT MEANS:
パシャッ
SPLASH

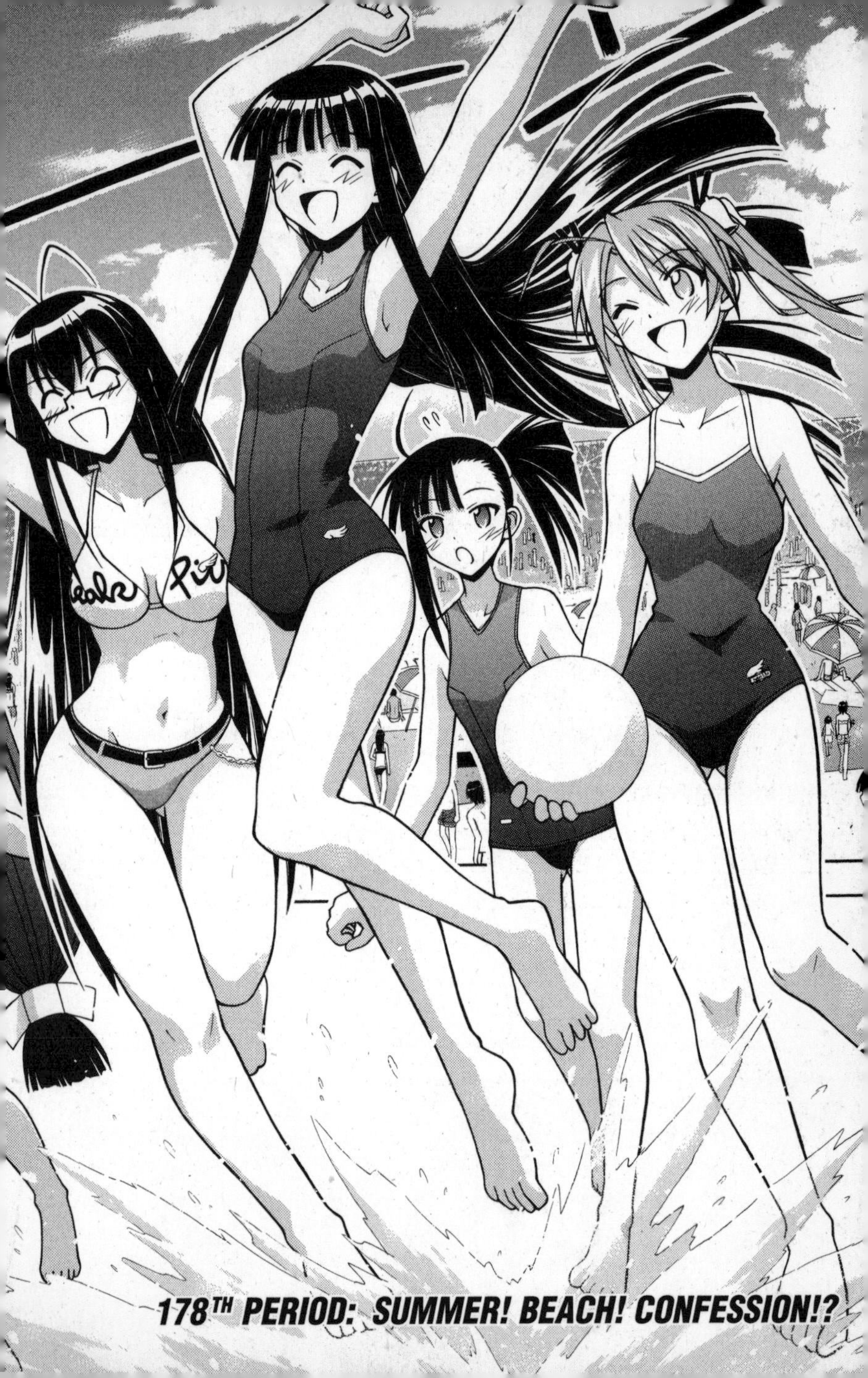

178TH PERIOD: SUMMER! BEACH! CONFESSION!?

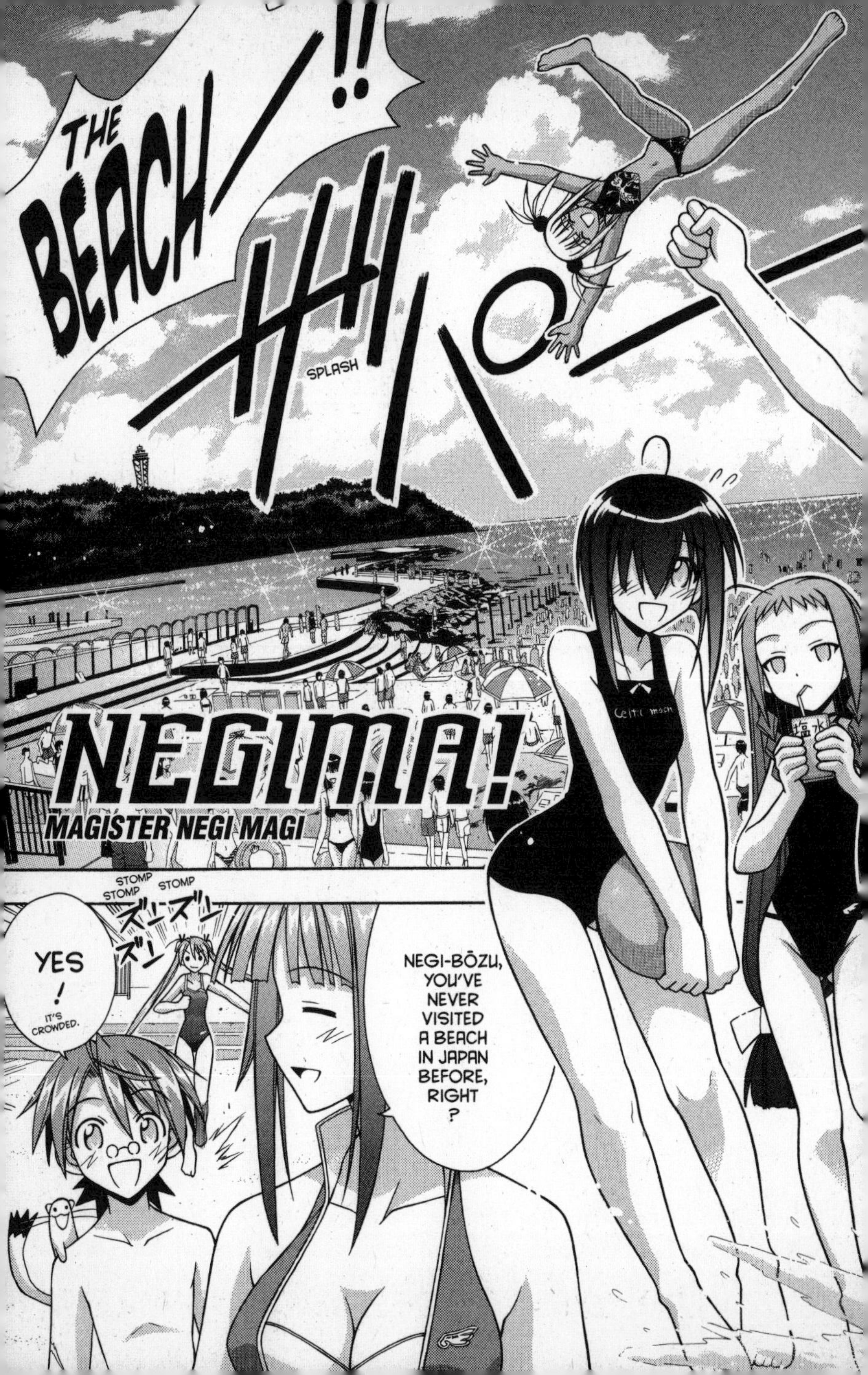

THE BEACH—!!
SPLASH
NEGIMA!
MAGISTER NEGI MAGI
NEGI-BŌZU, YOU'VE NEVER VISITED A BEACH IN JAPAN BEFORE, RIGHT?
STOMP STOMP STOMP
ズンズン ズン
YES! IT'S CROWDED.

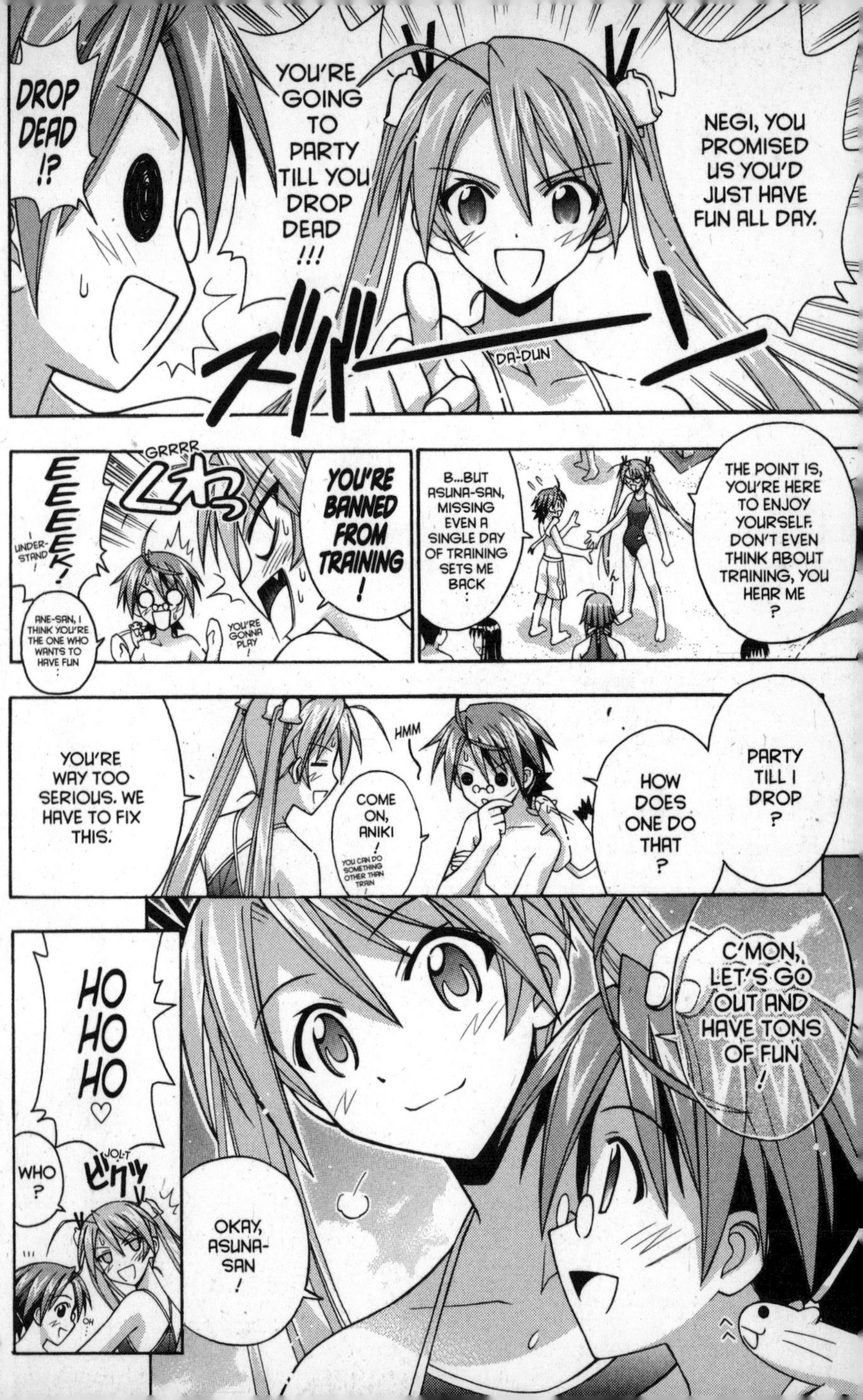
NEGI, YOU PROMISED US YOU'D JUST HAVE FUN ALL DAY.
YOU'RE GOING TO PARTY TILL YOU DROP DEAD !!!
DA-DUN
DROP DEAD !?
THE POINT IS, YOU'RE HERE TO ENJOY YOURSELF. DON'T EVEN THINK ABOUT TRAINING, YOU HEAR ME ?
B...BUT ASUNA-SAN, MISSING EVEN A SINGLE DAY OF TRAINING SETS ME BACK
YOU'RE BANNED FROM TRAINING !
YOU'RE GONNA PLAY !
GRRRR
EEEEEK!
I UNDERSTAND !
ANE-SAN, I THINK YOU'RE THE ONE WHO WANTS TO HAVE FUN
PARTY TILL I DROP ?
HOW DOES ONE DO THAT ?
HMM
COME ON, ANIKI !
YOU CAN DO SOMETHING OTHER THAN TRAIN
YOU'RE WAY TOO SERIOUS. WE HAVE TO FIX THIS.
C'MON, LET'S GO OUT AND HAVE TONS OF FUN !
OKAY, ASUNA-SAN !
HO HO HO ♡
JOLT
WHO ?
OH

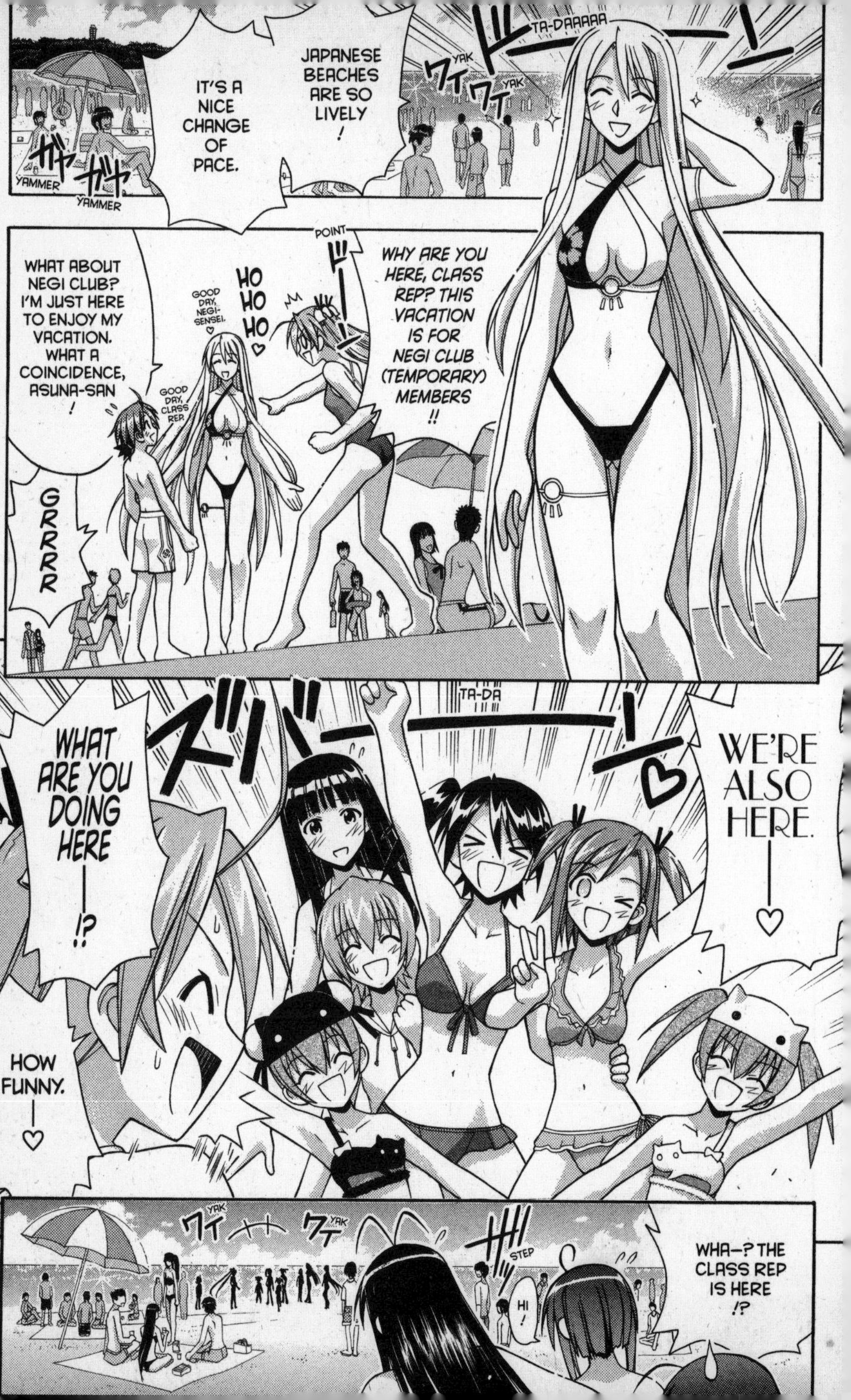

TA-DAAAAA
YAK YAK
JAPANESE BEACHES ARE SO LIVELY!
IT'S A NICE CHANGE OF PACE.
YAMMER YAMMER
WHY ARE YOU HERE, CLASS REP? THIS VACATION IS FOR NEGI CLUB (TEMPORARY) MEMBERS!!
POINT
HO HO HO ♡
GOOD DAY, NEGI-SENSEI.
GOOD DAY, CLASS REP.
WHAT ABOUT NEGI CLUB? I'M JUST HERE TO ENJOY MY VACATION. WHAT A COINCIDENCE, ASUNA-SAN!
GRRRR
TA-DA
WE'RE ALSO HERE. ♡
WHAT ARE YOU DOING HERE!?
HOW FUNNY. ♡
WHA-? THE CLASS REP IS HERE!?
STEP
HI!
YAK YAK

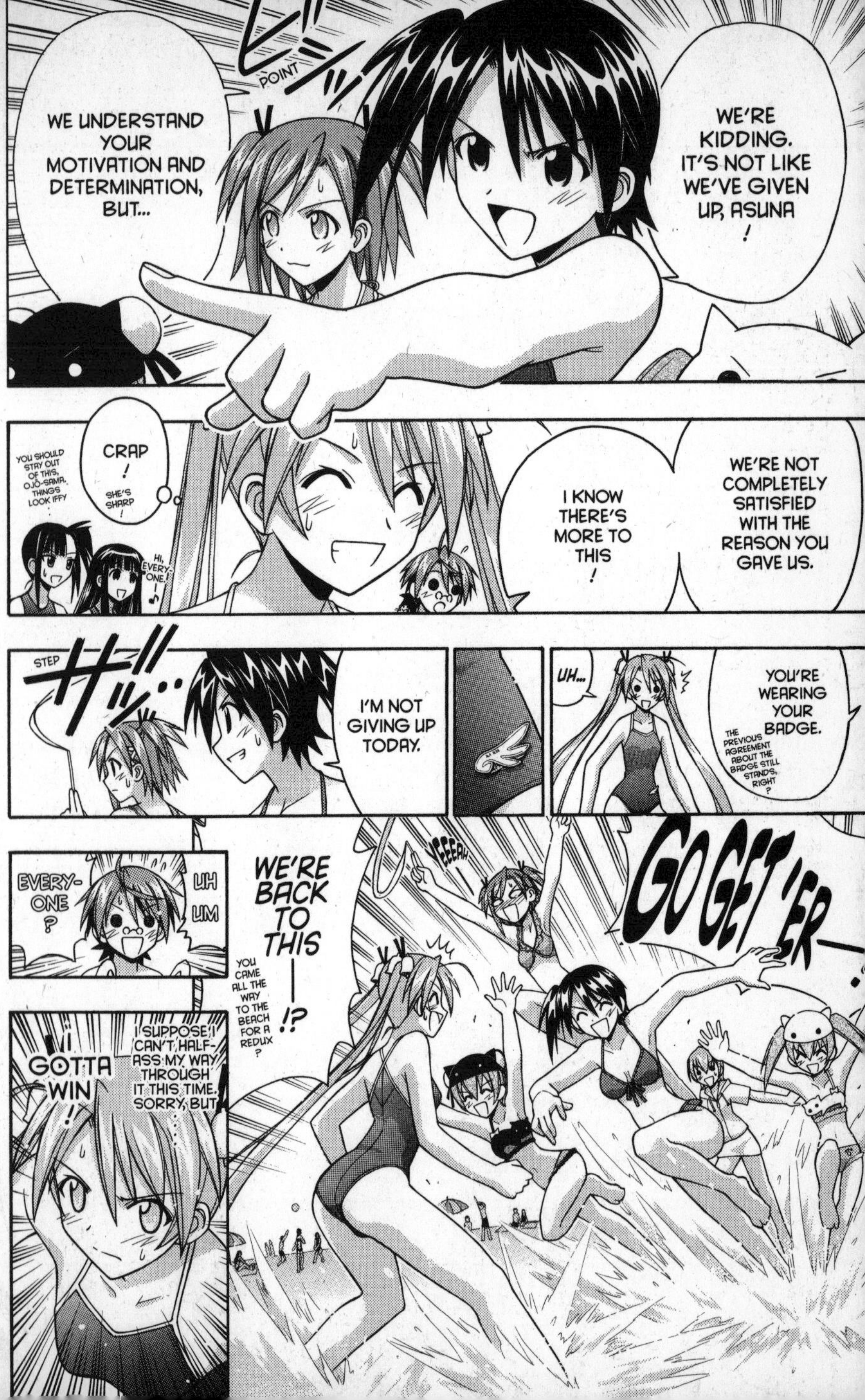
WE'RE KIDDING. IT'S NOT LIKE WE'VE GIVEN UP, ASUNA!
POINT
WE UNDERSTAND YOUR MOTIVATION AND DETERMINATION, BUT...
WE'RE NOT COMPLETELY SATISFIED WITH THE REASON YOU GAVE US.
I KNOW THERE'S MORE TO THIS!
CRAP!
SHE'S SHARP!
HI, EVERYONE!
YOU SHOULD STAY OUT OF THIS, OJŌ-SAMA. THINGS LOOK IFFY.
YOU'RE WEARING YOUR BADGE.
THE PREVIOUS AGREEMENT ABOUT THE BADGE STILL STANDS, RIGHT?
UH...
I'M NOT GIVING UP TODAY.
STEP
GO GET 'ER—!
YEEEAAH
WE'RE BACK TO THIS—!?
YOU CAME ALL THE WAY TO THE BEACH FOR A REDUX?
UH
UM
EVERYONE?
I SUPPOSE I CAN'T HALF-ASS MY WAY THROUGH IT THIS TIME. SORRY, BUT...
I GOTTA WIN!

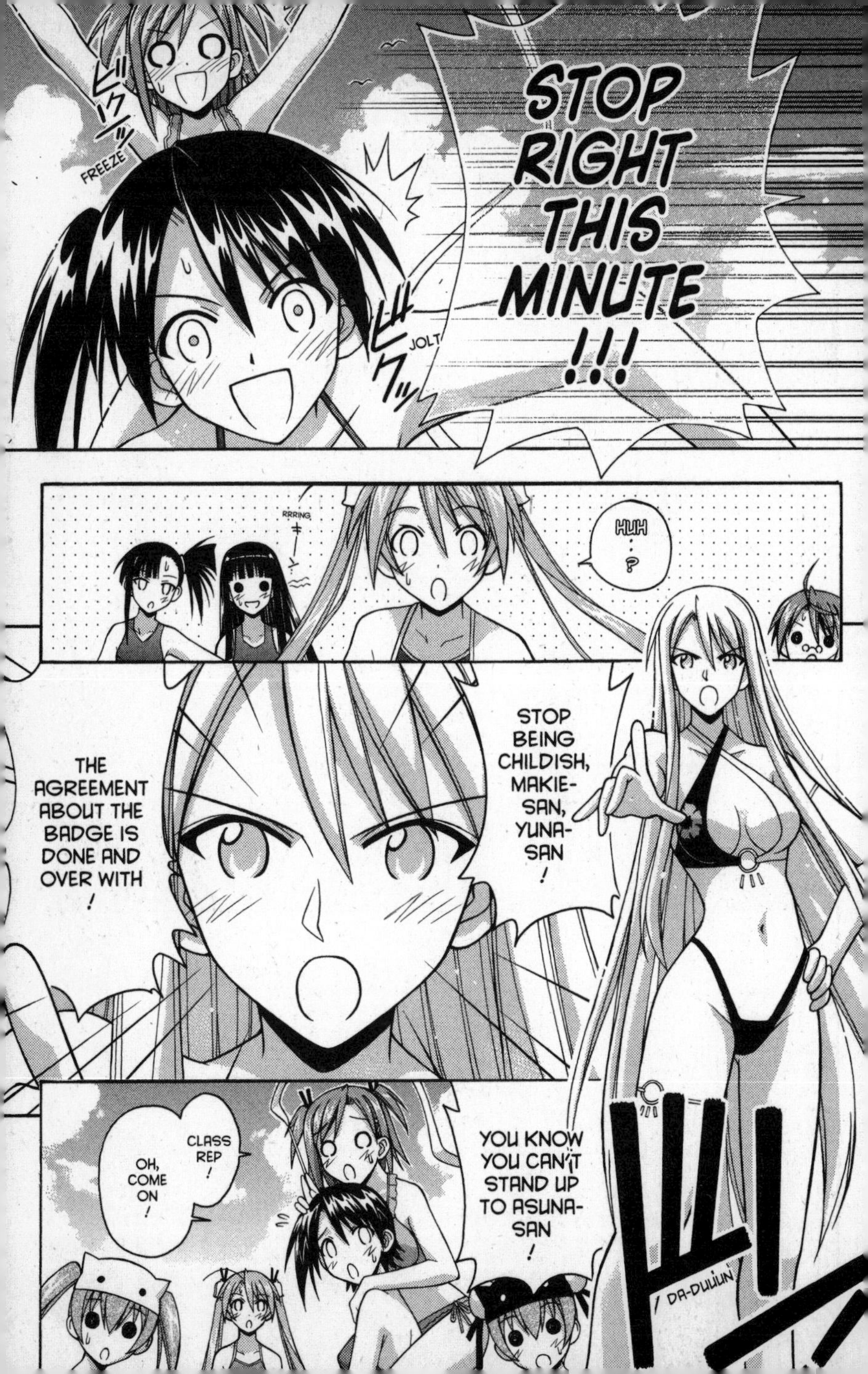
STOP RIGHT THIS MINUTE !!!
FREEZE
JOLT
HUH . . . ?
RRRING
STOP BEING CHILDISH, MAKIE-SAN, YUNA-SAN !
THE AGREEMENT ABOUT THE BADGE IS DONE AND OVER WITH !
YOU KNOW YOU CAN'T STAND UP TO ASUNA-SAN !
DA-DUUUN
CLASS REP !
OH, COME ON !

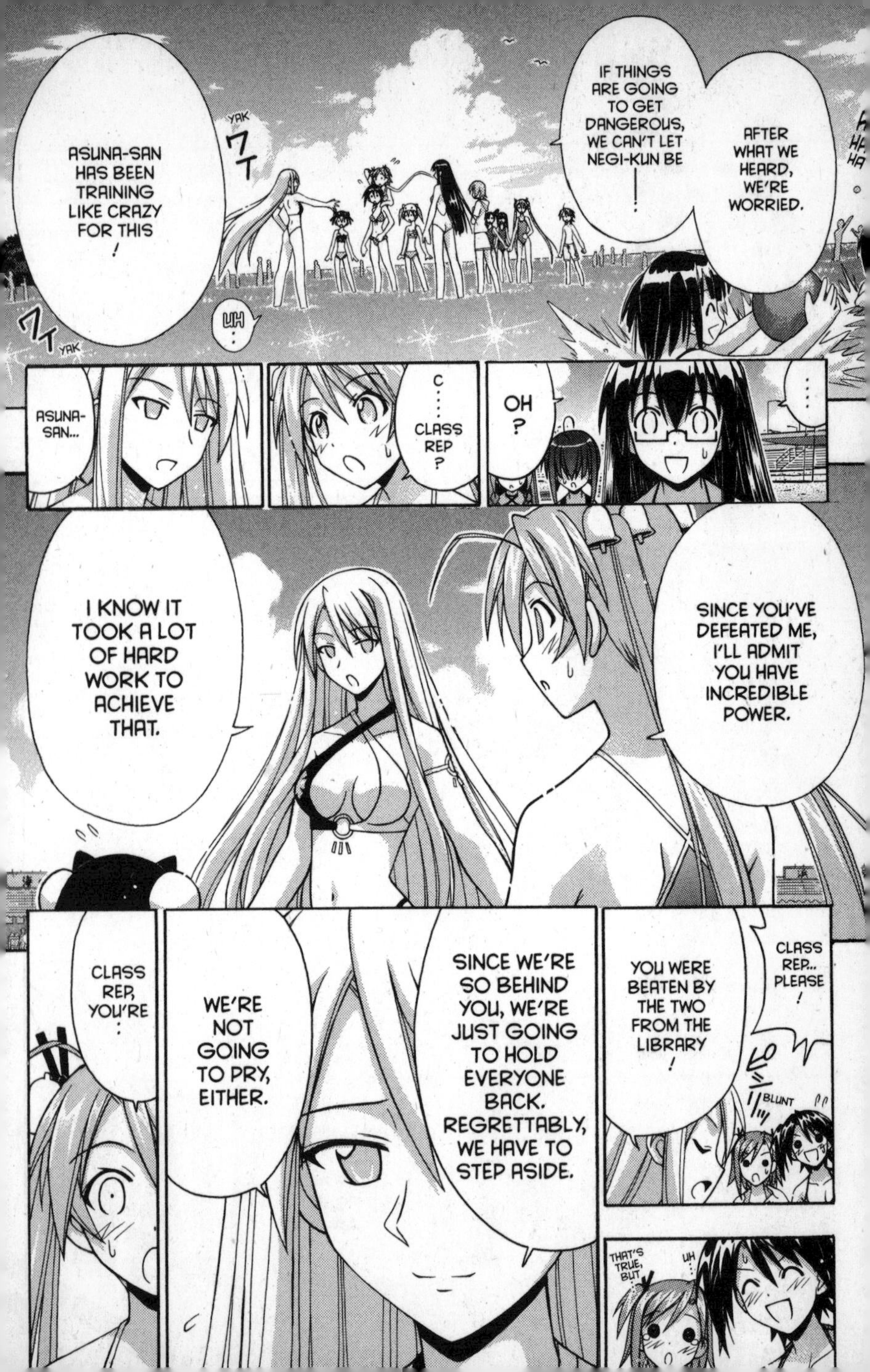
AFTER WHAT WE HEARD, WE'RE WORRIED.
IF THINGS ARE GOING TO GET DANGEROUS, WE CAN'T LET NEGI-KUN BE!
HA HA HA
YAK
ASUNA-SAN HAS BEEN TRAINING LIKE CRAZY FOR THIS!
UH...
YAK
...
OH?
C... CLASS REP?
ASUNA-SAN...
SINCE YOU'VE DEFEATED ME, I'LL ADMIT YOU HAVE INCREDIBLE POWER.
I KNOW IT TOOK A LOT OF HARD WORK TO ACHIEVE THAT.
CLASS REP... PLEASE!
YOU WERE BEATEN BY THE TWO FROM THE LIBRARY!
BLUNT
UH...
THAT'S TRUE, BUT
SINCE WE'RE SO BEHIND YOU, WE'RE JUST GOING TO HOLD EVERYONE BACK. REGRETTABLY, WE HAVE TO STEP ASIDE.
WE'RE NOT GOING TO PRY, EITHER.
CLASS REP, YOU'RE...

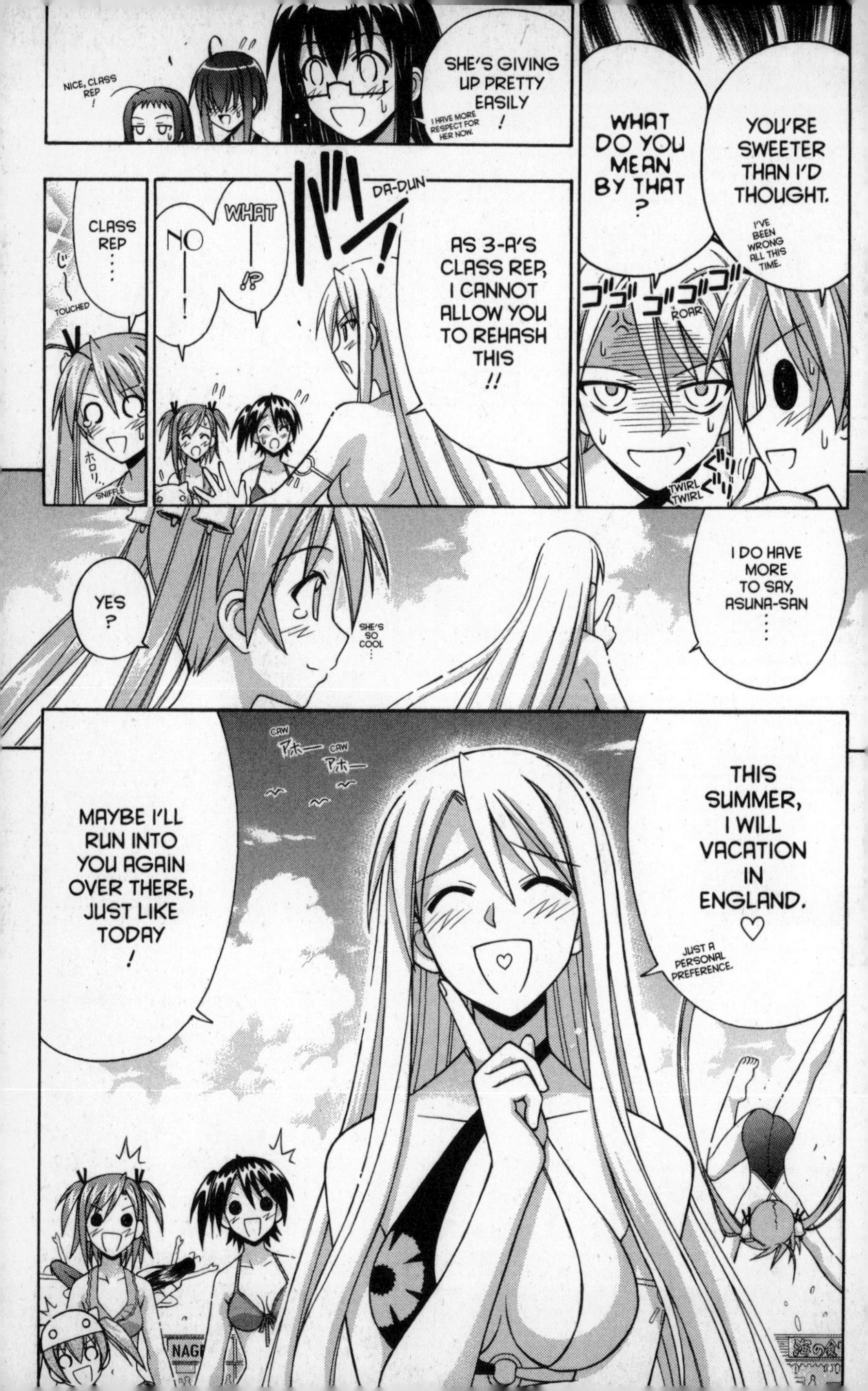
YOU'RE SWEETER THAN I'D THOUGHT.
I'VE BEEN WRONG ALL THIS TIME.
WHAT DO YOU MEAN BY THAT?
ROAR
TWIRL TWIRL
SHE'S GIVING UP PRETTY EASILY!
I HAVE MORE RESPECT FOR HER NOW.
NICE, CLASS REP!
DA-DUN
AS 3-A'S CLASS REP, I CANNOT ALLOW YOU TO REHASH THIS!!
WHAT—!?
NO—!
CLASS REP......
TOUCHED
SNIFFLE
I DO HAVE MORE TO SAY, ASUNA-SAN...
SHE'S SO COOL...
YES?
CAW CAW
THIS SUMMER, I WILL VACATION IN ENGLAND. ♡
JUST A PERSONAL PREFERENCE.
MAYBE I'LL RUN INTO YOU AGAIN OVER THERE, JUST LIKE TODAY!

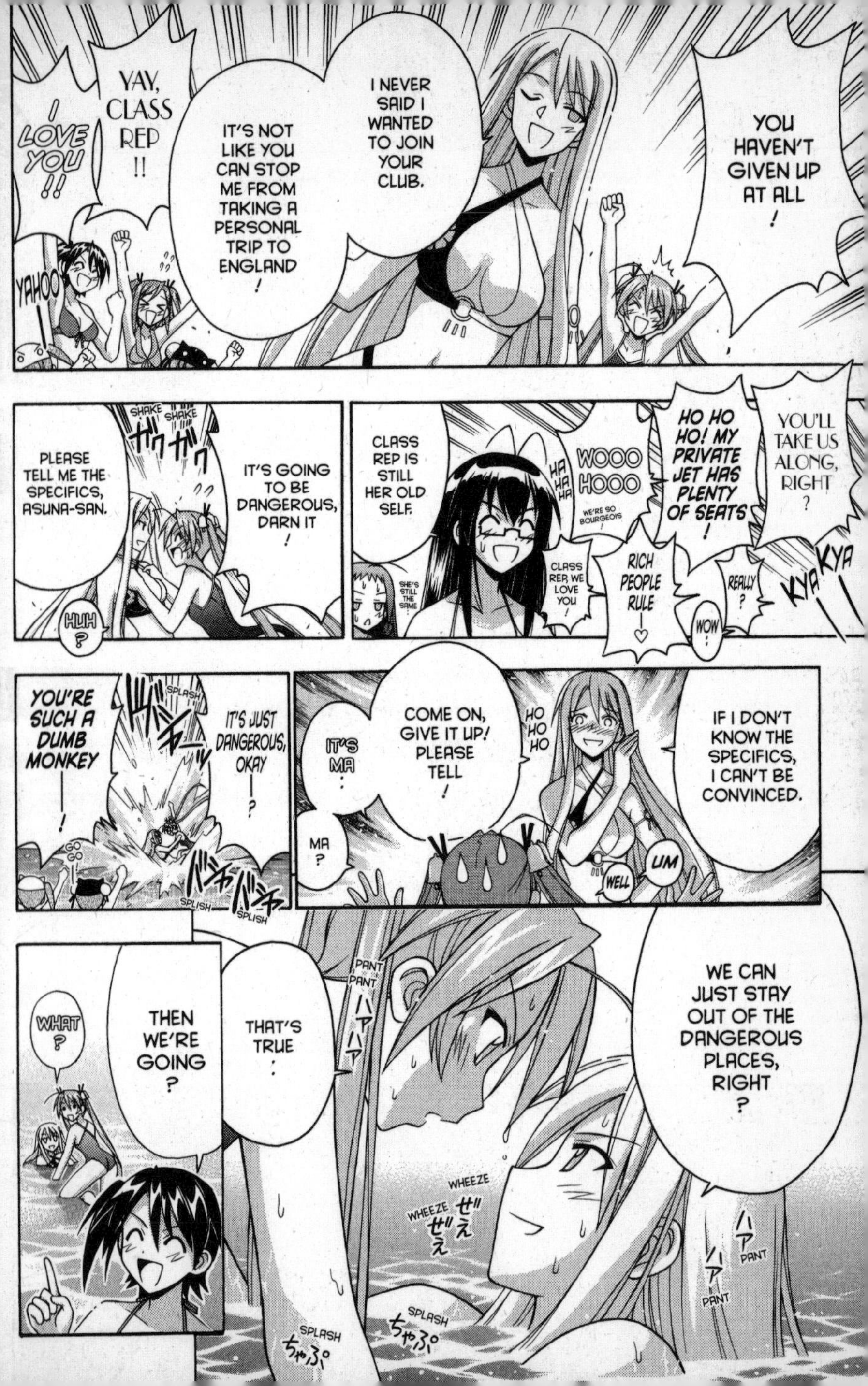
YOU HAVEN'T GIVEN UP AT ALL!
I NEVER SAID I WANTED TO JOIN YOUR CLUB.
IT'S NOT LIKE YOU CAN STOP ME FROM TAKING A PERSONAL TRIP TO ENGLAND!
YAY, CLASS REP!!
I LOVE YOU!!
YAHOO!
YOU'LL TAKE US ALONG, RIGHT?
HO HO HO! MY PRIVATE JET HAS PLENTY OF SEATS!
KYA KYA
WOOO HOOO
HA HA HA
WE'RE SO BOURGEOIS!
REALLY?
RICH PEOPLE RULE ♡
WOW!
CLASS REP IS STILL HER OLD SELF.
CLASS REP, WE LOVE YOU!
SHE'S STILL THE SAME
SHAKE SHAKE
IT'S GOING TO BE DANGEROUS, DARN IT!
PLEASE TELL ME THE SPECIFICS, ASUNA-SAN.
HUH?
IF I DON'T KNOW THE SPECIFICS, I CAN'T BE CONVINCED.
HO HO HO
COME ON, GIVE IT UP! PLEASE TELL!
UM
WELL
IT'S MA...
MA?
SPLASH
IT'S JUST DANGEROUS, OKAY—?
YOU'RE SUCH A DUMB MONKEY—!
GO GO!
SPLISH
SPLISH
WE CAN JUST STAY OUT OF THE DANGEROUS PLACES, RIGHT?
PANT PANT
PANT
PANT
WHEEZE
WHEEZE
THAT'S TRUE...
THEN WE'RE GOING?
WHAT?
SPLASH
SPLASH

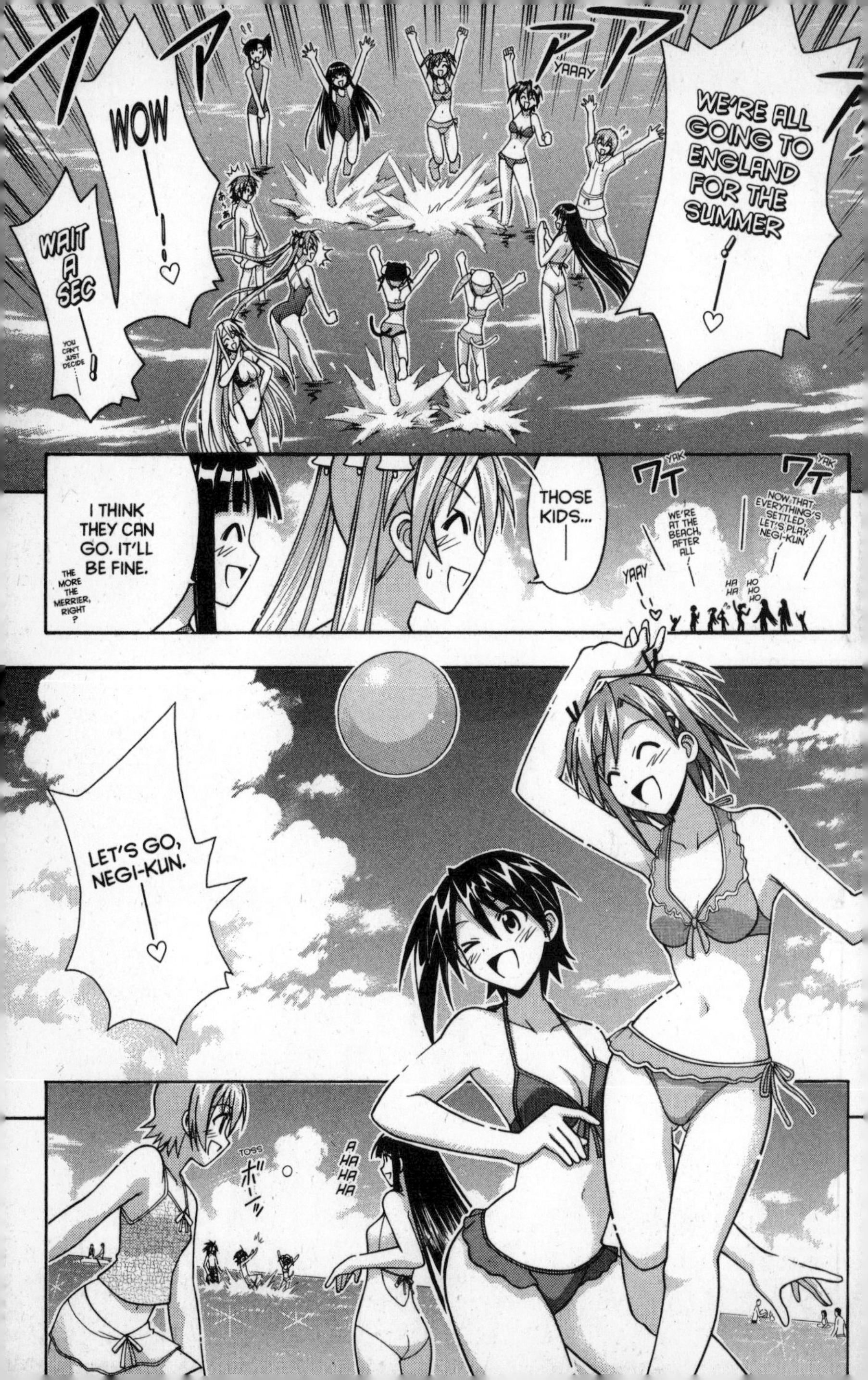
WE'RE ALL GOING TO ENGLAND FOR THE SUMMER!
YAAAY
WOW!
WAIT A SEC!
YOU CAN'T JUST DECIDE...
YAK
NOW THAT EVERYTHING'S SETTLED, LET'S PLAY, NEGI-KUN!
YAK
WE'RE AT THE BEACH, AFTER ALL!
HO HO HO
HA HA
YAAY
THOSE KIDS...
I THINK THEY CAN GO. IT'LL BE FINE.
THE MORE THE MERRIER, RIGHT?
LET'S GO, NEGI-KUN.
A HA HA HA
TOSS

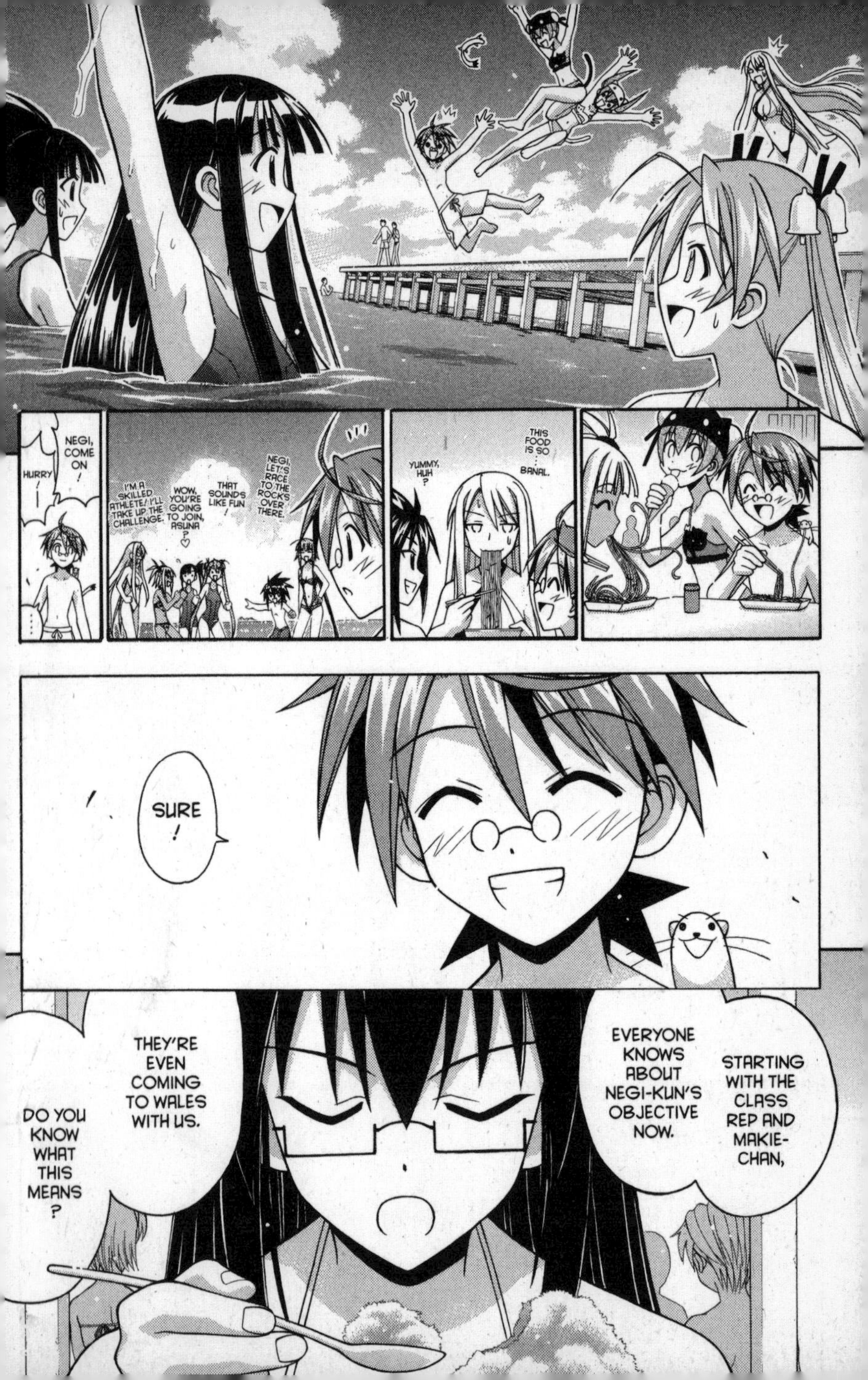
THIS FOOD IS SO... BANAL.
YUMMY, HUH?
NEGI, LET'S RACE TO THE ROCKS OVER THERE.
THAT SOUNDS LIKE FUN!
WOW, YOU'RE GOING TO JOIN, ASUNA ♡
I'M A SKILLED ATHLETE! I'LL TAKE UP THE CHALLENGE.
NEGI, COME ON!
HURRY!
SURE!
STARTING WITH THE CLASS REP AND MAKIE-CHAN,
EVERYONE KNOWS ABOUT NEGI-KUN'S OBJECTIVE NOW.
THEY'RE EVEN COMING TO WALES WITH US.
DO YOU KNOW WHAT THIS MEANS?

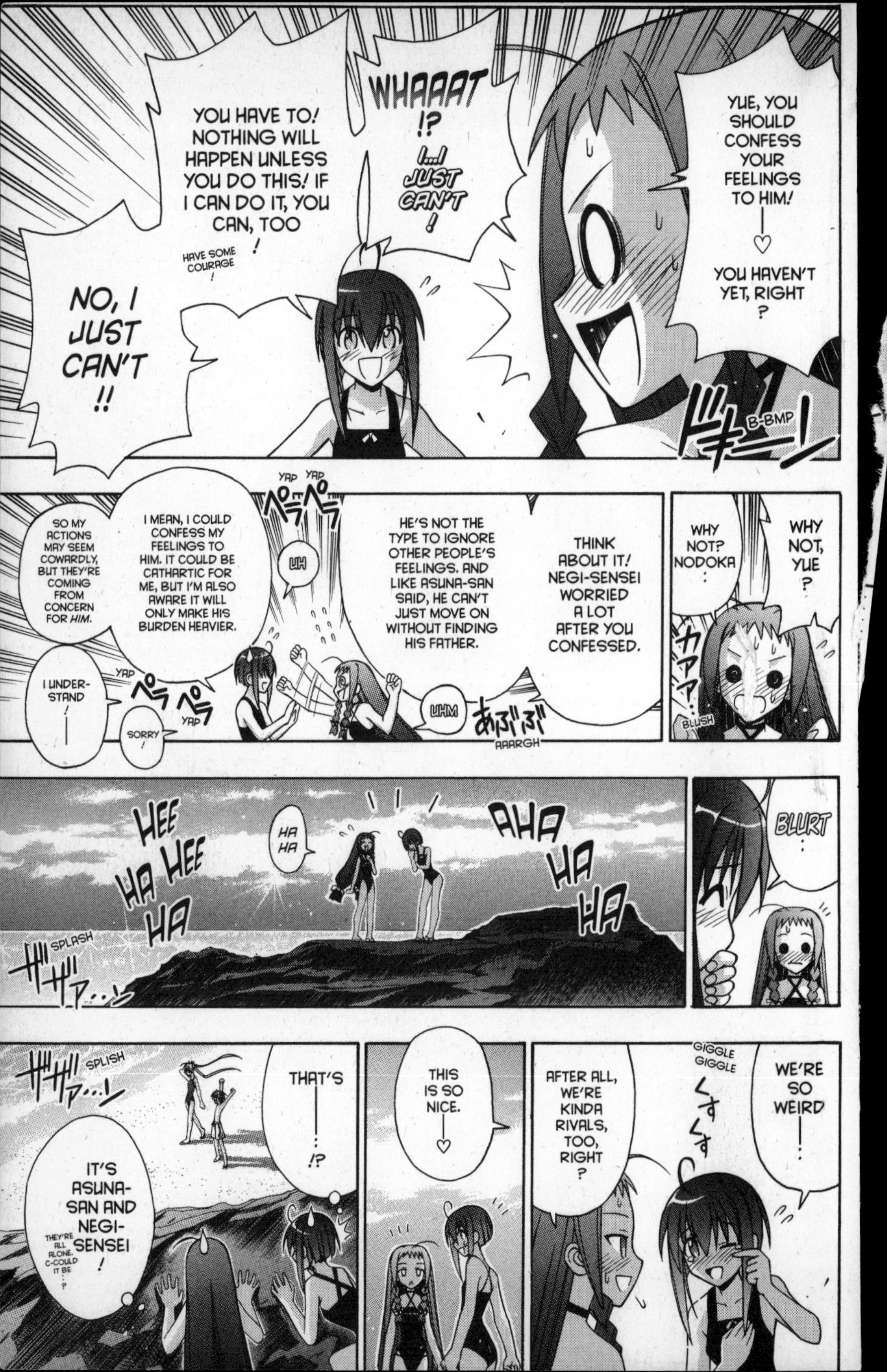
YUE, YOU SHOULD CONFESS YOUR FEELINGS TO HIM! ♡
YOU HAVEN'T YET, RIGHT?
B-BMP
WHAAAT!?
I...I JUST CAN'T!
YOU HAVE TO! NOTHING WILL HAPPEN UNLESS YOU DO THIS! IF I CAN DO IT, YOU CAN, TOO!
HAVE SOME COURAGE!
NO, I JUST CAN'T!!
WHY NOT, YUE?
WHY NOT? NODOKA...
BLUSH
THINK ABOUT IT! NEGI-SENSEI WORRIED A LOT AFTER YOU CONFESSED.
HE'S NOT THE TYPE TO IGNORE OTHER PEOPLE'S FEELINGS. AND LIKE ASUNA-SAN SAID, HE CAN'T JUST MOVE ON WITHOUT FINDING HIS FATHER.
YAP YAP
UH
I MEAN, I COULD CONFESS MY FEELINGS TO HIM. IT COULD BE CATHARTIC FOR ME, BUT I'M ALSO AWARE IT WILL ONLY MAKE HIS BURDEN HEAVIER.
SO MY ACTIONS MAY SEEM COWARDLY, BUT THEY'RE COMING FROM CONCERN FOR *HIM*.
UHM
AAARGH
YAP YAP
SORRY!
I UNDER-STAND!
BLURT...
AHA HA HA HA
HA HA
HEE HA HEE HA HA
SPLASH
WE'RE SO WEIRD...
GIGGLE GIGGLE
AFTER ALL, WE'RE KINDA RIVALS, TOO, RIGHT?
THIS IS SO NICE. ♡
THAT'S...!?
SPLASH
IT'S ASUNA-SAN AND NEGI-SENSEI!
THEY'RE ALL ALONE. C-COULD IT BE...?

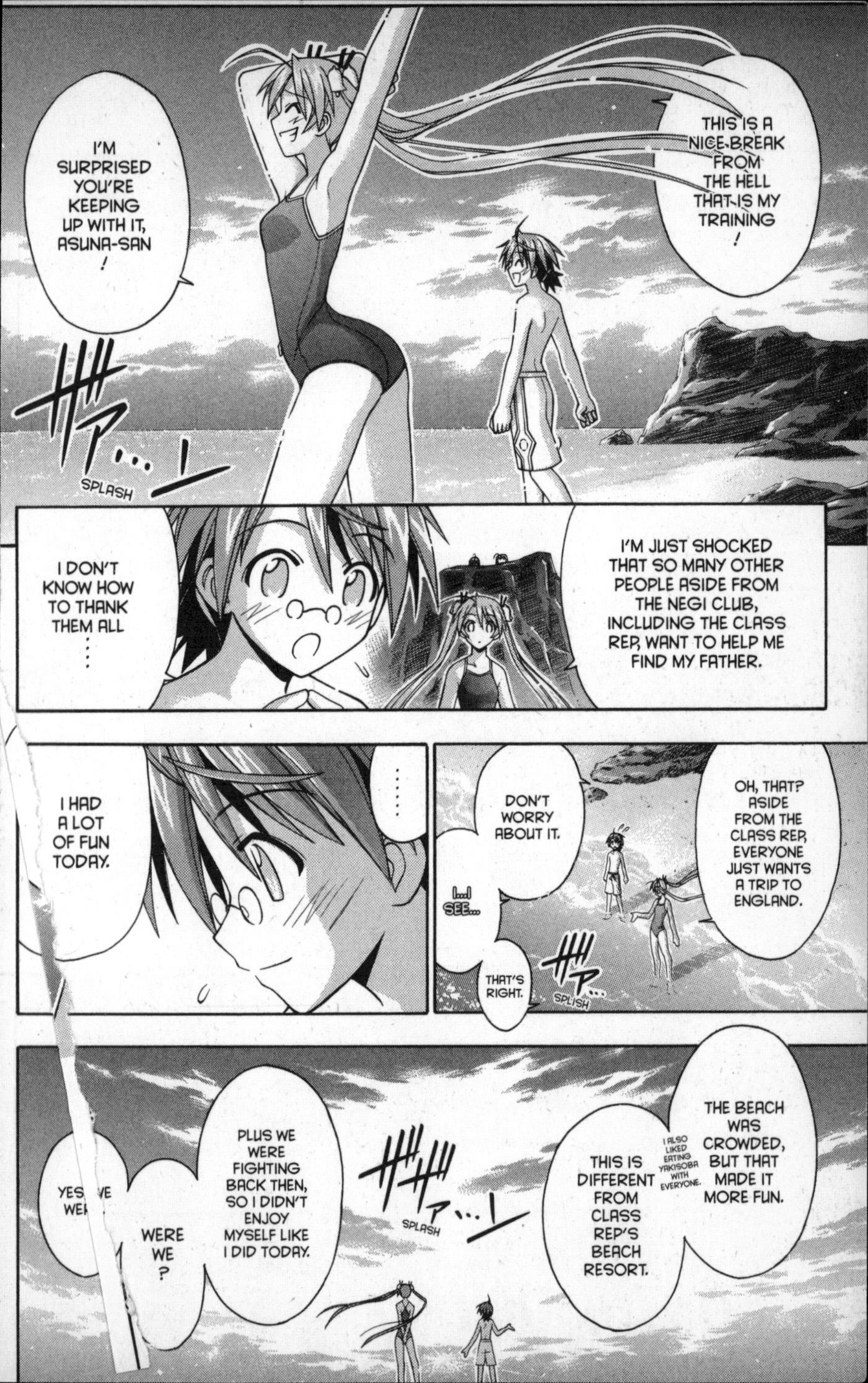
THIS IS A NICE BREAK FROM THE HELL THAT IS MY TRAINING!
I'M SURPRISED YOU'RE KEEPING UP WITH IT, ASUNA-SAN!
SPLASH
I'M JUST SHOCKED THAT SO MANY OTHER PEOPLE ASIDE FROM THE NEGI CLUB, INCLUDING THE CLASS REP, WANT TO HELP ME FIND MY FATHER.
I DON'T KNOW HOW TO THANK THEM ALL....
OH, THAT? ASIDE FROM THE CLASS REP, EVERYONE JUST WANTS A TRIP TO ENGLAND.
DON'T WORRY ABOUT IT.
I...I SEE...
THAT'S RIGHT.
SPLASH
......
I HAD A LOT OF FUN TODAY.
THE BEACH WAS CROWDED, BUT THAT MADE IT MORE FUN.
I ALSO LIKED EATING YAKISOBA WITH EVERYONE.
THIS IS DIFFERENT FROM CLASS REP'S BEACH RESORT.
SPLASH
PLUS WE WERE FIGHTING BACK THEN, SO I DIDN'T ENJOY MYSELF LIKE I DID TODAY.
WERE WE?
YES, WE WE

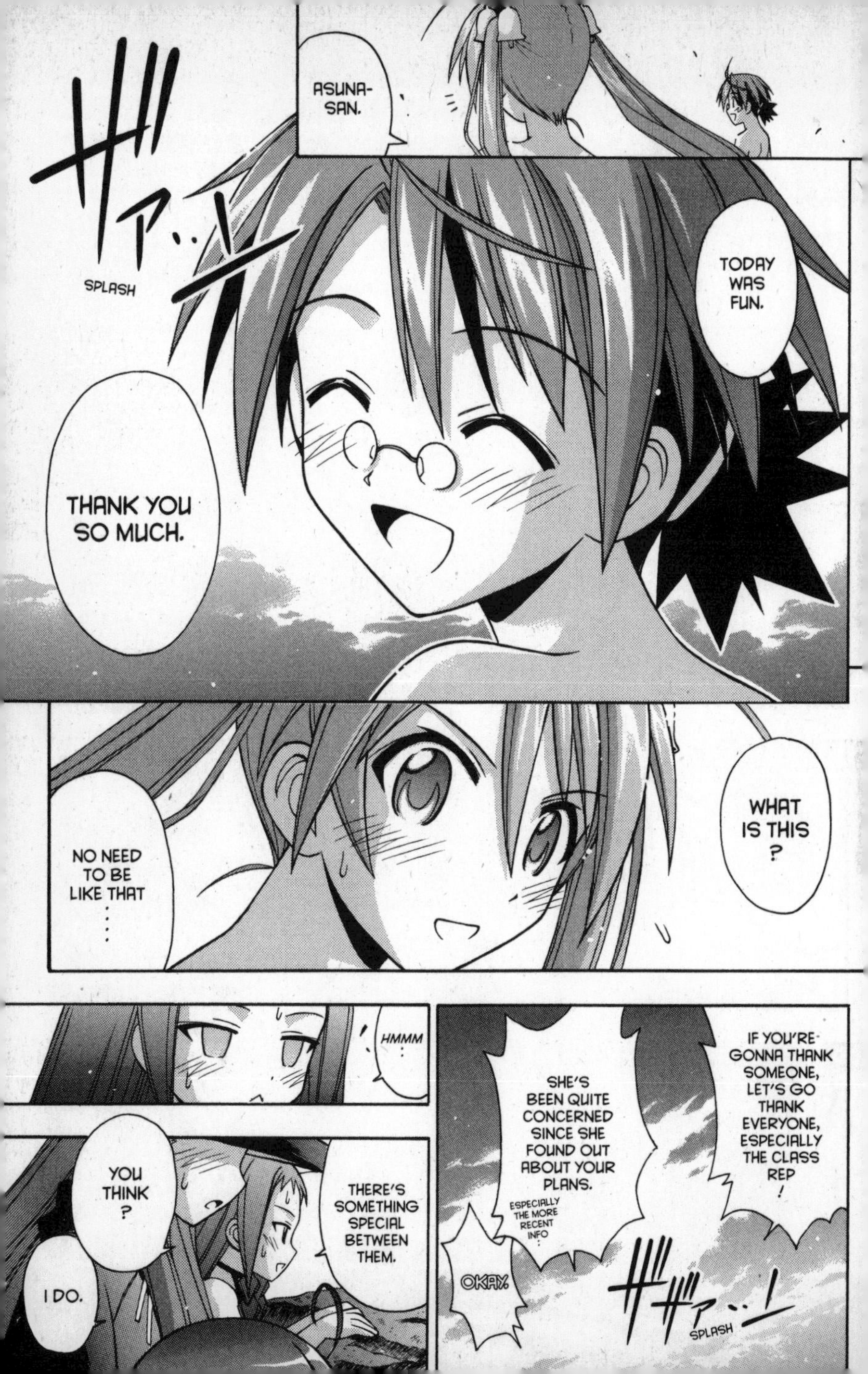

ASUNA-SAN.
SPLASH
TODAY WAS FUN.
THANK YOU SO MUCH.
WHAT IS THIS?
NO NEED TO BE LIKE THAT...
IF YOU'RE GONNA THANK SOMEONE, LET'S GO THANK EVERYONE, ESPECIALLY THE CLASS REP!
SHE'S BEEN QUITE CONCERNED SINCE SHE FOUND OUT ABOUT YOUR PLANS.
ESPECIALLY THE MORE RECENT INFO:
OKAY.
SPLASH
HMMM:
THERE'S SOMETHING SPECIAL BETWEEN THEM.
YOU THINK?
I DO.

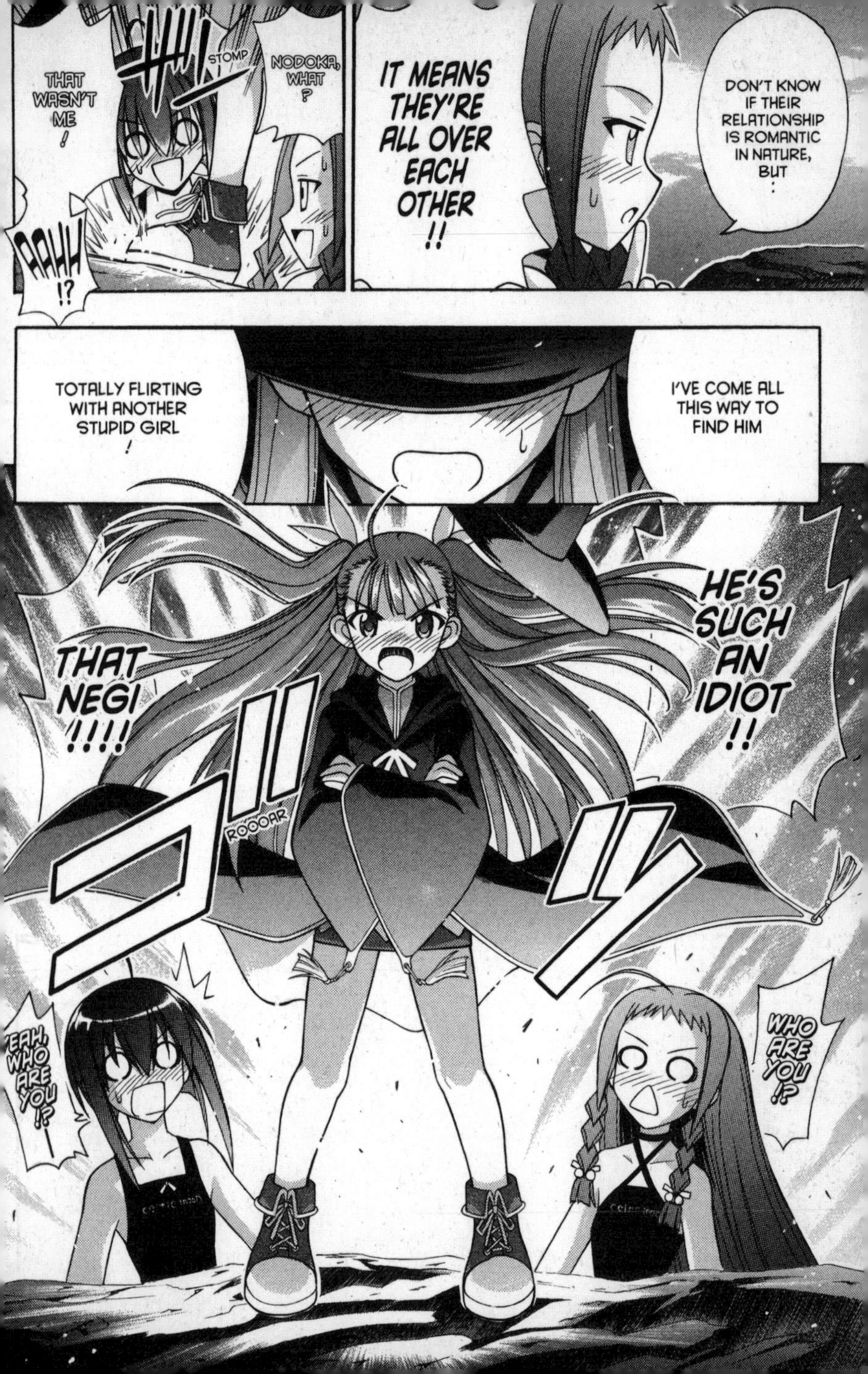
DON'T KNOW IF THEIR RELATIONSHIP IS ROMANTIC IN NATURE, BUT :
IT MEANS THEY'RE ALL OVER EACH OTHER !!
NODOKA, WHAT ?
STOMP
THAT WASN'T ME !
AAHH !?
I'VE COME ALL THIS WAY TO FIND HIM
TOTALLY FLIRTING WITH ANOTHER STUPID GIRL !
HE'S SUCH AN IDIOT !!
THAT NEGI !!!!
ROOOAR
WHO ARE YOU !?
EAH, WHO ARE YOU !?

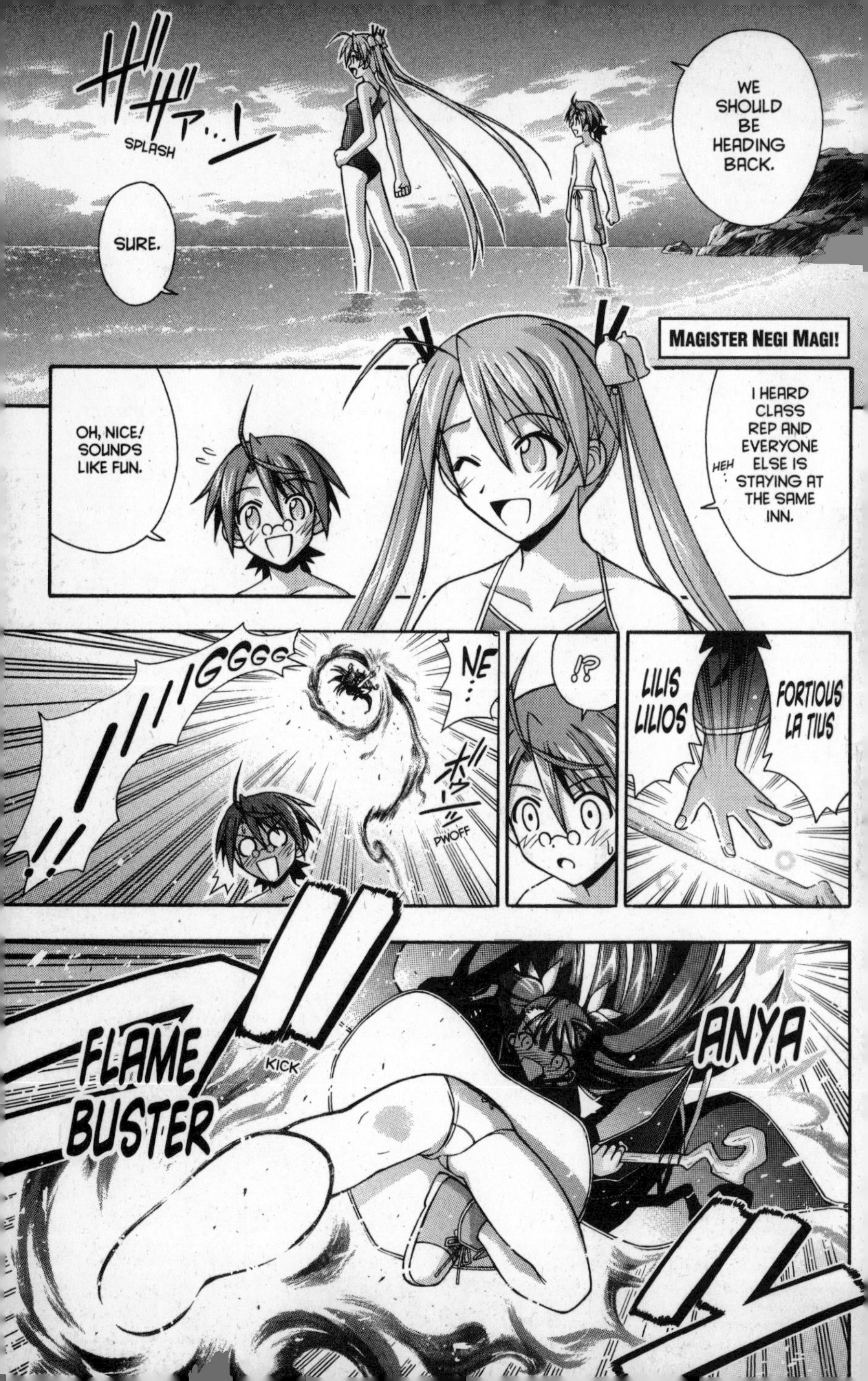
WE SHOULD BE HEADING BACK.
SPLASH
SURE.
MAGISTER NEGI MAGI!
I HEARD CLASS REP AND EVERYONE ELSE IS STAYING AT THE SAME INN.
HEH
OH, NICE! SOUNDS LIKE FUN.
LILIS LILIOS
FORTIOUS LA TIUS
!?
NE...
PWOFF
IGGGG!!
ANYA
FLAME BUSTER
KICK

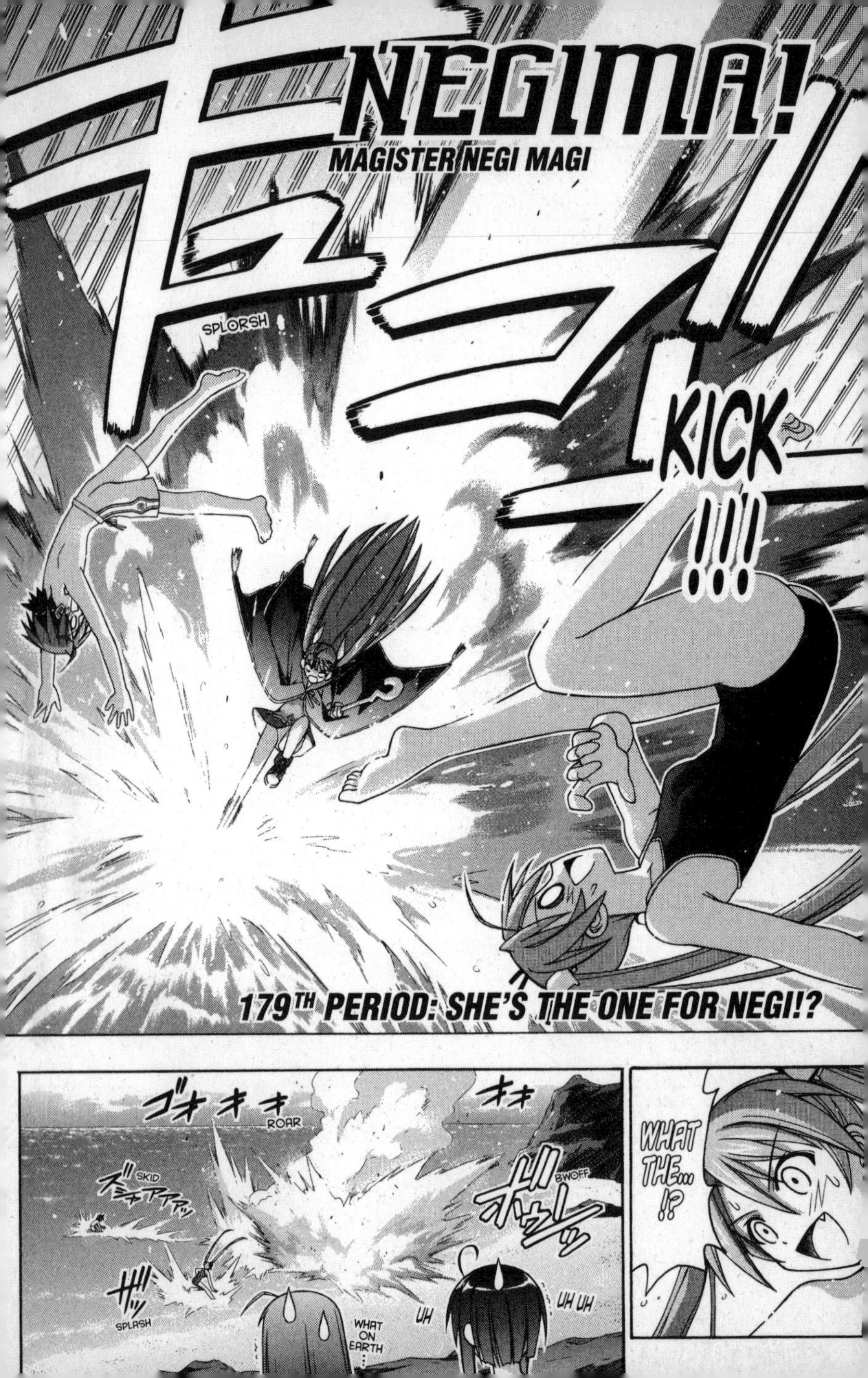
NEGIMA!
MAGISTER NEGI MAGI
SPLORSH
KICK!!!
179TH PERIOD: SHE'S THE ONE FOR NEGI!?
WHAT THE... !?
ROAR
SKID
BWOFF
SPLASH
WHAT ON EARTH
UH
UH UH

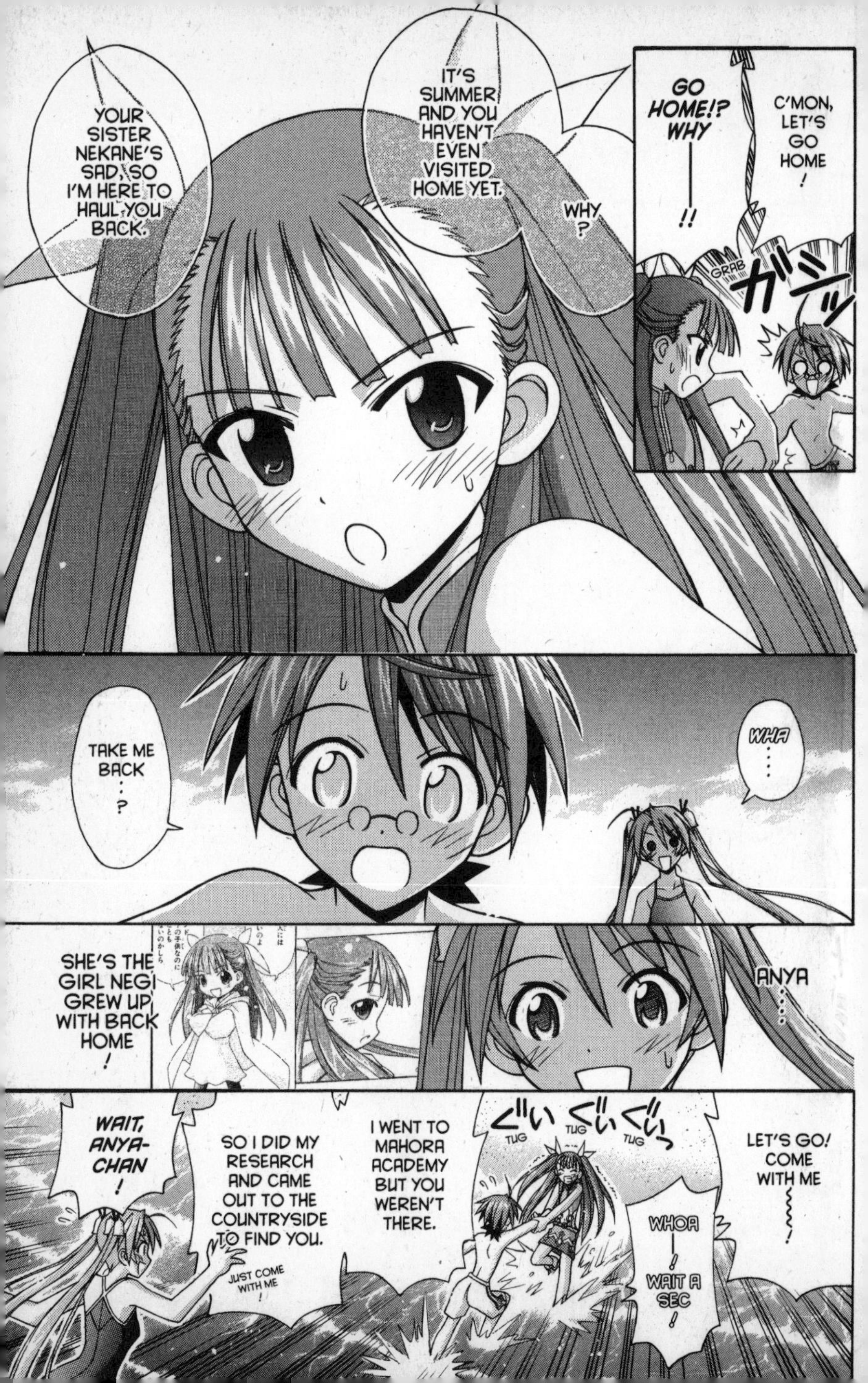
C'MON, LET'S GO HOME!
GO HOME!? WHY——!!
GRAB
ガシッ
WHY?
IT'S SUMMER AND YOU HAVEN'T EVEN VISITED HOME YET.
YOUR SISTER NEKANE'S SAD, SO I'M HERE TO HAUL YOU BACK.
WHA...
TAKE ME BACK...?
ANYA...
SHE'S THE GIRL NEGI GREW UP WITH BACK HOME!
LET'S GO! COME WITH ME~!
WHOA! WAIT A SEC!
ぐい ぐい ぐいっ
TUG TUG TUG
I WENT TO MAHORA ACADEMY BUT YOU WEREN'T THERE.
SO I DID MY RESEARCH AND CAME OUT TO THE COUNTRYSIDE TO FIND YOU.
JUST COME WITH ME!
WAIT, ANYA-CHAN!

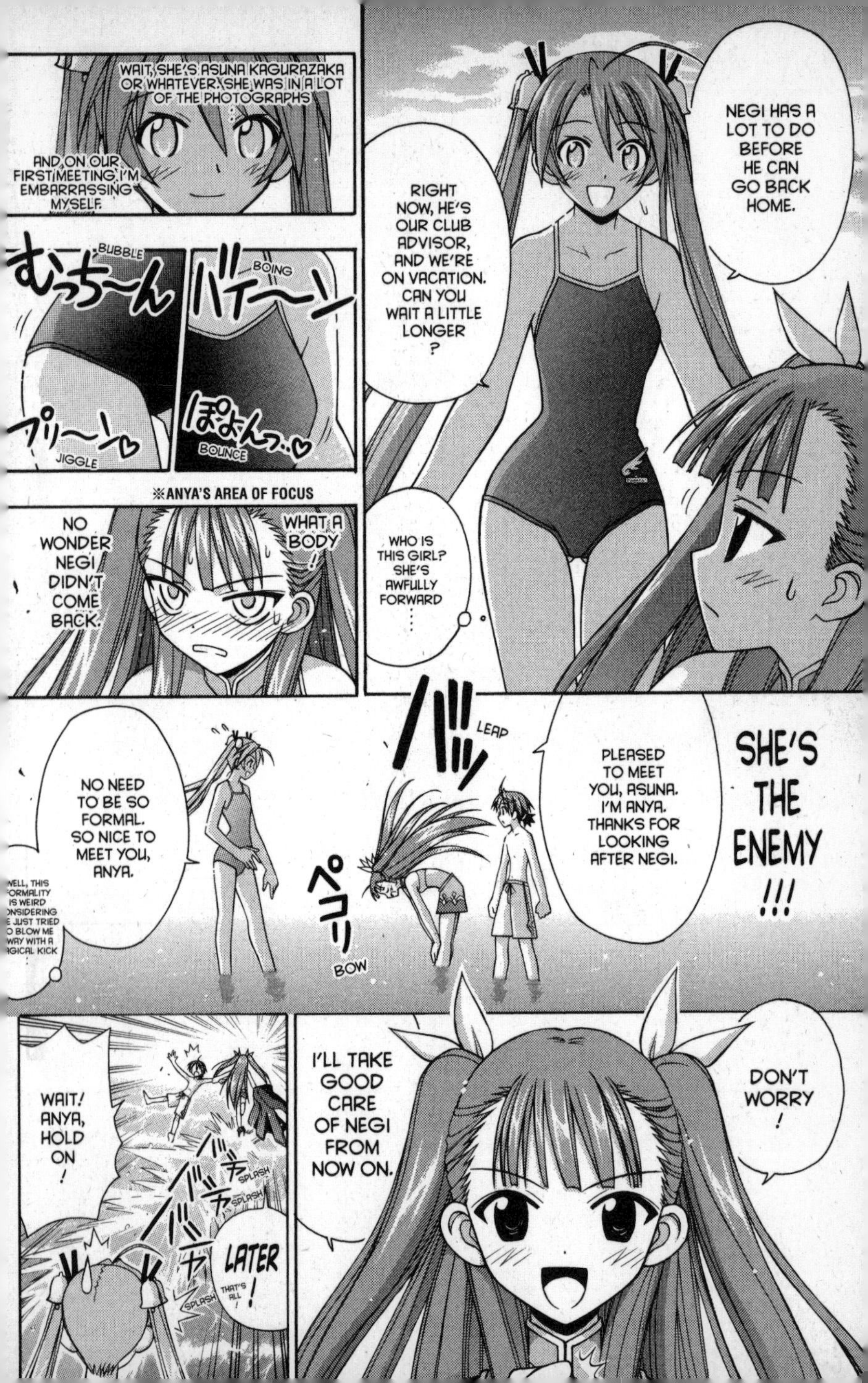
NEGI HAS A LOT TO DO BEFORE HE CAN GO BACK HOME.
RIGHT NOW, HE'S OUR CLUB ADVISOR, AND WE'RE ON VACATION. CAN YOU WAIT A LITTLE LONGER ?
WHO IS THIS GIRL? SHE'S AWFULLY FORWARD ...
WAIT, SHE'S ASUNA KAGURAZAKA OR WHATEVER. SHE WAS IN A LOT OF THE PHOTOGRAPHS ...
AND ON OUR FIRST MEETING, I'M EMBARRASSING MYSELF.
バイーン BOING
ぽよんっ BOUNCE
むっちーん BUBBLE
プリーン JIGGLE
※ANYA'S AREA OF FOCUS
WHAT A BODY !
NO WONDER NEGI DIDN'T COME BACK.
SHE'S THE ENEMY !!!
PLEASED TO MEET YOU, ASUNA. I'M ANYA. THANKS FOR LOOKING AFTER NEGI.
バッ LEAP
ペコリ BOW
NO NEED TO BE SO FORMAL. SO NICE TO MEET YOU, ANYA.
WELL, THIS FORMALITY IS WEIRD
DON'T WORRY !
I'LL TAKE GOOD CARE OF NEGI FROM NOW ON.
WAIT! ANYA, HOLD ON !
SPLASH
SPLASH
SPLASH
LATER !
THAT'S ALL

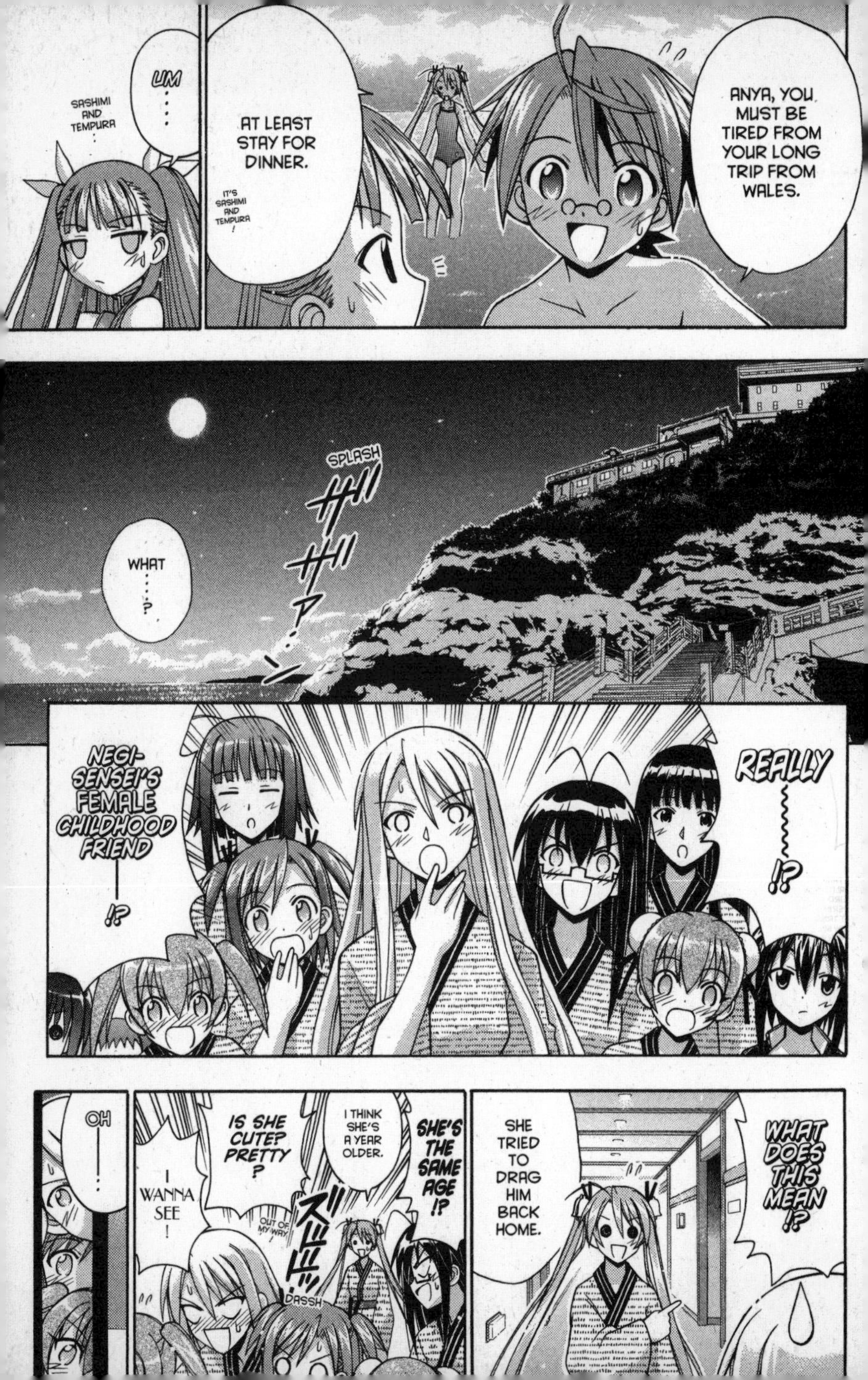
ANYA, YOU MUST BE TIRED FROM YOUR LONG TRIP FROM WALES.
AT LEAST STAY FOR DINNER.
IT'S SASHIMI AND TEMPURA!
UM ...
SASHIMI AND TEMPURA ...
SPLASH
WHAT ...?
REALLY ~~~!?
NEGI-SENSEI'S FEMALE CHILDHOOD FRIEND —!?
WHAT DOES THIS MEAN!?
SHE TRIED TO DRAG HIM BACK HOME.
SHE'S THE SAME AGE!?
I THINK SHE'S A YEAR OLDER.
IS SHE CUTE? PRETTY?
OUT OF MY WAY
DASSH
I WANNA SEE!
OH —!

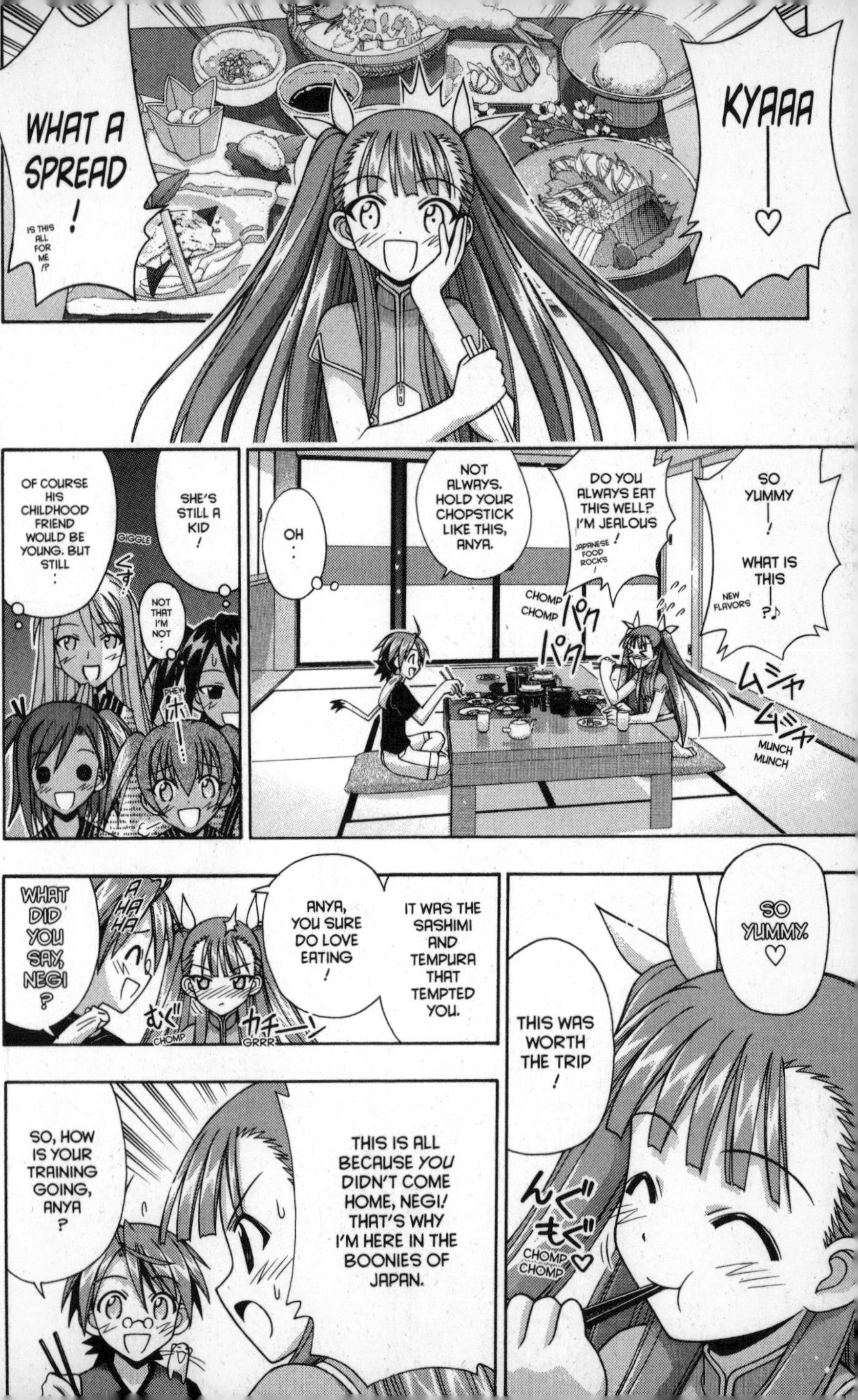
KYAAA ♡
WHAT A SPREAD!
IS THIS ALL FOR ME!?
SO YUMMY! WHAT IS THIS!?♪
NEW FLAVORS
MUNCH MUNCH
DO YOU ALWAYS EAT THIS WELL? I'M JEALOUS!
JAPANESE FOOD ROCKS!
CHOMP CHOMP
NOT ALWAYS. HOLD YOUR CHOPSTICK LIKE THIS, ANYA.
OH...
SHE'S STILL A KID!
OF COURSE HIS CHILDHOOD FRIEND WOULD BE YOUNG. BUT STILL...
GIGGLE
NOT THAT I'M NOT...
PHEW
SO YUMMY. ♡
THIS WAS WORTH THE TRIP!
CHOMP CHOMP ♡
IT WAS THE SASHIMI AND TEMPURA THAT TEMPTED YOU.
ANYA, YOU SURE DO LOVE EATING!
GRRR
WHAT DID YOU SAY, NEGI?
CHOMP
THIS IS ALL BECAUSE YOU DIDN'T COME HOME, NEGI! THAT'S WHY I'M HERE IN THE BOONIES OF JAPAN.
SO, HOW IS YOUR TRAINING GOING, ANYA?

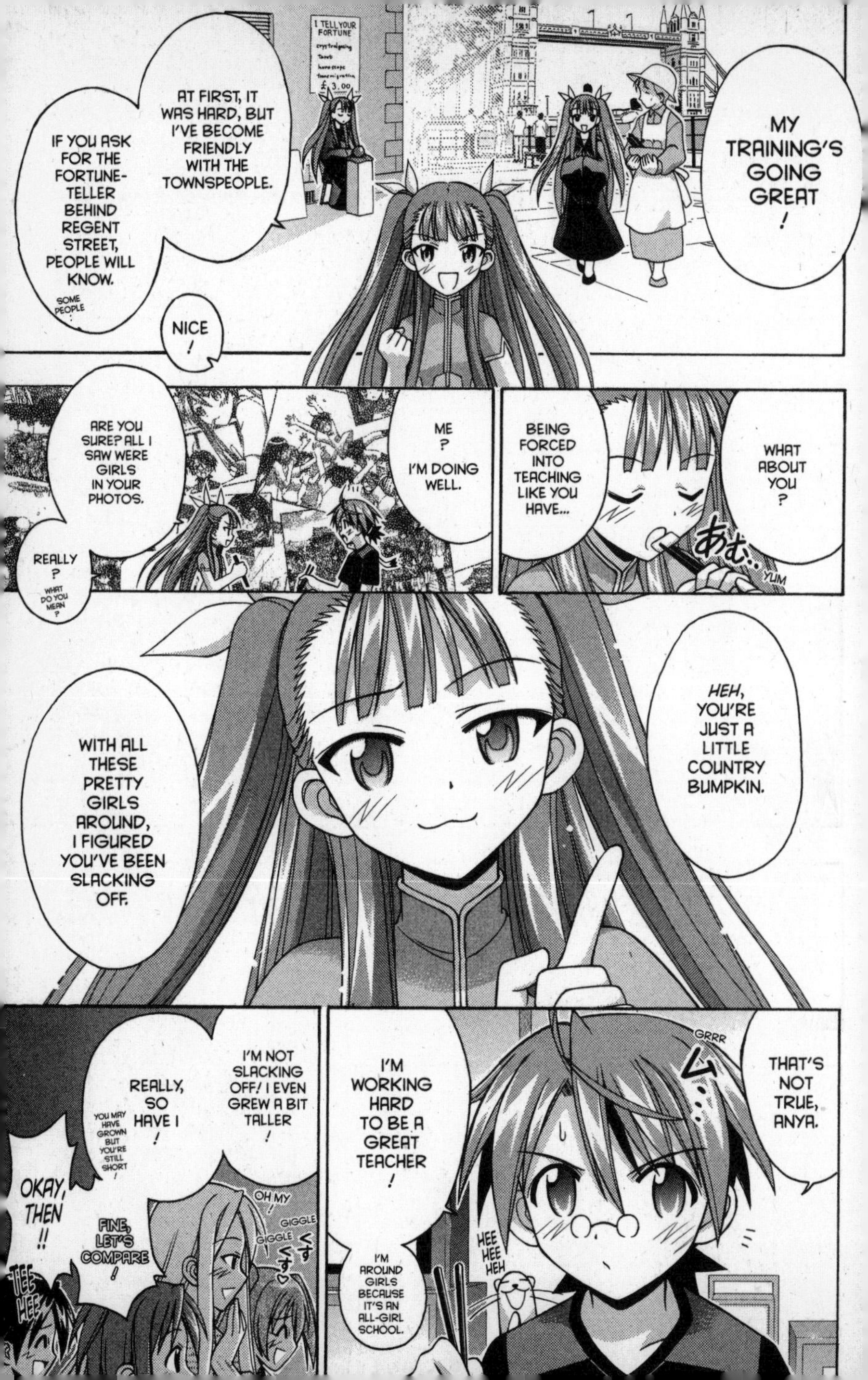
MY TRAINING'S GOING GREAT!
AT FIRST, IT WAS HARD, BUT I'VE BECOME FRIENDLY WITH THE TOWNSPEOPLE.
IF YOU ASK FOR THE FORTUNE-TELLER BEHIND REGENT STREET, PEOPLE WILL KNOW.
SOME PEOPLE...
I TELL YOUR FORTUNE
£3.00
NICE!
WHAT ABOUT YOU?
あむ… YUM
BEING FORCED INTO TEACHING LIKE YOU HAVE...
ME? I'M DOING WELL.
ARE YOU SURE? ALL I SAW WERE GIRLS IN YOUR PHOTOS.
REALLY?
WHAT DO YOU MEAN?
HEH, YOU'RE JUST A LITTLE COUNTRY BUMPKIN.
WITH ALL THESE PRETTY GIRLS AROUND, I FIGURED YOU'VE BEEN SLACKING OFF.
THAT'S NOT TRUE, ANYA.
ム… GRRR
I'M WORKING HARD TO BE A GREAT TEACHER!
HEE HEE HEH
I'M AROUND GIRLS BECAUSE IT'S AN ALL-GIRL SCHOOL.
I'M NOT SLACKING OFF! I EVEN GREW A BIT TALLER!
REALLY, SO HAVE I!
YOU MAY HAVE GROWN BUT YOU'RE STILL SHORT!
OH MY!
GIGGLE GIGGLE くすくす♡
OKAY, THEN!!
FINE, LET'S COMPARE!
TEE HEE

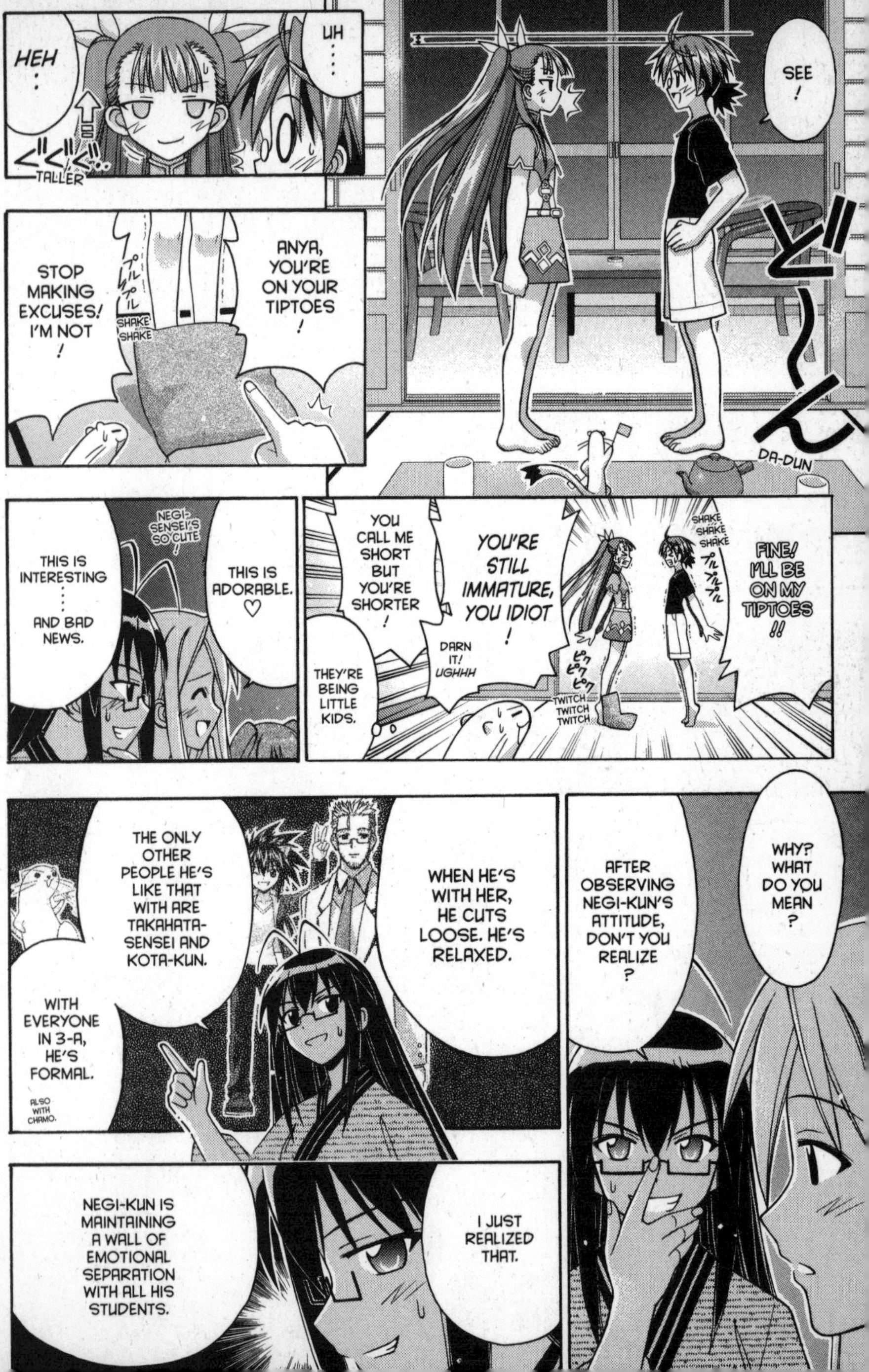
SEE!
DA-DUN
HEH...
UH....
TALLER
ANYA, YOU'RE ON YOUR TIPTOES!
STOP MAKING EXCUSES! I'M NOT!
SHAKE SHAKE
FINE! I'LL BE ON MY TIPTOES!!
SHAKE SHAKE SHAKE
YOU'RE STILL IMMATURE, YOU IDIOT!
DARN IT! UGHHH
YOU CALL ME SHORT BUT YOU'RE SHORTER!
THEY'RE BEING LITTLE KIDS.
TWITCH TWITCH TWITCH
THIS IS ADORABLE. ♡
NEGI-SENSEI'S SO CUTE!
THIS IS INTERESTING... AND BAD NEWS.
WHY? WHAT DO YOU MEAN?
AFTER OBSERVING NEGI-KUN'S ATTITUDE, DON'T YOU REALIZE?
WHEN HE'S WITH HER, HE CUTS LOOSE. HE'S RELAXED.
THE ONLY OTHER PEOPLE HE'S LIKE THAT WITH ARE TAKAHATA-SENSEI AND KOTA-KUN.
WITH EVERYONE IN 3-A, HE'S FORMAL.
ALSO WITH CHAMO.
I JUST REALIZED THAT.
NEGI-KUN IS MAINTAINING A WALL OF EMOTIONAL SEPARATION WITH ALL HIS STUDENTS.

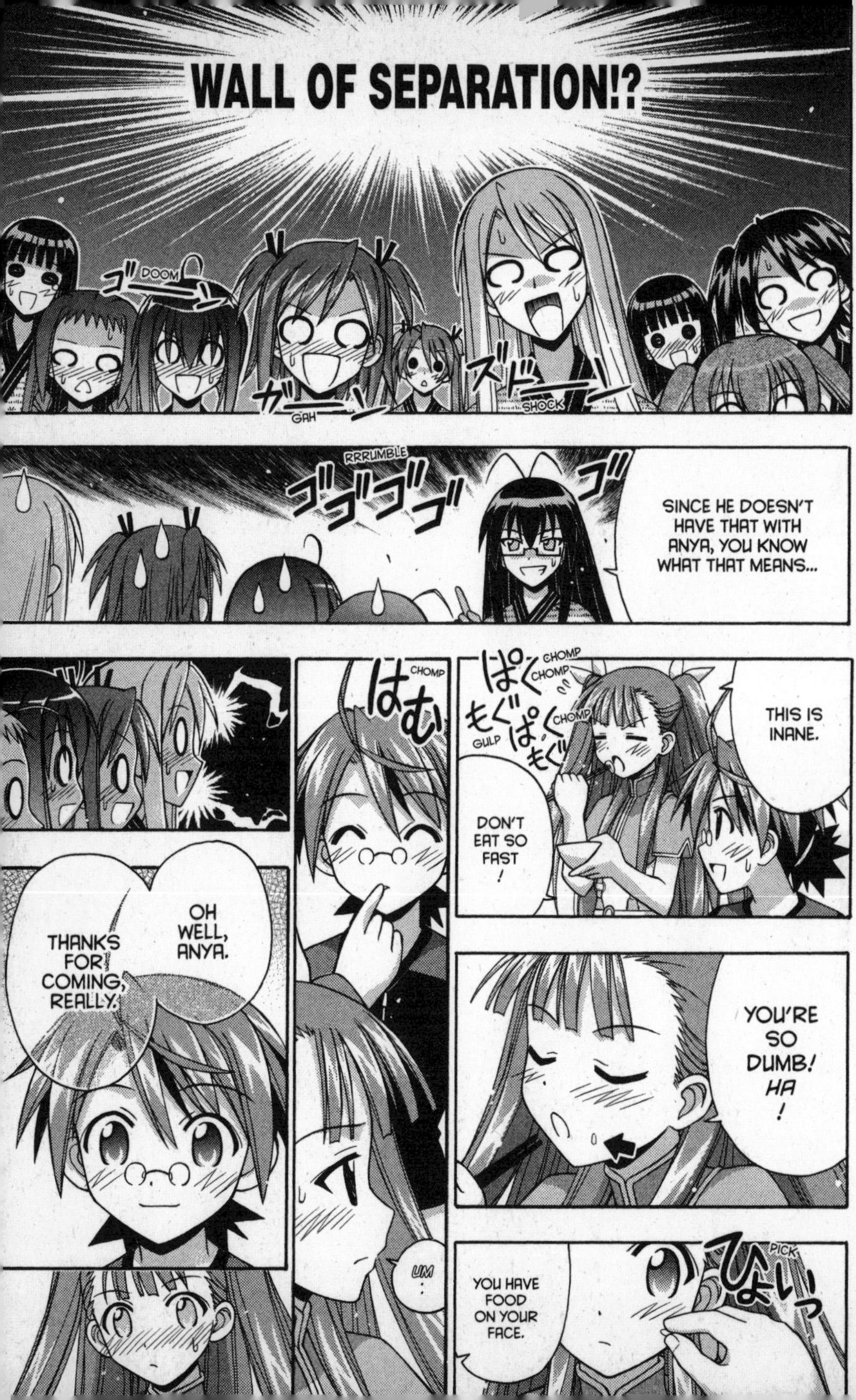
WALL OF SEPARATION!?
ズドーン SHOCK
ガーン GAH
ゴ DOOM
ゴゴゴゴ RRRUMBLE
SINCE HE DOESN'T HAVE THAT WITH ANYA, YOU KNOW WHAT THAT MEANS...
THIS IS INANE.
ぱく CHOMP
もぐ GULP
ぱく CHOMP
もぐ CHOMP
DON'T EAT SO FAST!
はむ CHOMP
YOU'RE SO DUMB! HA!
OH WELL, ANYA.
THANKS FOR COMING, REALLY.
ひょいっ PICK
YOU HAVE FOOD ON YOUR FACE.
UM...

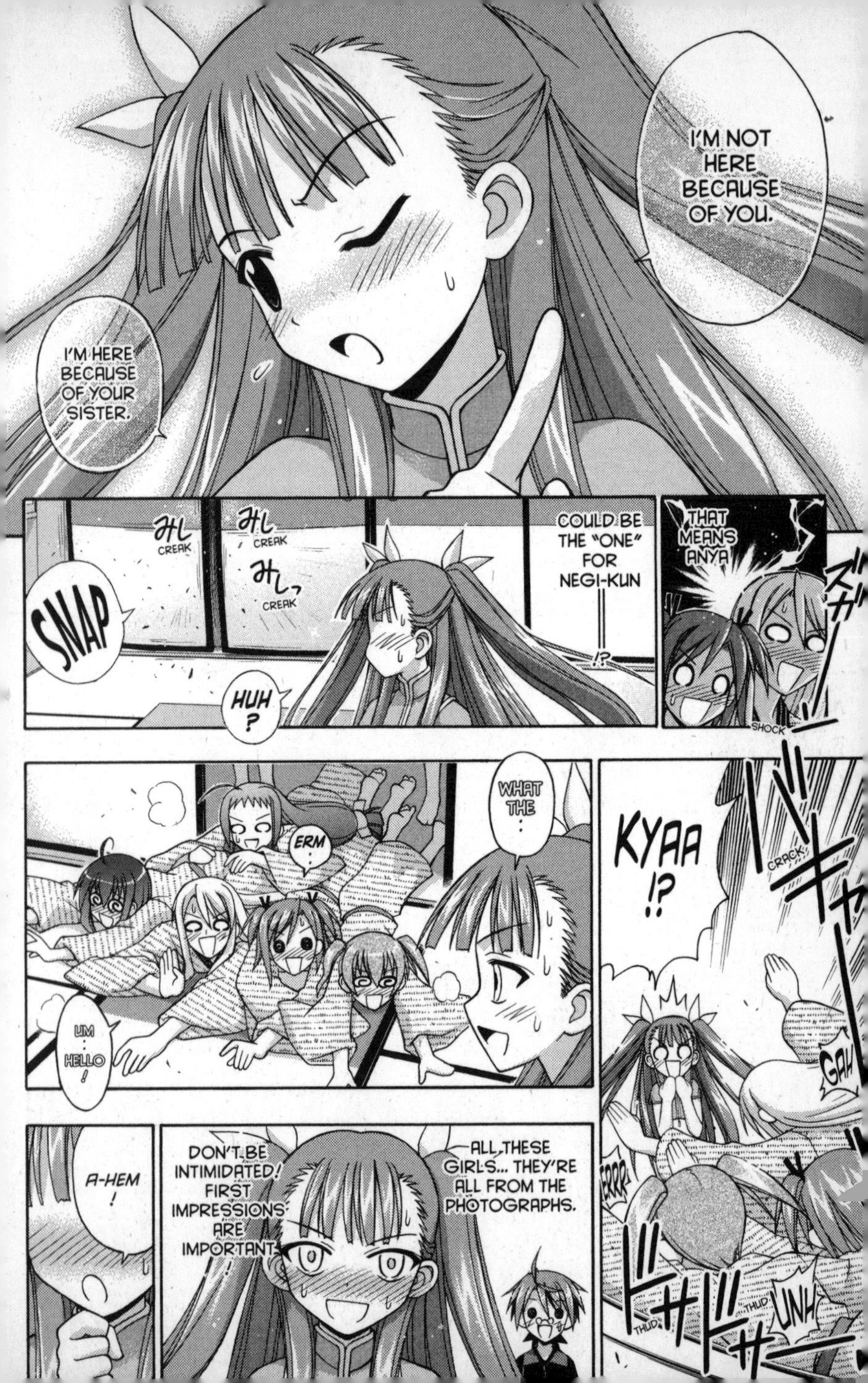
I'M NOT HERE BECAUSE OF YOU.
I'M HERE BECAUSE OF YOUR SISTER.
THAT MEANS ANYA
SHOCK
COULD BE THE "ONE" FOR NEGI-KUN ||| !?
みし CREAK
みし CREAK
みしっ CREAK
SNAP
HUH?
KYAA !?
CRACK
GAH
ERRR
THUD
THUD
UNH
WHAT THE . .
ERM . .
UM . . HELLO!
ALL THESE GIRLS... THEY'RE ALL FROM THE PHOTOGRAPHS.
DON'T BE INTIMIDATED! FIRST IMPRESSIONS ARE IMPORTANT
A-HEM!

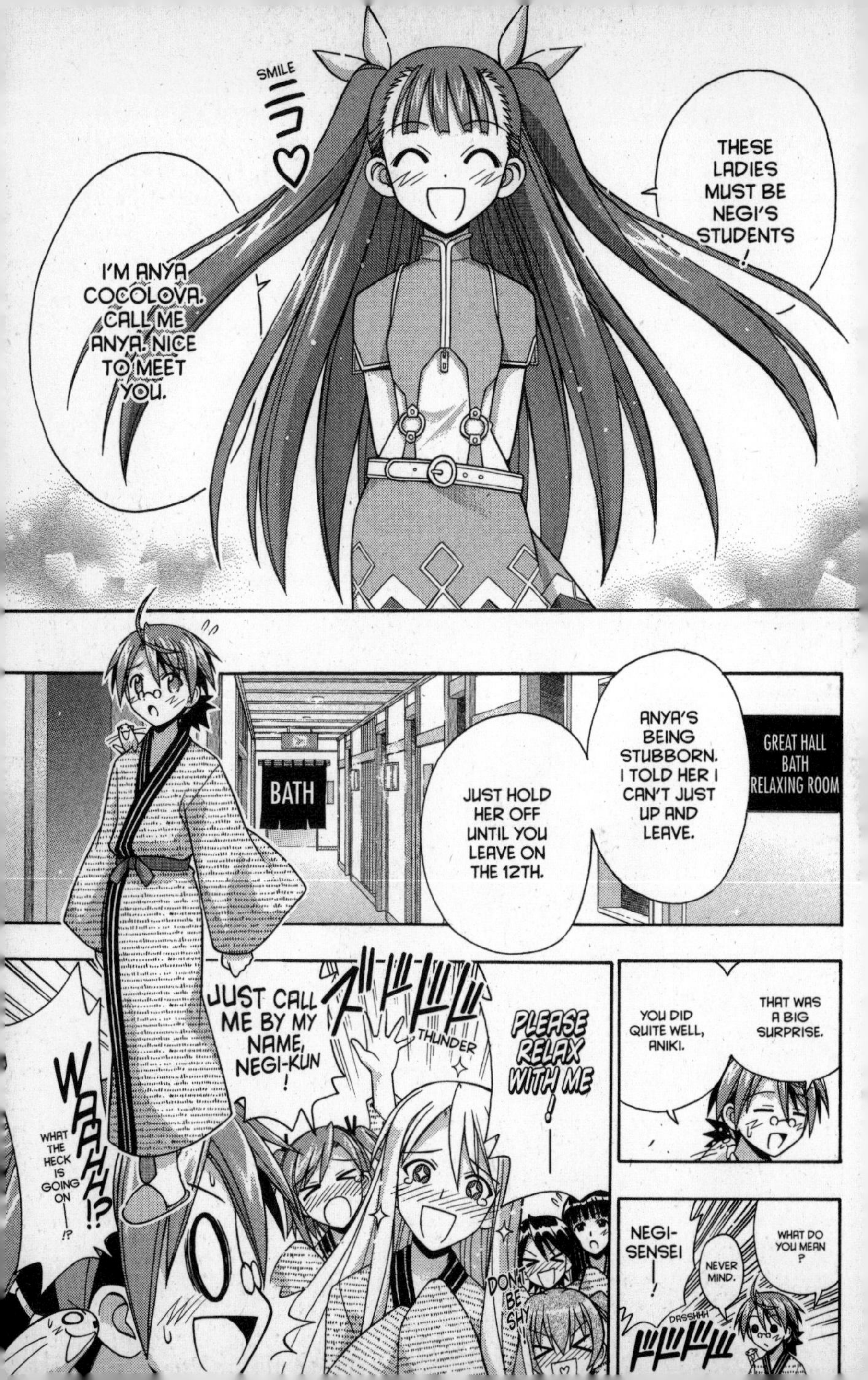
THESE LADIES MUST BE NEGI'S STUDENTS!
SMILE
I'M ANYA COCOLOVA. CALL ME ANYA. NICE TO MEET YOU.
GREAT HALL BATH RELAXING ROOM
ANYA'S BEING STUBBORN. I TOLD HER I CAN'T JUST UP AND LEAVE.
JUST HOLD HER OFF UNTIL YOU LEAVE ON THE 12TH.
BATH
THAT WAS A BIG SURPRISE.
YOU DID QUITE WELL, ANIKI.
WHAT DO YOU MEAN?
NEVER MIND.
NEGI-SENSEI!
DASSHHH
PLEASE RELAX WITH ME!
THUNDER
JUST CALL ME BY MY NAME, NEGI-KUN!
WAAAHH!?
WHAT THE HECK IS GOING ON!?
DON'T BE SHY!

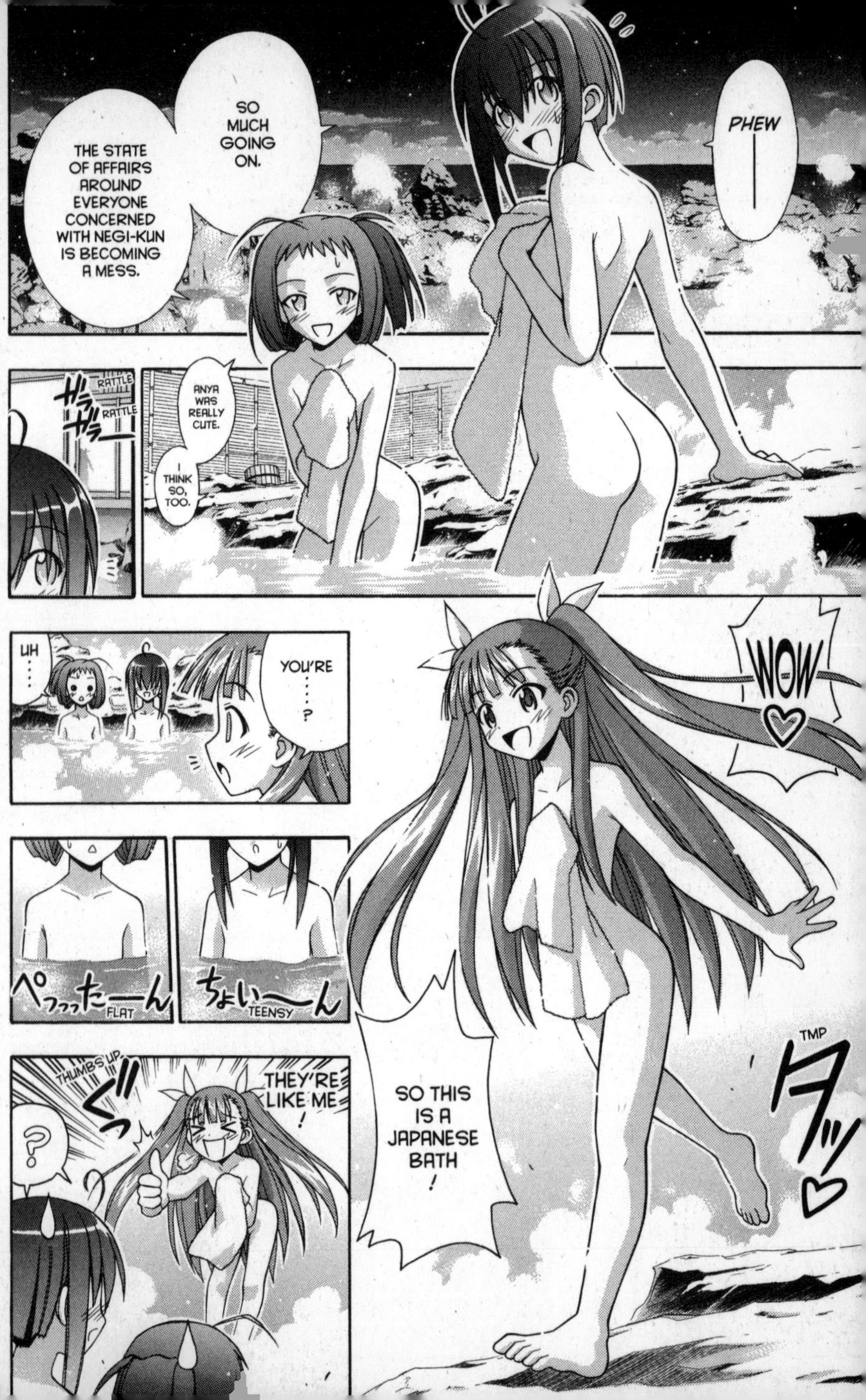
PHEW —
SO MUCH GOING ON.
THE STATE OF AFFAIRS AROUND EVERYONE CONCERNED WITH NEGI-KUN IS BECOMING A MESS.
ANYA WAS REALLY CUTE.
I THINK SO, TOO.
ガラガラー
RATTLE RATTLE
WOW ♥
ダッ
TMP
SO THIS IS A JAPANESE BATH!
YOU'RE...?
UH...
ちょい〜ん
TEENSY
ぺっっったーん
FLAT
ぐっ
THUMBS UP
THEY'RE LIKE ME!
?

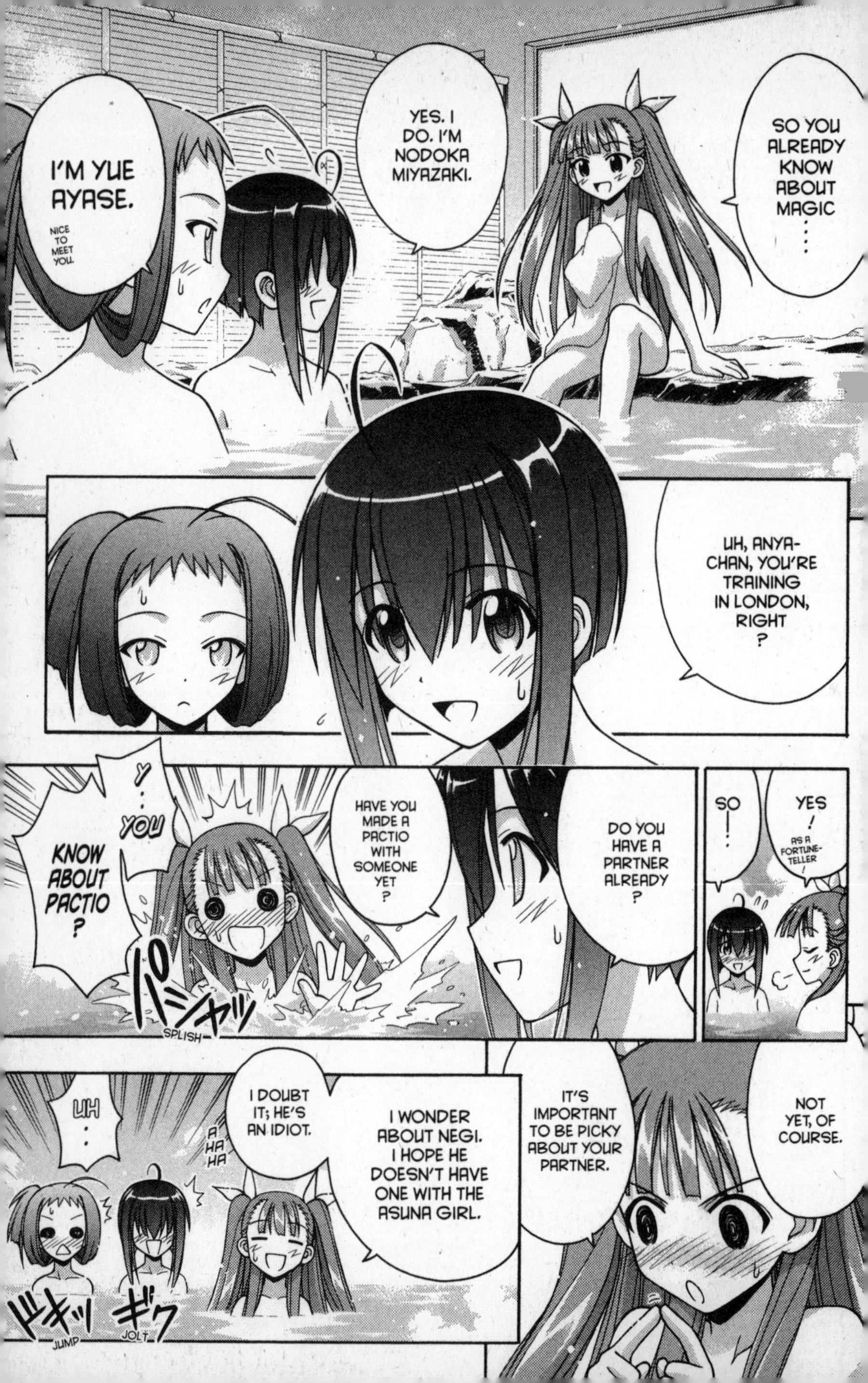
SO YOU ALREADY KNOW ABOUT MAGIC...
YES. I DO. I'M NODOKA MIYAZAKI.
I'M YUE AYASE.
NICE TO MEET YOU.
UH, ANYA-CHAN, YOU'RE TRAINING IN LONDON, RIGHT?
YES! AS A FORTUNE-TELLER!
SO...!
DO YOU HAVE A PARTNER ALREADY?
HAVE YOU MADE A PACTIO WITH SOMEONE YET?
Y... YOU KNOW ABOUT PACTIO?
SPLISH
NOT YET, OF COURSE.
IT'S IMPORTANT TO BE PICKY ABOUT YOUR PARTNER.
I WONDER ABOUT NEGI. I HOPE HE DOESN'T HAVE ONE WITH THE ASUNA GIRL.
I DOUBT IT; HE'S AN IDIOT.
A HA HA
UH...
JOLT
JUMP

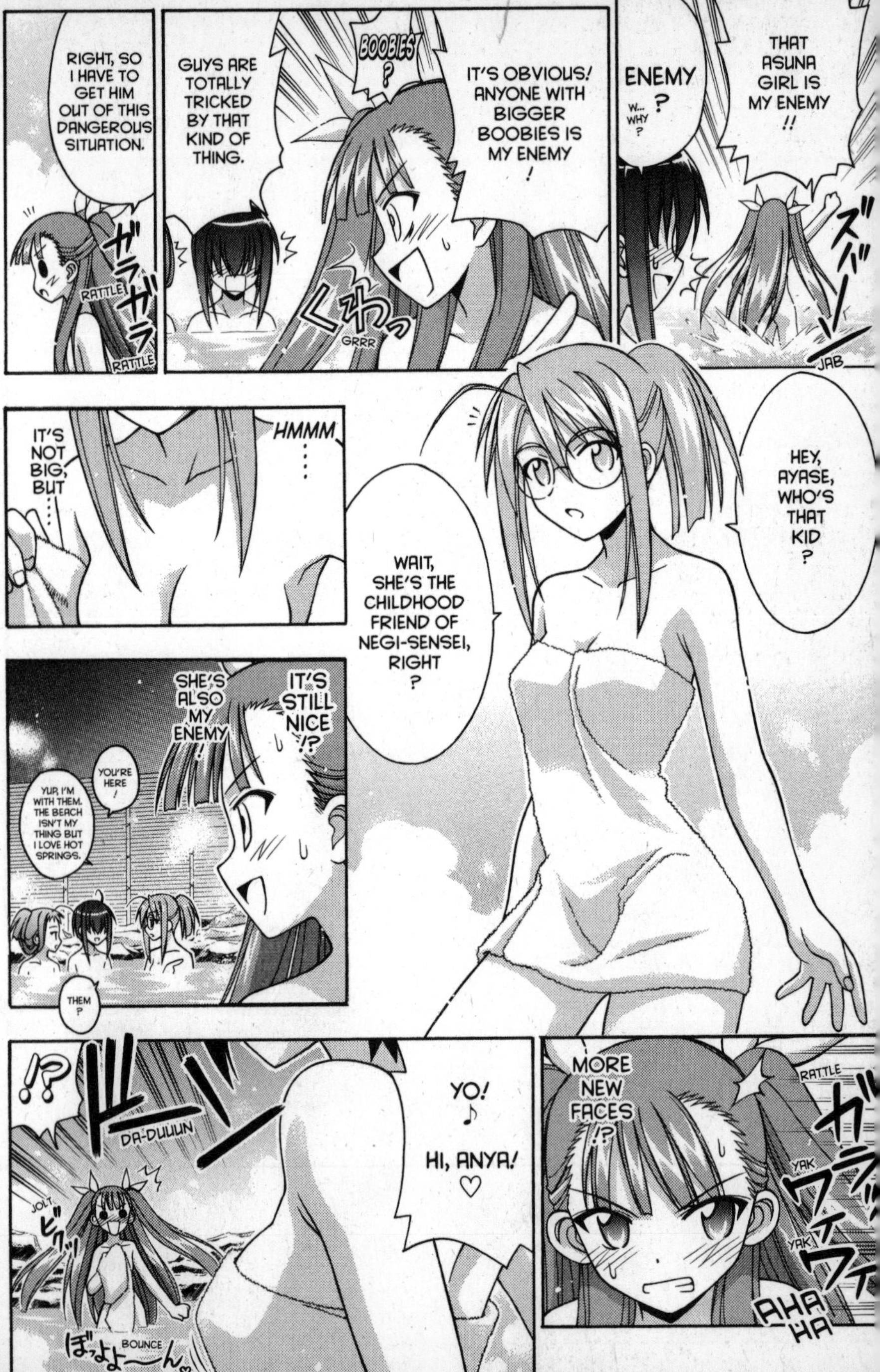
THAT ASUNA GIRL IS MY ENEMY !!
ENEMY ?
W... WHY ?
JAB
BOOBIES ?
IT'S OBVIOUS! ANYONE WITH BIGGER BOOBIES IS MY ENEMY !
GUYS ARE TOTALLY TRICKED BY THAT KIND OF THING.
GRRR
RIGHT, SO I HAVE TO GET HIM OUT OF THIS DANGEROUS SITUATION.
RATTLE
RATTLE
HEY, AYASE, WHO'S THAT KID ?
WAIT, SHE'S THE CHILDHOOD FRIEND OF NEGI-SENSEI, RIGHT ?
HMMM ....
IT'S NOT BIG, BUT ....
IT'S STILL NICE !?
SHE'S ALSO MY ENEMY !
YOU'RE HERE !
YUP, I'M WITH THEM. THE BEACH ISN'T MY THING BUT I LOVE HOT SPRINGS.
THEM ?
MORE NEW FACES !?
RATTLE
YAK
YAK
AHA HA
YO! ♪
HI, ANYA! ♡
!?
DA-DUUUN
JOLT
BOUNCE

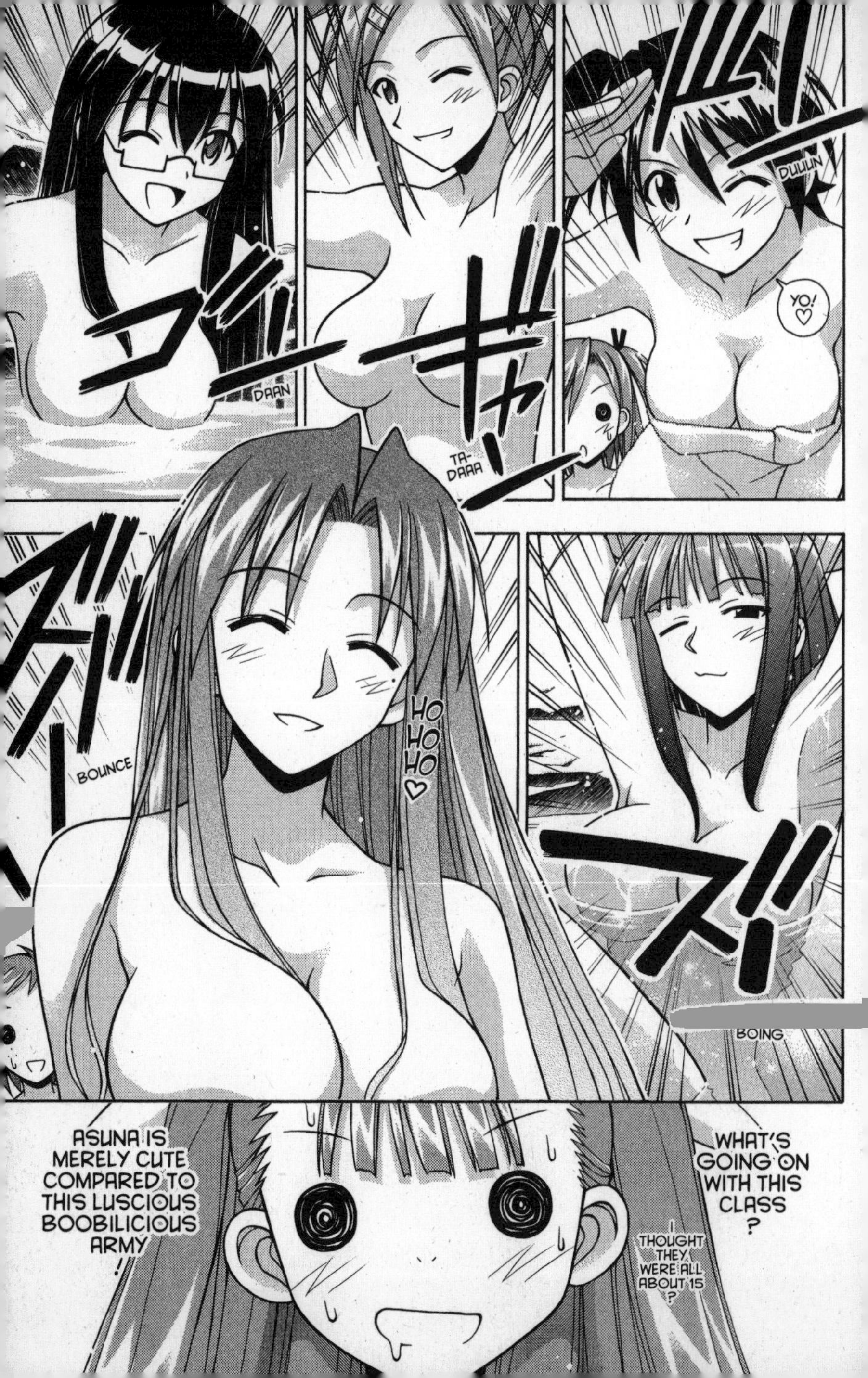
DUUUN
YO! ♡
TA-DAAA
DAAN
BOING
HO HO HO ♡
BOUNCE
WHAT'S GOING ON WITH THIS CLASS?
I THOUGHT THEY WERE ALL ABOUT 15?
ASUNA IS MERELY CUTE COMPARED TO THIS LUSCIOUS BOOBILICIOUS ARMY!

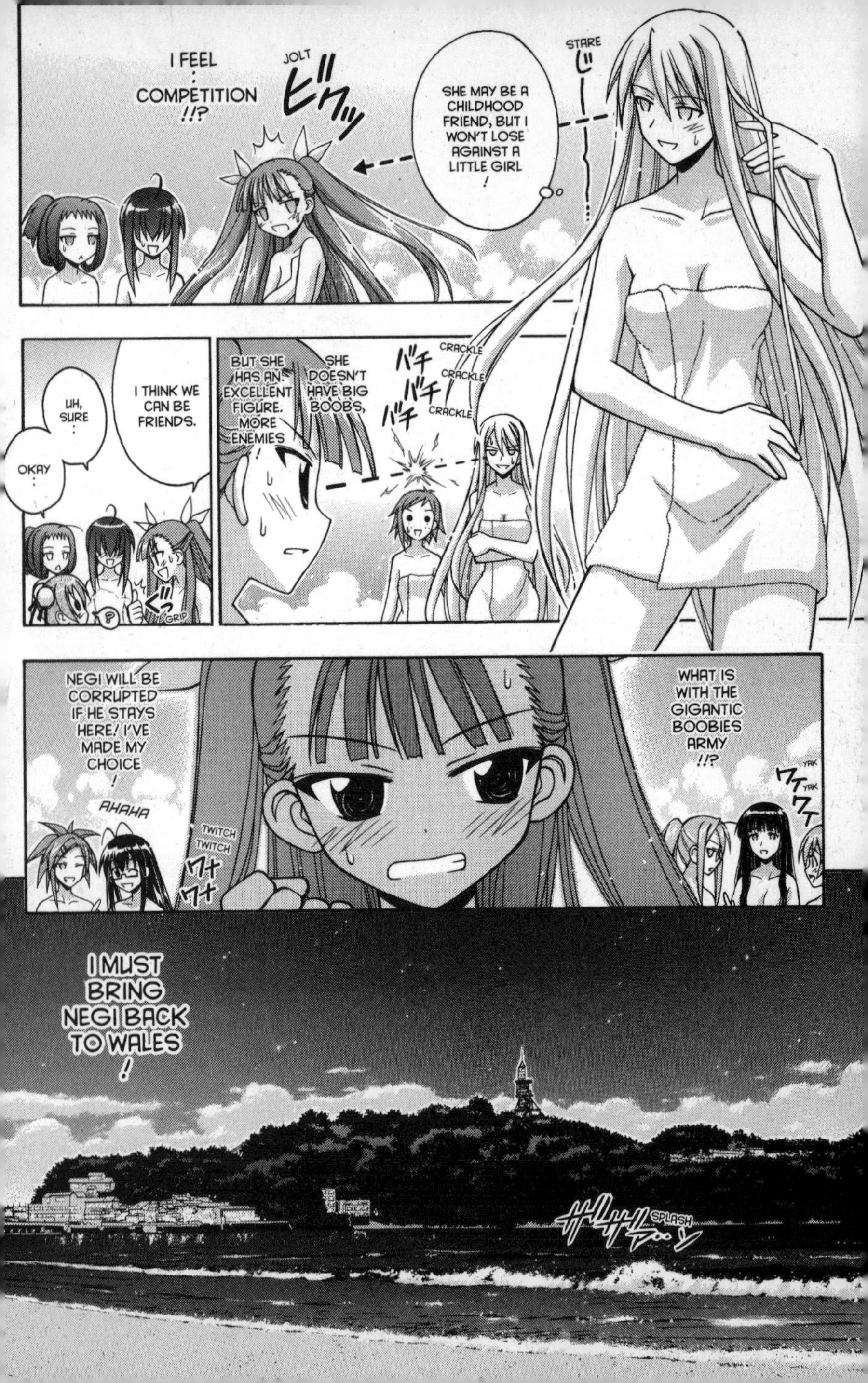
STARE
SHE MAY BE A CHILDHOOD FRIEND, BUT I WON'T LOSE AGAINST A LITTLE GIRL!
JOLT
I FEEL ... COMPETITION!!?
SHE DOESN'T HAVE BIG BOOBS,
BUT SHE HAS AN EXCELLENT FIGURE. MORE ENEMIES!
CRACKLE
CRACKLE
CRACKLE
I THINK WE CAN BE FRIENDS.
UH, SURE...
OKAY...
GRIP
WHAT IS WITH THE GIGANTIC BOOBIES ARMY!?
YAK YAK
NEGI WILL BE CORRUPTED IF HE STAYS HERE! I'VE MADE MY CHOICE!
AHAHA
TWITCH TWITCH
I MUST BRING NEGI BACK TO WALES!
SPLASH

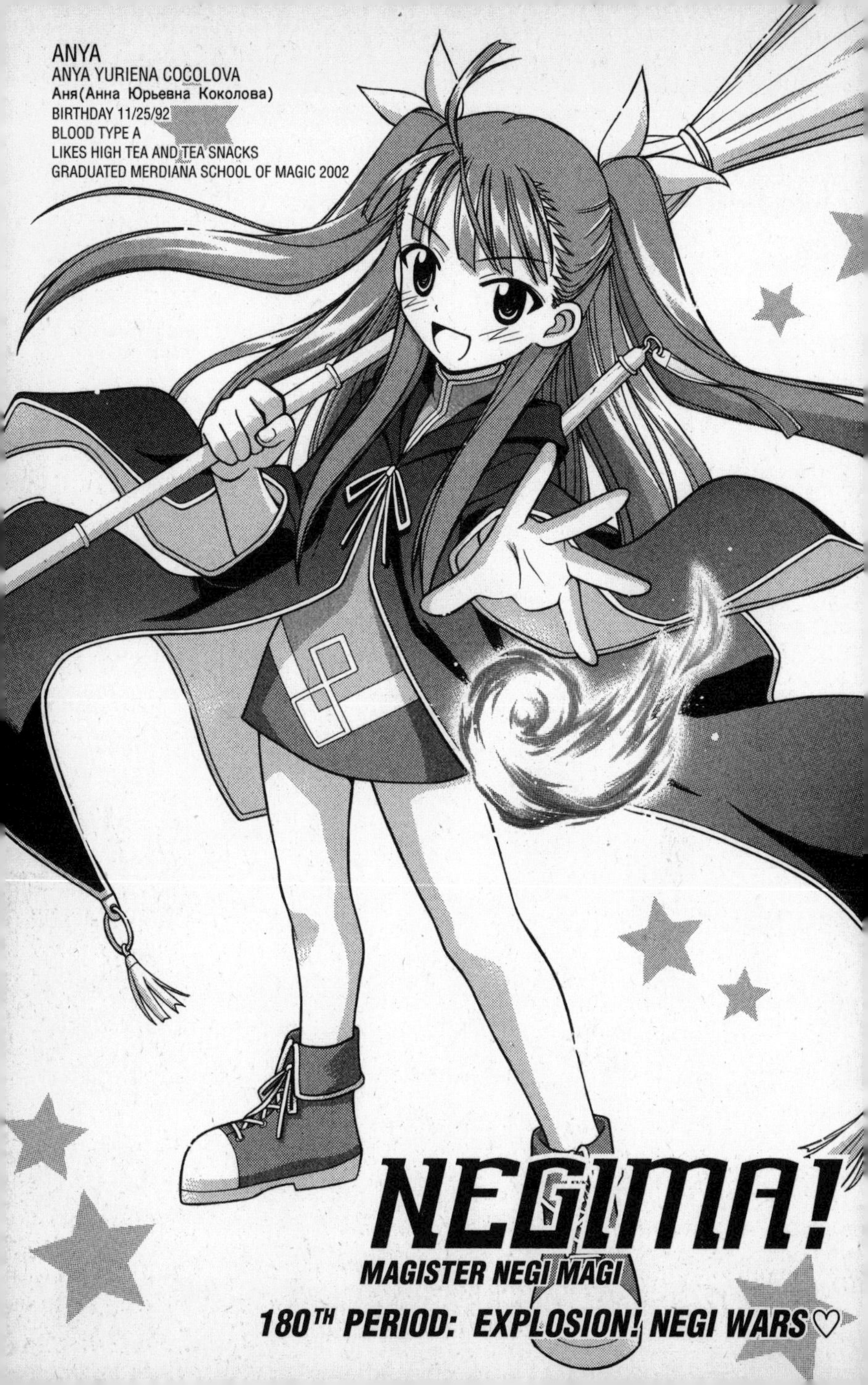
ANYA
ANYA YURIENA COCOLOVA
Аня(Анна Юрьевна Коколова)
BIRTHDAY 11/25/92
BLOOD TYPE A
LIKES HIGH TEA AND TEA SNACKS
GRADUATED MERDIANA SCHOOL OF MAGIC 2002
NEGIMA!
MAGISTER NEGI MAGI
180TH PERIOD: EXPLOSION! NEGI WARS♡

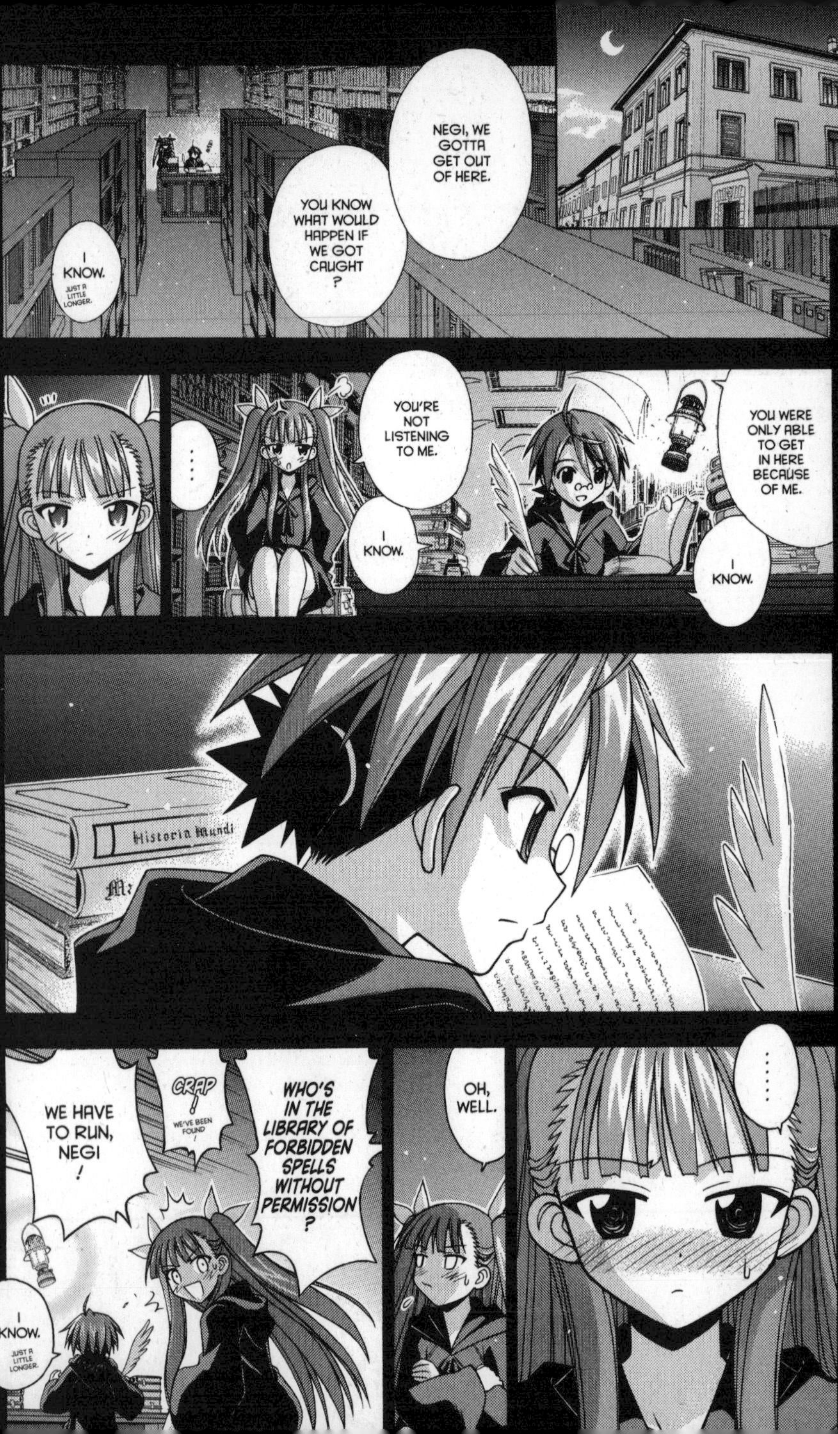
NEGI, WE GOTTA GET OUT OF HERE.
YOU KNOW WHAT WOULD HAPPEN IF WE GOT CAUGHT?
I KNOW.
JUST A LITTLE LONGER.
YOU WERE ONLY ABLE TO GET IN HERE BECAUSE OF ME.
I KNOW.
YOU'RE NOT LISTENING TO ME.
I KNOW.
....
Historia Mundi
......
OH, WELL.
WHO'S IN THE LIBRARY OF FORBIDDEN SPELLS WITHOUT PERMISSION?
CRAP!
WE'VE BEEN FOUND!
WE HAVE TO RUN, NEGI!
I KNOW.
JUST A LITTLE LONGER.

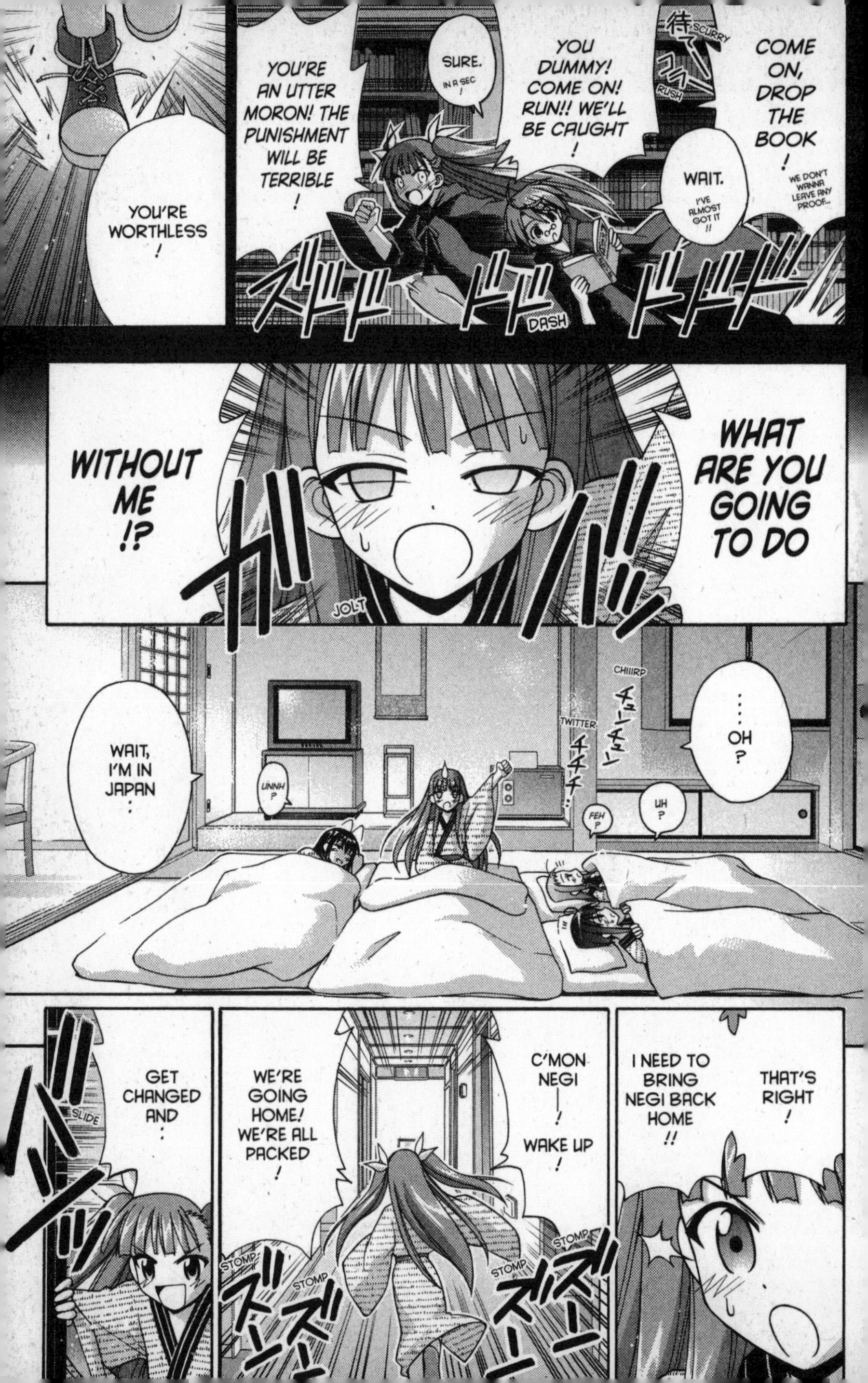
COME ON, DROP THE BOOK!
WE DON'T WANNA LEAVE ANY PROOF...
SCURRY
RUSH
WAIT.
I'VE ALMOST GOT IT!!
YOU DUMMY! COME ON! RUN!! WE'LL BE CAUGHT!
SURE.
IN A SEC!
YOU'RE AN UTTER MORON! THE PUNISHMENT WILL BE TERRIBLE!
DASH
YOU'RE WORTHLESS!
WHAT ARE YOU GOING TO DO
WITHOUT ME!?
JOLT
....OH?
CHIIIRP
TWITTER
UH?
FEH?
UNNH?
WAIT, I'M IN JAPAN:
THAT'S RIGHT!
I NEED TO BRING NEGI BACK HOME!!
STOMP
C'MON NEGI—! WAKE UP!
STOMP
WE'RE GOING HOME! WE'RE ALL PACKED!
STOMP
GET CHANGED AND:
SLIDE
STOMP

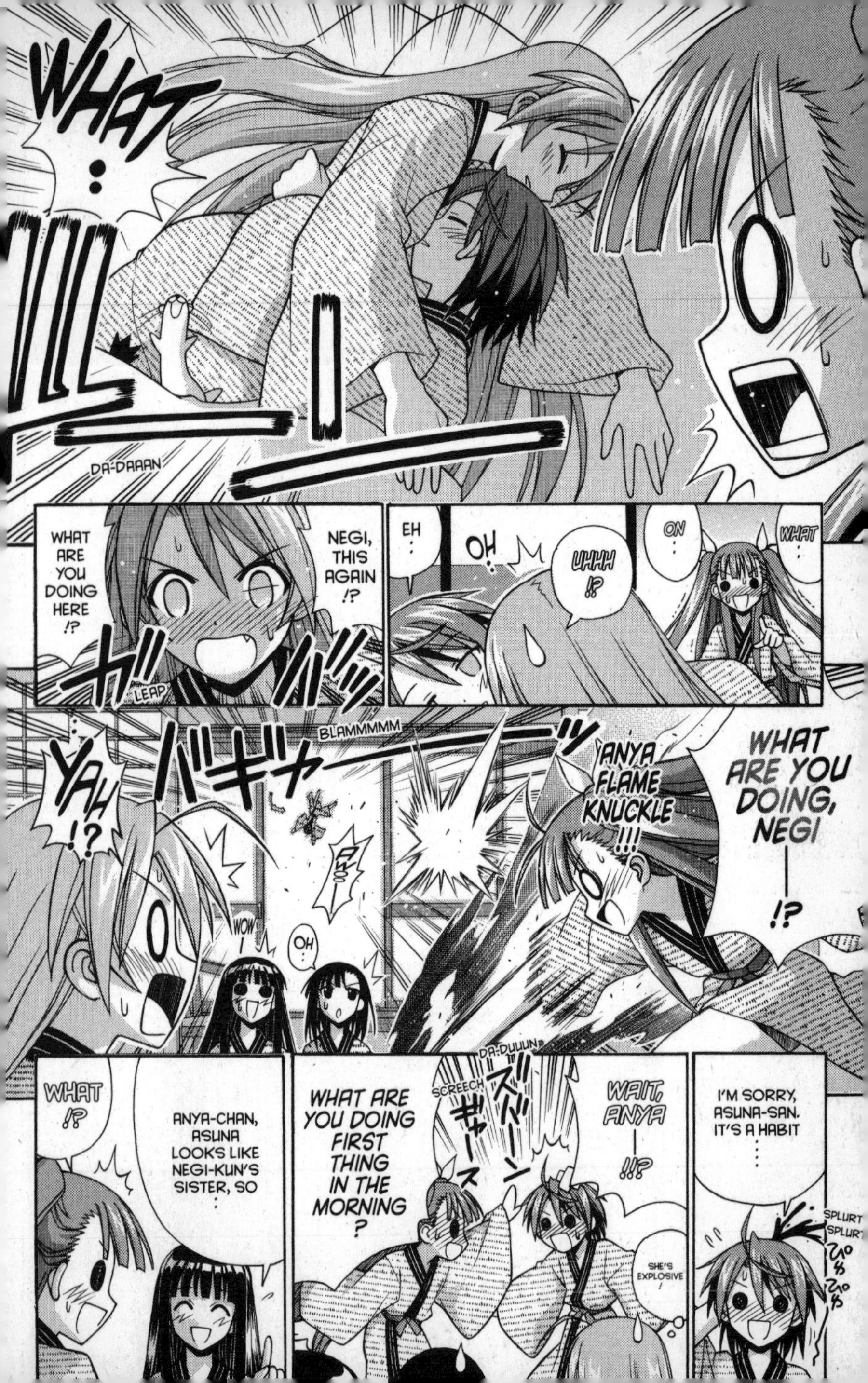
WHAT...!!!
DA-DAAAN
WHAT...
ON...
UHHH!?
OH!
EH...
NEGI, THIS AGAIN!?
WHAT ARE YOU DOING HERE!?
LEAP
WHAT ARE YOU DOING, NEGI—!?
ANYA FLAME KNUCKLE!!!
BLAMMMMM
バギャーッ
OH...
WOW!
YAH!?
I'M SORRY, ASUNA-SAN. IT'S A HABIT...
SPLURT
SPLURT
WAIT, ANYA—!!?
DA-DUUUN
SCREECH
SHE'S EXPLOSIVE!
WHAT ARE YOU DOING FIRST THING IN THE MORNING?
ANYA-CHAN, ASUNA LOOKS LIKE NEGI-KUN'S SISTER, SO...
WHAT!?

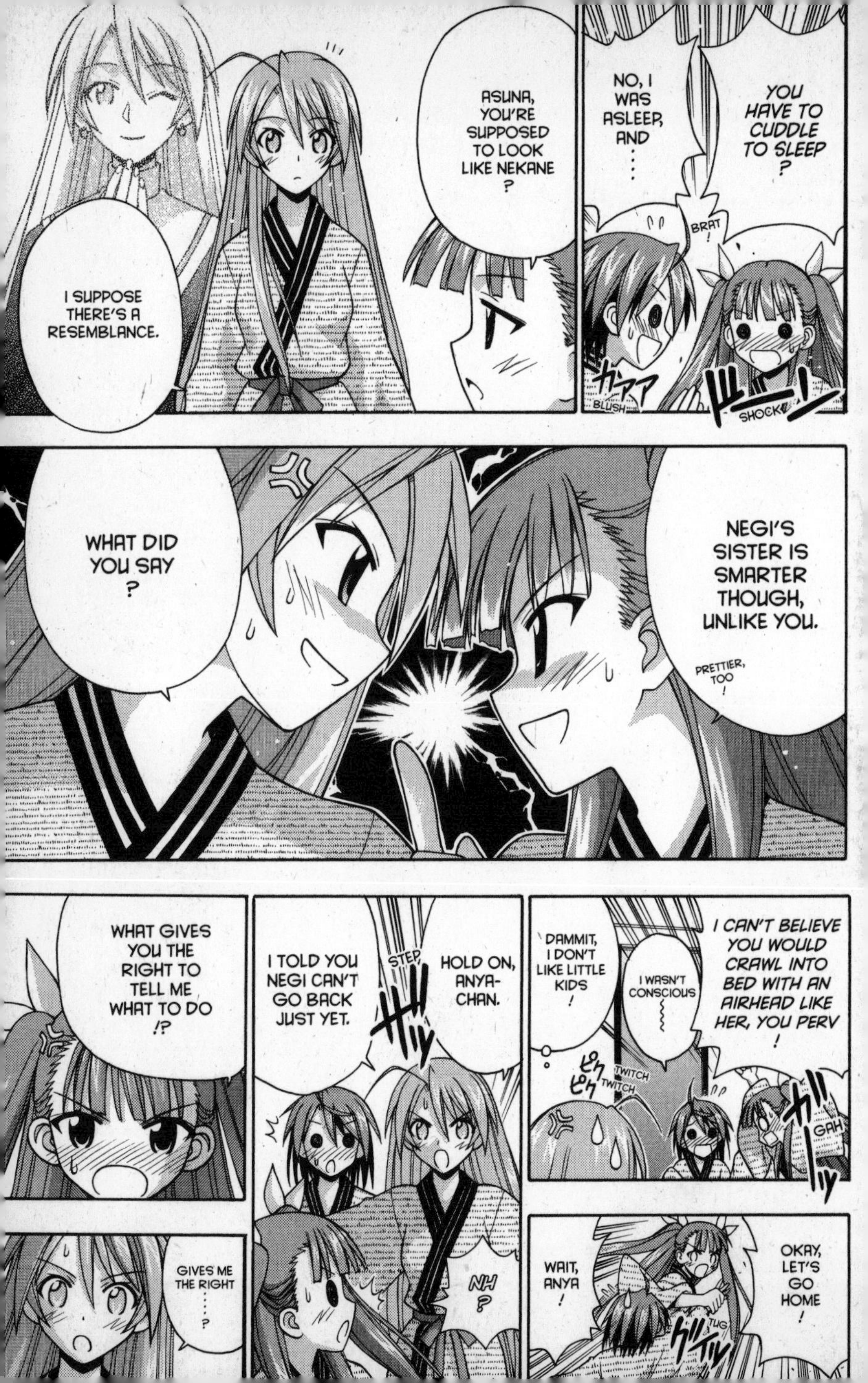
YOU HAVE TO CUDDLE TO SLEEP?
NO, I WAS ASLEEP, AND ....
BRAT!
BLUSH
SHOCK
ASUNA, YOU'RE SUPPOSED TO LOOK LIKE NEKANE?
I SUPPOSE THERE'S A RESEMBLANCE.
NEGI'S SISTER IS SMARTER THOUGH, UNLIKE YOU.
PRETTIER, TOO!
WHAT DID YOU SAY?
I CAN'T BELIEVE YOU WOULD CRAWL INTO BED WITH AN AIRHEAD LIKE HER, YOU PERV!
I WASN'T CONSCIOUS
DAMMIT, I DON'T LIKE LITTLE KIDS!
TWITCH TWITCH
GAH
OKAY, LET'S GO HOME!
WAIT, ANYA!
TUG
HOLD ON, ANYA-CHAN.
STEP
I TOLD YOU NEGI CAN'T GO BACK JUST YET.
NH?
WHAT GIVES YOU THE RIGHT TO TELL ME WHAT TO DO!?
GIVES ME THE RIGHT....?

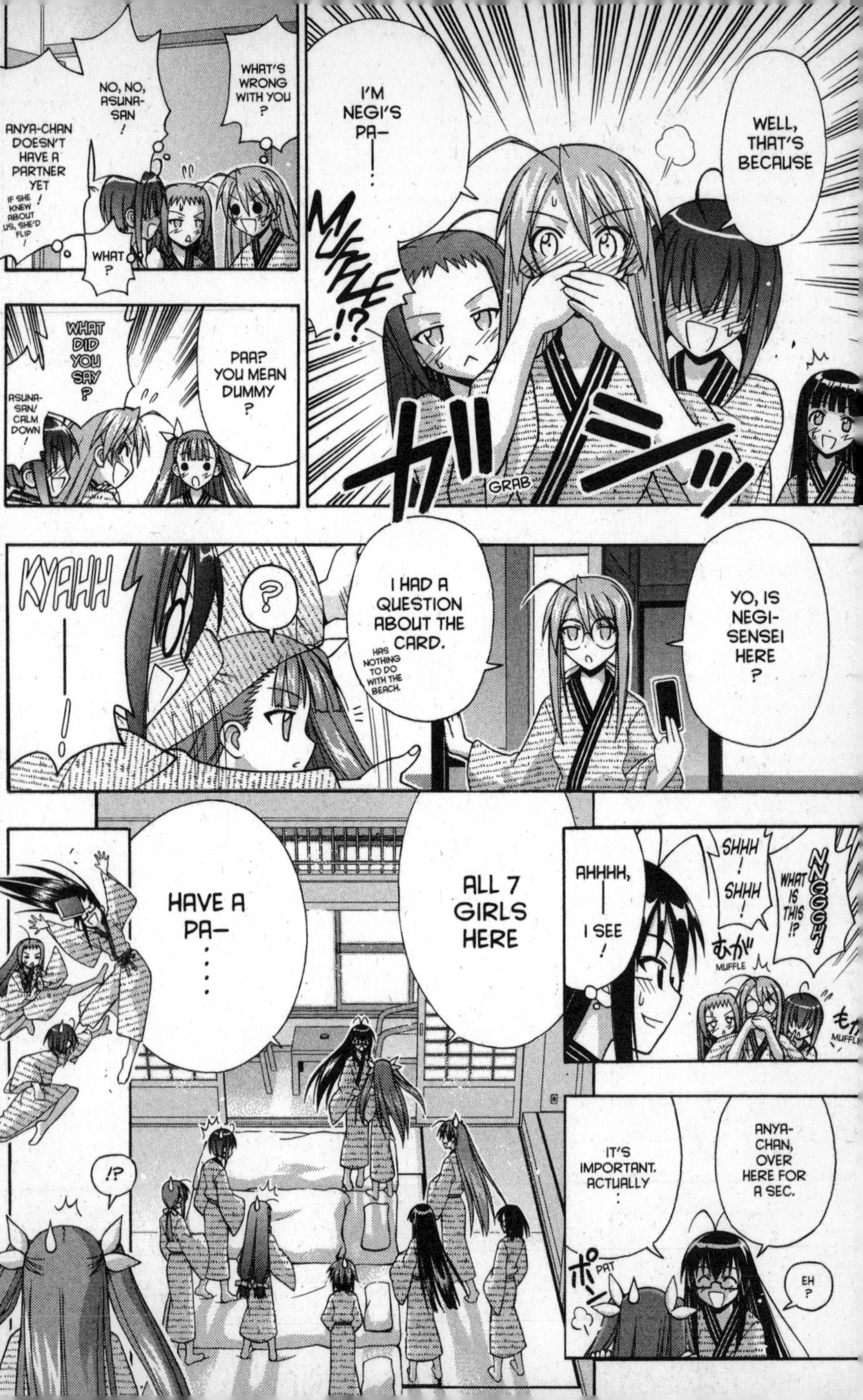

WELL, THAT'S BECAUSE
I'M NEGI'S PA—!
MUFFLE!?
GRAB
WHAT'S WRONG WITH YOU?
NO, NO, ASUNA-SAN!
ANYA-CHAN DOESN'T HAVE A PARTNER YET!
IF SHE KNEW ABOUT US, SHE'D FLIP!
WHAT?
PAA? YOU MEAN DUMMY?
WHAT DID YOU SAY?
ASUNA-SAN! CALM DOWN!
YO, IS NEGI-SENSEI HERE?
I HAD A QUESTION ABOUT THE CARD.
HAS NOTHING TO DO WITH THE BEACH.
?
KYAHH—!
NNGGGH!
WHAT IS THIS!?
SHHH! SHHH!
MUFFLE
MUFFLE
AHHHH,— I SEE!
ANYA-CHAN, OVER HERE FOR A SEC.
IT'S IMPORTANT. ACTUALLY...
PAT
EH?
ALL 7 GIRLS HERE
HAVE A PA—....
!?

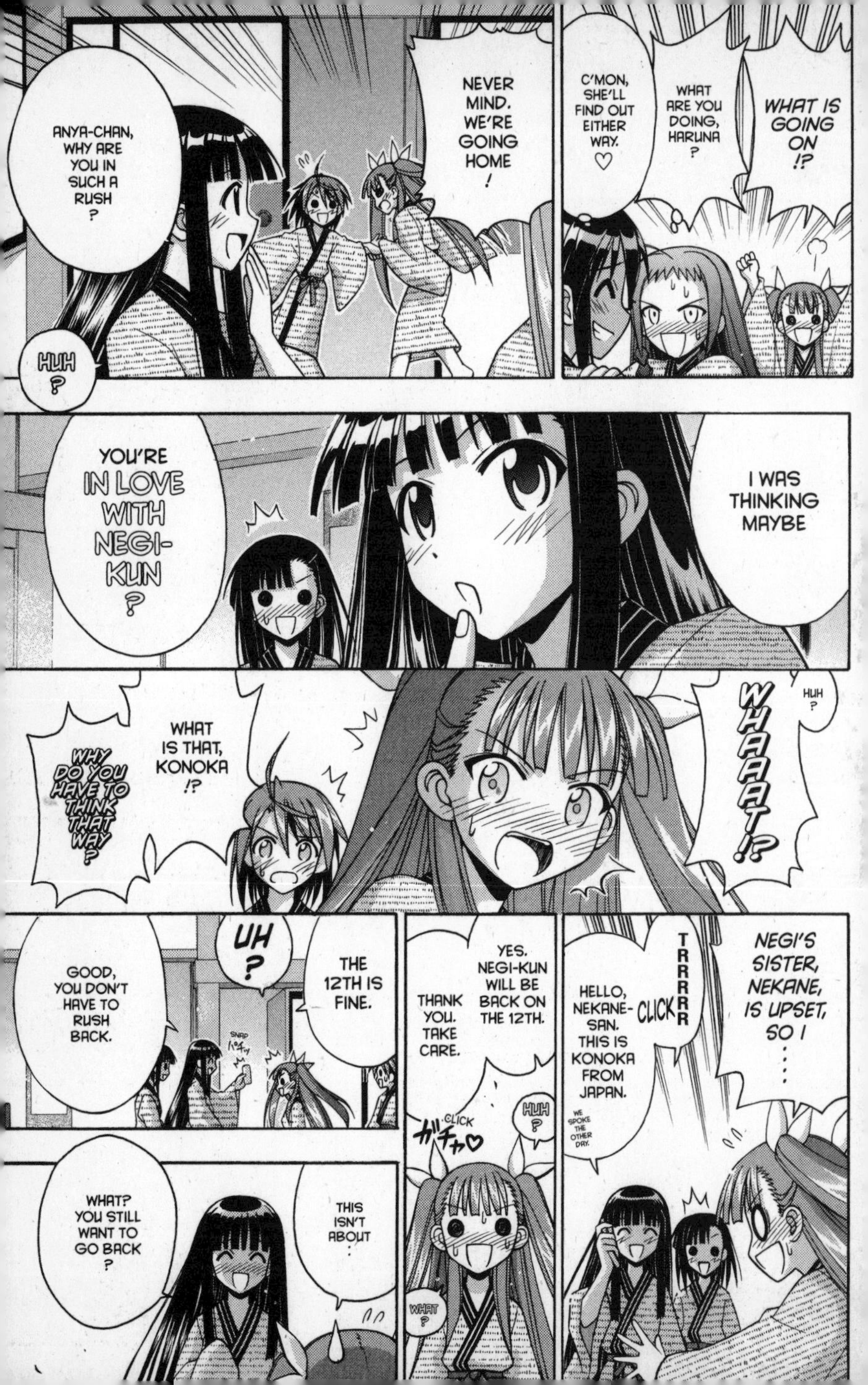
WHAT IS GOING ON !?
WHAT ARE YOU DOING, HARUNA ?
C'MON, SHE'LL FIND OUT EITHER WAY. ♡
NEVER MIND. WE'RE GOING HOME !
ANYA-CHAN, WHY ARE YOU IN SUCH A RUSH ?
HUH ?
I WAS THINKING MAYBE
YOU'RE IN LOVE WITH NEGI-KUN ?
HUH ?
WHAAAAT!?
WHAT IS THAT, KONOKA !?
WHY DO YOU HAVE TO THINK THAT WAY ?
NEGI'S SISTER, NEKANE, IS UPSET, SO I ....
TRRRRRR
CLICK
HELLO, NEKANE-SAN. THIS IS KONOKA FROM JAPAN.
WE SPOKE THE OTHER DAY.
YES. NEGI-KUN WILL BE BACK ON THE 12TH.
THANK YOU. TAKE CARE.
HUH ?
CLICK
ガチャ♡
WHAT ?
UH ?
THE 12TH IS FINE.
SNAP
GOOD, YOU DON'T HAVE TO RUSH BACK.
THIS ISN'T ABOUT :
WHAT? YOU STILL WANT TO GO BACK ?

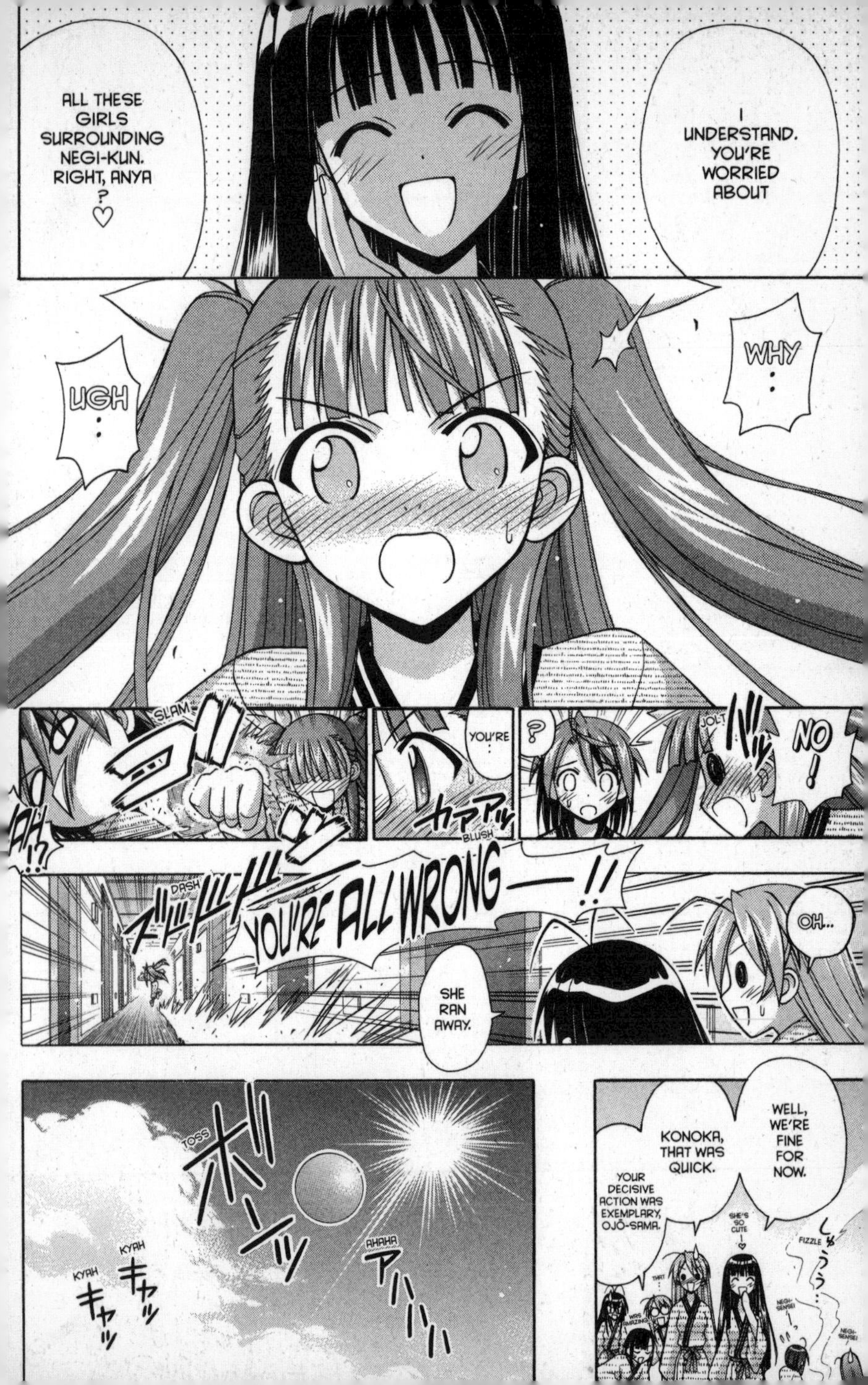

I UNDERSTAND. YOU'RE WORRIED ABOUT
ALL THESE GIRLS SURROUNDING NEGI-KUN. RIGHT, ANYA? ♡
WHY...
UGH...
NO!
JOLT
?
YOU'RE...
BLUSH
SLAM
AH!?
OH...
SHE RAN AWAY.
YOU'RE ALL WRONG—!!
DASH
WELL, WE'RE FINE FOR NOW.
KONOKA, THAT WAS QUICK.
YOUR DECISIVE ACTION WAS EXEMPLARY, OJŌ-SAMA.
SHE'S SO CUTE ♡
THAT... WAS AMAZING
FIZZLE
NEGI-SENSEI!
NEGI-SENSEI
TOSS
AHAHA
KYAH
KYAH

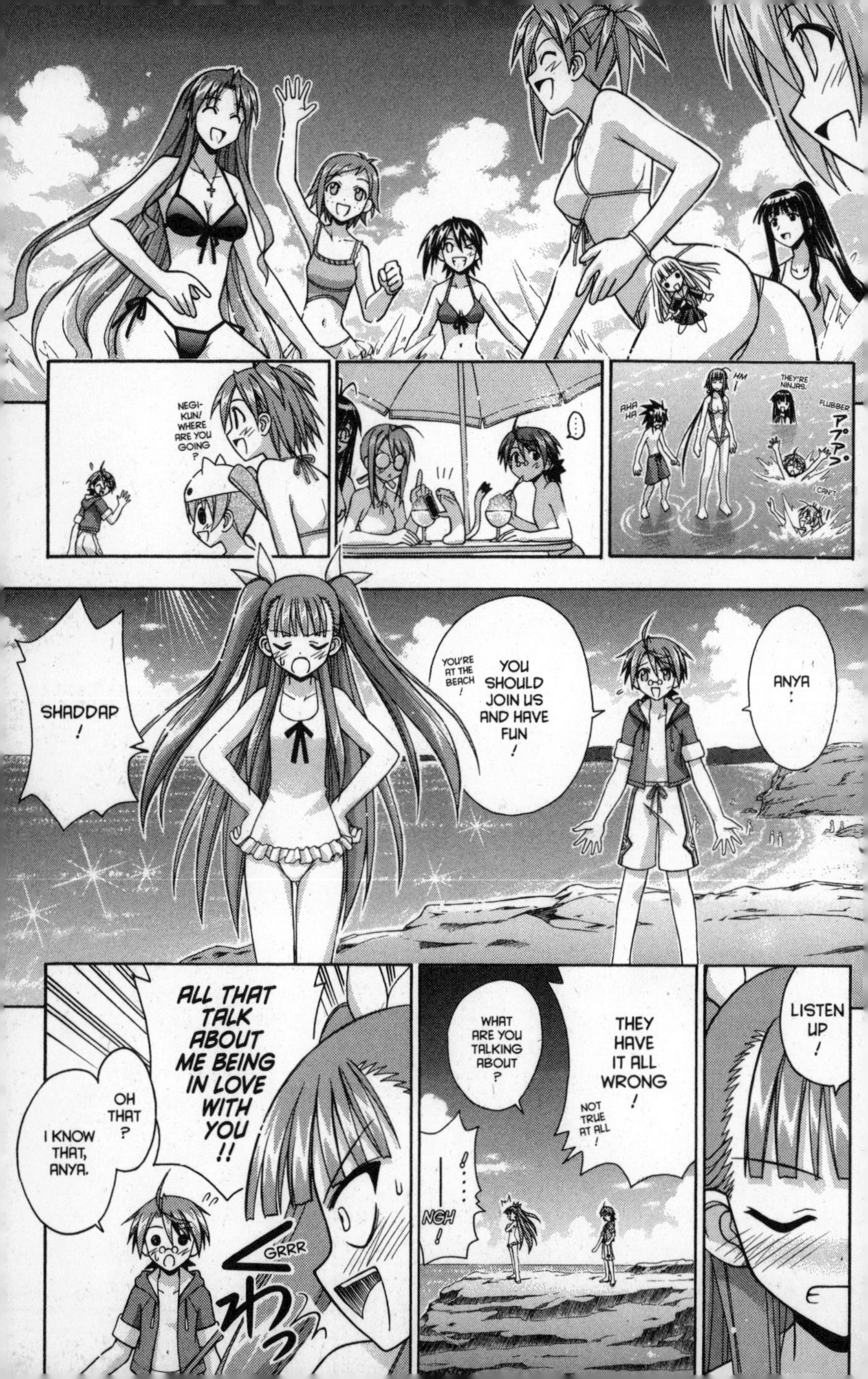
HM !
THEY'RE NINJAS.
AHA HA
FLUBBER
アプアプ
I CAN'T !
…
NEGI-KUN! WHERE ARE YOU GOING ?
ANYA !
YOU SHOULD JOIN US AND HAVE FUN !
YOU'RE AT THE BEACH !
SHADDAP !
LISTEN UP !
THEY HAVE IT ALL WRONG !
NOT TRUE AT ALL !
WHAT ARE YOU TALKING ABOUT ?
…!
NGH !
ALL THAT TALK ABOUT ME BEING IN LOVE WITH YOU !!
OH THAT ?
I KNOW THAT, ANYA.
GRRR

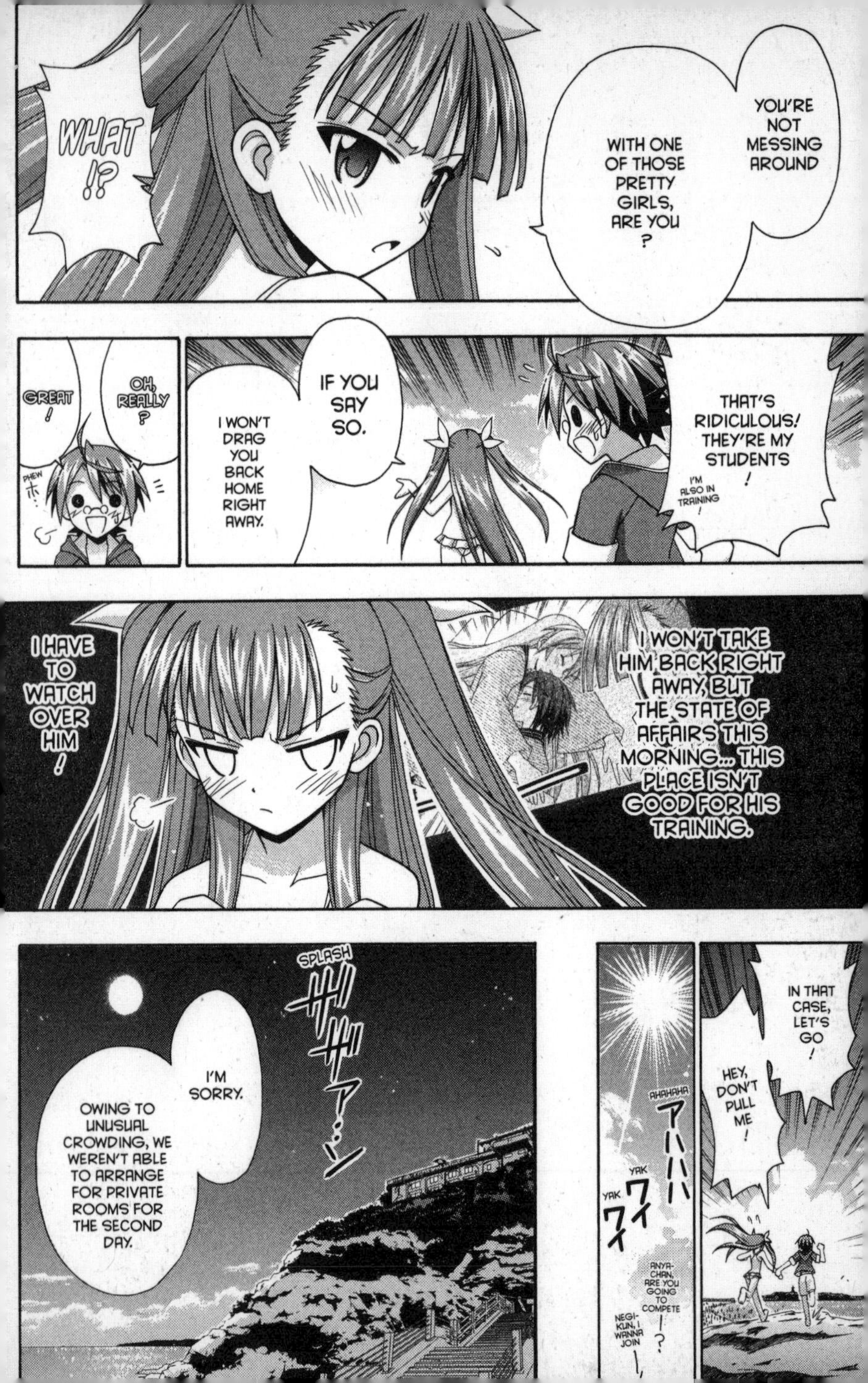
YOU'RE NOT MESSING AROUND
WITH ONE OF THOSE PRETTY GIRLS, ARE YOU?
WHAT!?
THAT'S RIDICULOUS! THEY'RE MY STUDENTS!
I'M ALSO IN TRAINING!
IF YOU SAY SO.
I WON'T DRAG YOU BACK HOME RIGHT AWAY.
OH, REALLY?
GREAT!
PHEW
I WON'T TAKE HIM BACK RIGHT AWAY, BUT THE STATE OF AFFAIRS THIS MORNING... THIS PLACE ISN'T GOOD FOR HIS TRAINING.
I HAVE TO WATCH OVER HIM!
IN THAT CASE, LET'S GO!
HEY, DON'T PULL ME!
AHAHAHA
YAK YAK
ANYA-CHAN, ARE YOU GOING TO COMPETE!?
NEGI-KUN, I WANNA JOIN!
SPLASH
I'M SORRY.
OWING TO UNUSUAL CROWDING, WE WEREN'T ABLE TO ARRANGE FOR PRIVATE ROOMS FOR THE SECOND DAY.

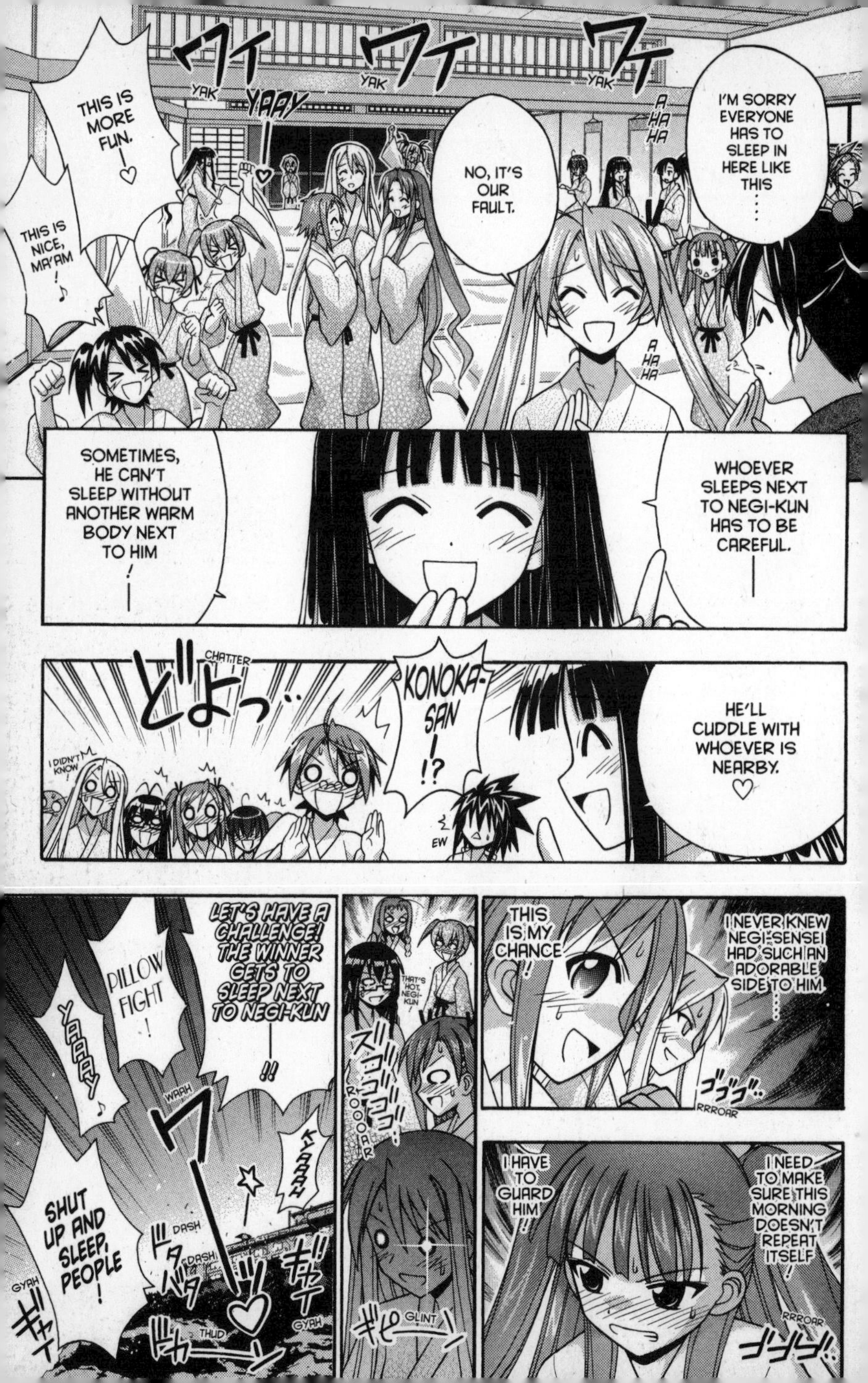
I'M SORRY EVERYONE HAS TO SLEEP IN HERE LIKE THIS....
A HA HA
YAK
NO, IT'S OUR FAULT.
A HA HA
YAK
YAK
YAAY!♡
THIS IS MORE FUN.♡
YAK
THIS IS NICE, MA'AM!♪
WHOEVER SLEEPS NEXT TO NEGI-KUN HAS TO BE CAREFUL.—
SOMETIMES, HE CAN'T SLEEP WITHOUT ANOTHER WARM BODY NEXT TO HIM!
HE'LL CUDDLE WITH WHOEVER IS NEARBY.♡
EW
KONOKA-SAN!!?
CHATTER
I DIDN'T KNOW!
I NEVER KNEW NEGI-SENSEI HAD SUCH AN ADORABLE SIDE TO HIM....
THIS IS MY CHANCE!
RRROAR
I NEED TO MAKE SURE THIS MORNING DOESN'T REPEAT ITSELF!
I HAVE TO GUARD HIM!
RRROAR
GLINT
THAT'S HOT, NEGI-KUN!
RRRROOOAR
LET'S HAVE A CHALLENGE! THE WINNER GETS TO SLEEP NEXT TO NEGI-KUN—!!
PILLOW FIGHT!
YAAAAY♪
WAAH
KYAAAH
GYAH
DASH
DASH
THUD
SHUT UP AND SLEEP, PEOPLE!
GYAH

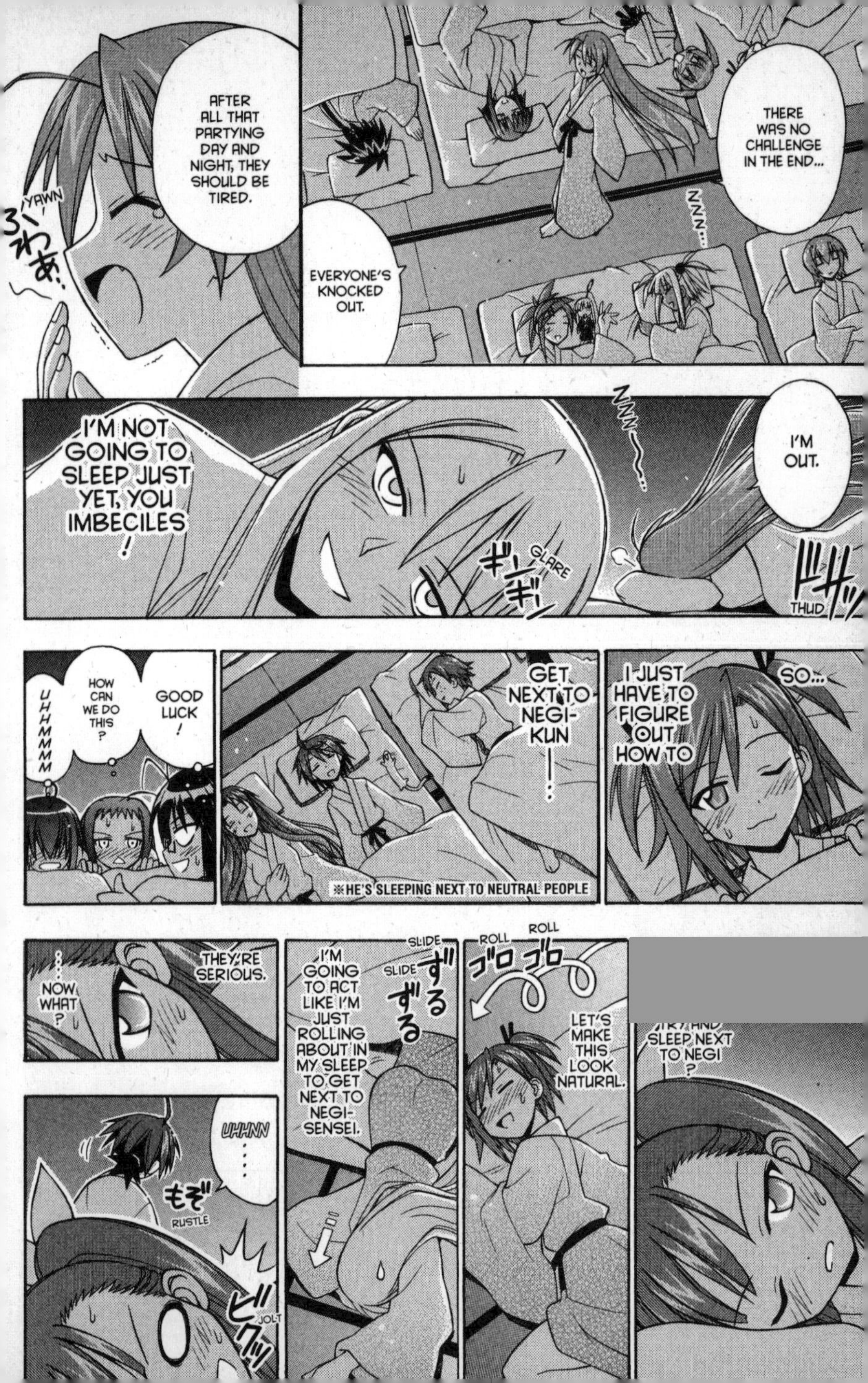
THERE WAS NO CHALLENGE IN THE END...
ZZZ...
EVERYONE'S KNOCKED OUT.
AFTER ALL THAT PARTYING DAY AND NIGHT, THEY SHOULD BE TIRED.
ふわあ
YAWN
I'M OUT.
ドサッ
THUD
ZZZ~...
ギンギン
GLARE
I'M NOT GOING TO SLEEP JUST YET, YOU IMBECILES!
SO...
I JUST HAVE TO FIGURE OUT HOW TO
GET NEXT TO NEGI-KUN...!
※HE'S SLEEPING NEXT TO NEUTRAL PEOPLE
GOOD LUCK!
HOW CAN WE DO THIS?
UHHMMMM
SLEEP NEXT TO NEGI ?
ゴロゴロ
ROLL ROLL
LET'S MAKE THIS LOOK NATURAL.
ずるずる
SLIDE SLIDE
I'M GOING TO ACT LIKE I'M JUST ROLLING ABOUT IN MY SLEEP TO GET NEXT TO NEGI-SENSEI.
THEY'RE SERIOUS.
...NOW WHAT?
UHHNN...
もぞ
RUSTLE
ビクッ
JOLT

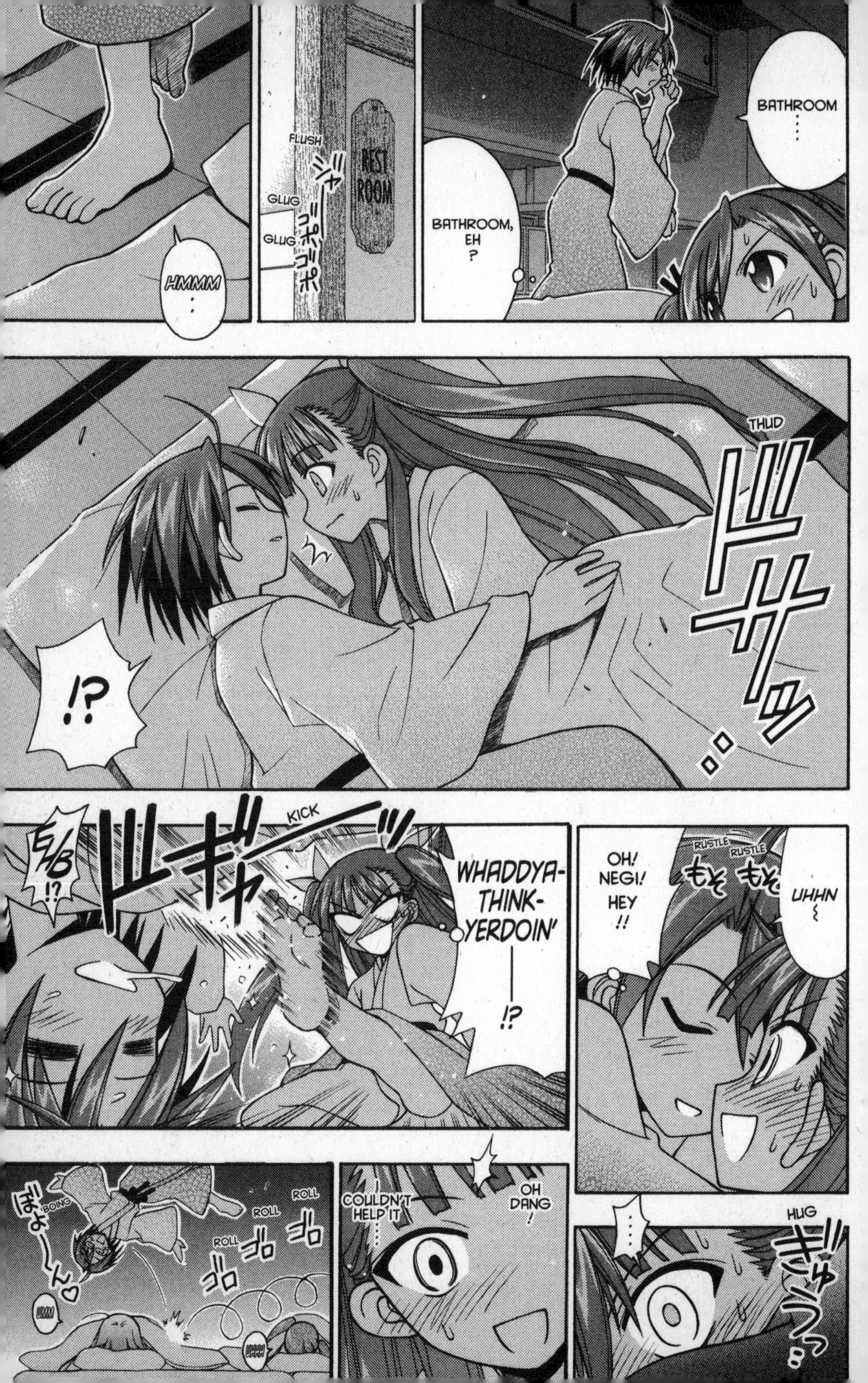
BATHROOM
....
BATHROOM, EH
?
FLUSH
ジャー
GLUG
GLUG
ゴポゴポ
REST ROOM
HMMM
:
THUD
ドサッ
!?
RUSTLE
RUSTLE
もそ もそ
UHHN
~
OH! NEGI! HEY !!
KICK
ドギャ
WHADDYA-THINK-YERDOIN'
——
!?
!?
HUG
ぎゅうっ
....
OH DANG
!
I COULDN'T HELP IT
....
ROLL
ゴロ
ROLL
ゴロ
ROLL
ゴロ
BOING
ぽよーん♡
UMM
UHHH

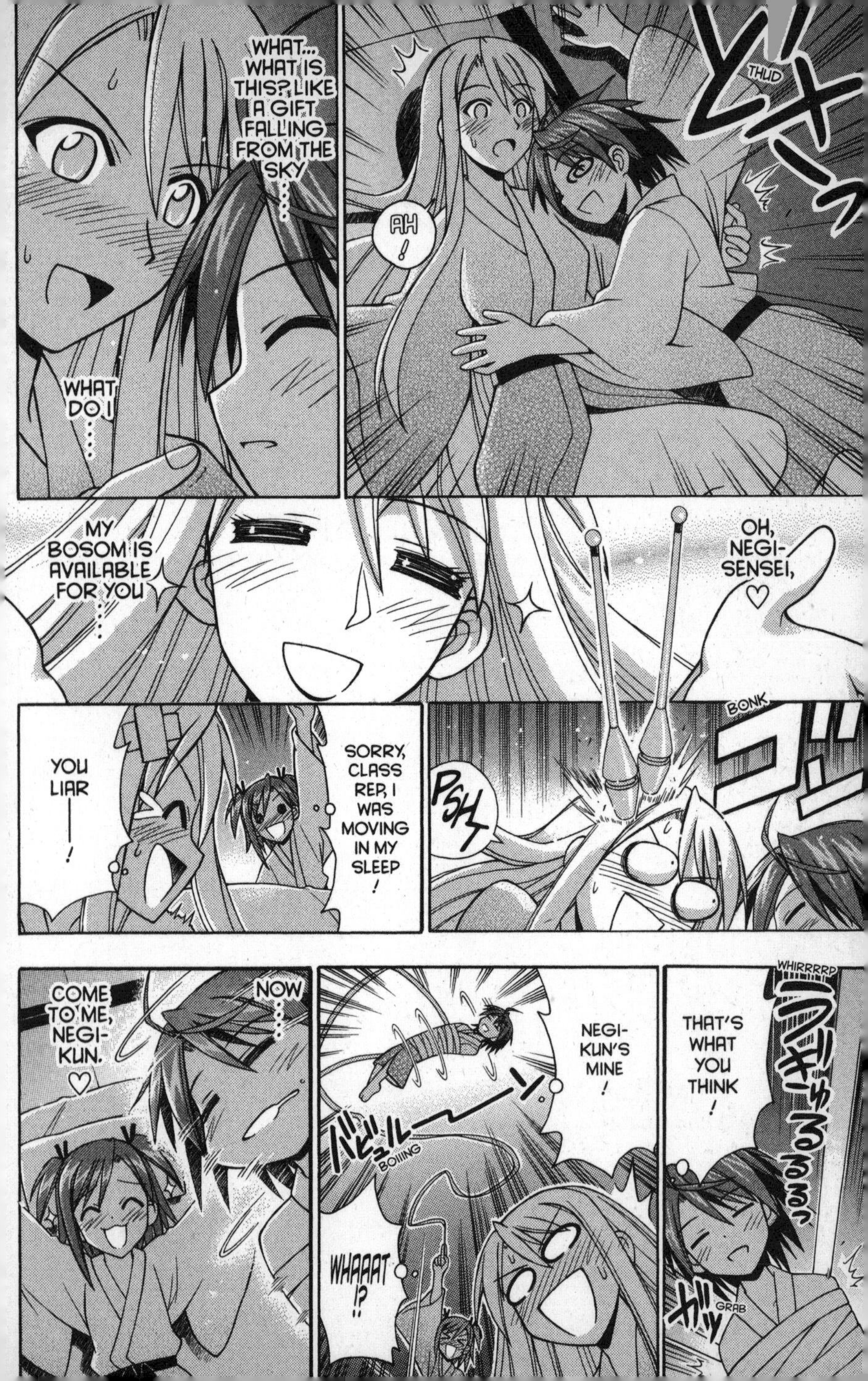
THUD
AH!
WHAT... WHAT IS THIS? LIKE A GIFT FALLING FROM THE SKY......
WHAT DO I...
OH, NEGI-SENSEI, ♡
MY BOSOM IS AVAILABLE FOR YOU...
BONK
PSHT
SORRY, CLASS REP, I WAS MOVING IN MY SLEEP!
YOU LIAR—!
WHIRRRRP
THAT'S WHAT YOU THINK!
GRAB
NEGI-KUN'S MINE!
BOIIING
WHAAAT!?
NOW...
COME TO ME, NEGI-KUN. ♡

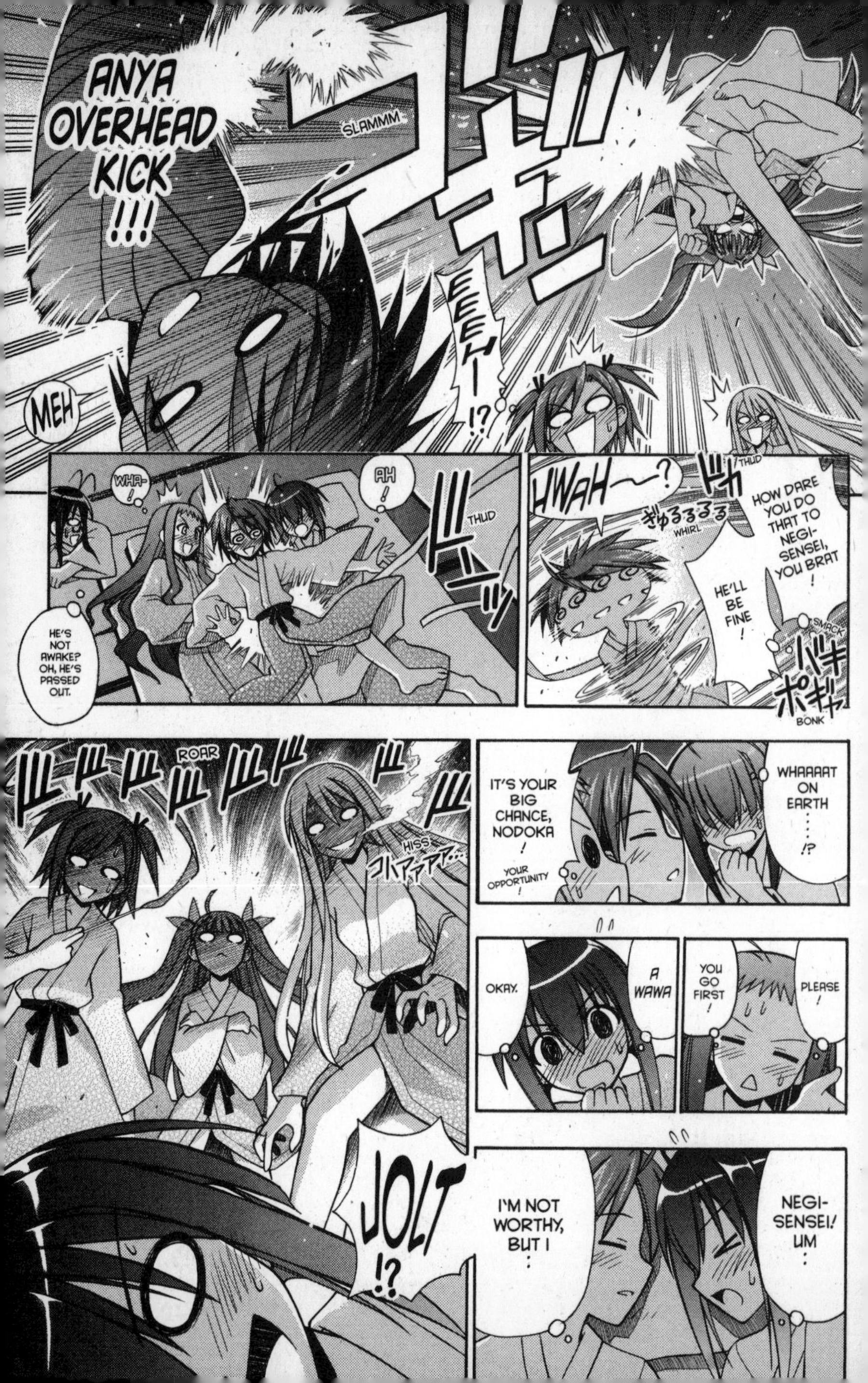

EEEEH—!?
SLAMMM
ANYA OVERHEAD KICK!!!
MEH
THUD
HOW DARE YOU DO THAT TO NEGI-SENSEI, YOU BRAT!
HWAH~~?
ぎゅるるるる
WHIRL
HE'LL BE FINE!
SMACK
BONK
AH!
THUD
WHA-!
HE'S NOT AWAKE? OH, HE'S PASSED OUT.
WHAAAAT ON EARTH.....!?
IT'S YOUR BIG CHANCE, NODOKA!
YOUR OPPORTUNITY!
PLEASE!
YOU GO FIRST!
A WAWA
OKAY.
NEGI-SENSEI! UM...
I'M NOT WORTHY, BUT I...
ROAR
HISS
JOLT!?

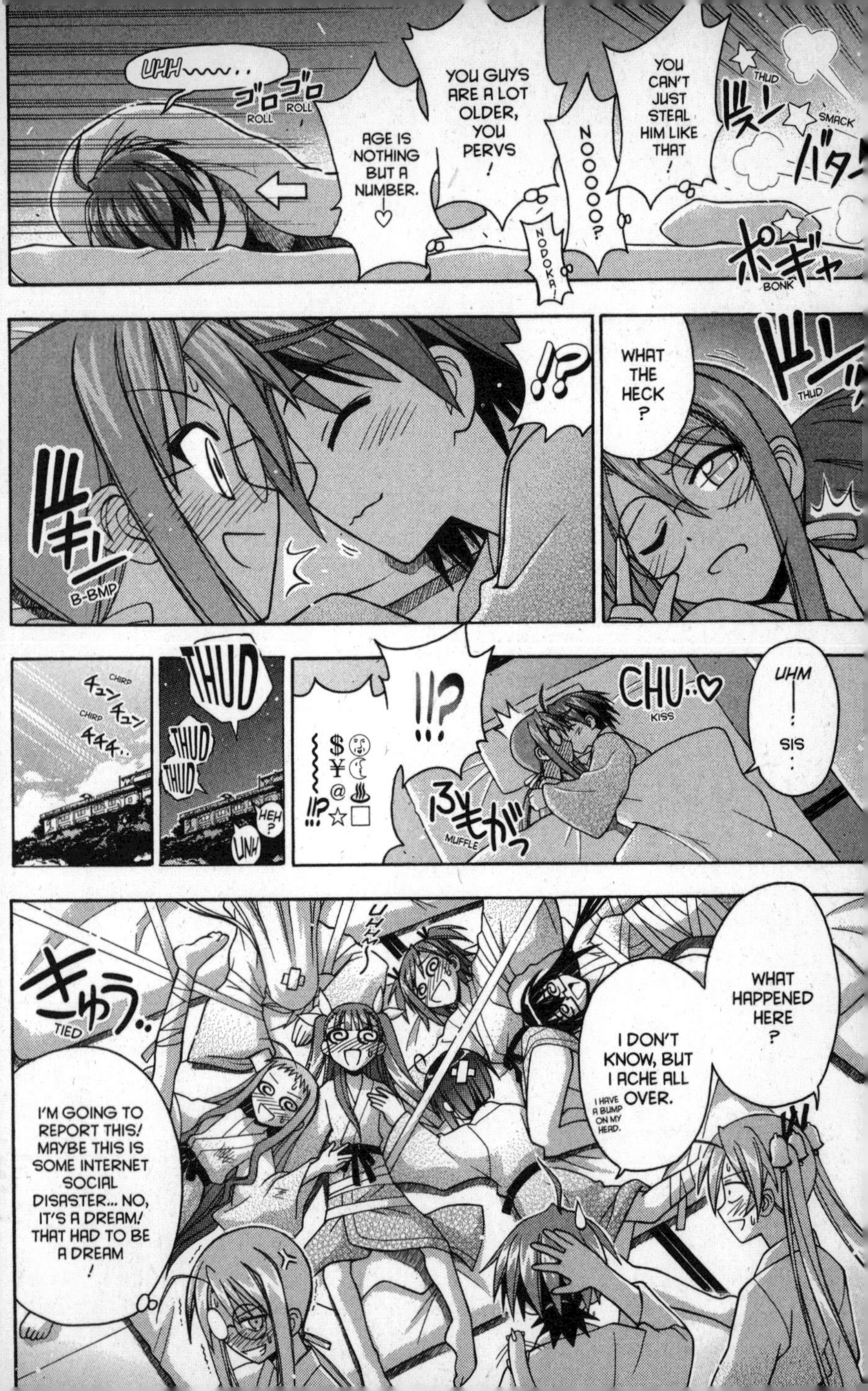
THUD
SMACK
BONK
YOU CAN'T JUST STEAL HIM LIKE THAT!
NOOOOOO?
NODOKA!
YOU GUYS ARE A LOT OLDER, YOU PERVS!
AGE IS NOTHING BUT A NUMBER. ♡
UHH~~..
ゴロゴロ
ROLL ROLL
THUD
WHAT THE HECK?
!!?
B-BMP
UHM... SIS...
CHU..♡
KISS
ふもがっ
MUFFLE
!!?
$ ¥ @ ☆ !!?
THUD
THUD THUD
HEH?
UNH
チュン チュン チチチ..
CHIRP CHIRP
WHAT HAPPENED HERE?
I DON'T KNOW, BUT I ACHE ALL OVER.
I HAVE A BUMP ON MY HEAD.
UHHM~
きゅう..
TIED
I'M GOING TO REPORT THIS! MAYBE THIS IS SOME INTERNET SOCIAL DISASTER... NO, IT'S A DREAM! THAT HAD TO BE A DREAM!

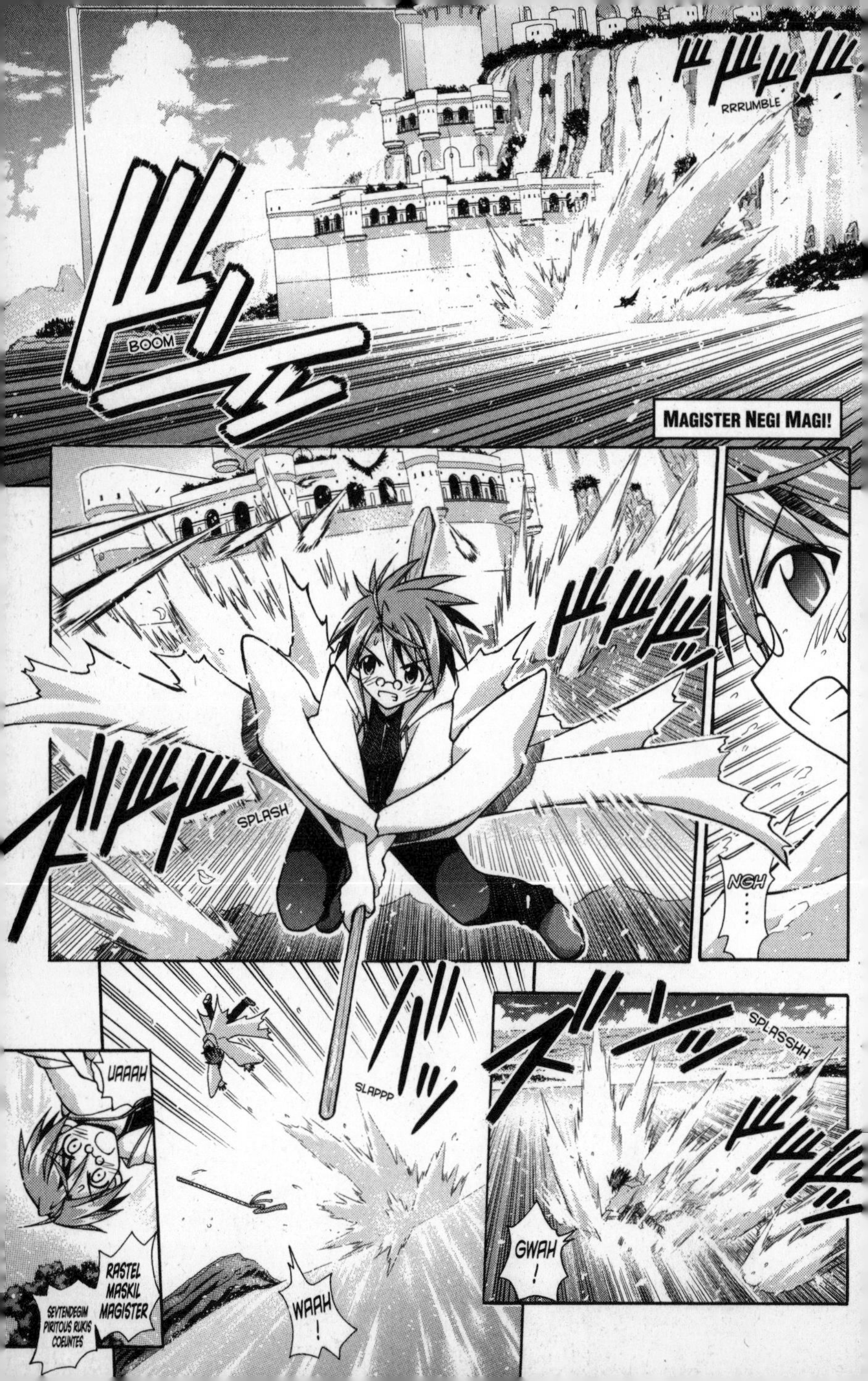
RRRUMBLE
BOOM
MAGISTER NEGI MAGI!
NGH ......
SPLASH
SPLASSHH
GWAH!
SLAPPP
WAAH!
UAAAH
RASTEL MASKIL MAGISTER
SEVTENDEGIM PIRITOUS RUKIS COEUNTES

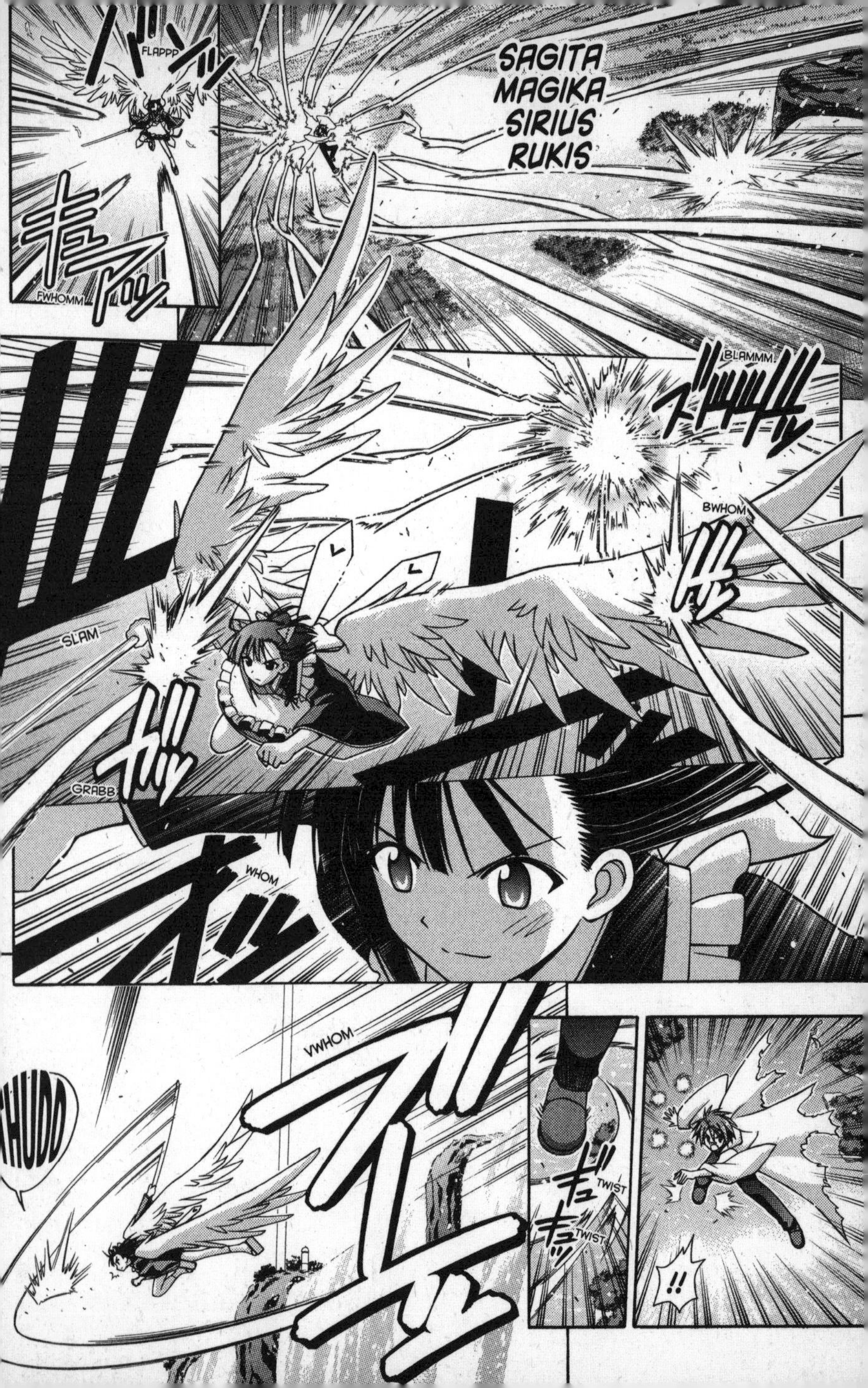
SAGITA MAGIKA SIRIUS RUKIS
FLAPPP
FWHOMM
BLAMMM
BWHOM
SLAM
GRABB
WHOM
!!
TWIST
TWIST
VWHOM
THUDD

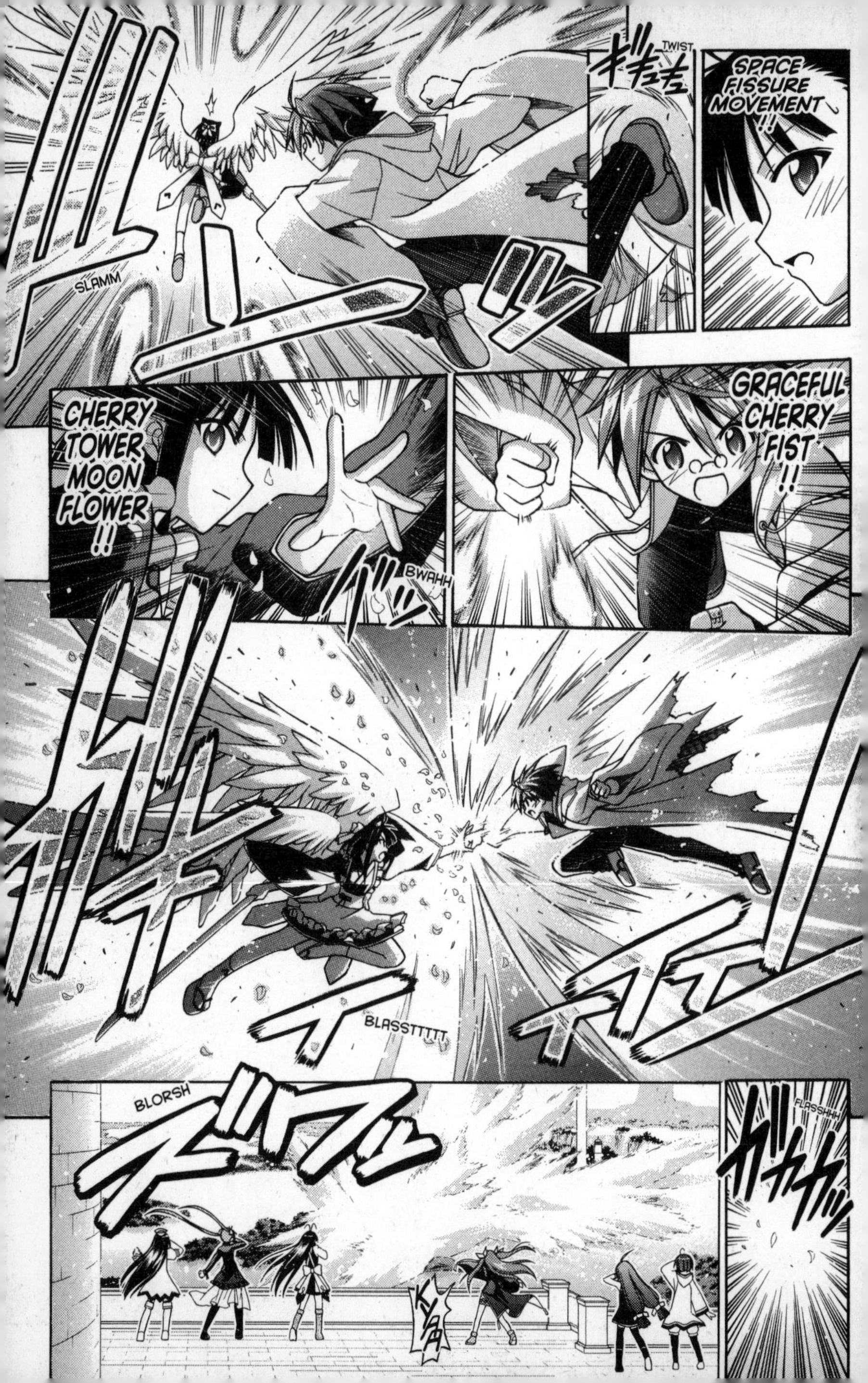
SPACE FISSURE MOVEMENT!!
TWIST
SLAMM
GRACEFUL CHERRY FIST!!
CHERRY TOWER MOON FLOWER!!
BWAHH
BLASSTTTTT
FLASSHHH
BLORSH

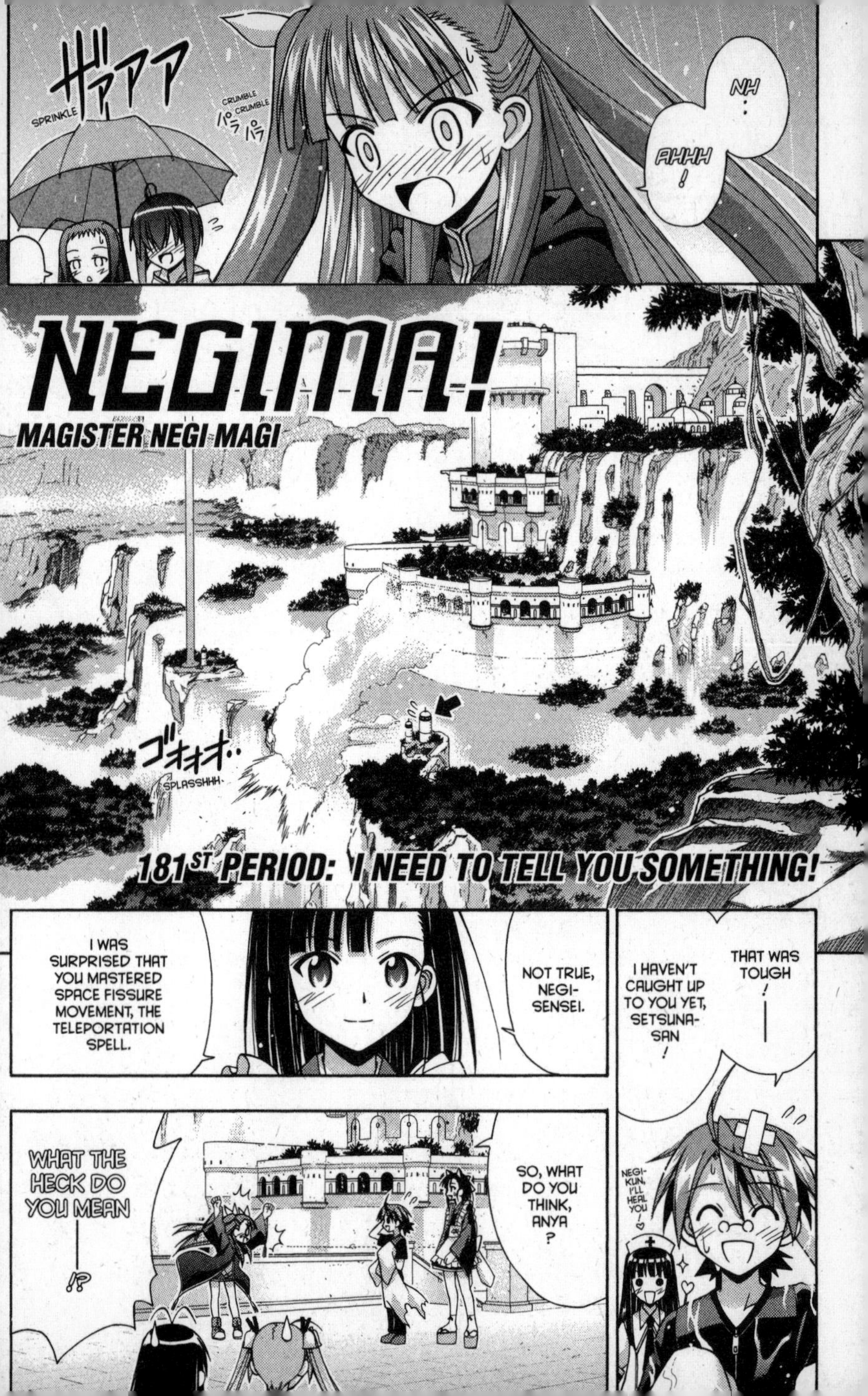
NH...
AHHH!
CRUMBLE CRUMBLE
パラパラ
SPRINKLE
ザァアア
NEGIMA!
MAGISTER NEGI MAGI
ゴォォォ
SPLASSHHH
181ST PERIOD: I NEED TO TELL YOU SOMETHING!
THAT WAS TOUGH!
I HAVEN'T CAUGHT UP TO YOU YET, SETSUNA-SAN!
NEGI-KUN, I'LL HEAL YOU ♡
NOT TRUE, NEGI-SENSEI.
I WAS SURPRISED THAT YOU MASTERED SPACE FISSURE MOVEMENT, THE TELEPORTATION SPELL.
SO, WHAT DO YOU THINK, ANYA?
WHAT THE HECK DO YOU MEAN——!?

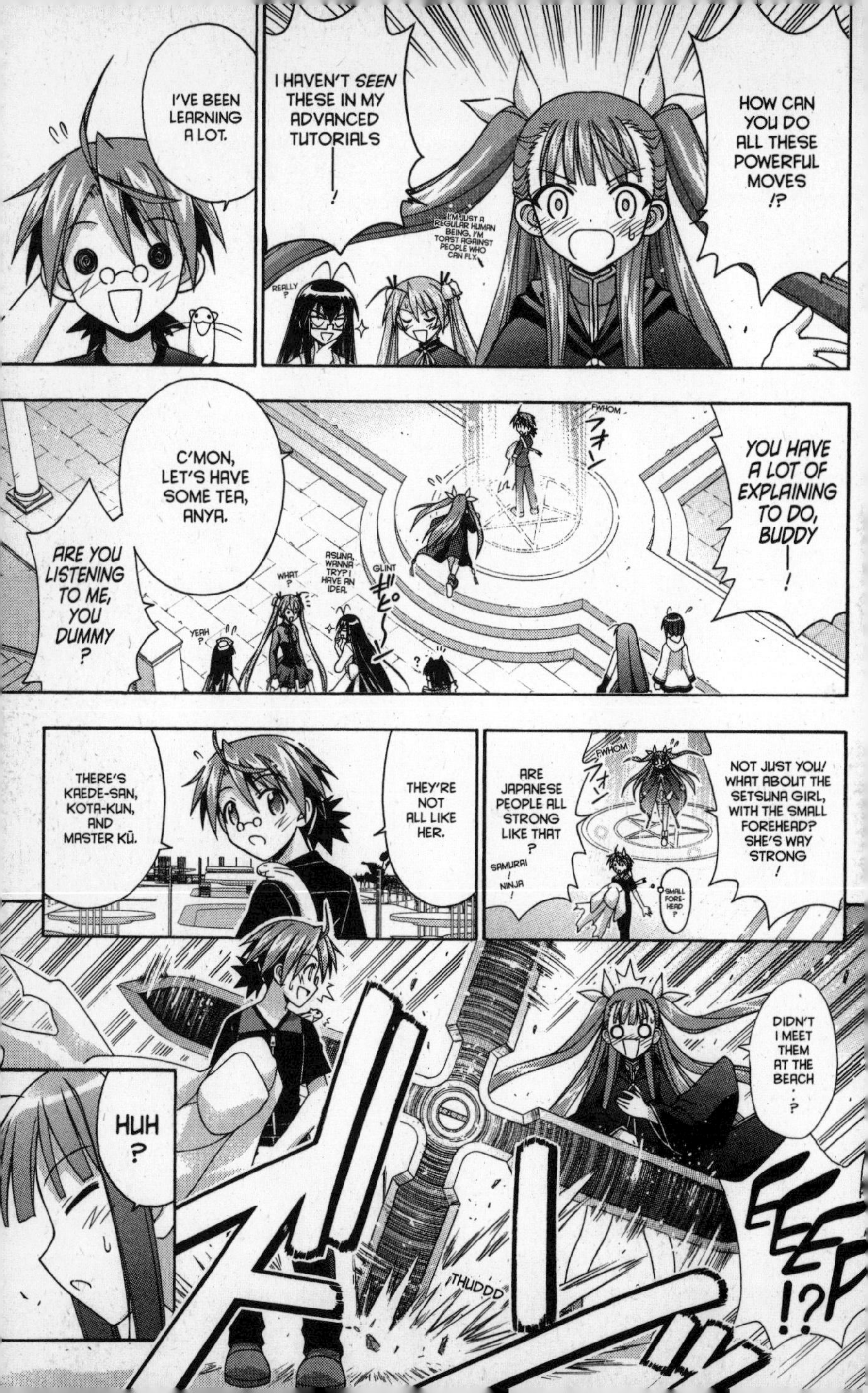
HOW CAN YOU DO ALL THESE POWERFUL MOVES !?
I HAVEN'T *SEEN* THESE IN MY ADVANCED TUTORIALS !
I'M JUST A REGULAR HUMAN BEING. I'M TOAST AGAINST PEOPLE WHO CAN FLY.
REALLY ?
I'VE BEEN LEARNING A LOT.
YOU HAVE A LOT OF EXPLAINING TO DO, BUDDY !
FWHOM
C'MON, LET'S HAVE SOME TEA, ANYA.
ASUNA, WANNA TRY? I HAVE AN IDEA.
WHAT ?
GLINT
YEAH ?
ARE YOU LISTENING TO ME, YOU DUMMY ?
NOT JUST YOU! WHAT ABOUT THE SETSUNA GIRL, WITH THE SMALL FOREHEAD? SHE'S WAY STRONG !
FWHOM
ARE JAPANESE PEOPLE ALL STRONG LIKE THAT ?
SAMURAI ! NINJA !
SMALL FOREHEAD ?
THEY'RE NOT ALL LIKE HER.
THERE'S KAEDE-SAN, KOTA-KUN, AND MASTER KŪ.
EEEP !?
DIDN'T I MEET THEM AT THE BEACH . . ?
THUDDD
HUH ?

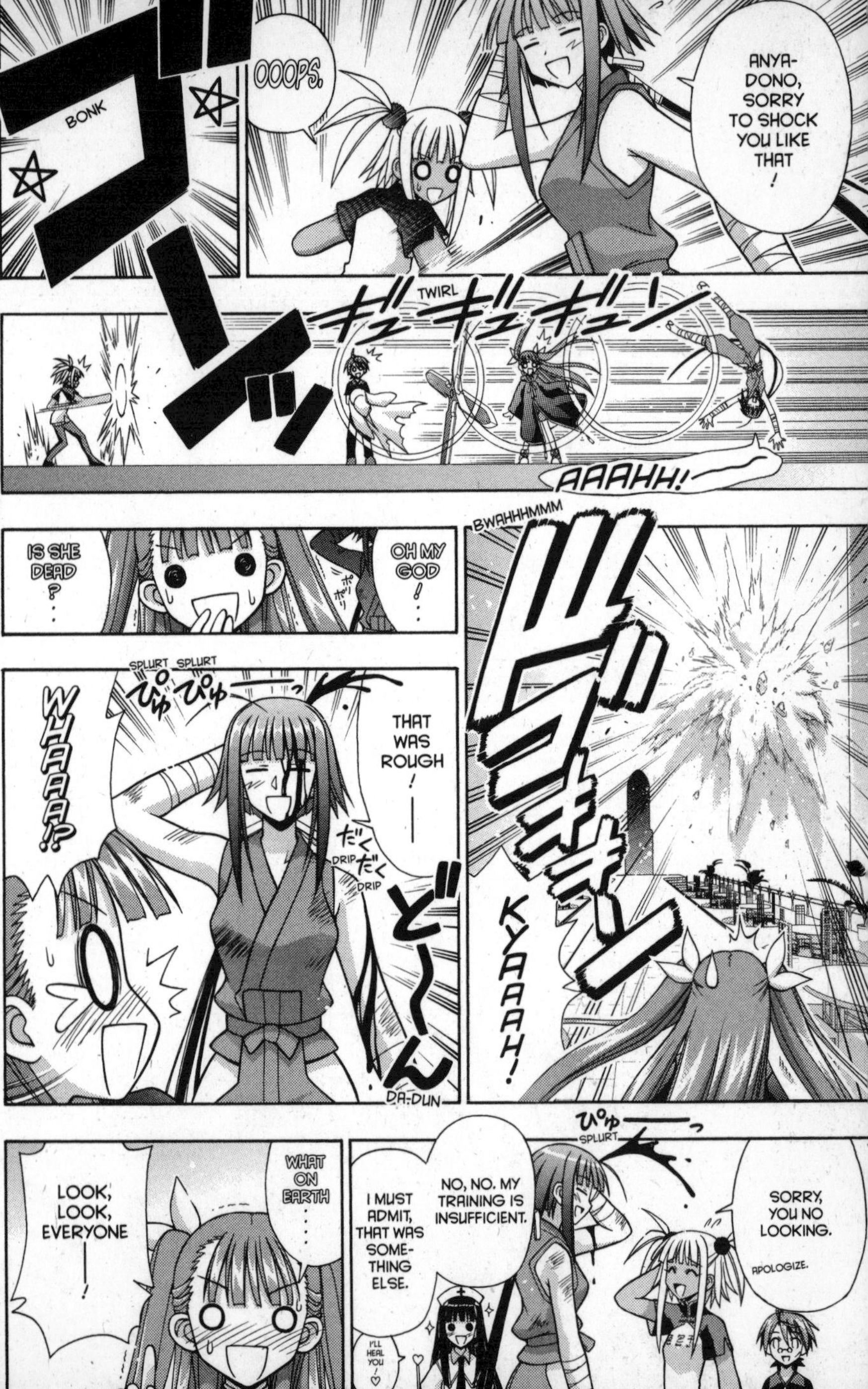

ANYA-DONO, SORRY TO SHOCK YOU LIKE THAT!
OOOPS.
BONK
TWIRL
AAAHH!
BWAHHHMMM
KYAAAAH!
OH MY GOD!...
IS SHE DEAD?...
SPLURT SPLURT
THAT WAS ROUGH!—
DRIP DRIP
DA-DUN
WHAAAAA!?
SORRY, YOU NO LOOKING.
APOLOGIZE.
SPLURT
NO, NO. MY TRAINING IS INSUFFICIENT.
I MUST ADMIT, THAT WAS SOMETHING ELSE.
I'LL HEAL YOU ♡
WHAT ON EARTH...
LOOK, LOOK, EVERYONE—!

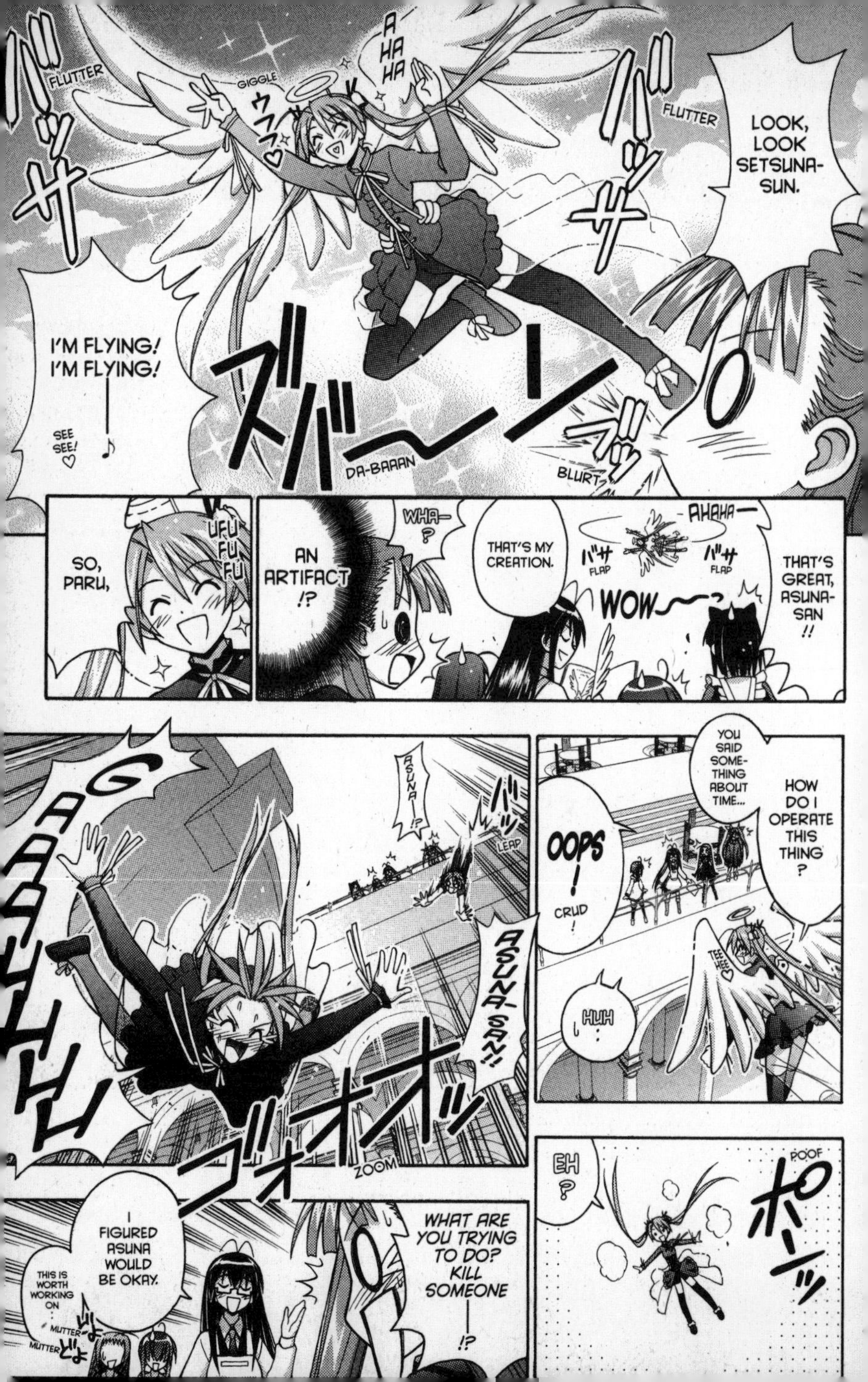
LOOK, LOOK SETSUNA-SUN.
FLUTTER
A HA HA
GIGGLE
FLUTTER
I'M FLYING! I'M FLYING! ♪
SEE SEE! ♡
DA-BAAAN
BLURT
AHAHA
THAT'S GREAT, ASUNA-SAN!!
WOW~~
FLAP
FLAP
THAT'S MY CREATION.
WHA-?
AN ARTIFACT!?
SO, PARU,
UFU FU FU
HOW DO I OPERATE THIS THING?
YOU SAID SOMETHING ABOUT TIME...
OOPS!
CRUD!
TEE HEE ♡
HUH
ASUNA-SAN!!
LEAP
ASUNA—!?
ZOOM
POOF
EH?
WHAT ARE YOU TRYING TO DO? KILL SOMEONE—!?
I FIGURED ASUNA WOULD BE OKAY.
THIS IS WORTH WORKING ON
MUTTER
MUTTER

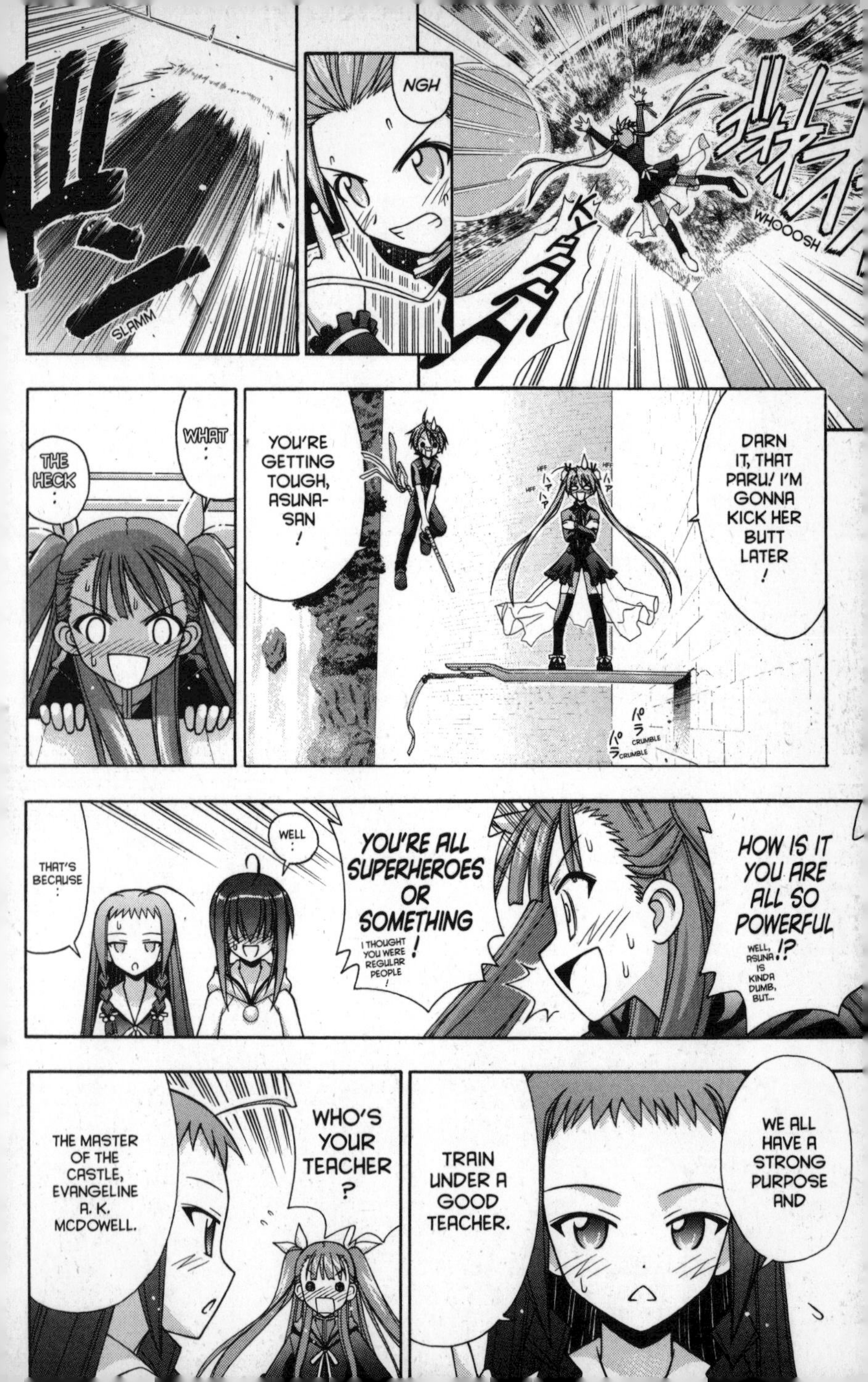
WHOOOSH
NGH
SLAMM
DARN IT, THAT PARU! I'M GONNA KICK HER BUTT LATER!
HFF HFF
CRUMBLE CRUMBLE
YOU'RE GETTING TOUGH, ASUNA-SAN!
WHAT...
THE HECK...
HOW IS IT YOU ARE ALL SO POWERFUL!?
WELL, ASUNA IS KINDA DUMB, BUT...
YOU'RE ALL SUPERHEROES OR SOMETHING!
I THOUGHT YOU WERE REGULAR PEOPLE!
WELL...
THAT'S BECAUSE...
WE ALL HAVE A STRONG PURPOSE AND
TRAIN UNDER A GOOD TEACHER.
WHO'S YOUR TEACHER?
THE MASTER OF THE CASTLE, EVANGELINE A. K. MCDOWELL.

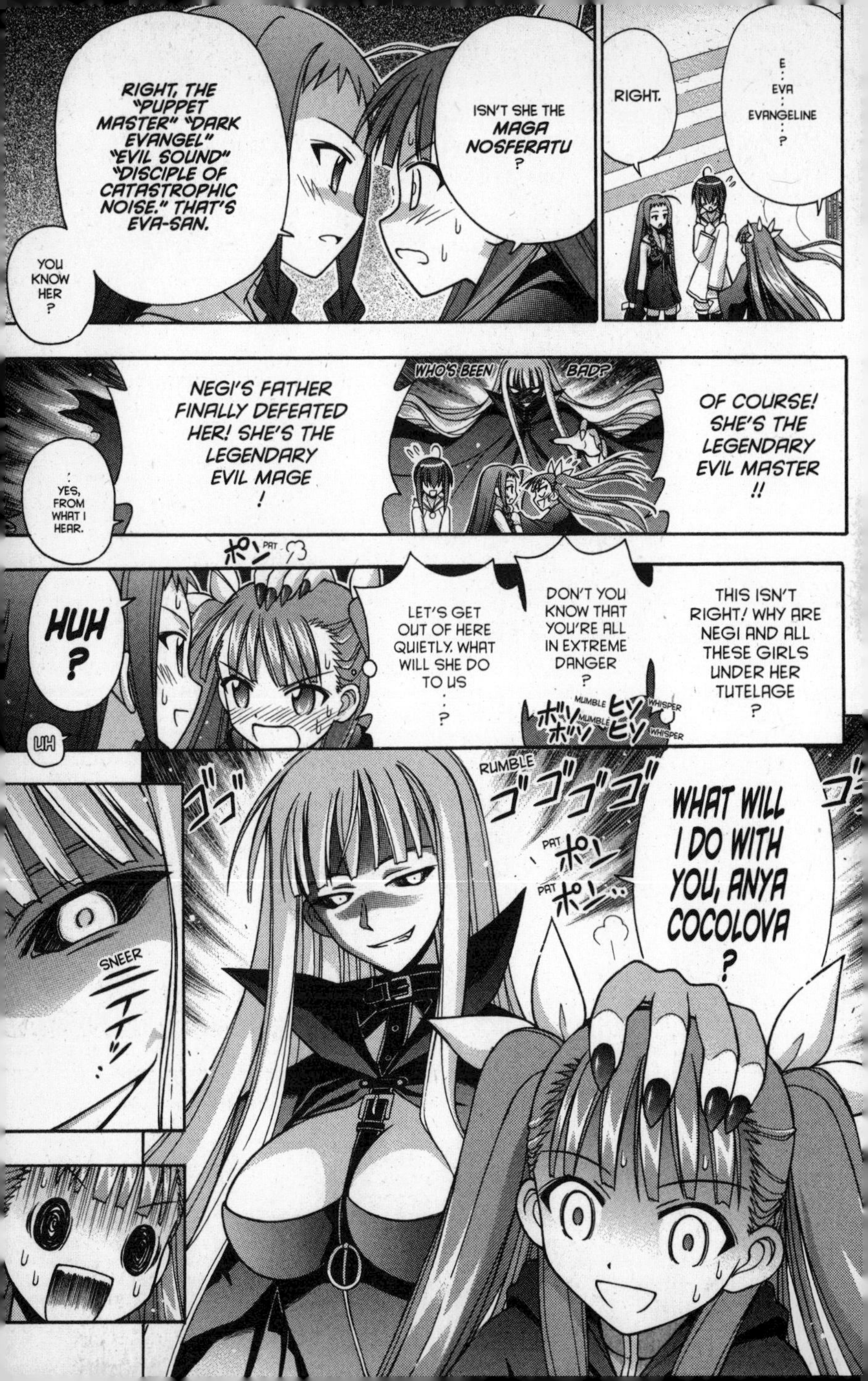
E... EVA... EVANGELINE...?
RIGHT.
ISN'T SHE THE MAGA NOSFERATU?
RIGHT, THE "PUPPET MASTER" "DARK EVANGEL" "EVIL SOUND" "DISCIPLE OF CATASTROPHIC NOISE." THAT'S EVA-SAN.
YOU KNOW HER?
OF COURSE! SHE'S THE LEGENDARY EVIL MASTER!!
WHO'S BEEN BAD?
NEGI'S FATHER FINALLY DEFEATED HER! SHE'S THE LEGENDARY EVIL MAGE!
...YES, FROM WHAT I HEAR.
THIS ISN'T RIGHT! WHY ARE NEGI AND ALL THESE GIRLS UNDER HER TUTELAGE?
DON'T YOU KNOW THAT YOU'RE ALL IN EXTREME DANGER?
ヒソヒソ WHISPER WHISPER
ボソボソ MUMBLE MUMBLE
LET'S GET OUT OF HERE QUIETLY. WHAT WILL SHE DO TO US...?
ポン PAT
HUH?
UH
ゴゴゴゴ RUMBLE
WHAT WILL I DO WITH YOU, ANYA COCOLOVA?
ポン PAT
ポン PAT
SNEER

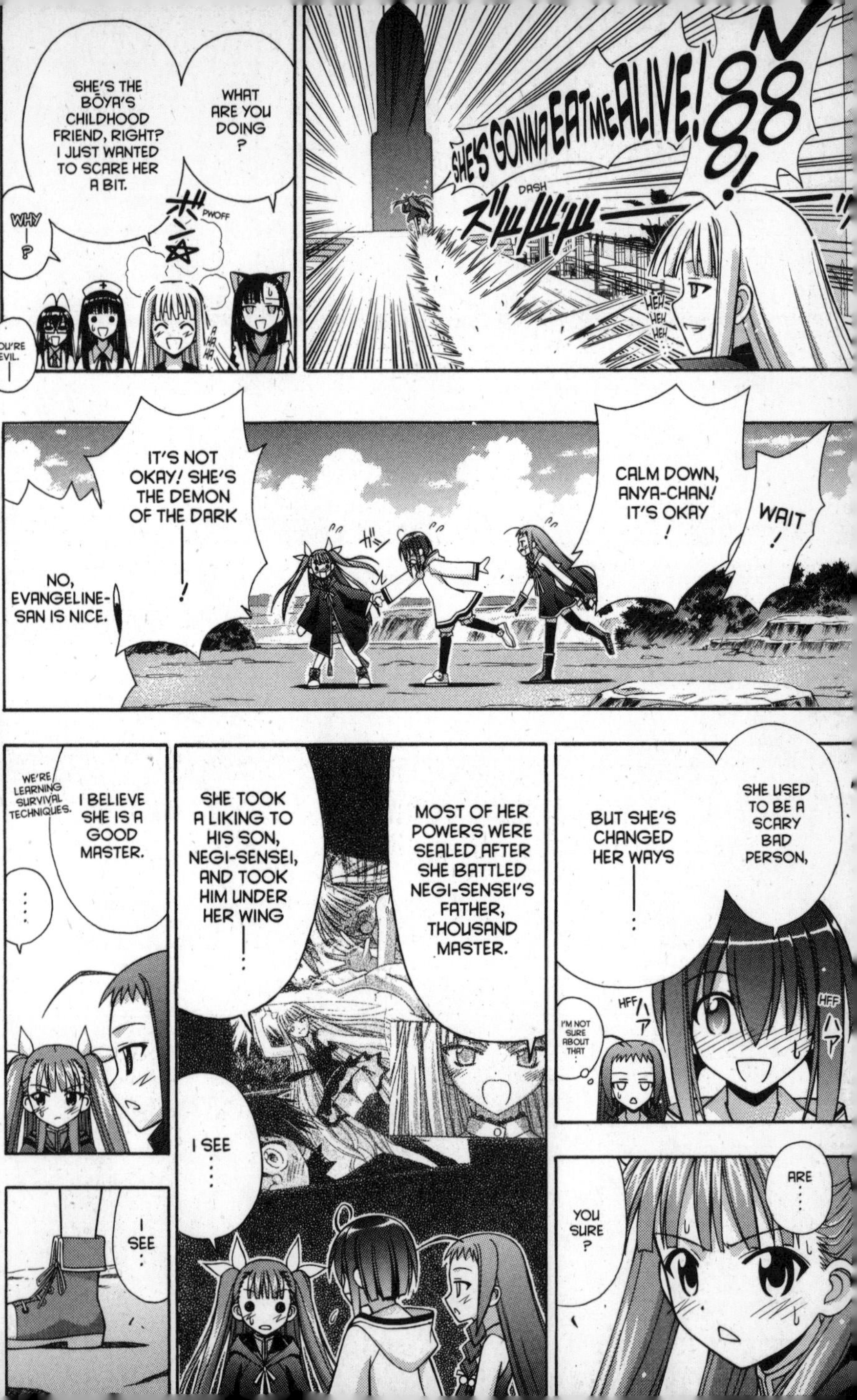
NOOO!!
SHE'S GONNA EAT ME ALIVE!
DASH
HEH HEH HEH
WHAT ARE YOU DOING?
SHE'S THE BŌYA'S CHILDHOOD FRIEND, RIGHT? I JUST WANTED TO SCARE HER A BIT.
PWOFF
WHY—?
A HA HA
YOU'RE EVIL.—
WAIT!
CALM DOWN, ANYA-CHAN! IT'S OKAY!
IT'S NOT OKAY! SHE'S THE DEMON OF THE DARK—!
NO, EVANGELINE-SAN IS NICE.
SHE USED TO BE A SCARY BAD PERSON,
BUT SHE'S CHANGED HER WAYS—...
HFF
HFF
I'M NOT SURE ABOUT THAT...
ARE...
YOU SURE?
MOST OF HER POWERS WERE SEALED AFTER SHE BATTLED NEGI-SENSEI'S FATHER, THOUSAND MASTER.
SHE TOOK A LIKING TO HIS SON, NEGI-SENSEI, AND TOOK HIM UNDER HER WING—...
I SEE...
I BELIEVE SHE IS A GOOD MASTER.
WE'RE LEARNING SURVIVAL TECHNIQUES.
...?
I SEE...

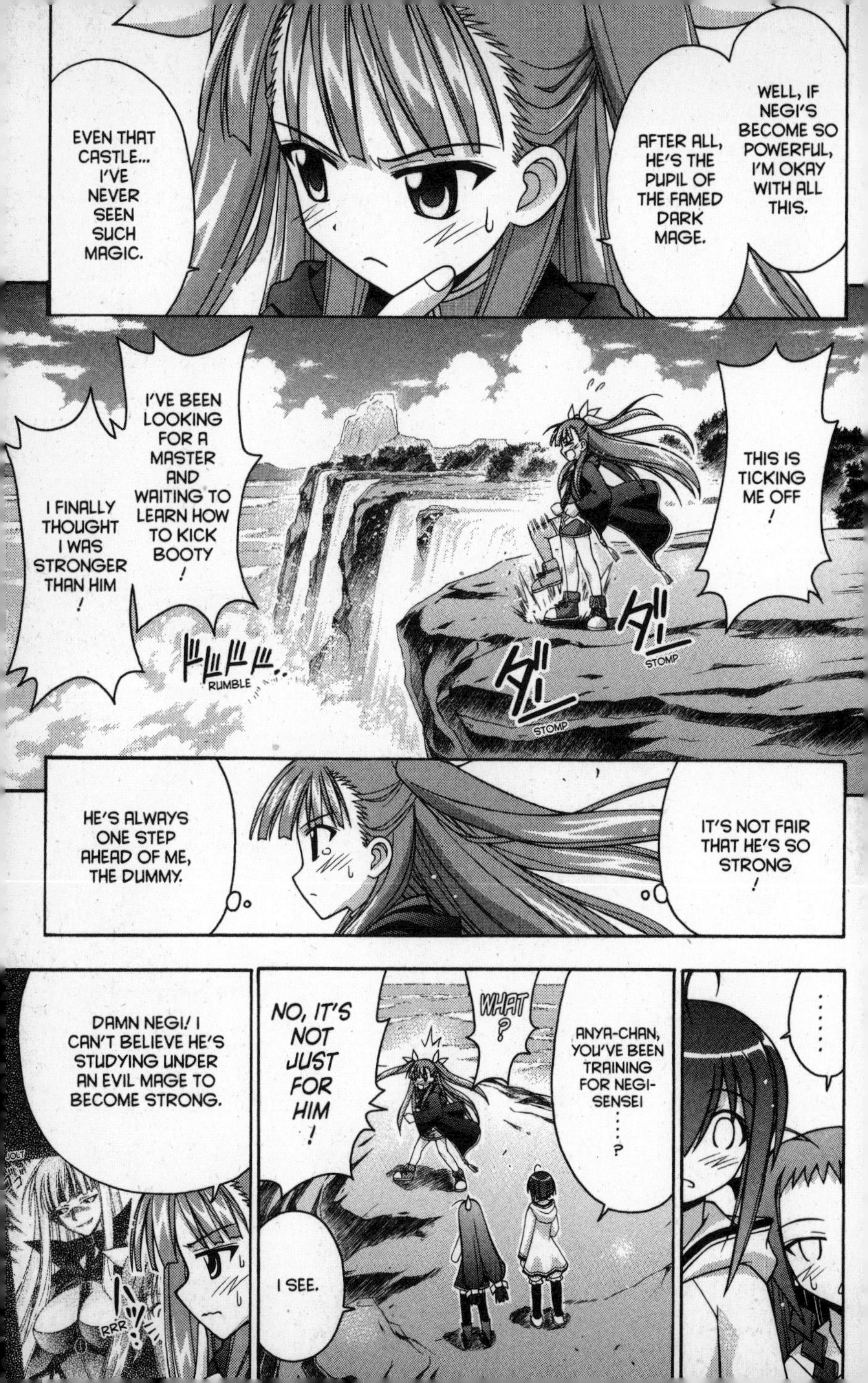
WELL, IF NEGI'S BECOME SO POWERFUL, I'M OKAY WITH ALL THIS.
AFTER ALL, HE'S THE PUPIL OF THE FAMED DARK MAGE.
EVEN THAT CASTLE... I'VE NEVER SEEN SUCH MAGIC.
THIS IS TICKING ME OFF!
STOMP
STOMP
I'VE BEEN LOOKING FOR A MASTER AND WAITING TO LEARN HOW TO KICK BOOTY!
I FINALLY THOUGHT I WAS STRONGER THAN HIM!
RUMBLE
IT'S NOT FAIR THAT HE'S SO STRONG!
HE'S ALWAYS ONE STEP AHEAD OF ME, THE DUMMY.
......
ANYA-CHAN, YOU'VE BEEN TRAINING FOR NEGI-SENSEI.....?
WHAT?
NO, IT'S NOT JUST FOR HIM!
I SEE.
DAMN NEGI! I CAN'T BELIEVE HE'S STUDYING UNDER AN EVIL MAGE TO BECOME STRONG.
JOLT
RRR

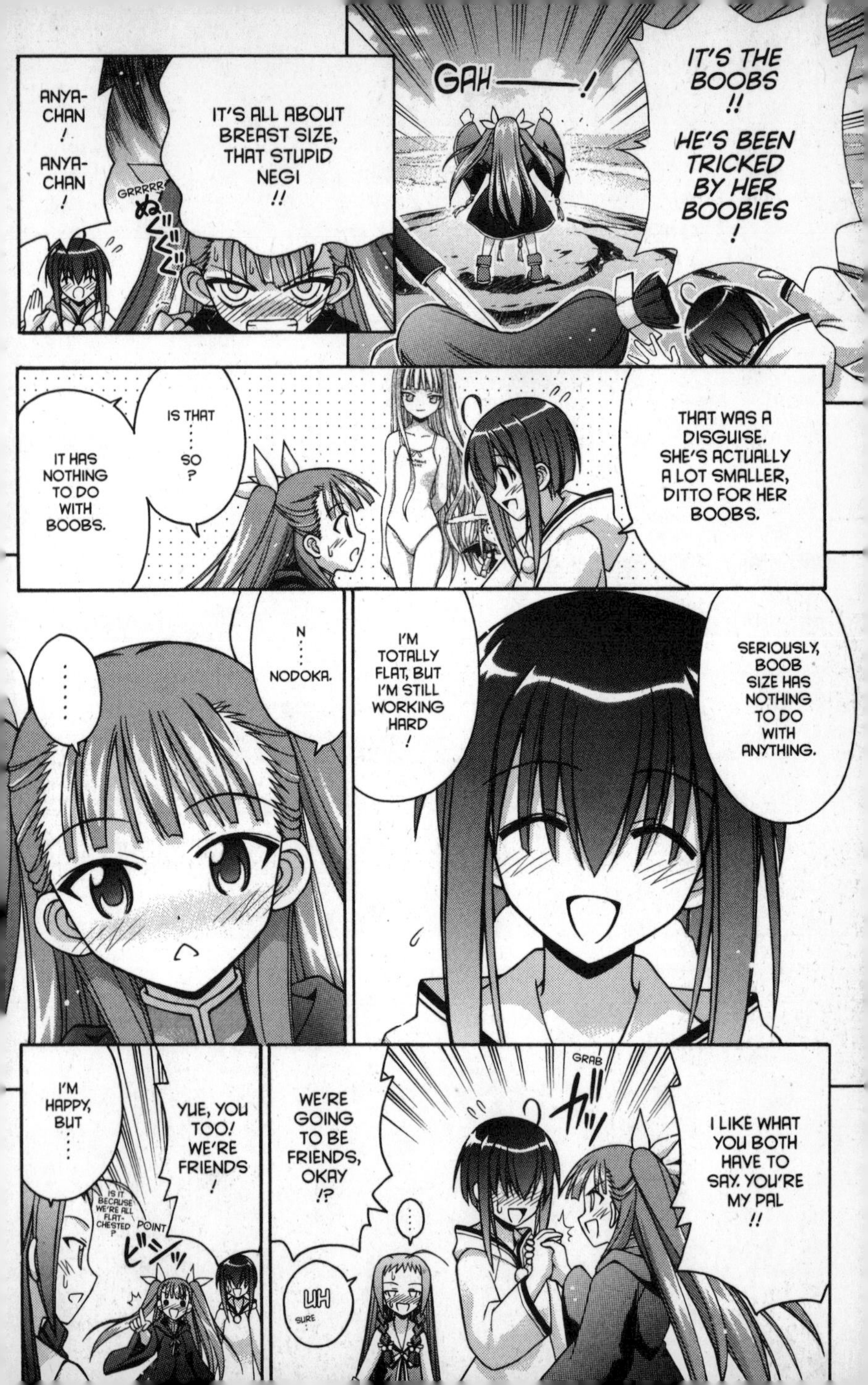
IT'S THE BOOBS!!
HE'S BEEN TRICKED BY HER BOOBIES!
GAH——!
IT'S ALL ABOUT BREAST SIZE, THAT STUPID NEGI!!
GRRRRR
ぬぐぐぐ
ANYA-CHAN! ANYA-CHAN!
THAT WAS A DISGUISE. SHE'S ACTUALLY A LOT SMALLER, DITTO FOR HER BOOBS.
IS THAT... SO?
IT HAS NOTHING TO DO WITH BOOBS.
SERIOUSLY, BOOB SIZE HAS NOTHING TO DO WITH ANYTHING.
I'M TOTALLY FLAT, BUT I'M STILL WORKING HARD!
N... NODOKA.
......
I LIKE WHAT YOU BOTH HAVE TO SAY. YOU'RE MY PAL!!
GRAB
ガッ
WE'RE GOING TO BE FRIENDS, OKAY!?
...
UH
SURE
YUE, YOU TOO! WE'RE FRIENDS!
I'M HAPPY, BUT...
IS IT BECAUSE WE'RE ALL FLAT-CHESTED?
POINT
ビシッ

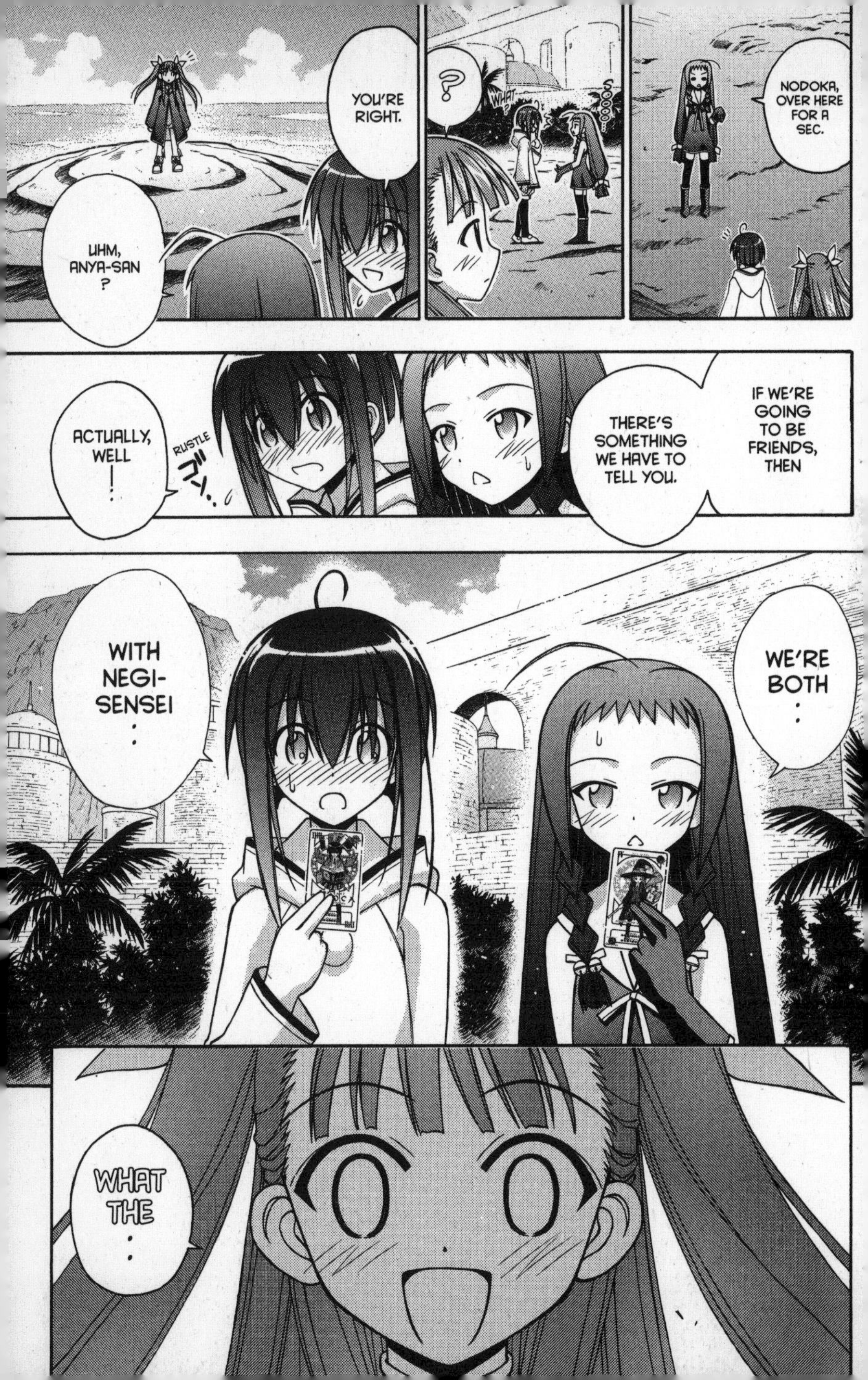
NODOKA, OVER HERE FOR A SEC.
?
WHAT
YOU'RE RIGHT.
UHM, ANYA-SAN?
IF WE'RE GOING TO BE FRIENDS, THEN
THERE'S SOMETHING WE HAVE TO TELL YOU.
RUSTLE
ACTUALLY, WELL!
WE'RE BOTH..
WITH NEGI-SENSEI..
WHAT THE..

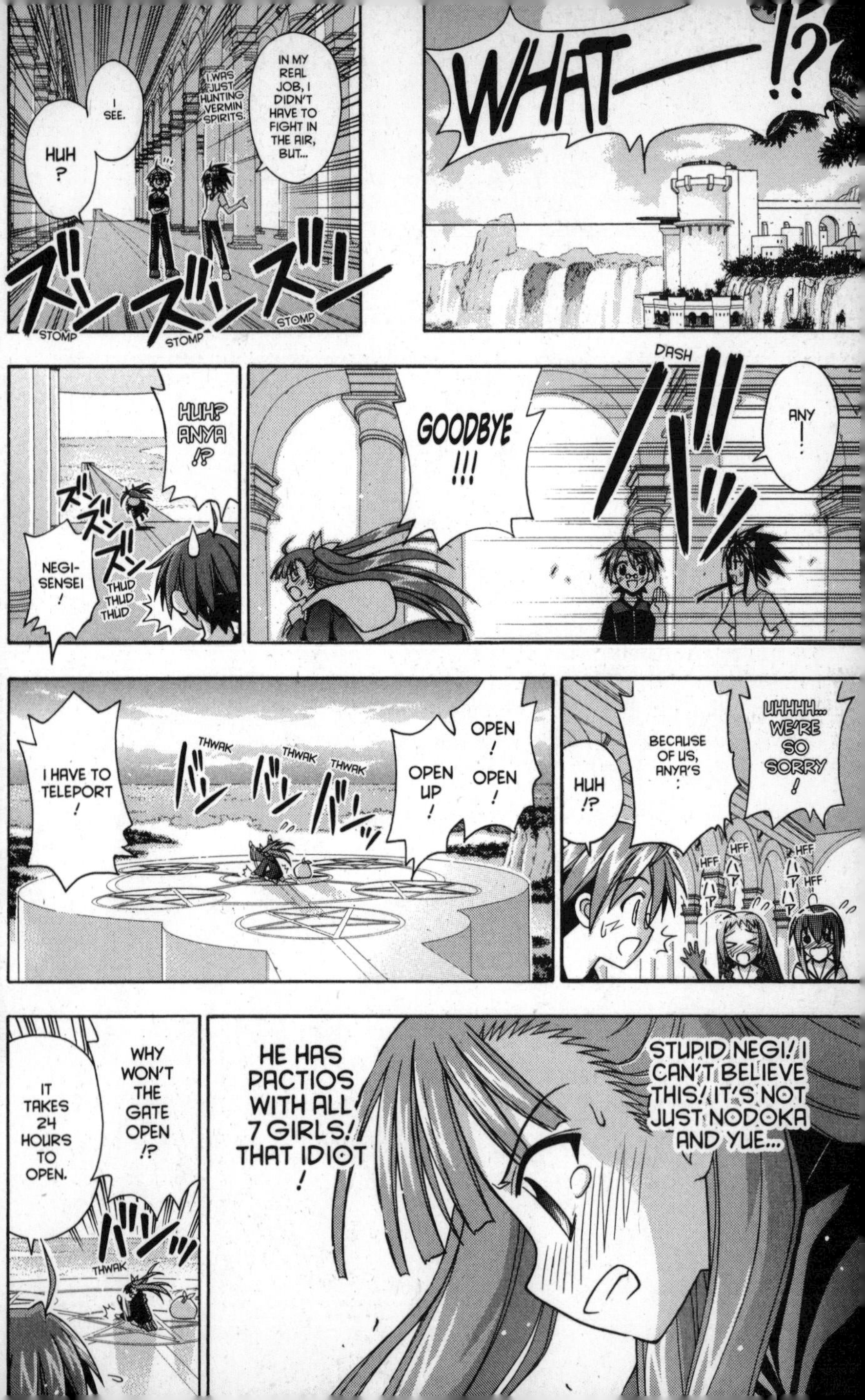
WHAT—!?
IN MY REAL JOB, I DIDN'T HAVE TO FIGHT IN THE AIR, BUT...
I WAS JUST HUNTING VERMIN SPIRITS.
I SEE.
HUH?
STOMP
STOMP
STOMP
DASH
ANY!
GOODBYE!!!
HUH? ANYA!?
NEGI-SENSEI!
THUD THUD THUD
UHHHH... WE'RE SO SORRY!
BECAUSE OF US, ANYA'S:
HUH!?
HFF
HFF
HFF
HFF
OPEN! OPEN!
OPEN UP!
THWAK
THWAK
THWAK
I HAVE TO TELEPORT!
STUPID NEGI! I CAN'T BELIEVE THIS! IT'S NOT JUST NODOKA AND YUE...
HE HAS PACTIOS WITH ALL 7 GIRLS! THAT IDIOT!
WHY WON'T THE GATE OPEN!?
IT TAKES 24 HOURS TO OPEN.
THWAK

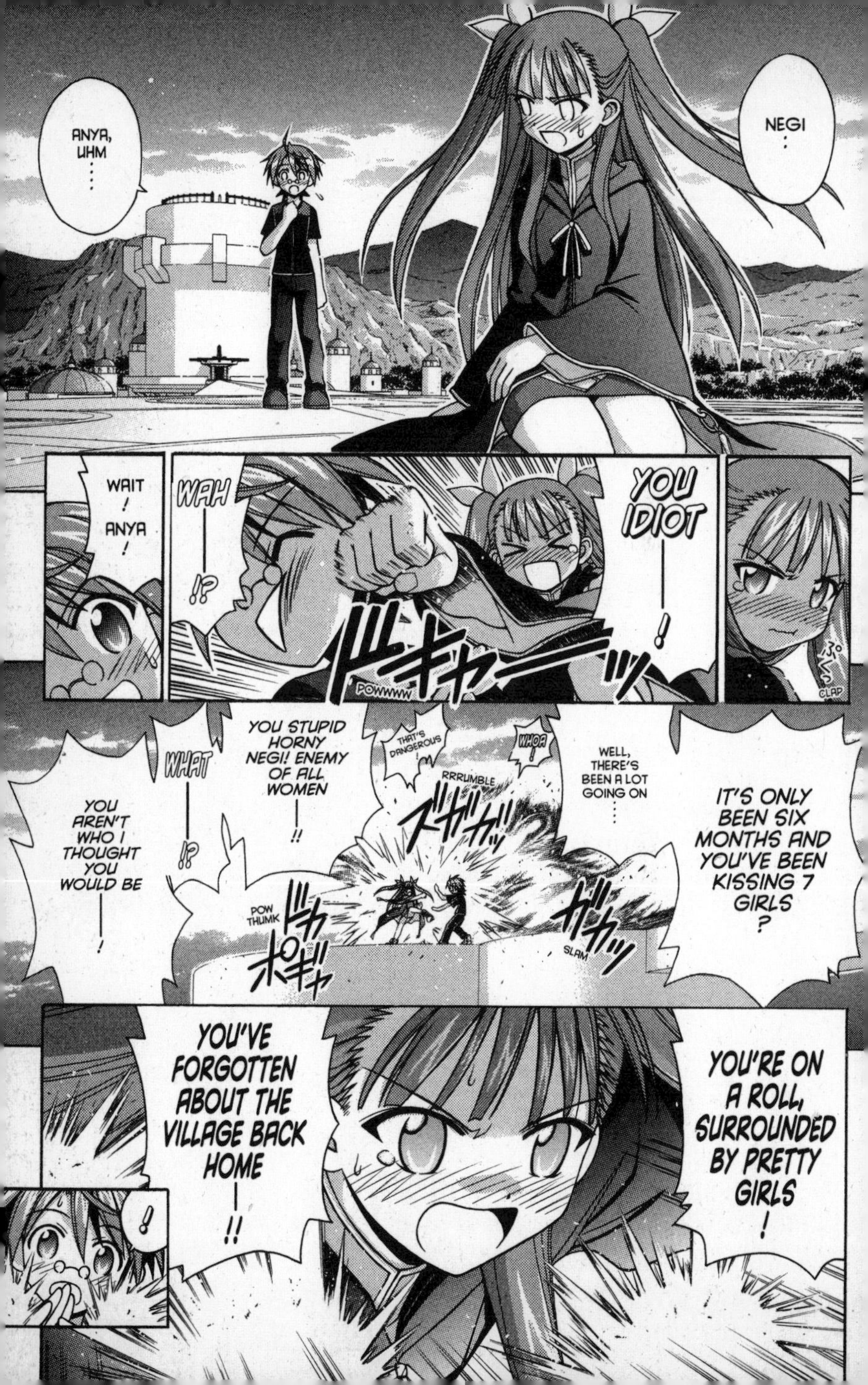
NEGI ...
ANYA, UHM ......
ぷくっ
CLAP
YOU IDIOT—!
WAH—!?
ドギャーッ
POWWWW
WAIT! ANYA!
IT'S ONLY BEEN SIX MONTHS AND YOU'VE BEEN KISSING 7 GIRLS?
WELL, THERE'S BEEN A LOT GOING ON ......
WHOA!
THAT'S DANGEROUS!
RRRUMBLE
ズガガッ
YOU STUPID HORNY NEGI! ENEMY OF ALL WOMEN—!!
WHAT—!?
YOU AREN'T WHO I THOUGHT YOU WOULD BE—!
ガガッ
SLAM
ドカ ポギャ
POW THUMK
YOU'RE ON A ROLL, SURROUNDED BY PRETTY GIRLS!
YOU'VE FORGOTTEN ABOUT THE VILLAGE BACK HOME—!!
!

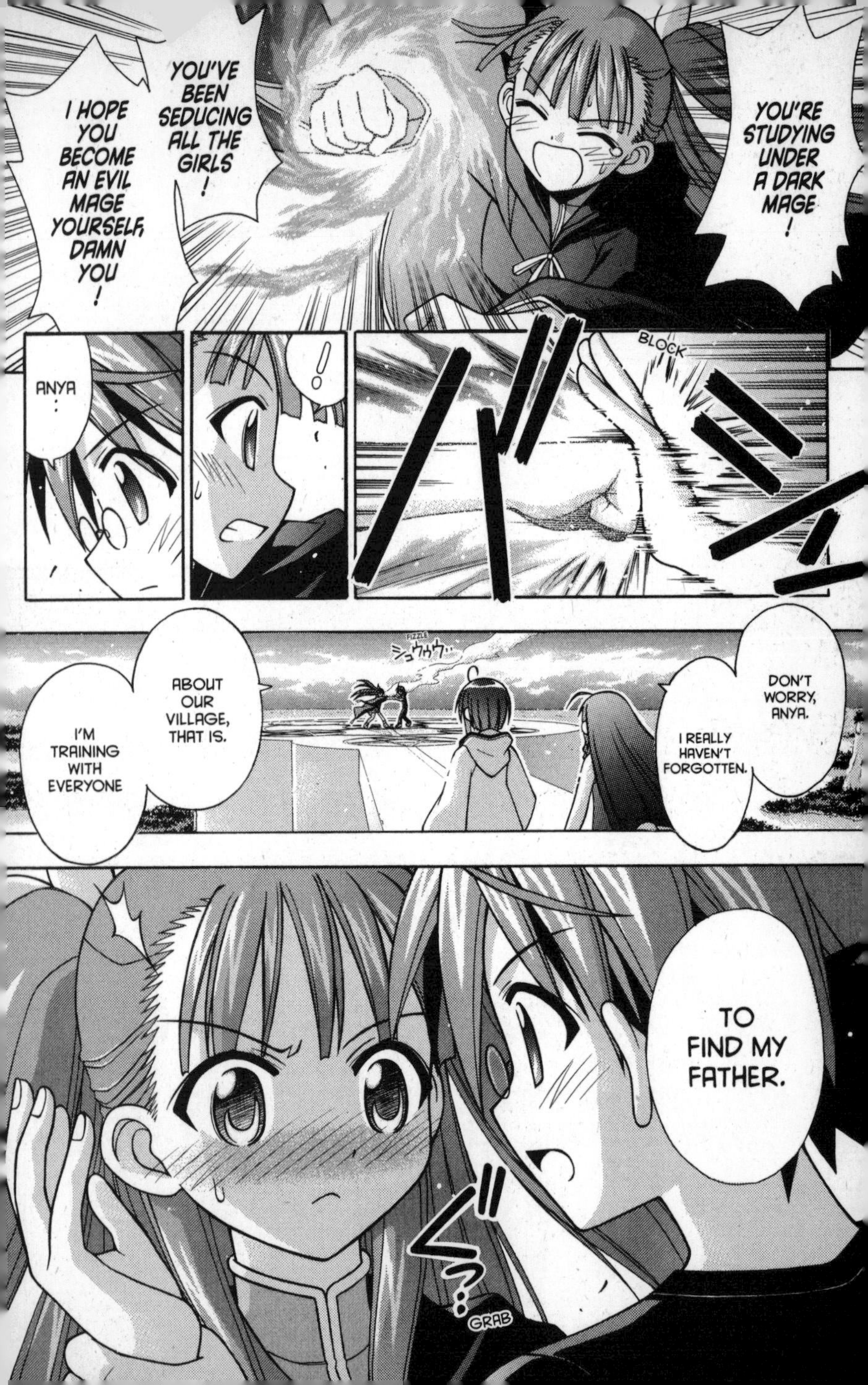
YOU'RE STUDYING UNDER A DARK MAGE!
YOU'VE BEEN SEDUCING ALL THE GIRLS!
I HOPE YOU BECOME AN EVIL MAGE YOURSELF, DAMN YOU!
BLOCK
!
ANYA...
DON'T WORRY, ANYA.
I REALLY HAVEN'T FORGOTTEN.
FIZZLE
ABOUT OUR VILLAGE, THAT IS.
I'M TRAINING WITH EVERYONE
TO FIND MY FATHER.
GRAB

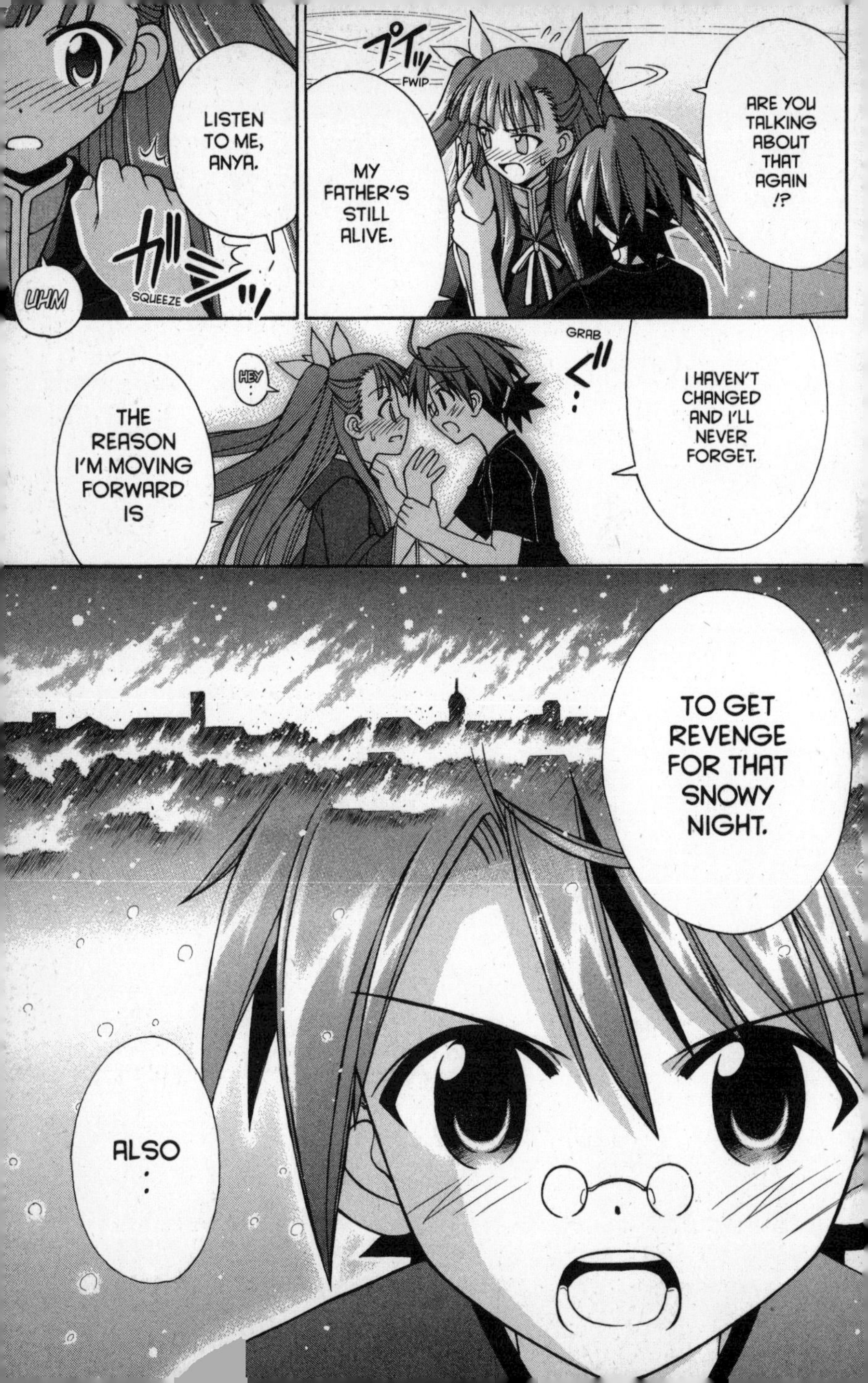
ARE YOU TALKING ABOUT THAT AGAIN !?
プイッ
FWIP
MY FATHER'S STILL ALIVE.
LISTEN TO ME, ANYA.
SQUEEZE
UHM
GRAB
I HAVEN'T CHANGED AND I'LL NEVER FORGET.
HEY
THE REASON I'M MOVING FORWARD IS
TO GET REVENGE FOR THAT SNOWY NIGHT.
ALSO . . .

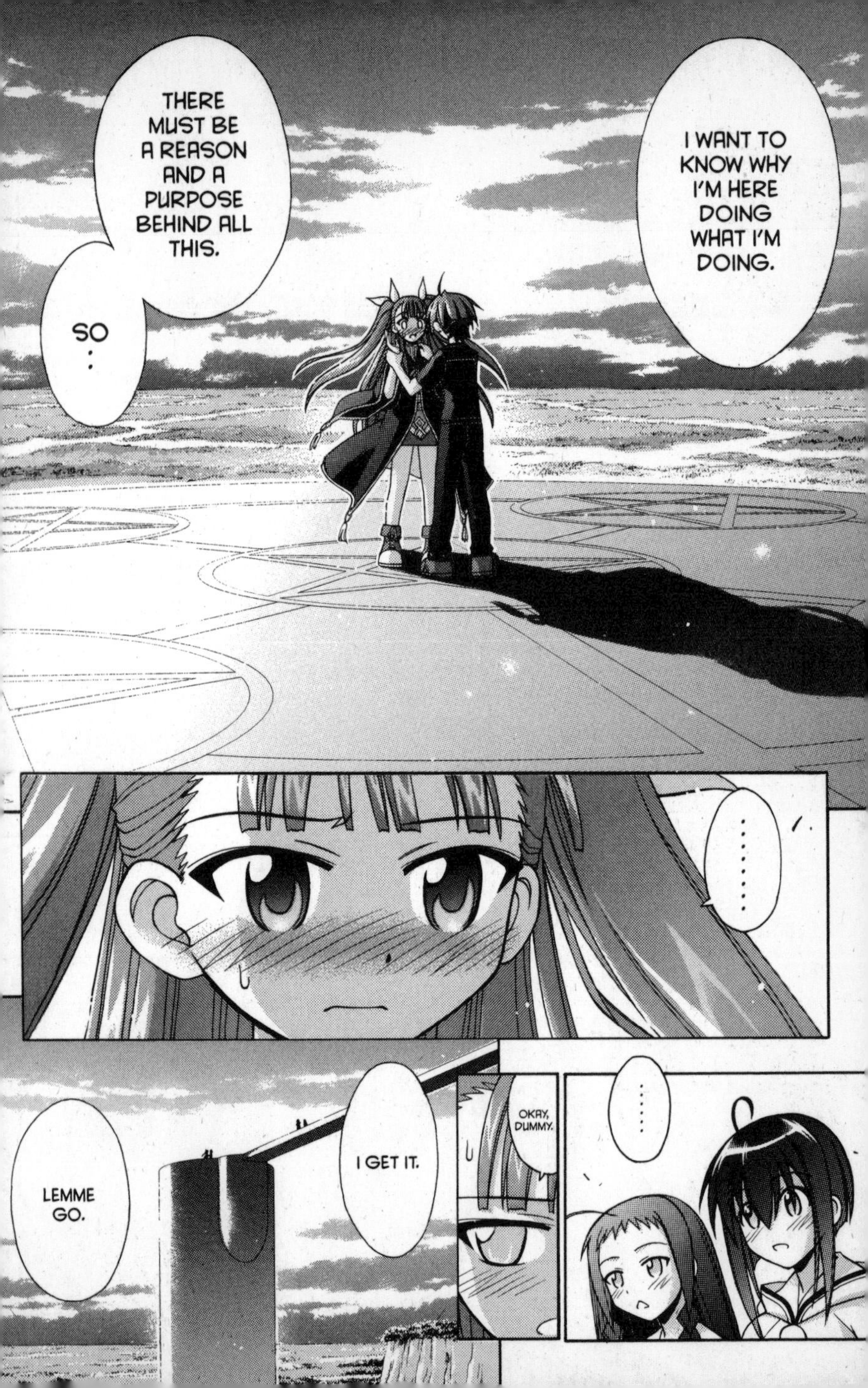
I WANT TO KNOW WHY I'M HERE DOING WHAT I'M DOING.
THERE MUST BE A REASON AND A PURPOSE BEHIND ALL THIS.
SO . . .
......
......
OKAY, DUMMY.
I GET IT.
LEMME GO.

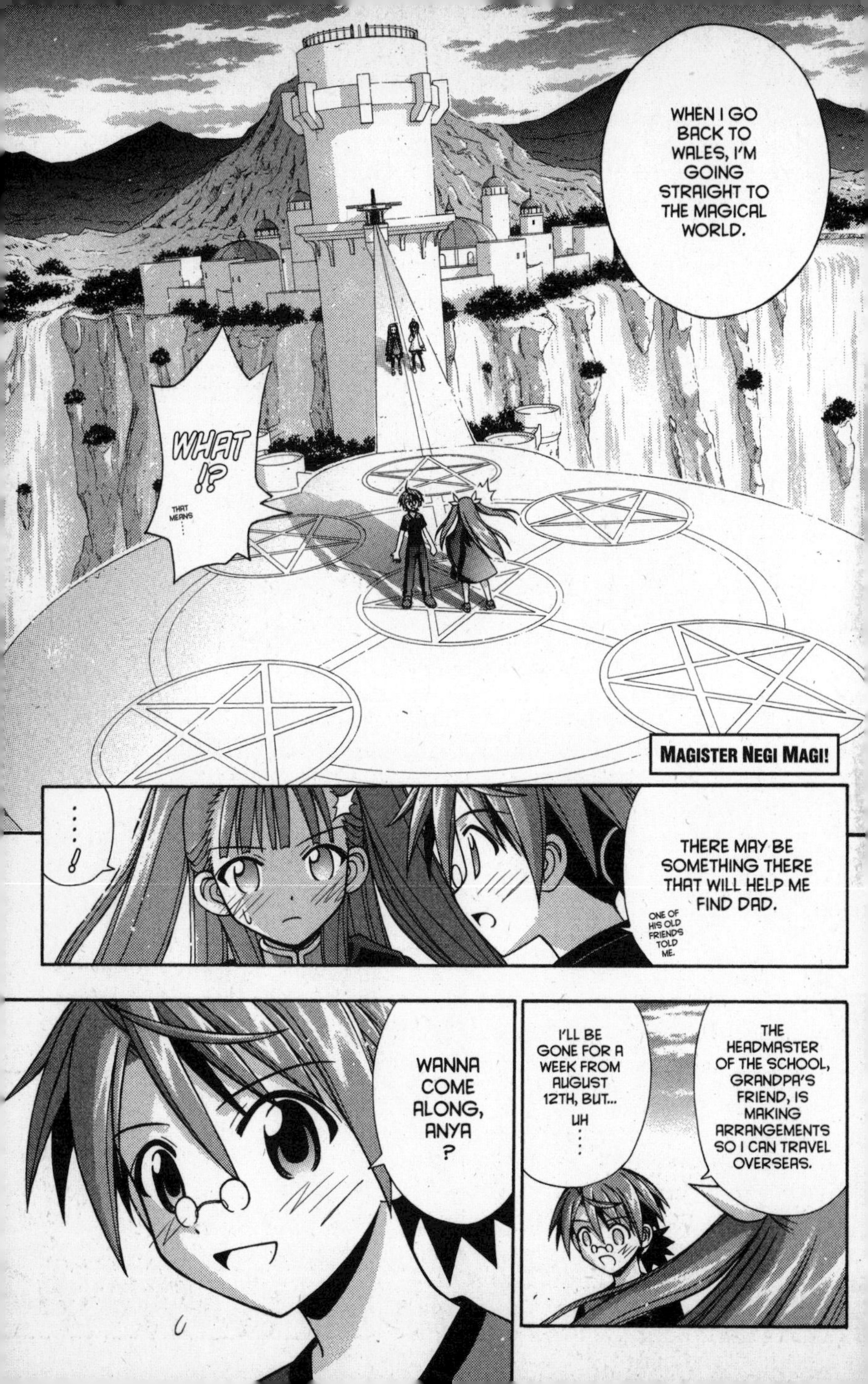
WHEN I GO BACK TO WALES, I'M GOING STRAIGHT TO THE MAGICAL WORLD.
WHAT !?
THAT MEANS....
MAGISTER NEGI MAGI!
THERE MAY BE SOMETHING THERE THAT WILL HELP ME FIND DAD.
ONE OF HIS OLD FRIENDS TOLD ME.
....!
THE HEADMASTER OF THE SCHOOL, GRANDPA'S FRIEND, IS MAKING ARRANGEMENTS SO I CAN TRAVEL OVERSEAS.
I'LL BE GONE FOR A WEEK FROM AUGUST 12TH, BUT...
UH ....
WANNA COME ALONG, ANYA ?

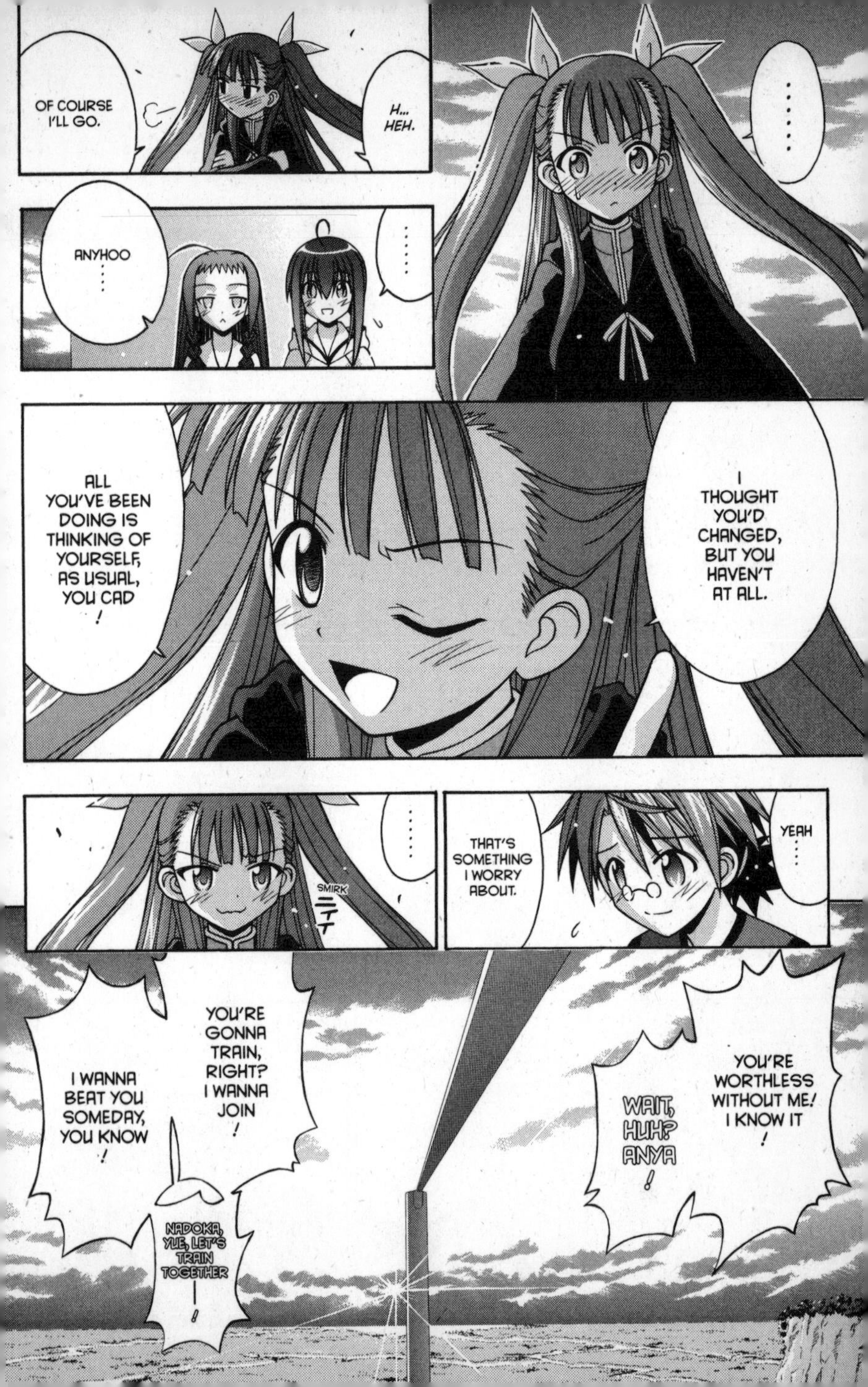
......
H... HEH.
OF COURSE I'LL GO.
......
ANYHOO ......
I THOUGHT YOU'D CHANGED, BUT YOU HAVEN'T AT ALL.
ALL YOU'VE BEEN DOING IS THINKING OF YOURSELF, AS USUAL, YOU CAD!
YEAH ......
THAT'S SOMETHING I WORRY ABOUT.
......
SMIRK
YOU'RE WORTHLESS WITHOUT ME! I KNOW IT!
WAIT, HUH? ANYA!
YOU'RE GONNA TRAIN, RIGHT? I WANNA JOIN!
I WANNA BEAT YOU SOMEDAY, YOU KNOW!
NADOKA, YUE, LET'S TRAIN TOGETHER—!

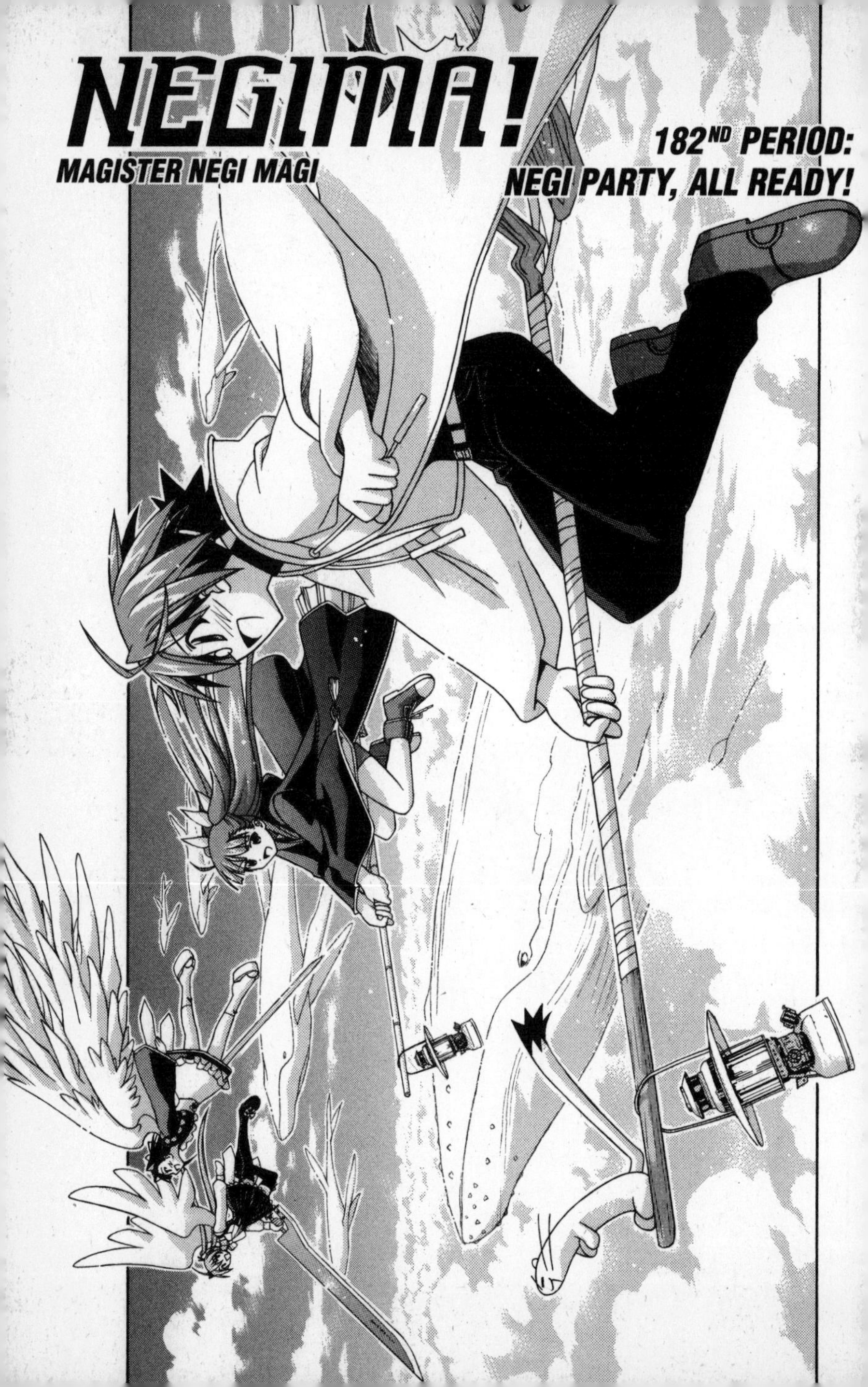
NEGIMA!
MAGISTER NEGI MAGI
182ND PERIOD:
NEGI PARTY, ALL READY!

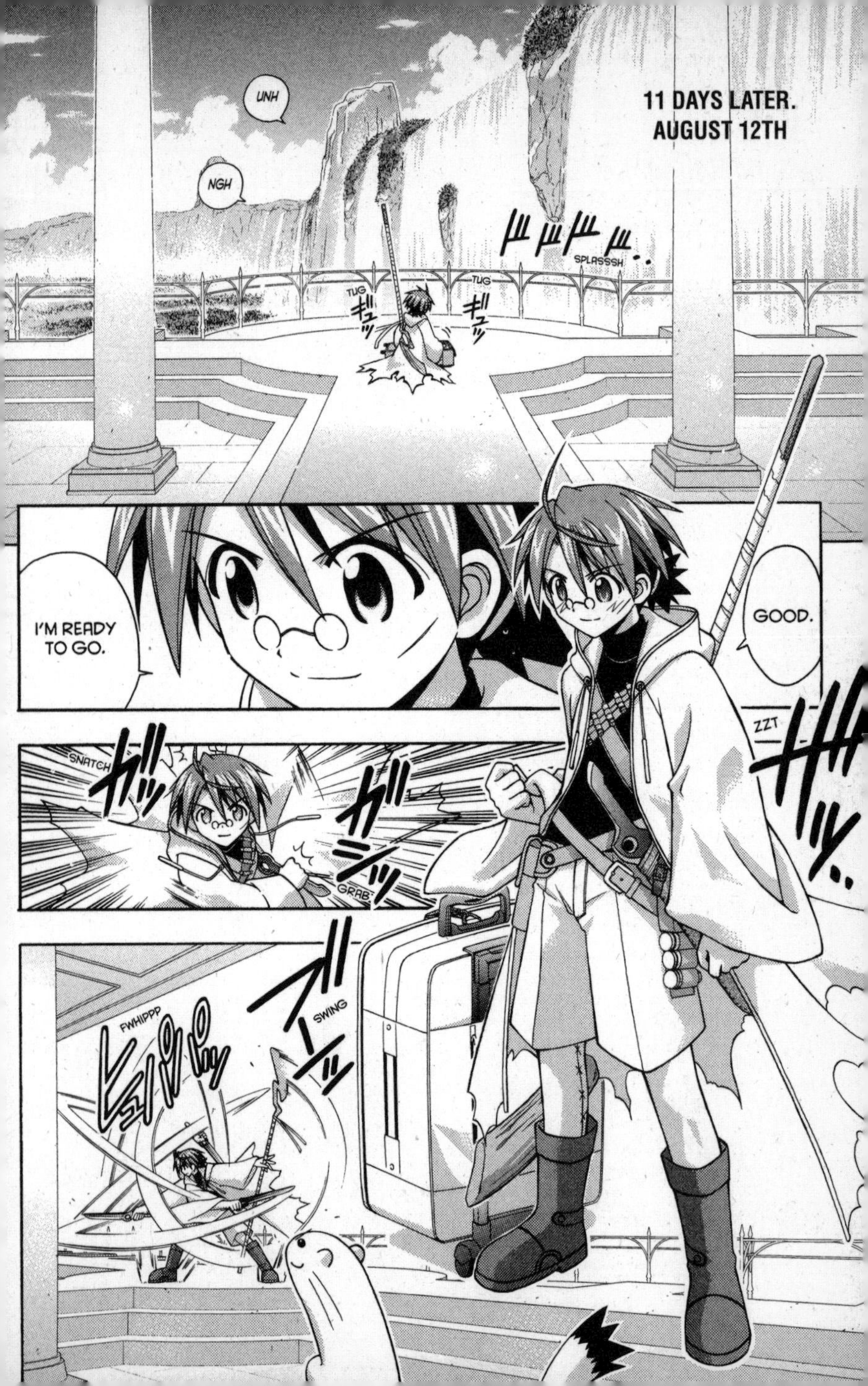

11 DAYS LATER.
AUGUST 12TH
UNH
SPLASSSH
NGH
TUG
TUG
GOOD.
ZZT
I'M READY TO GO.
SNATCH
GRAB
SWING
FWHIPPP

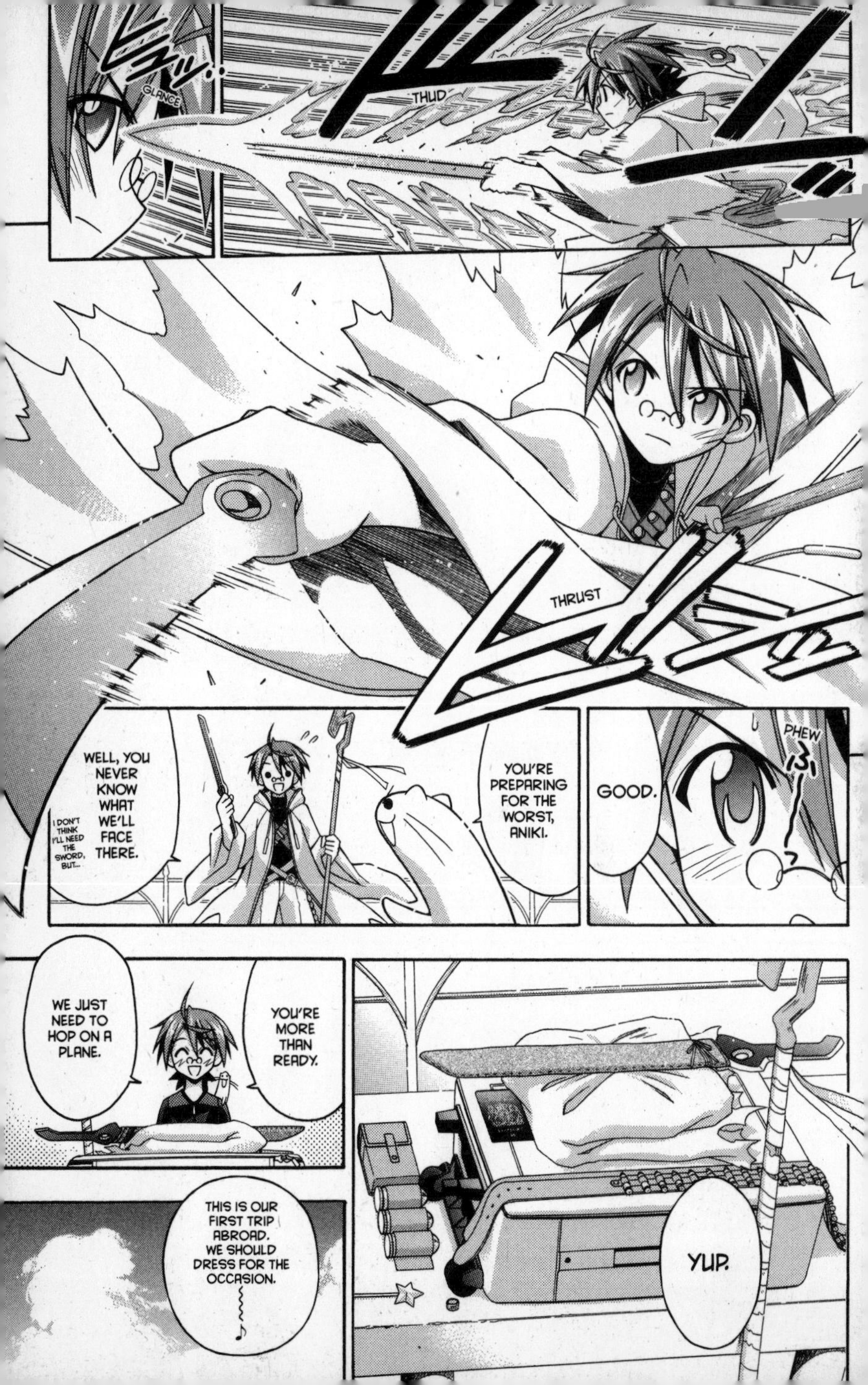
THUD
GLANCE
THRUST
PHEW
GOOD.
YOU'RE PREPARING FOR THE WORST, ANIKI.
WELL, YOU NEVER KNOW WHAT WE'LL FACE THERE.
I DON'T THINK I'LL NEED THE SWORD, BUT...
YUP.
YOU'RE MORE THAN READY.
WE JUST NEED TO HOP ON A PLANE.
THIS IS OUR FIRST TRIP ABROAD. WE SHOULD DRESS FOR THE OCCASION. ♪

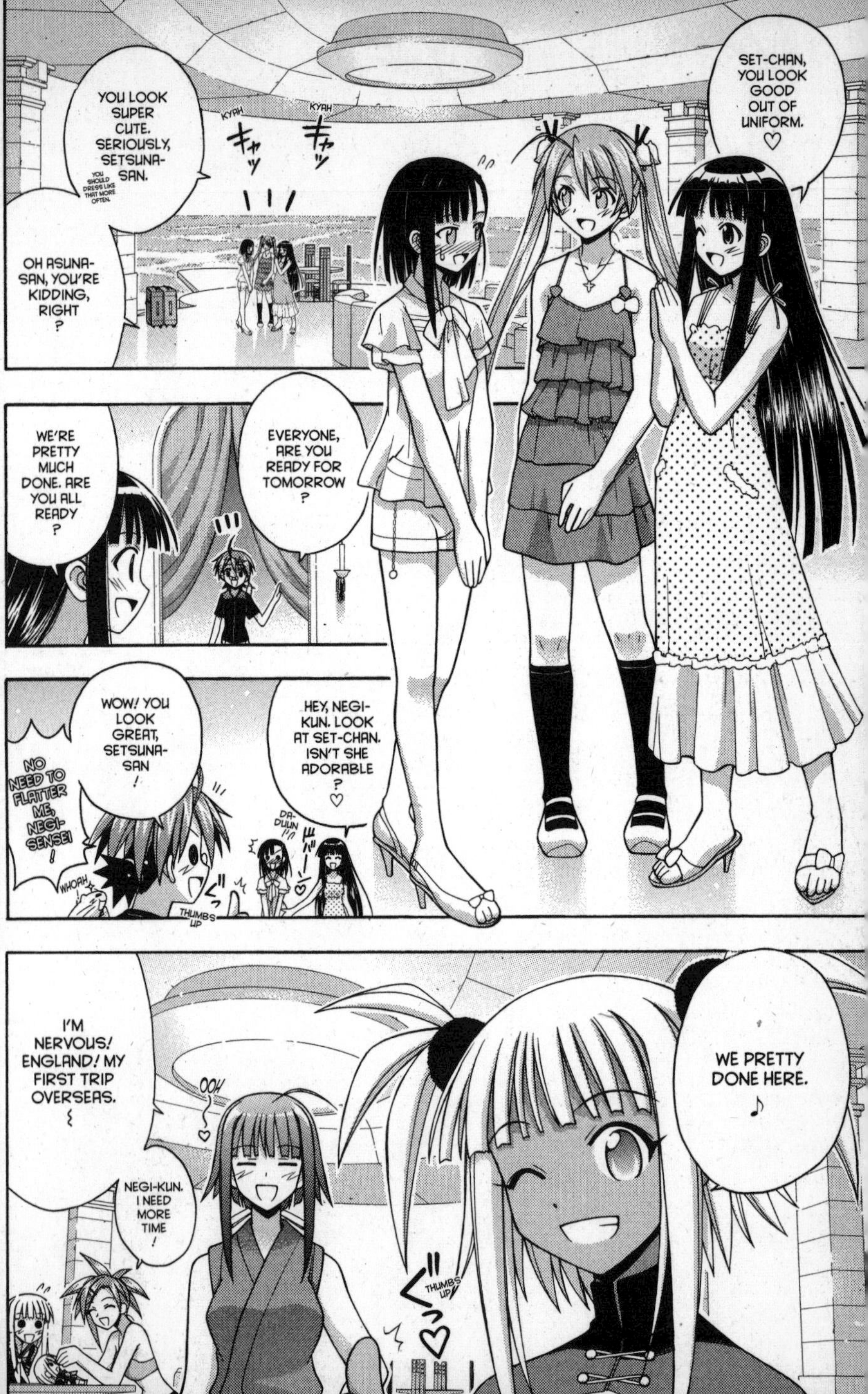
SET-CHAN, YOU LOOK GOOD OUT OF UNIFORM. ♡
KYAH
KYAH
YOU LOOK SUPER CUTE. SERIOUSLY, SETSUNA-SAN.
YOU SHOULD DRESS LIKE THAT MORE OFTEN.
OH ASUNA-SAN, YOU'RE KIDDING, RIGHT?
EVERYONE, ARE YOU READY FOR TOMORROW?
WE'RE PRETTY MUCH DONE. ARE YOU ALL READY?
HEY, NEGI-KUN. LOOK AT SET-CHAN. ISN'T SHE ADORABLE? ♡
DA-DUUN
WOW! YOU LOOK GREAT, SETSUNA-SAN!
NO NEED TO FLATTER ME, NEGI-SENSEI!
WHOAH
THUMBS UP
WE PRETTY DONE HERE. ♪
THUMBS UP
I'M NERVOUS! ENGLAND! MY FIRST TRIP OVERSEAS.
OOH
NEGI-KUN. I NEED MORE TIME!

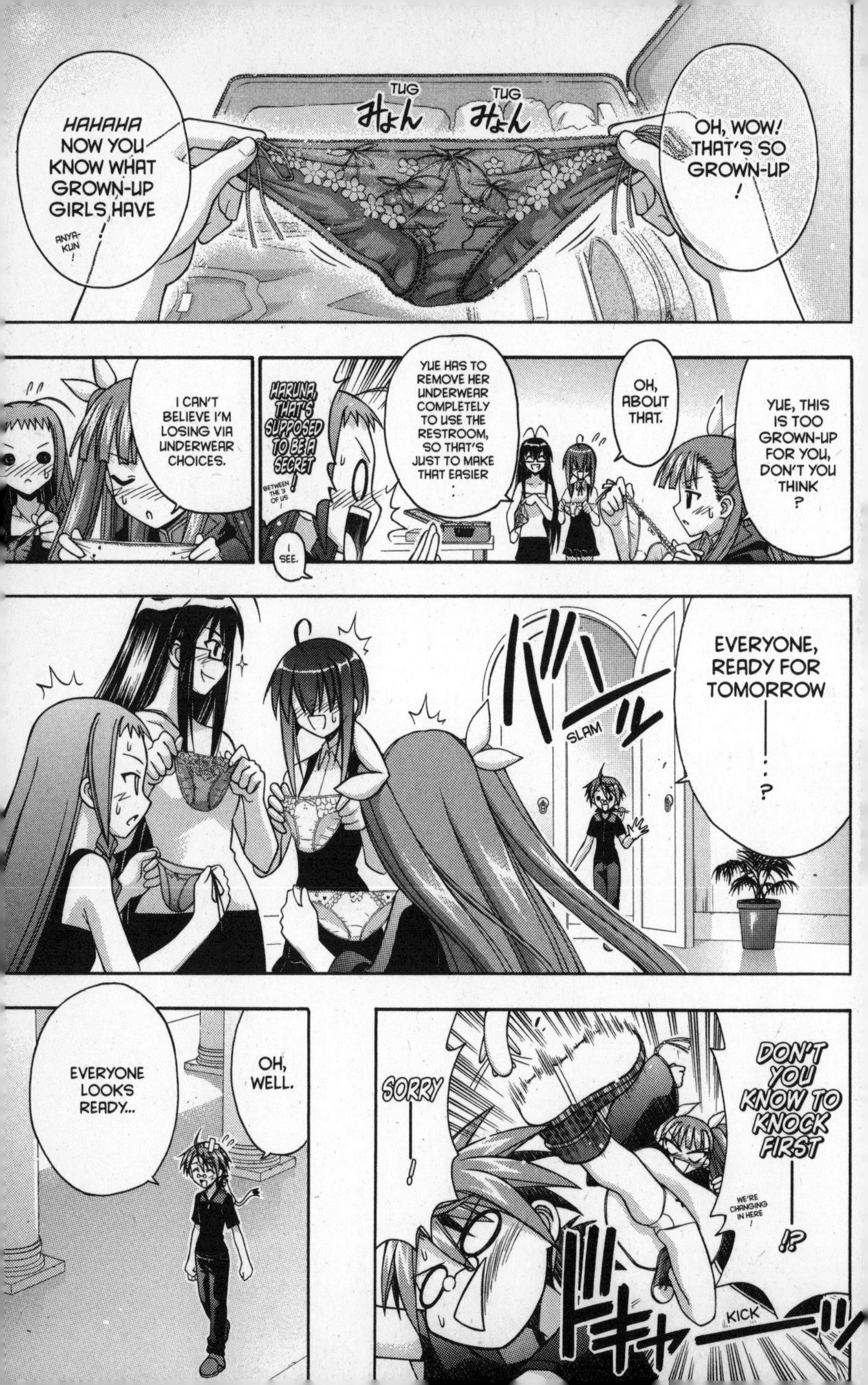
OH, WOW! THAT'S SO GROWN-UP!
TUG
みょん
TUG
みょん
HAHAHA NOW YOU KNOW WHAT GROWN-UP GIRLS HAVE!
ANYA-KUN!
YUE, THIS IS TOO GROWN-UP FOR YOU, DON'T YOU THINK?
OH, ABOUT THAT.
YUE HAS TO REMOVE HER UNDERWEAR COMPLETELY TO USE THE RESTROOM, SO THAT'S JUST TO MAKE THAT EASIER...
HARUNA, THAT'S SUPPOSED TO BE A SECRET!
BETWEEN THE 3 OF US!
I SEE.
I CAN'T BELIEVE I'M LOSING VIA UNDERWEAR CHOICES.
EVERYONE, READY FOR TOMORROW...?
バーン
SLAM
DON'T YOU KNOW TO KNOCK FIRST!?
WE'RE CHANGING IN HERE!
SORRY!
ドキャーッ
KICK
OH, WELL.
EVERYONE LOOKS READY...

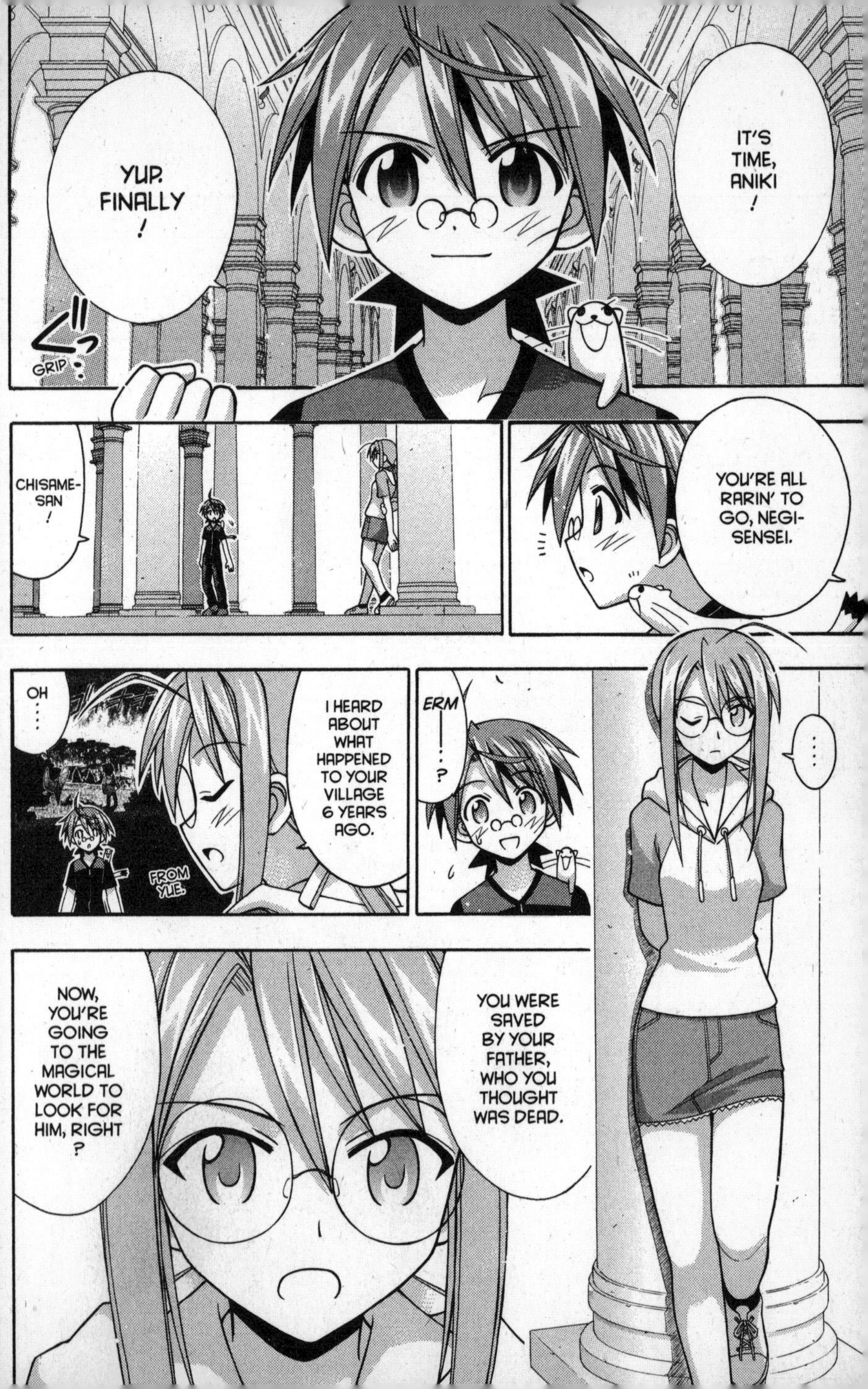
IT'S TIME, ANIKI!
YUP. FINALLY!
GRIP
YOU'RE ALL RARIN' TO GO, NEGI-SENSEI.
CHISAME-SAN!
....
ERM ...?
I HEARD ABOUT WHAT HAPPENED TO YOUR VILLAGE 6 YEARS AGO.
FROM YUE.
OH....
YOU WERE SAVED BY YOUR FATHER, WHO YOU THOUGHT WAS DEAD.
NOW, YOU'RE GOING TO THE MAGICAL WORLD TO LOOK FOR HIM, RIGHT?

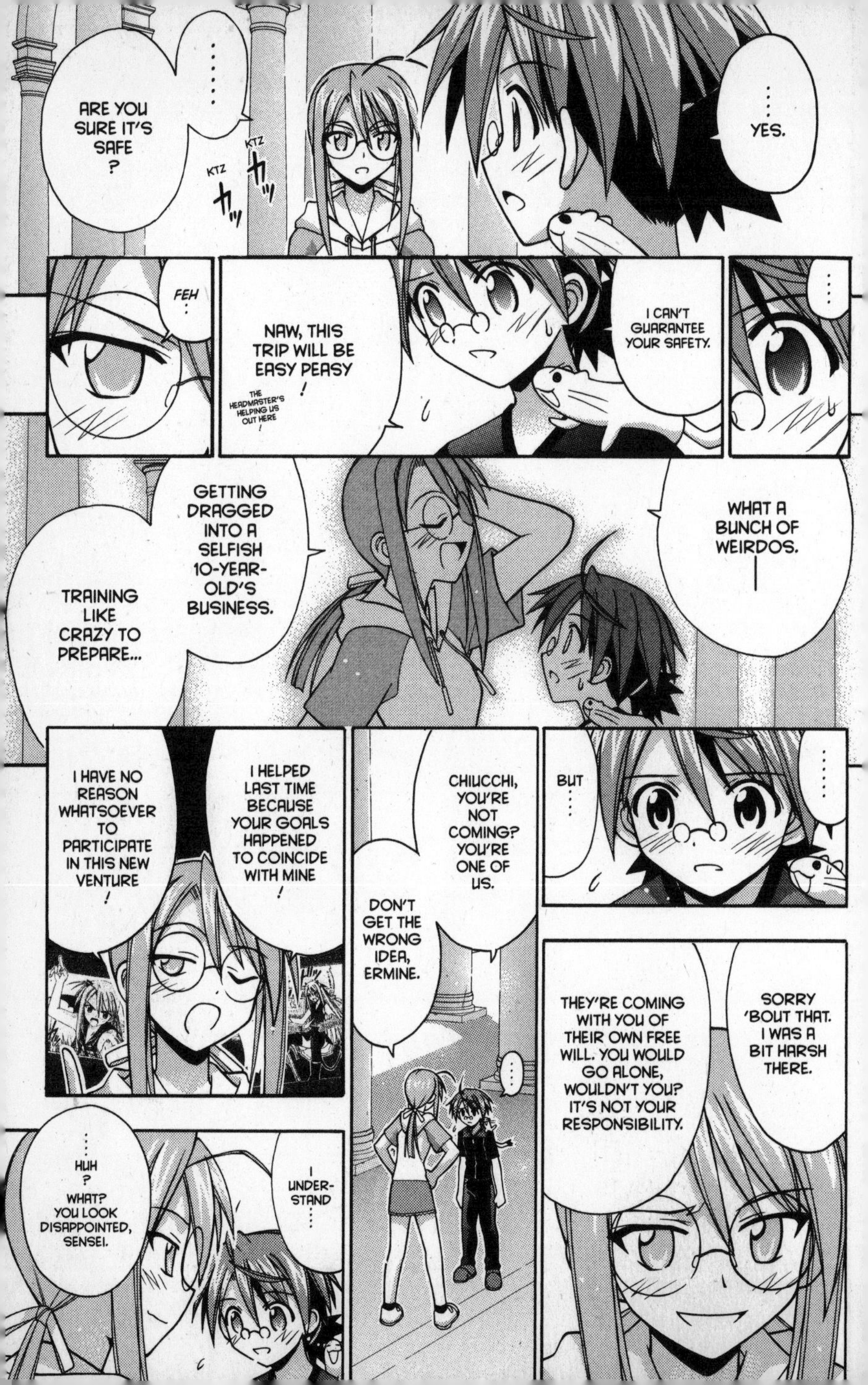
......YES.
......ARE YOU SURE IT'S SAFE?
KTZ
KTZ
......
I CAN'T GUARANTEE YOUR SAFETY.
NAW, THIS TRIP WILL BE EASY PEASY!
THE HEADMASTER'S HELPING US OUT HERE!
FEH...
WHAT A BUNCH OF WEIRDOS.
GETTING DRAGGED INTO A SELFISH 10-YEAR-OLD'S BUSINESS.
TRAINING LIKE CRAZY TO PREPARE...
......
BUT......
SORRY 'BOUT THAT. I WAS A BIT HARSH THERE.
THEY'RE COMING WITH YOU OF THEIR OWN FREE WILL. YOU WOULD GO ALONE, WOULDN'T YOU? IT'S NOT YOUR RESPONSIBILITY.
CHIUCCHI, YOU'RE NOT COMING? YOU'RE ONE OF US.
DON'T GET THE WRONG IDEA, ERMINE.
...
I HELPED LAST TIME BECAUSE YOUR GOALS HAPPENED TO COINCIDE WITH MINE!
I HAVE NO REASON WHATSOEVER TO PARTICIPATE IN THIS NEW VENTURE!
I UNDERSTAND......
......HUH? WHAT? YOU LOOK DISAPPOINTED, SENSEI.

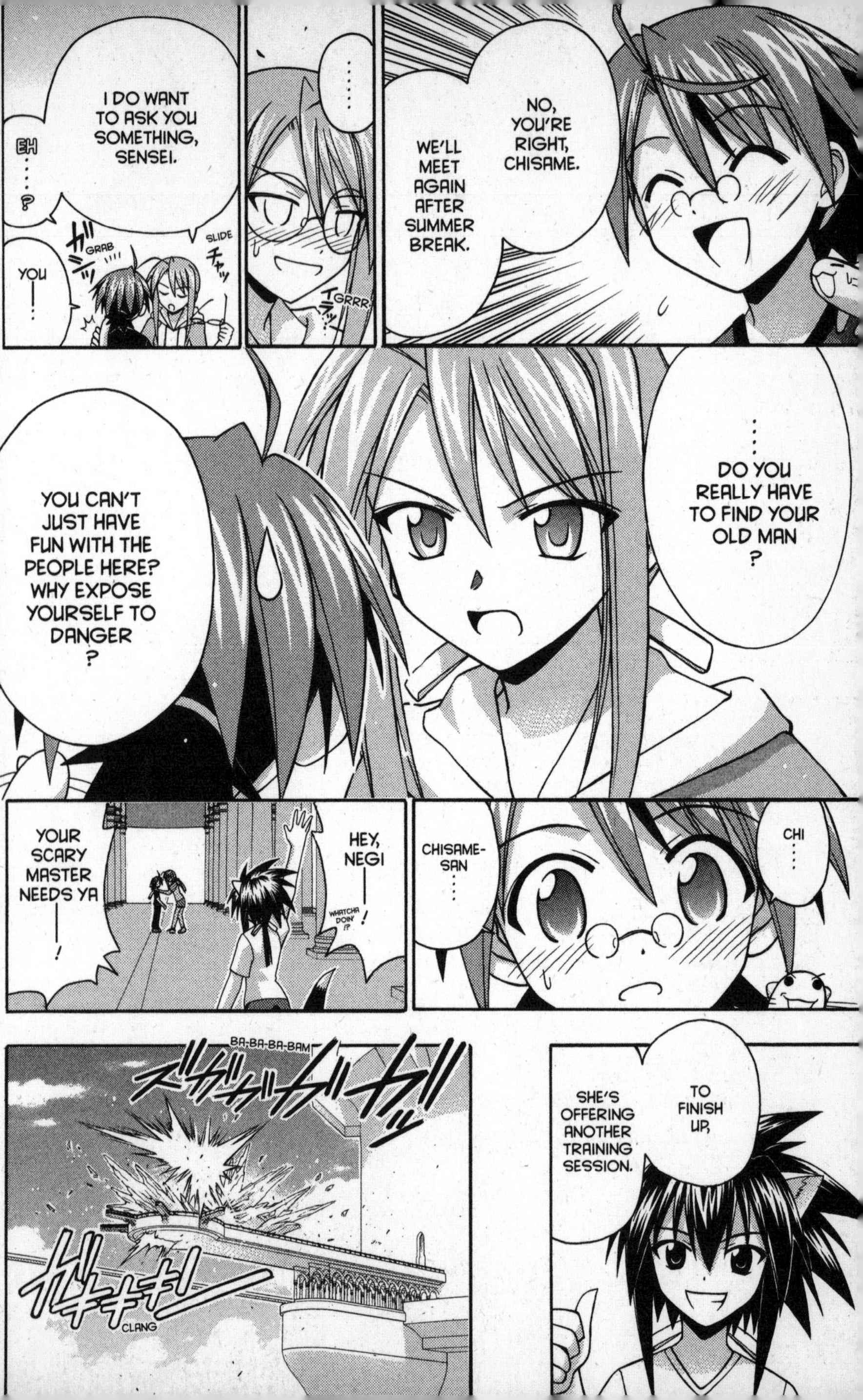
NO, YOU'RE RIGHT, CHISAME.
WE'LL MEET AGAIN AFTER SUMMER BREAK.
......
GRRR
I DO WANT TO ASK YOU SOMETHING, SENSEI.
EH.....?
SLIDE
GRAB
YOU—...!
......
DO YOU REALLY HAVE TO FIND YOUR OLD MAN?
YOU CAN'T JUST HAVE FUN WITH THE PEOPLE HERE? WHY EXPOSE YOURSELF TO DANGER?
CHI......
CHISAME-SAN......
HEY, NEGI—!
WHATCHA DOIN' !?
YOUR SCARY MASTER NEEDS YA—!
TO FINISH UP,
SHE'S OFFERING ANOTHER TRAINING SESSION.
BA-BA-BA-BAM
CLANG

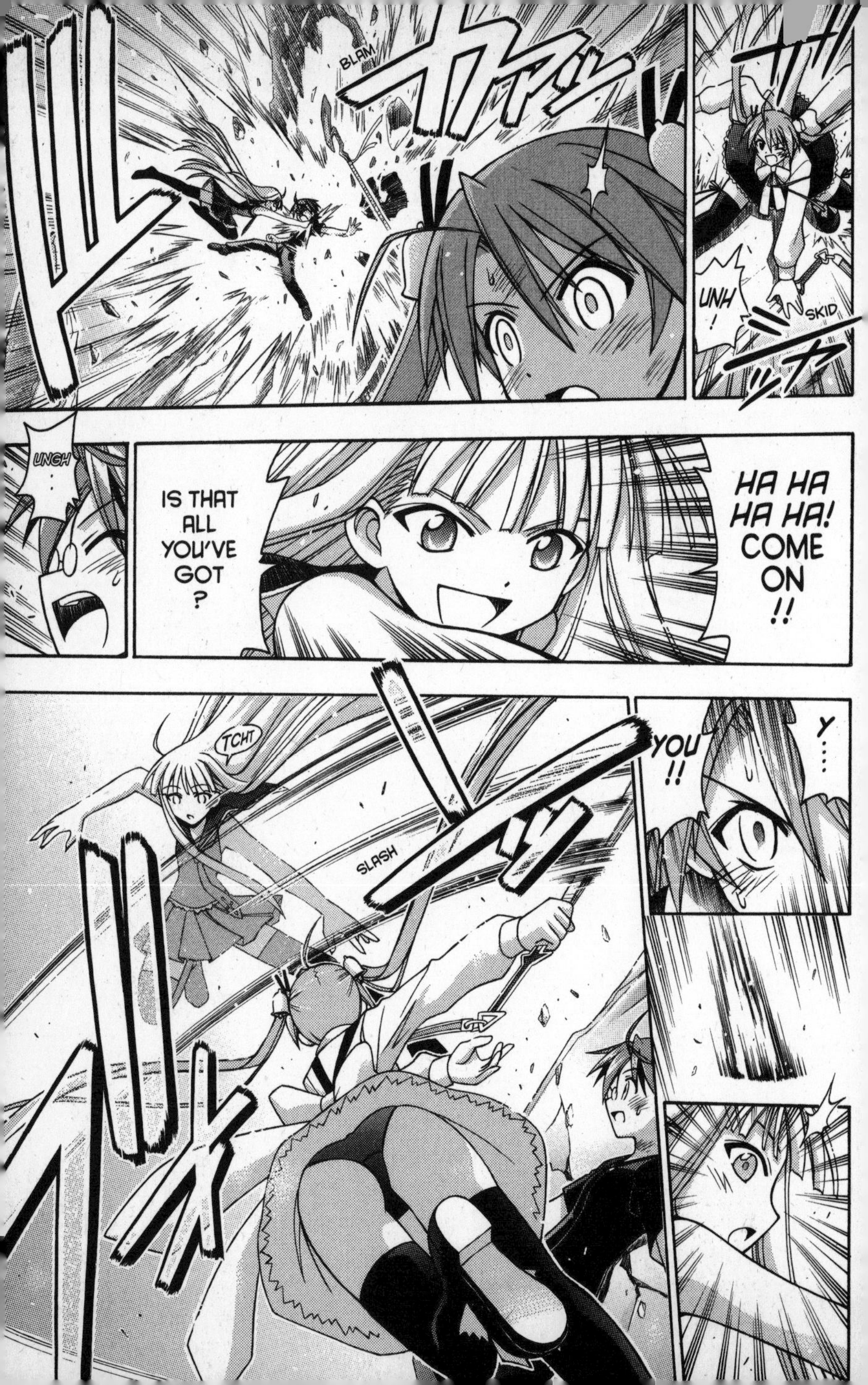
UNH!
SKID
BLAM
HA HA HA HA! COME ON!!
IS THAT ALL YOU'VE GOT?
UNGH
Y....
YOU!!
TCHT
SLASH

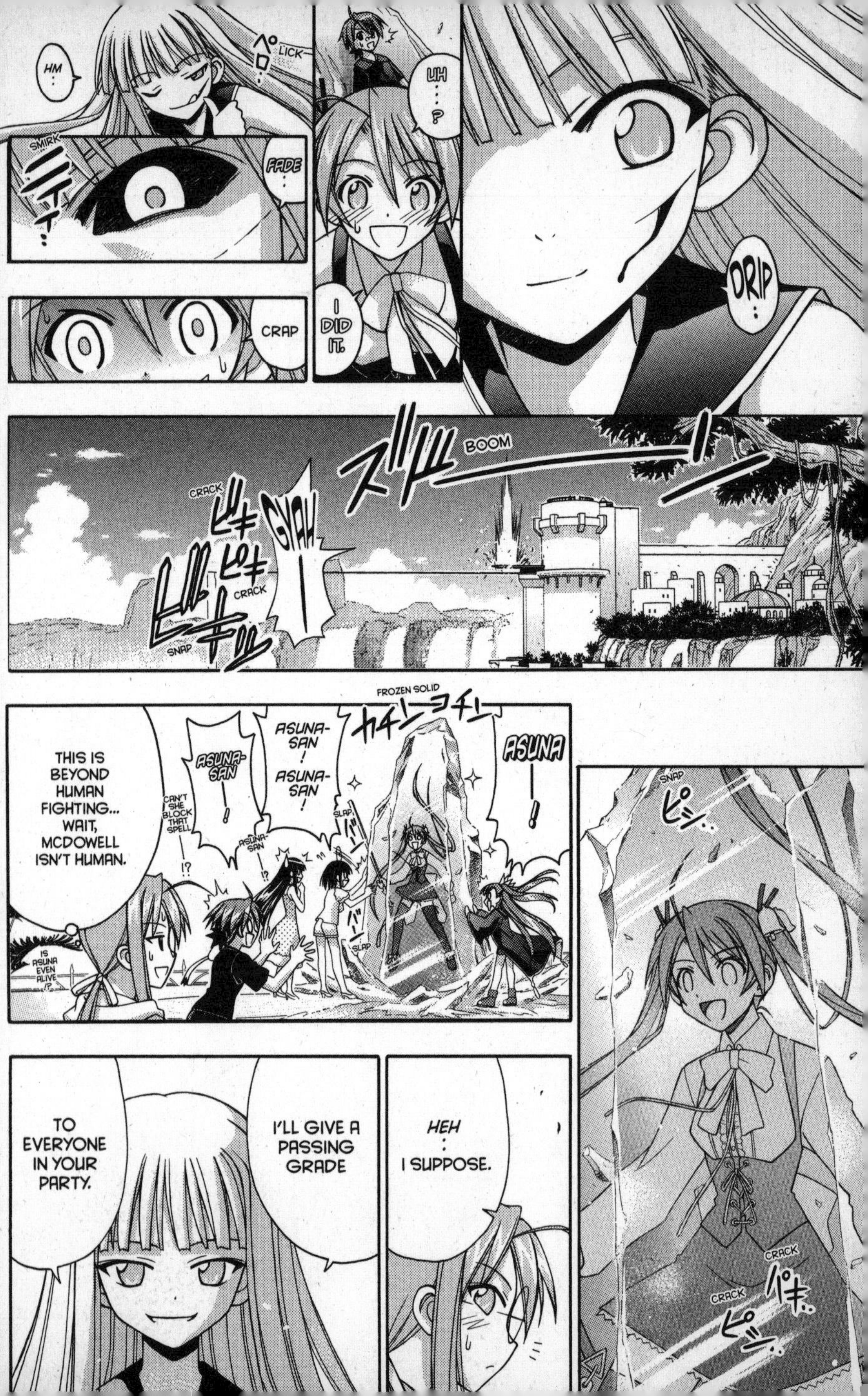
DRIP
UH...?
I DID IT.
HM...
LICK
SMIRK
FADE...
CRAP
BOOM
GYAH!
CRACK
CRACK
SNAP
SNAP
CRACK
CRACK
FROZEN SOLID
ASUNA!
ASUNA-SAN! ASUNA-SAN!
SLAP
SLAP
ASUNA-SAN!
CAN'T SHE BLOCK THAT SPELL!?
ASUNA-SAN!?
THIS IS BEYOND HUMAN FIGHTING... WAIT, MCDOWELL ISN'T HUMAN.
IS ASUNA EVEN ALIVE!?
HEH... I SUPPOSE.
I'LL GIVE A PASSING GRADE
TO EVERYONE IN YOUR PARTY.

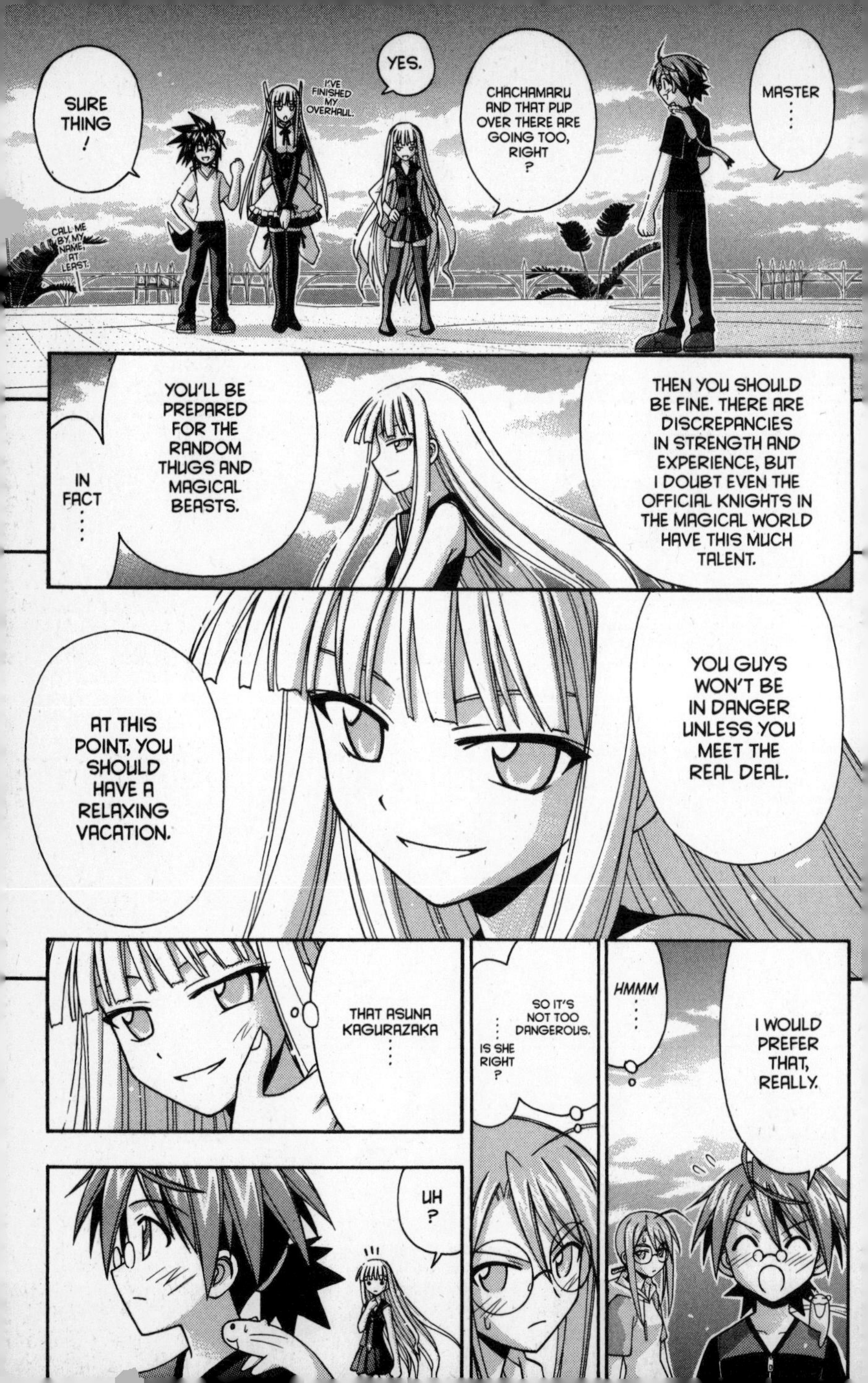
MASTER ....
CHACHAMARU AND THAT PUP OVER THERE ARE GOING TOO, RIGHT?
YES.
I'VE FINISHED MY OVERHAUL.
SURE THING!
CALL ME BY MY NAME, AT LEAST.
THEN YOU SHOULD BE FINE. THERE ARE DISCREPANCIES IN STRENGTH AND EXPERIENCE, BUT I DOUBT EVEN THE OFFICIAL KNIGHTS IN THE MAGICAL WORLD HAVE THIS MUCH TALENT.
YOU'LL BE PREPARED FOR THE RANDOM THUGS AND MAGICAL BEASTS.
IN FACT ....
YOU GUYS WON'T BE IN DANGER UNLESS YOU MEET THE REAL DEAL.
AT THIS POINT, YOU SHOULD HAVE A RELAXING VACATION.
I WOULD PREFER THAT, REALLY.
HMMM ....
SO IT'S NOT TOO DANGEROUS.
.... IS SHE RIGHT?
THAT ASUNA KAGURAZAKA ....
UH?

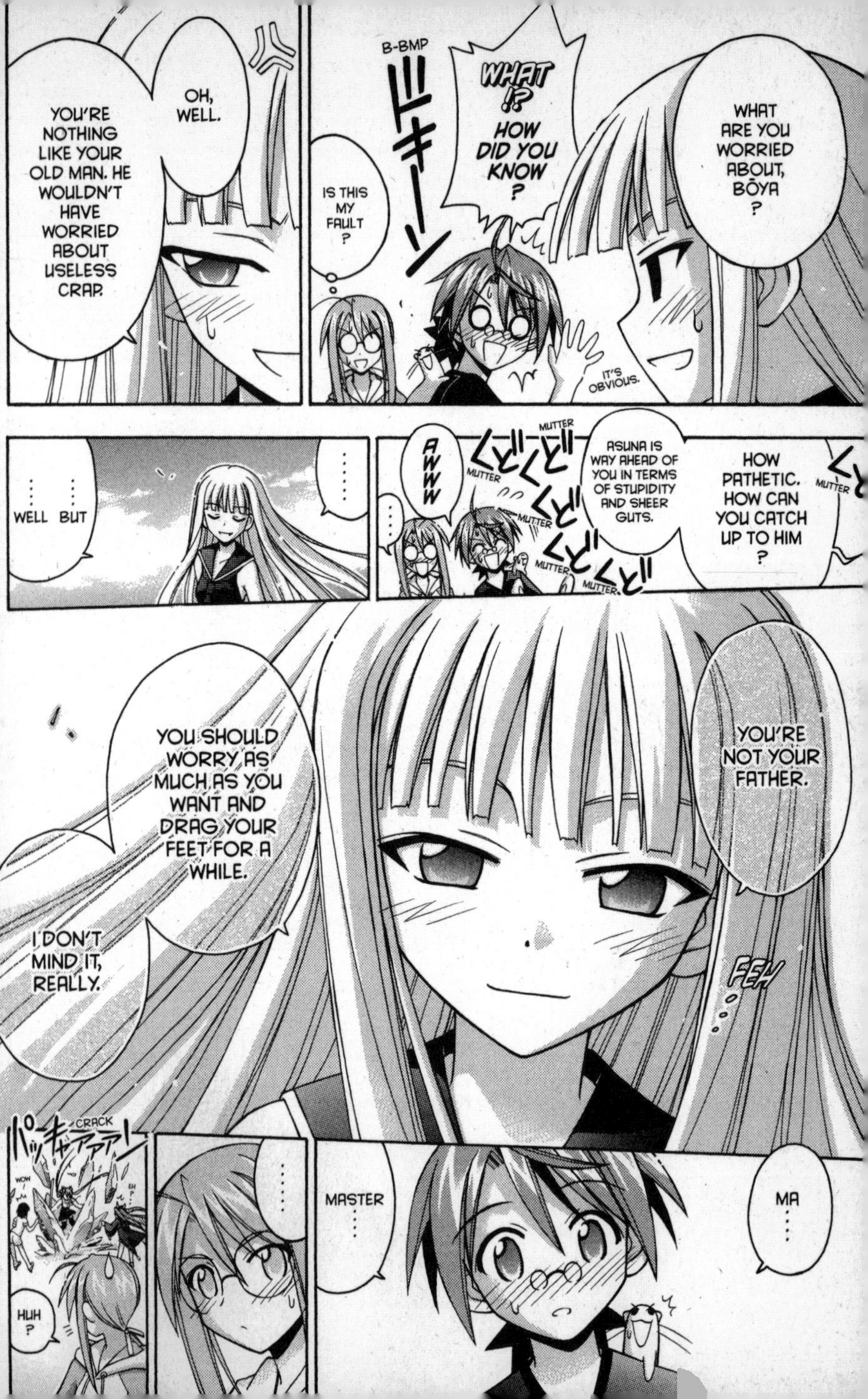
WHAT ARE YOU WORRIED ABOUT, BŌYA?
B-BMP
WHAT!? HOW DID YOU KNOW?
IT'S OBVIOUS.
IS THIS MY FAULT?
OH, WELL.
YOU'RE NOTHING LIKE YOUR OLD MAN. HE WOULDN'T HAVE WORRIED ABOUT USELESS CRAP.
MUTTER
HOW PATHETIC. HOW CAN YOU CATCH UP TO HIM?
ASUNA IS WAY AHEAD OF YOU IN TERMS OF STUPIDITY AND SHEER GUTS.
MUTTER
MUTTER
MUTTER
MUTTER
MUTTER
MUTTER
AWWW
...
......
... WELL ... BUT
YOU'RE NOT YOUR FATHER.
FEH
YOU SHOULD WORRY AS MUCH AS YOU WANT AND DRAG YOUR FEET FOR A WHILE.
I DON'T MIND IT, REALLY.
MA...
MASTER...
......
CRACK
EH
WOW
HUH?

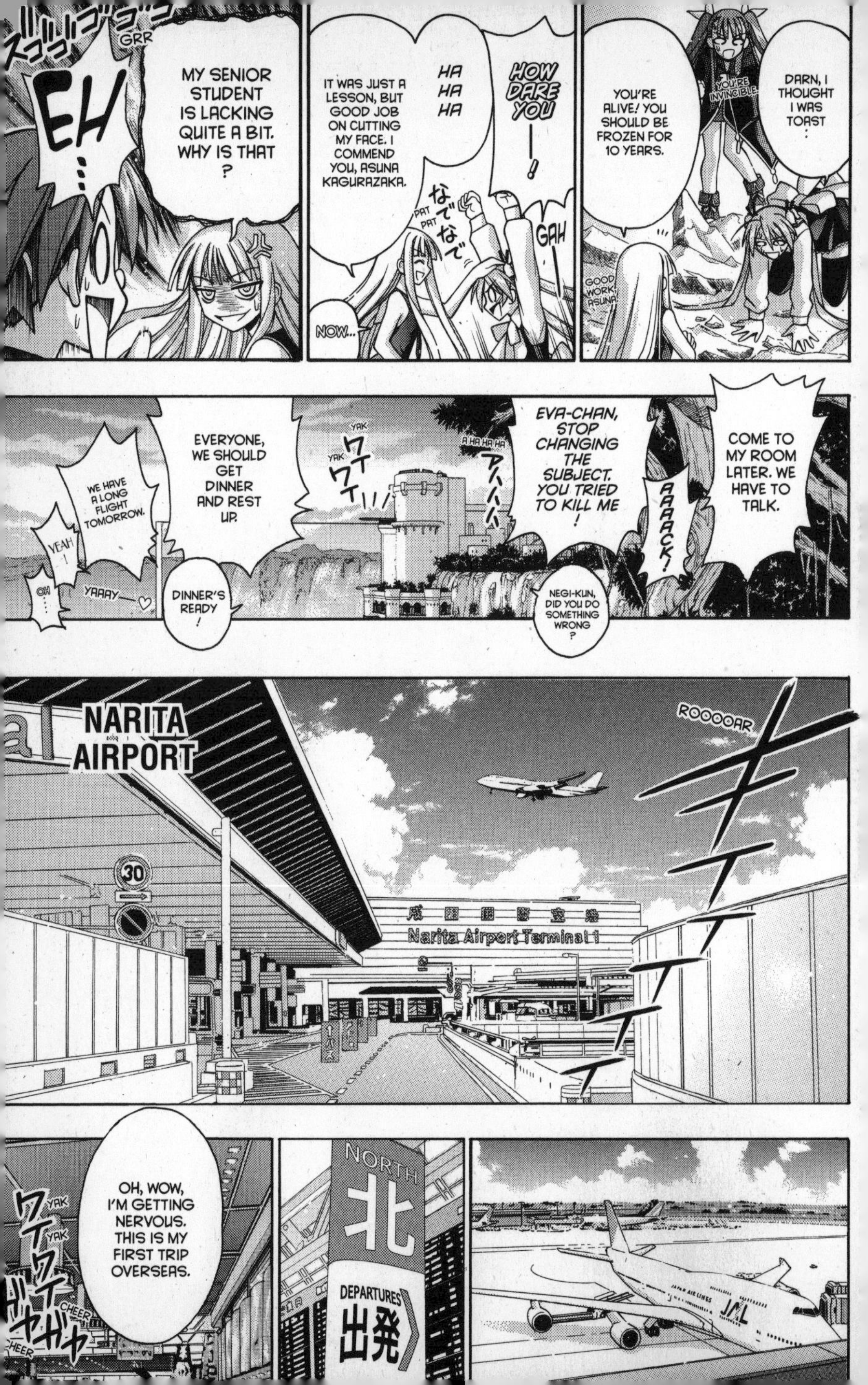
DARN, I THOUGHT I WAS TOAST :
YOU'RE INVINCIBLE.
YOU'RE ALIVE! YOU SHOULD BE FROZEN FOR 10 YEARS.
GOOD WORK, ASUNA.
HOW DARE YOU —!
GAH
HA HA HA
IT WAS JUST A LESSON, BUT GOOD JOB ON CUTTING MY FACE. I COMMEND YOU, ASUNA KAGURAZAKA.
なでなで
PAT PAT
NOW...
GRR
MY SENIOR STUDENT IS LACKING QUITE A BIT. WHY IS THAT ?
EH...
COME TO MY ROOM LATER. WE HAVE TO TALK.
AAAACK!
EVA-CHAN, STOP CHANGING THE SUBJECT. YOU TRIED TO KILL ME !
NEGI-KUN, DID YOU DO SOMETHING WRONG ?
アハハハ
A HA HA HA
ワイワイ
YAK YAK
EVERYONE, WE SHOULD GET DINNER AND REST UP.
DINNER'S READY !
WE HAVE A LONG FLIGHT TOMORROW.
YEAH !
YAAAY♡
OH.....
ROOOOAR
NARITA AIRPORT
30
成田国際空港
Narita Airport Terminal 1
NORTH
北
DEPARTURES
出発
JAPAN AIR LINES
JAL
OH, WOW, I'M GETTING NERVOUS. THIS IS MY FIRST TRIP OVERSEAS.
ワイワイ
YAK YAK
ガヤガヤ
CHEER CHEER

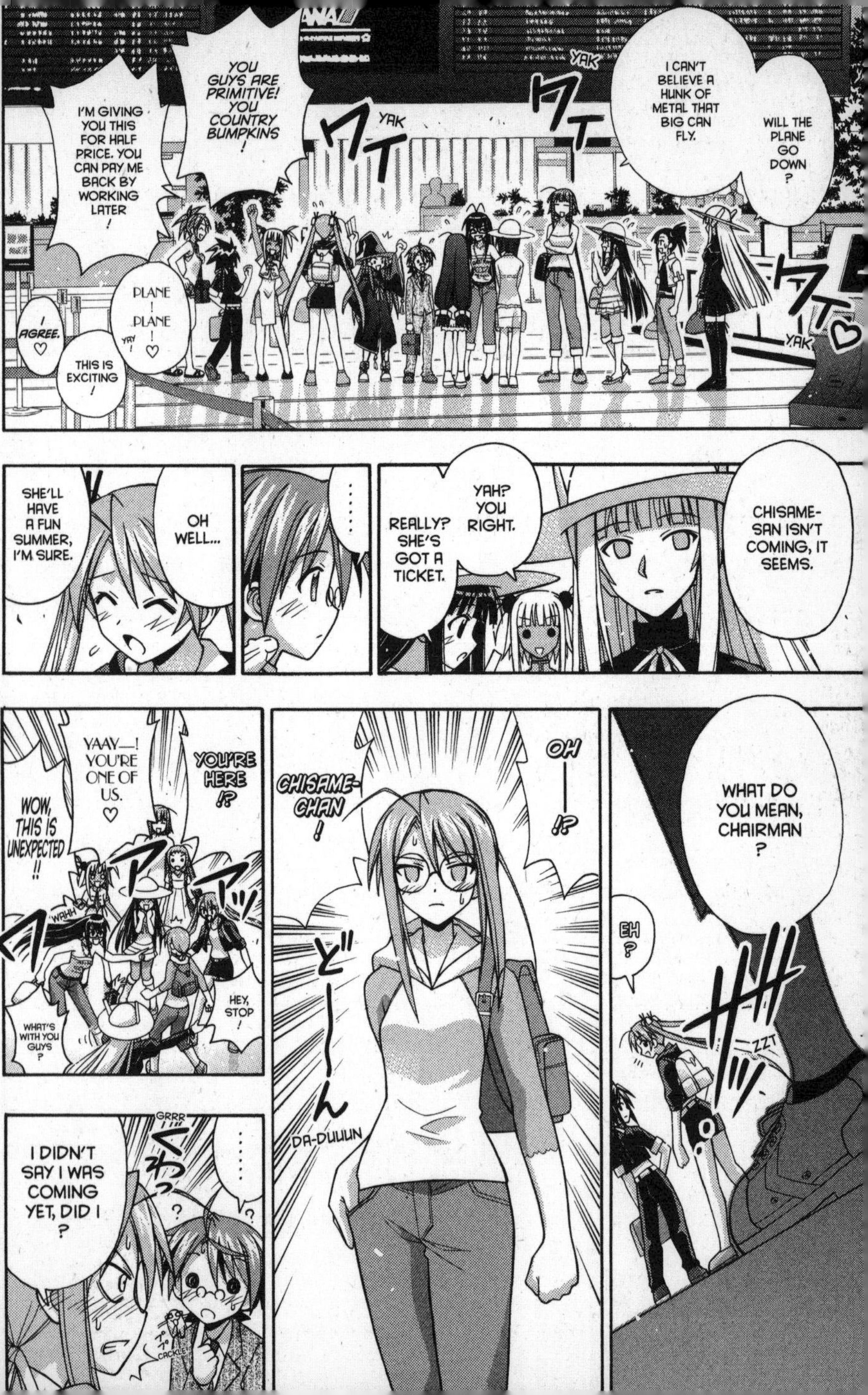
YAK
I CAN'T BELIEVE A HUNK OF METAL THAT BIG CAN FLY.
WILL THE PLANE GO DOWN?
YAK
YAK
YOU GUYS ARE PRIMITIVE! YOU COUNTRY BUMPKINS!
I'M GIVING YOU THIS FOR HALF PRICE. YOU CAN PAY ME BACK BY WORKING LATER!
PLANE! PLANE! ♡
YAY!
THIS IS EXCITING!
I AGREE. ♡
CHISAME-SAN ISN'T COMING, IT SEEMS.
YAH? YOU RIGHT.
REALLY? SHE'S GOT A TICKET.
......
OH WELL...
SHE'LL HAVE A FUN SUMMER, I'M SURE.
WHAT DO YOU MEAN, CHAIRMAN?
EH?
ZZT
OH—!?
CHISAME-CHAN!
DA-DUUUN
YOU'RE HERE!?
YAAY—! YOU'RE ONE OF US. ♡
WOW, THIS IS UNEXPECTED!!
WAHH
HEY, STOP!
WHAT'S WITH YOU GUYS?
......
GRRR
I DIDN'T SAY I WAS COMING YET, DID I?
CACKLE

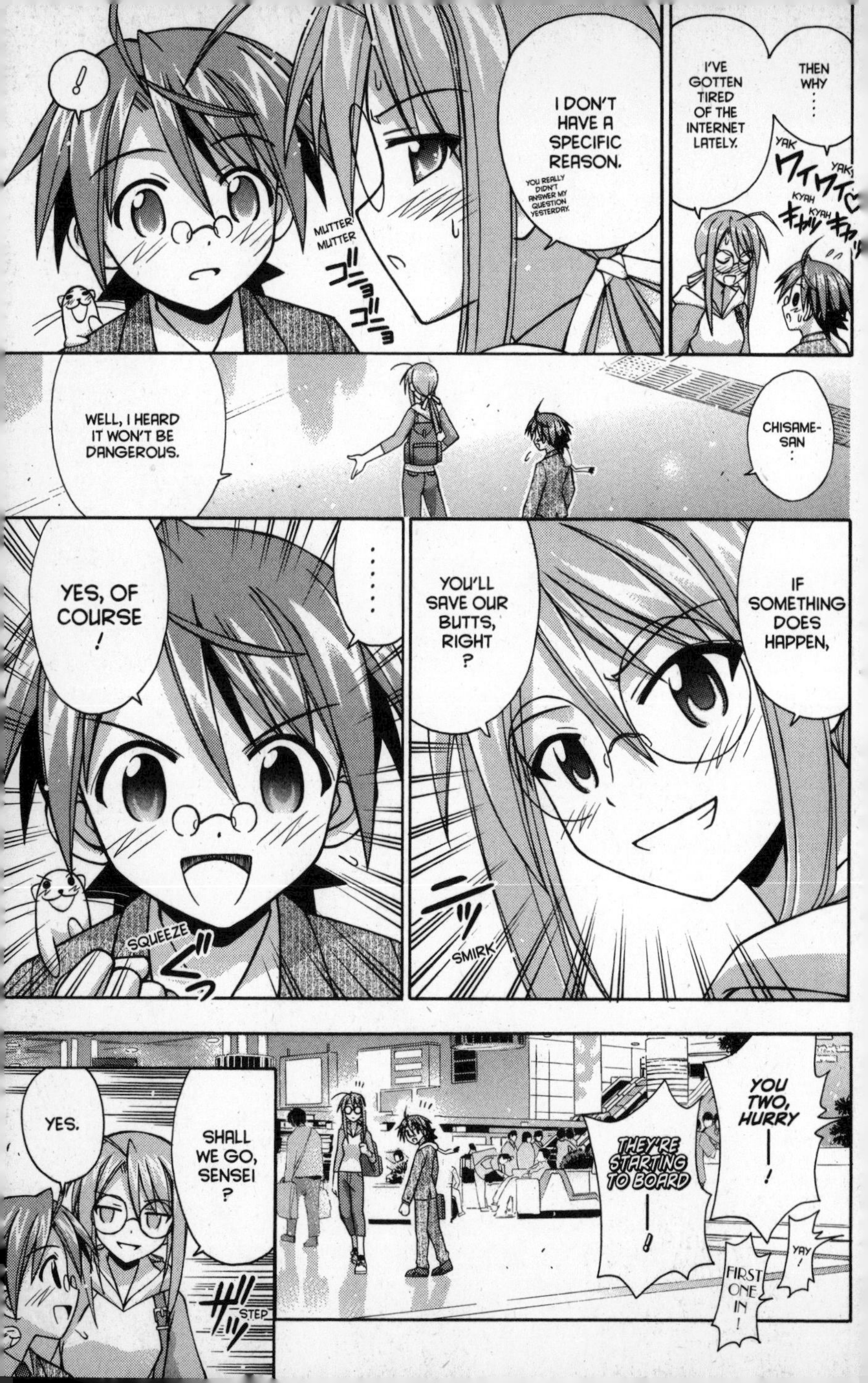
THEN WHY ...
I'VE GOTTEN TIRED OF THE INTERNET LATELY.
YAK YAK
KYAH KYAH
!
I DON'T HAVE A SPECIFIC REASON.
YOU REALLY DIDN'T ANSWER MY QUESTION YESTERDAY.
MUTTER MUTTER
CHISAME-SAN ...
WELL, I HEARD IT WON'T BE DANGEROUS.
IF SOMETHING DOES HAPPEN,
YOU'LL SAVE OUR BUTTS, RIGHT?
SMIRK
......
YES, OF COURSE!
SQUEEZE
YOU TWO, HURRY!
THEY'RE STARTING TO BOARD!
YAY!
FIRST ONE IN!
SHALL WE GO, SENSEI?
YES.
STEP

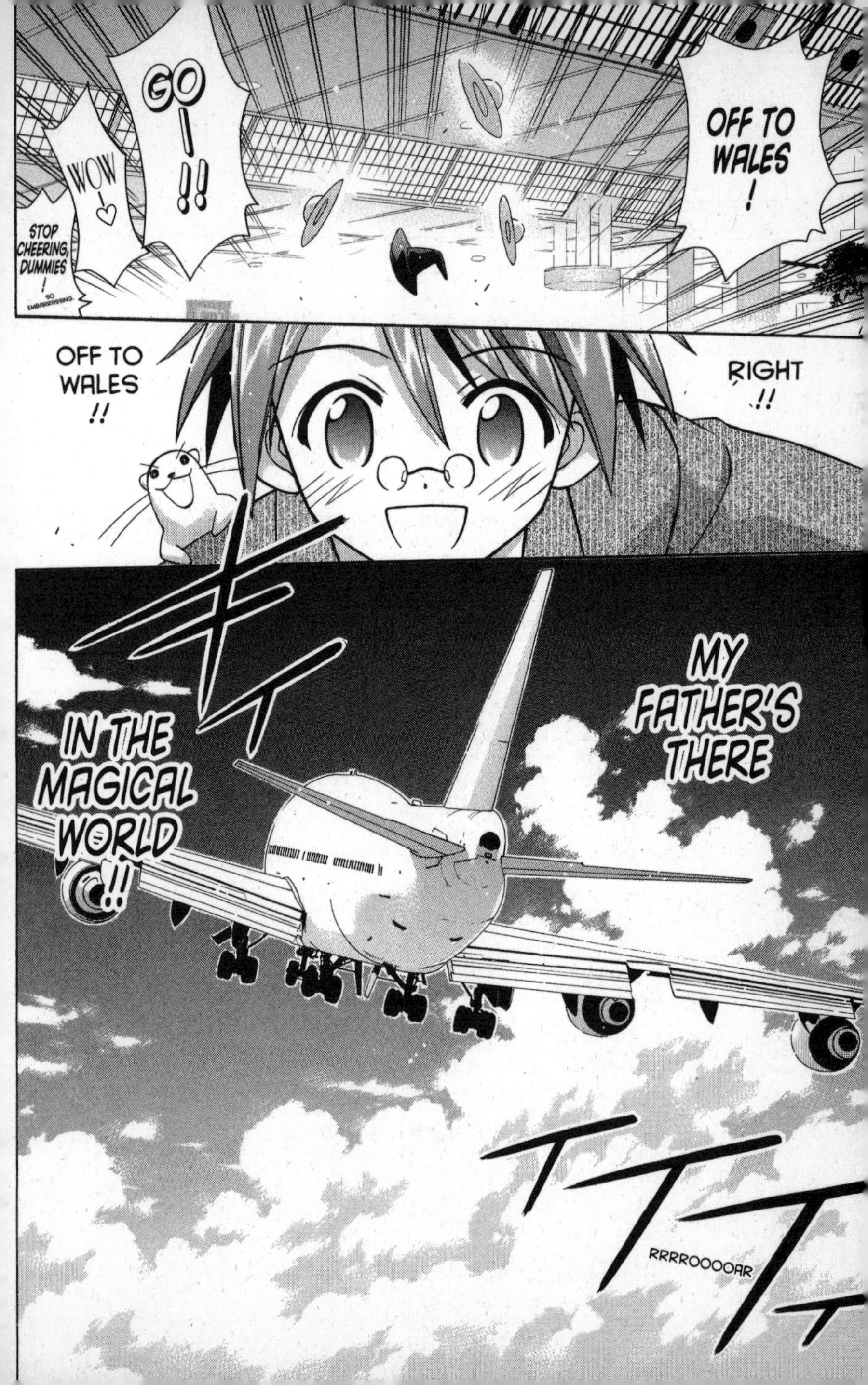
OFF TO WALES !
GO I !!
WOW ♡
STOP CHEERING, DUMMIES !
SO EMBARRASSING.
RIGHT !!
OFF TO WALES !!
MY FATHER'S THERE
IN THE MAGICAL WORLD !!
RRRROOOOAR

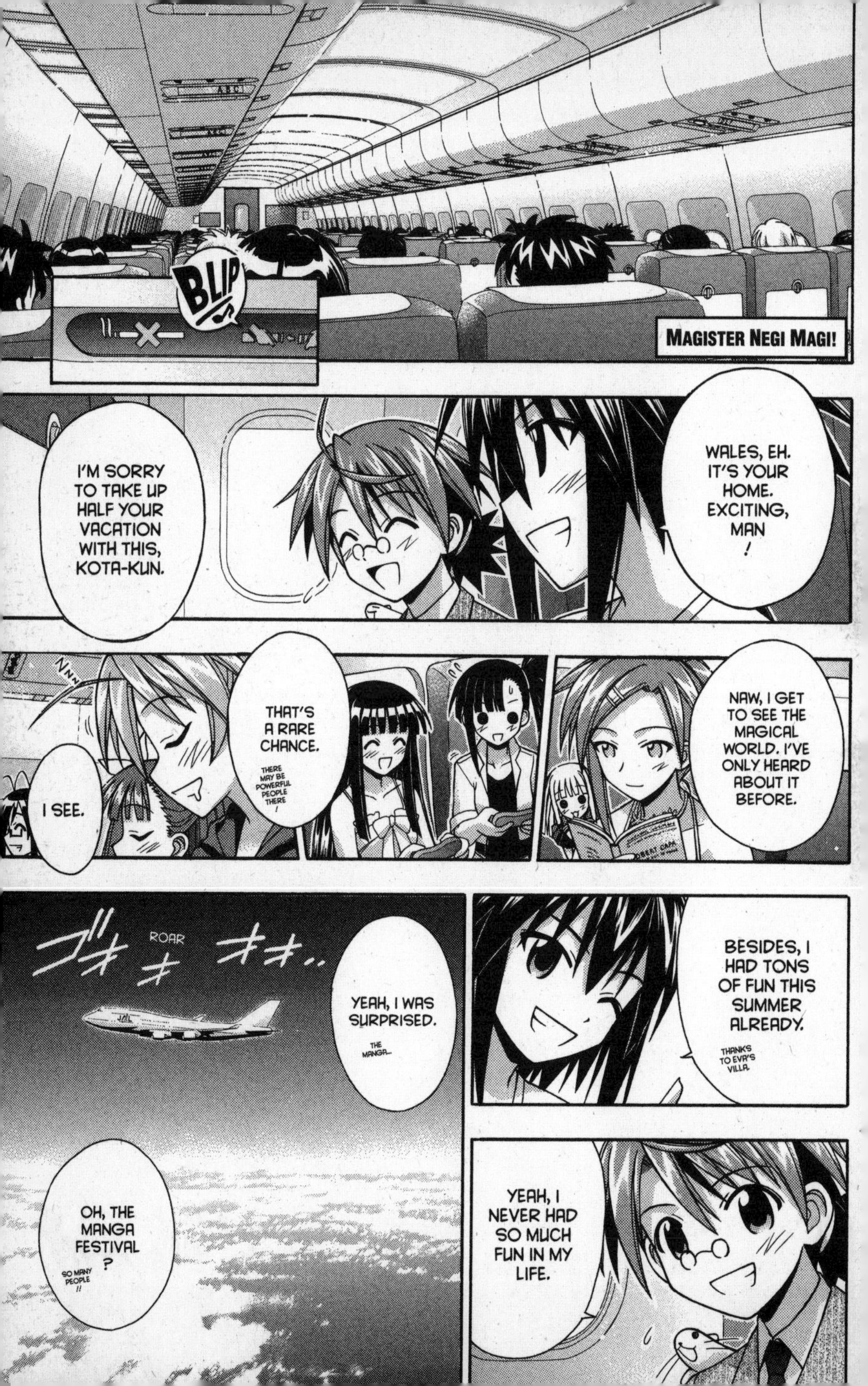
BLIP
MAGISTER NEGI MAGI!
WALES, EH. IT'S YOUR HOME. EXCITING, MAN!
I'M SORRY TO TAKE UP HALF YOUR VACATION WITH THIS, KOTA-KUN.
NAW, I GET TO SEE THE MAGICAL WORLD. I'VE ONLY HEARD ABOUT IT BEFORE.
THAT'S A RARE CHANCE.
THERE MAY BE POWERFUL PEOPLE THERE!
I SEE.
BESIDES, I HAD TONS OF FUN THIS SUMMER ALREADY.
THANKS TO EVA'S VILLA.
YEAH, I NEVER HAD SO MUCH FUN IN MY LIFE.
ROAR
YEAH, I WAS SURPRISED.
THE MANGA...
OH, THE MANGA FESTIVAL?
SO MANY PEOPLE!!

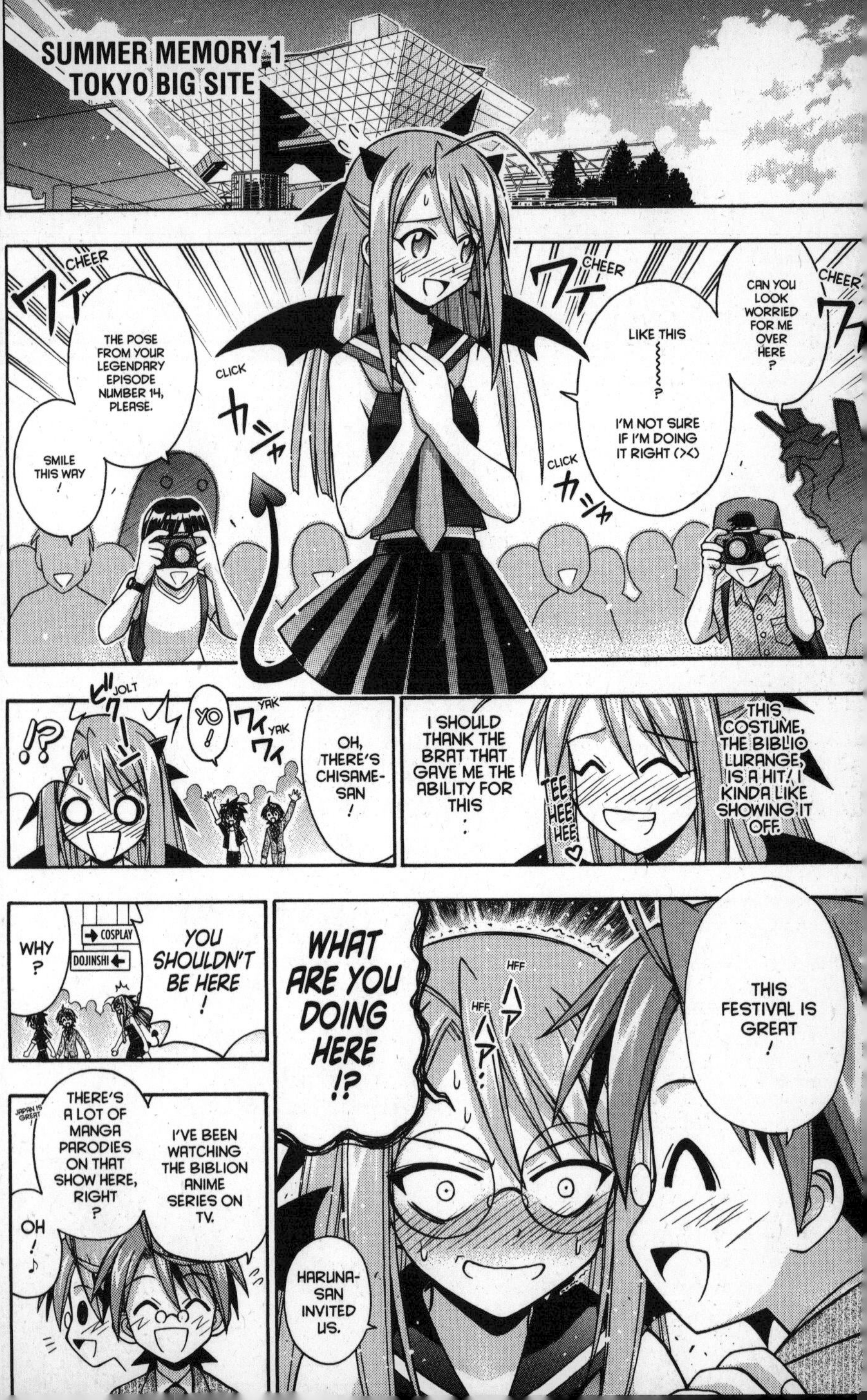
SUMMER MEMORY 1
TOKYO BIG SITE
CHEER
CAN YOU LOOK WORRIED FOR ME OVER HERE?
CHEER
LIKE THIS ......?
I'M NOT SURE IF I'M DOING IT RIGHT (><)
CLICK
CLICK
THE POSE FROM YOUR LEGENDARY EPISODE NUMBER 14, PLEASE.
CHEER
SMILE THIS WAY!
THIS COSTUME, THE BIBLIO LURANGE, IS A HIT! I KINDA LIKE SHOWING IT OFF.
TEE HEE HEE
I SHOULD THANK THE BRAT THAT GAVE ME THE ABILITY FOR THIS..
OH, THERE'S CHISAME-SAN!
YAK YAK
YO!
JOLT
!?
THIS FESTIVAL IS GREAT!
HFF
HFF
WHAT ARE YOU DOING HERE!?
HARUNA-SAN INVITED US.
YOU SHOULDN'T BE HERE!
COSPLAY
DOJINSHI
WHY?
I'VE BEEN WATCHING THE BIBLION ANIME SERIES ON TV.
THERE'S A LOT OF MANGA PARODIES ON THAT SHOW HERE, RIGHT?
JAPAN IS GREAT!
OH!♪

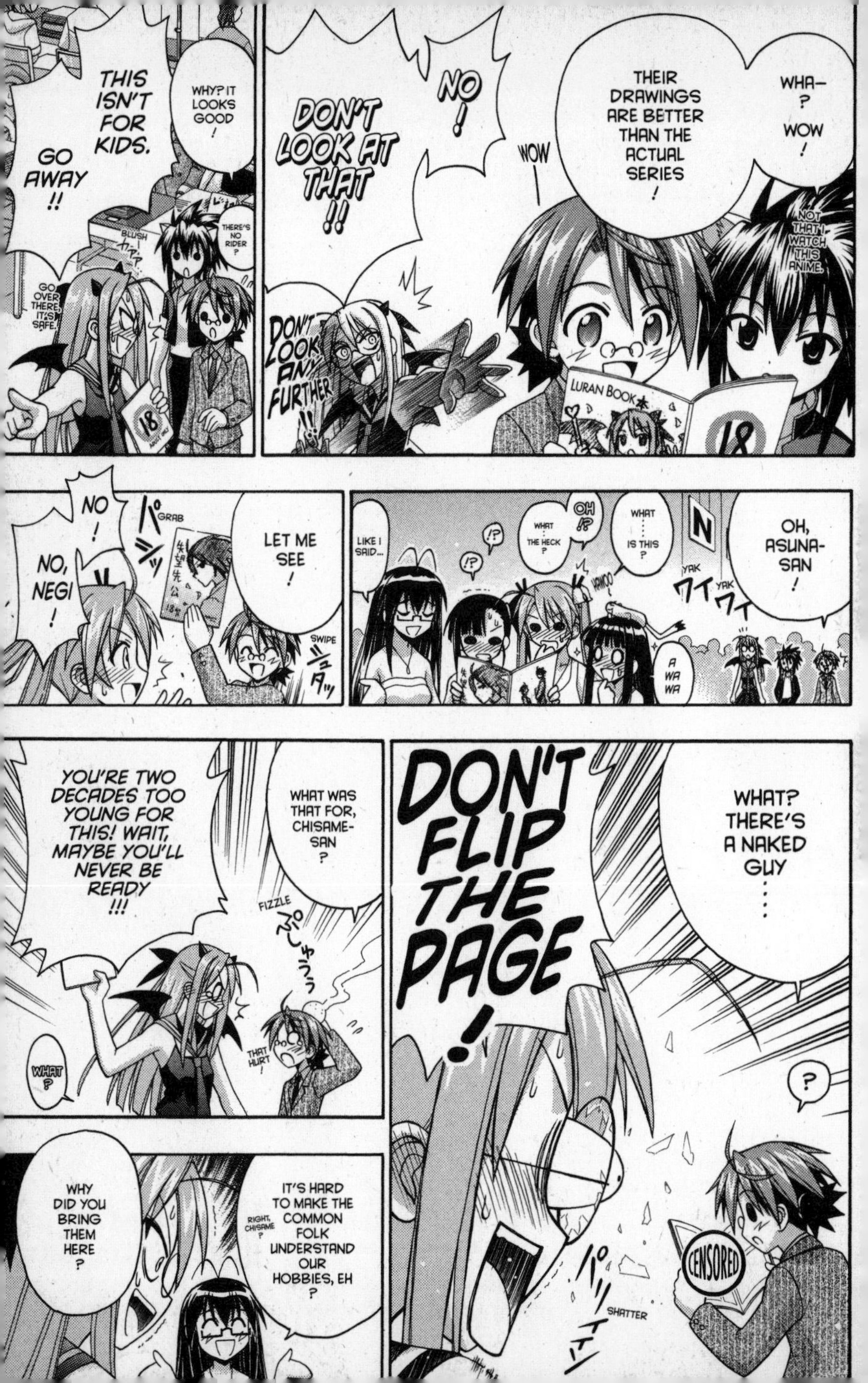
WHA— ? WOW !
THEIR DRAWINGS ARE BETTER THAN THE ACTUAL SERIES !
WOW !
NOT THAT I WATCH THIS ANIME.
NO !
DON'T LOOK AT THAT !!
DON'T LOOK ANY FURTHER !!
LURAN BOOK
18
WHY? IT LOOKS GOOD !
THIS ISN'T FOR KIDS.
GO AWAY !!
THERE'S NO RIDER ?
BLUSH
GO OVER THERE, IT'S SAFE.
18
OH, ASUNA-SAN !
YAK
YAK
WHAT ... IS THIS ?
OH !?
WHAT THE HECK ?
YAHOO
!?
!?
A WA WA
LIKE I SAID...
LET ME SEE !
GRAB
NO !
NO, NEGI !
SWIPE
WHAT? THERE'S A NAKED GUY ....
DON'T FLIP THE PAGE !
?
CENSORED
SHATTER
WHAT WAS THAT FOR, CHISAME-SAN ?
YOU'RE TWO DECADES TOO YOUNG FOR THIS! WAIT, MAYBE YOU'LL NEVER BE READY !!!
FIZZLE
THAT HURT !
WHAT ?
IT'S HARD TO MAKE THE COMMON FOLK UNDERSTAND OUR HOBBIES, EH ?
RIGHT, CHISAME ?
WHY DID YOU BRING THEM HERE ?

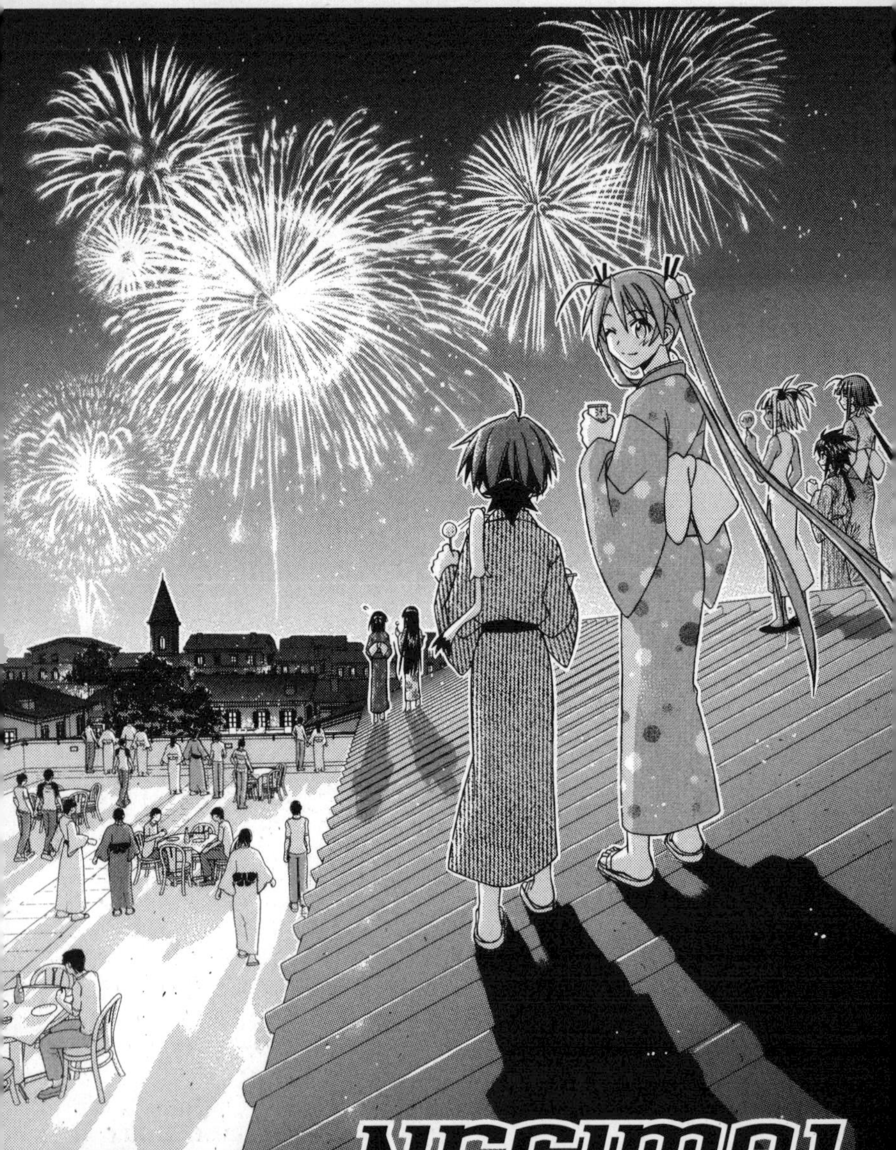
NEGIMA!

MAGISTER NEGI MAGI

183RD PERIOD: FULL OF MEMORIES ♡

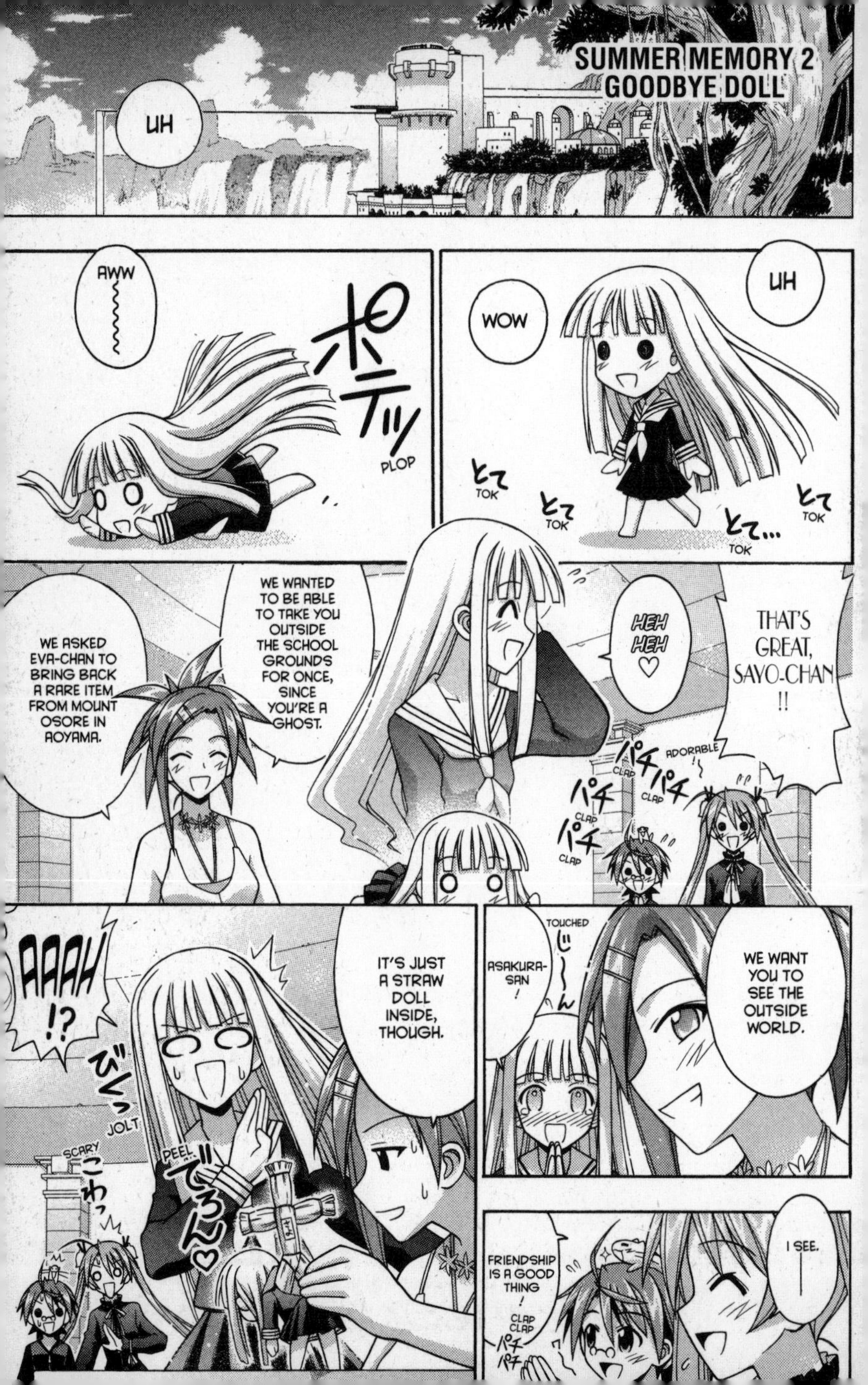
SUMMER MEMORY 2
GOODBYE DOLL
UH
UH
WOW
とて TOK
とて TOK
とて... TOK
とて TOK
AWW~
ポテッ PLOP
THAT'S GREAT, SAYO-CHAN!!
HEH HEH ♥
パチパチ CLAP CLAP
パチパチ CLAP CLAP
ADORABLE!
WE WANTED TO BE ABLE TO TAKE YOU OUTSIDE THE SCHOOL GROUNDS FOR ONCE, SINCE YOU'RE A GHOST.
WE ASKED EVA-CHAN TO BRING BACK A RARE ITEM FROM MOUNT OSORE IN AOYAMA.
WE WANT YOU TO SEE THE OUTSIDE WORLD.
ASAKURA-SAN!
じ～ん TOUCHED
I SEE.
FRIENDSHIP IS A GOOD THING!
パチパチ CLAP CLAP
IT'S JUST A STRAW DOLL INSIDE, THOUGH.
AAAH!?
びくっ JOLT
でろん♥ PEEL
こわっ SCARY

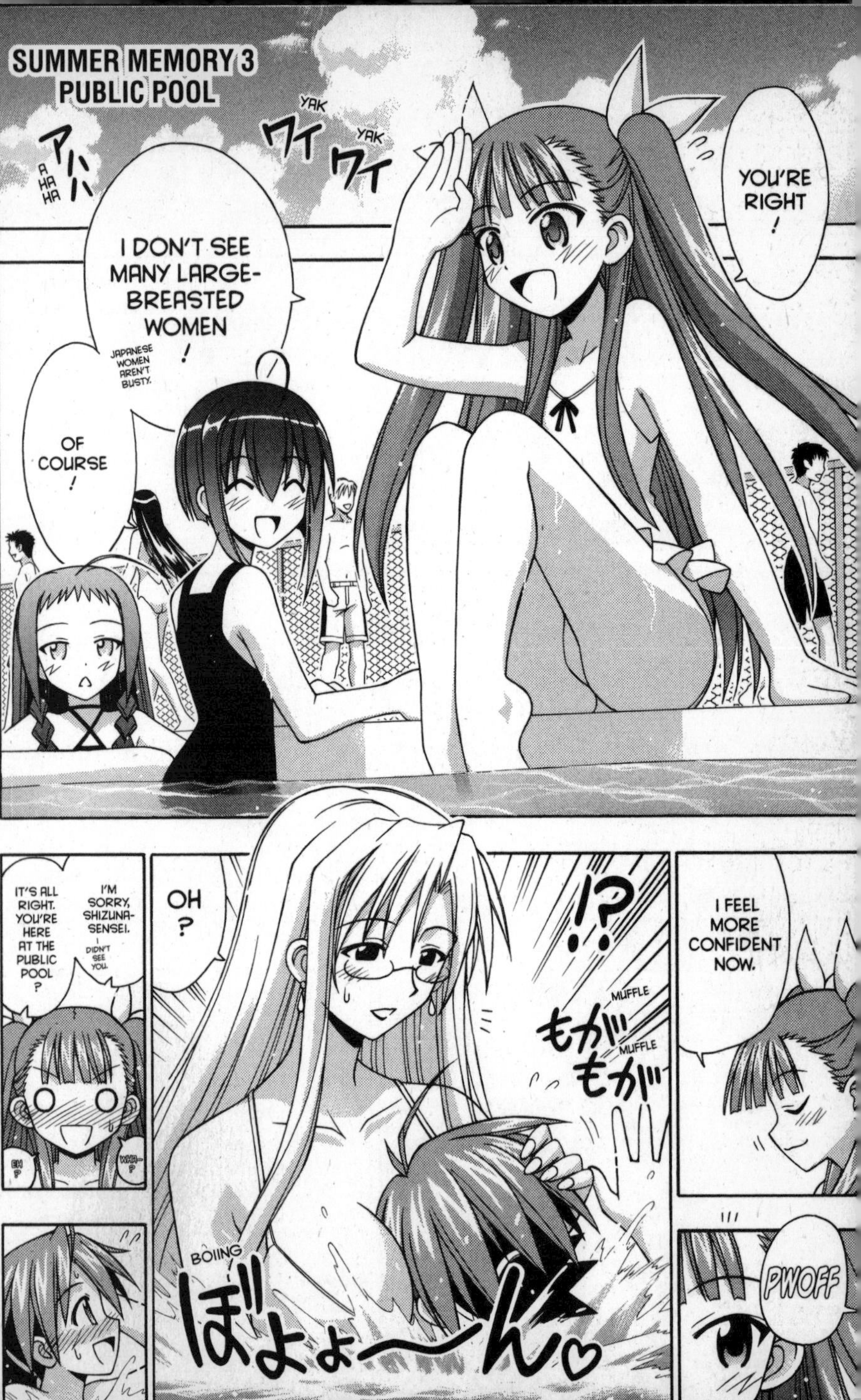
SUMMER MEMORY 3
PUBLIC POOL
YOU'RE RIGHT!
YAK ワイ YAK ワイ
I DON'T SEE MANY LARGE-BREASTED WOMEN!
A HA HA アハハ
JAPANESE WOMEN AREN'T BUSTY.
OF COURSE!
I FEEL MORE CONFIDENT NOW.
PWOFF
!?
MUFFLE もが MUFFLE もが
OH?
BOIING ぼよょ〜ん♡
I'M SORRY, SHIZUNA-SENSEI.
I DIDN'T SEE YOU.
IT'S ALL RIGHT. YOU'RE HERE AT THE PUBLIC POOL?
EH?
WHA-?

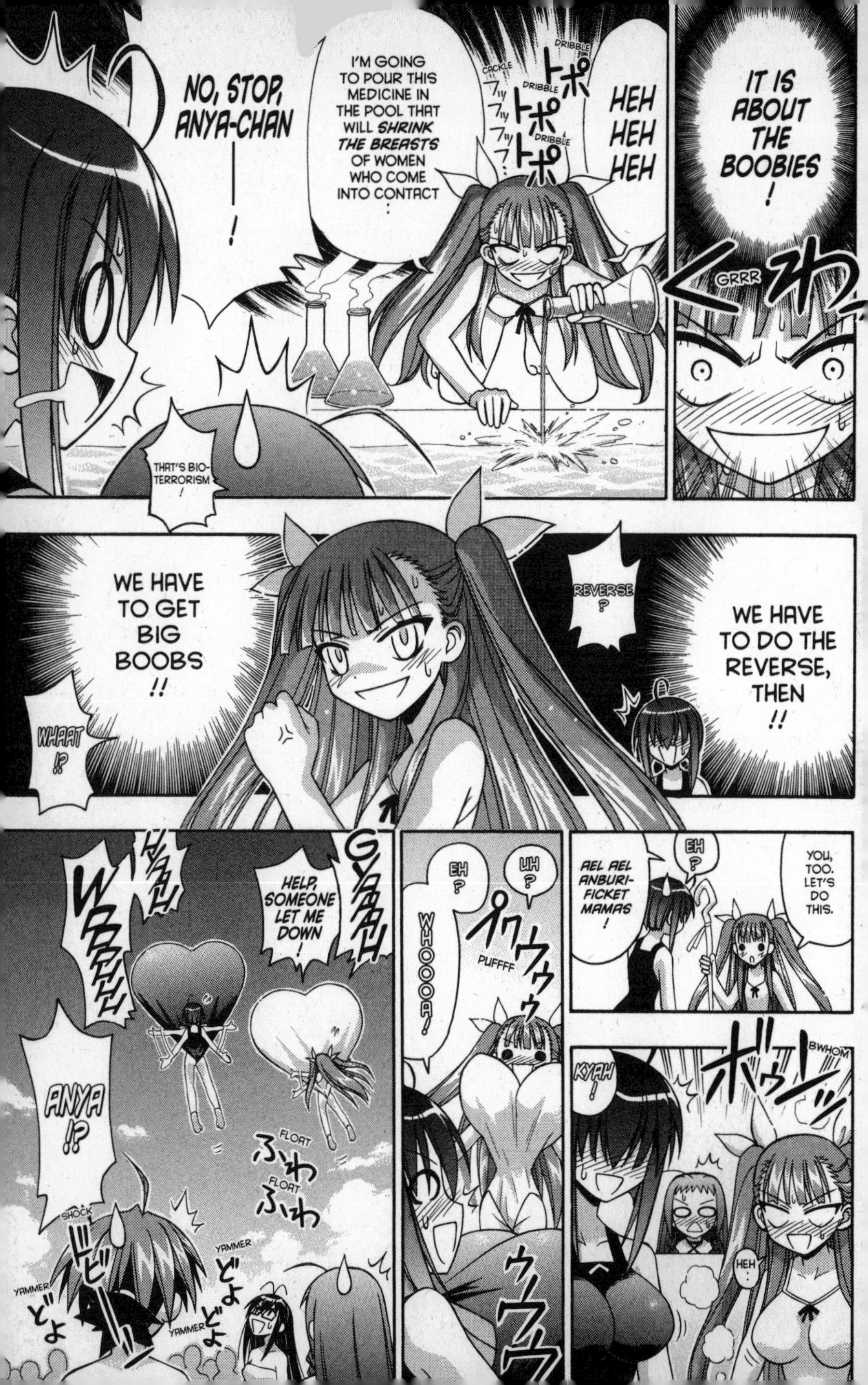
IT IS ABOUT THE BOOBIES!
くわっ
GRRR
HEH HEH HEH
トポ
DRIBBLE
トポ
DRIBBLE
トポ
DRIBBLE
フッフッフッフ…
CACKLE
I'M GOING TO POUR THIS MEDICINE IN THE POOL THAT WILL SHRINK THE BREASTS OF WOMEN WHO COME INTO CONTACT…
NO, STOP, ANYA-CHAN—!
THAT'S BIO-TERRORISM!
WE HAVE TO DO THE REVERSE, THEN!!
REVERSE?
WE HAVE TO GET BIG BOOBS!!
WHAAT!?
YOU, TOO. LET'S DO THIS.
EH?
AEL AEL ANBURI-FICKET MAMAS!
ボウンッ
BWHOM
KYAH!
HEH…
UH?
EH?
WHOOOOA!
プクウウウ
PUFFFF
GYAAAH
HELP, SOMEONE LET ME DOWN!
WAAAAH
ANYA!?
ふわ
FLOAT
ふわ
FLOAT
ドビ
SHOCK
どよ
YAMMER
どよ
YAMMER
どよ
YAMMER

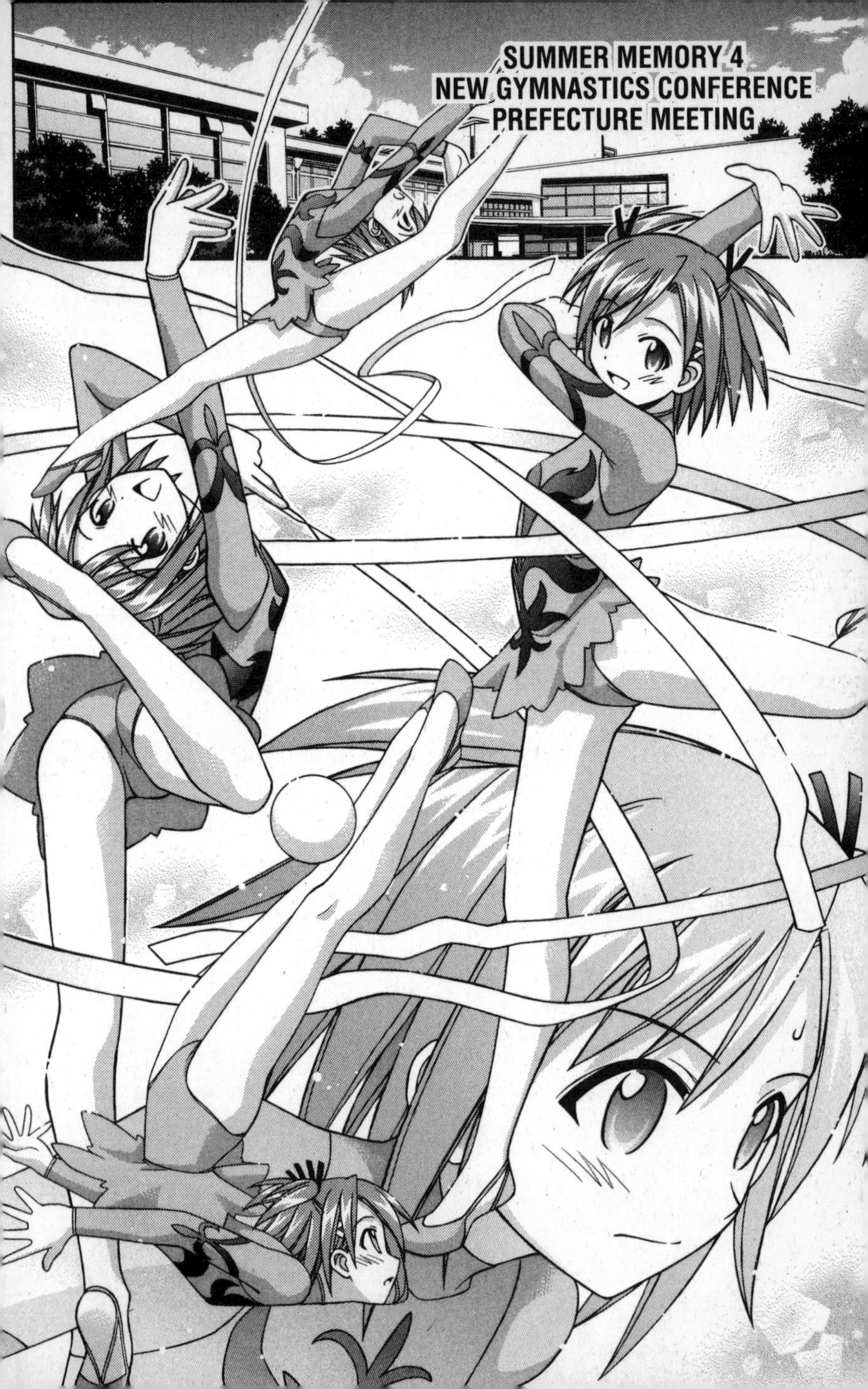
SUMMER MEMORY 4
NEW GYMNASTICS CONFERENCE
PREFECTURE MEETING

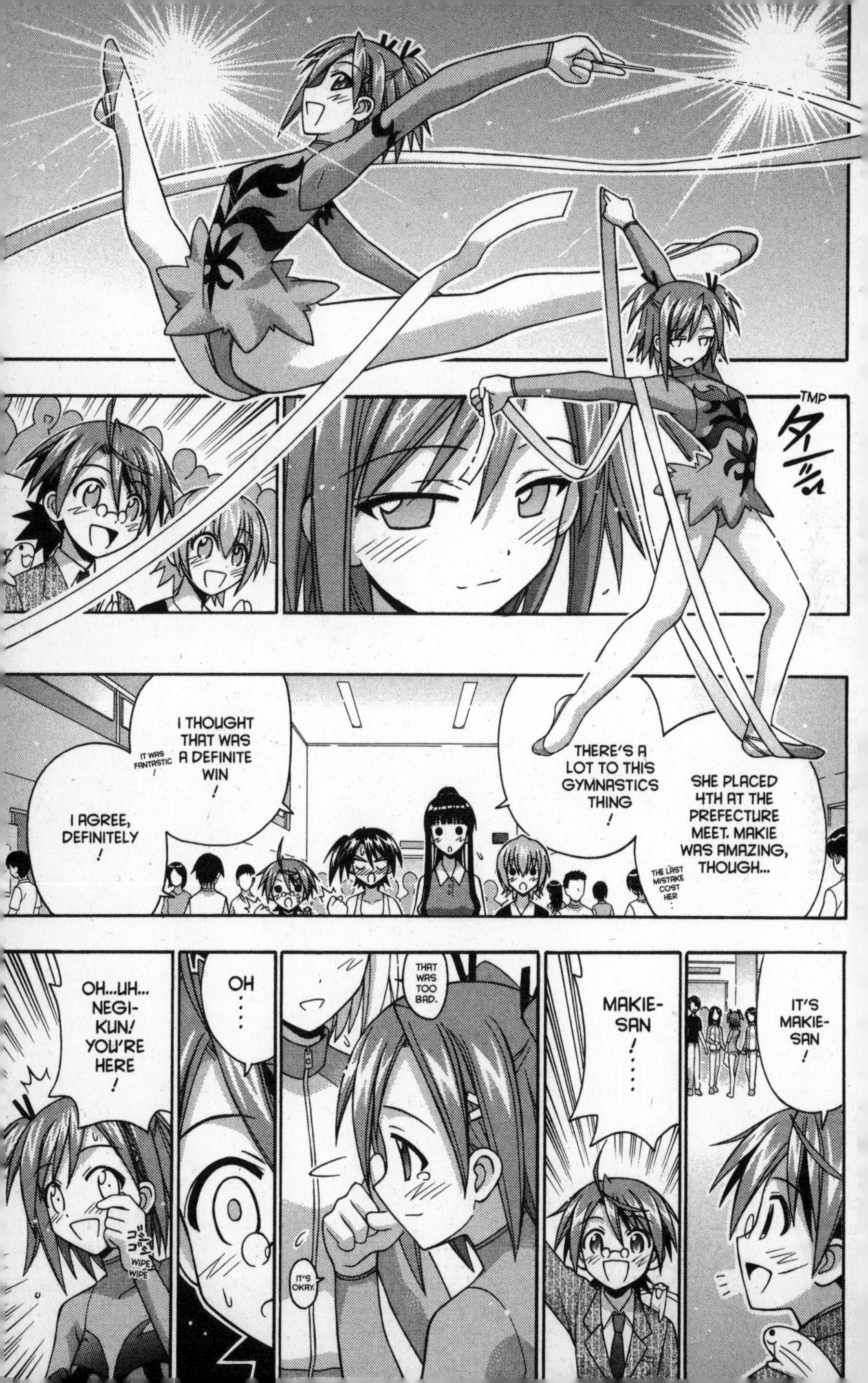
TMP
SHE PLACED 4TH AT THE PREFECTURE MEET. MAKIE WAS AMAZING, THOUGH...
THE LAST MISTAKE COST HER!
THERE'S A LOT TO THIS GYMNASTICS THING!
I THOUGHT THAT WAS A DEFINITE WIN!
IT WAS FANTASTIC!
I AGREE, DEFINITELY!
IT'S MAKIE-SAN!
MAKIE-SAN...!
THAT WAS TOO BAD.
IT'S OKAY.
OH...
OH...UH... NEGI-KUN! YOU'RE HERE!
WIPE WIPE

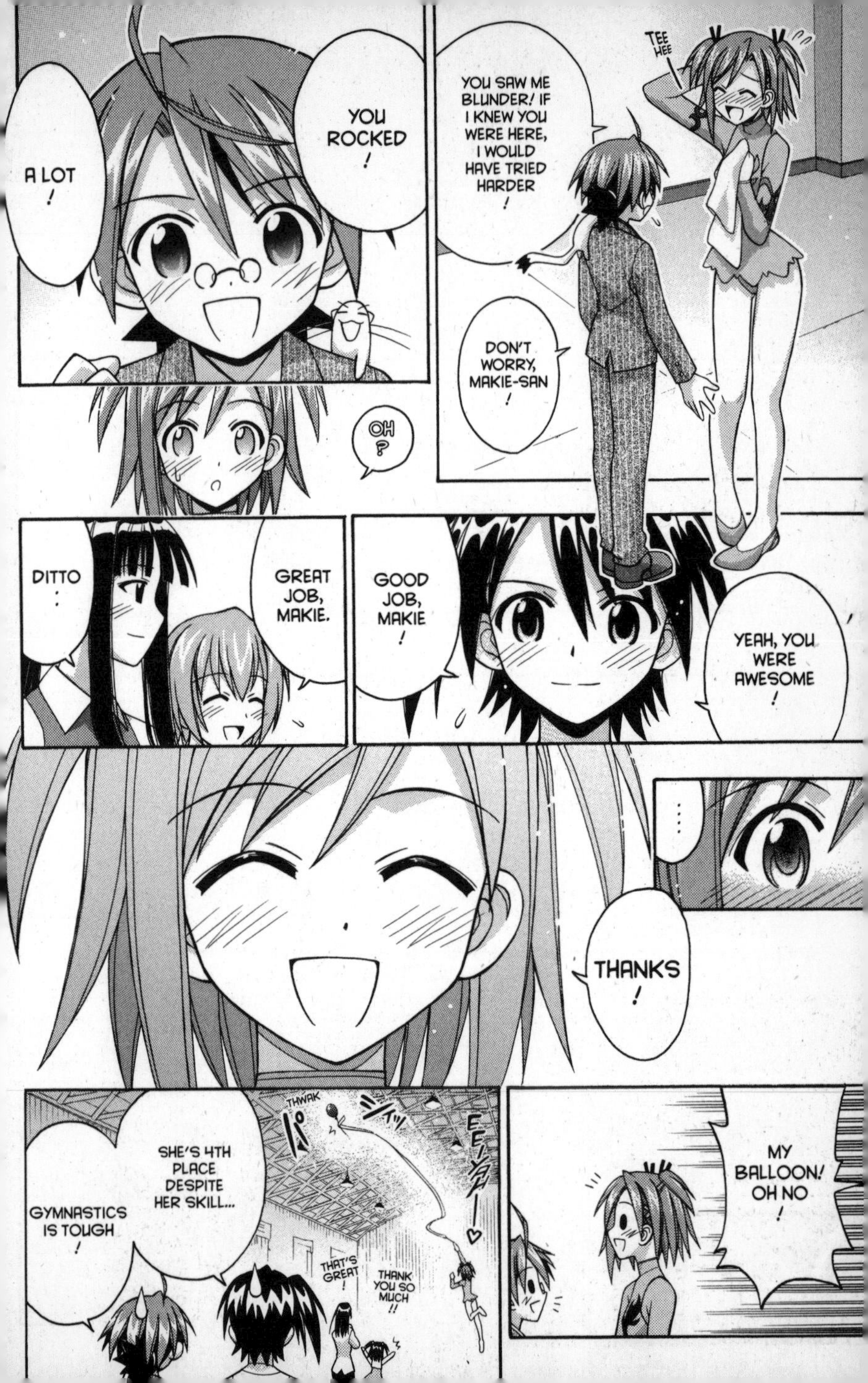
TEE HEE
YOU SAW ME BLUNDER! IF I KNEW YOU WERE HERE, I WOULD HAVE TRIED HARDER!
DON'T WORRY, MAKIE-SAN!
YOU ROCKED!
A LOT!
OH?
YEAH, YOU WERE AWESOME!
GOOD JOB, MAKIE!
GREAT JOB, MAKIE.
DITTO:
....
THANKS!
MY BALLOON! OH NO!
THWAK
EEYAA!
THAT'S GREAT!
THANK YOU SO MUCH!!
SHE'S 4TH PLACE DESPITE HER SKILL...
GYMNASTICS IS TOUGH!

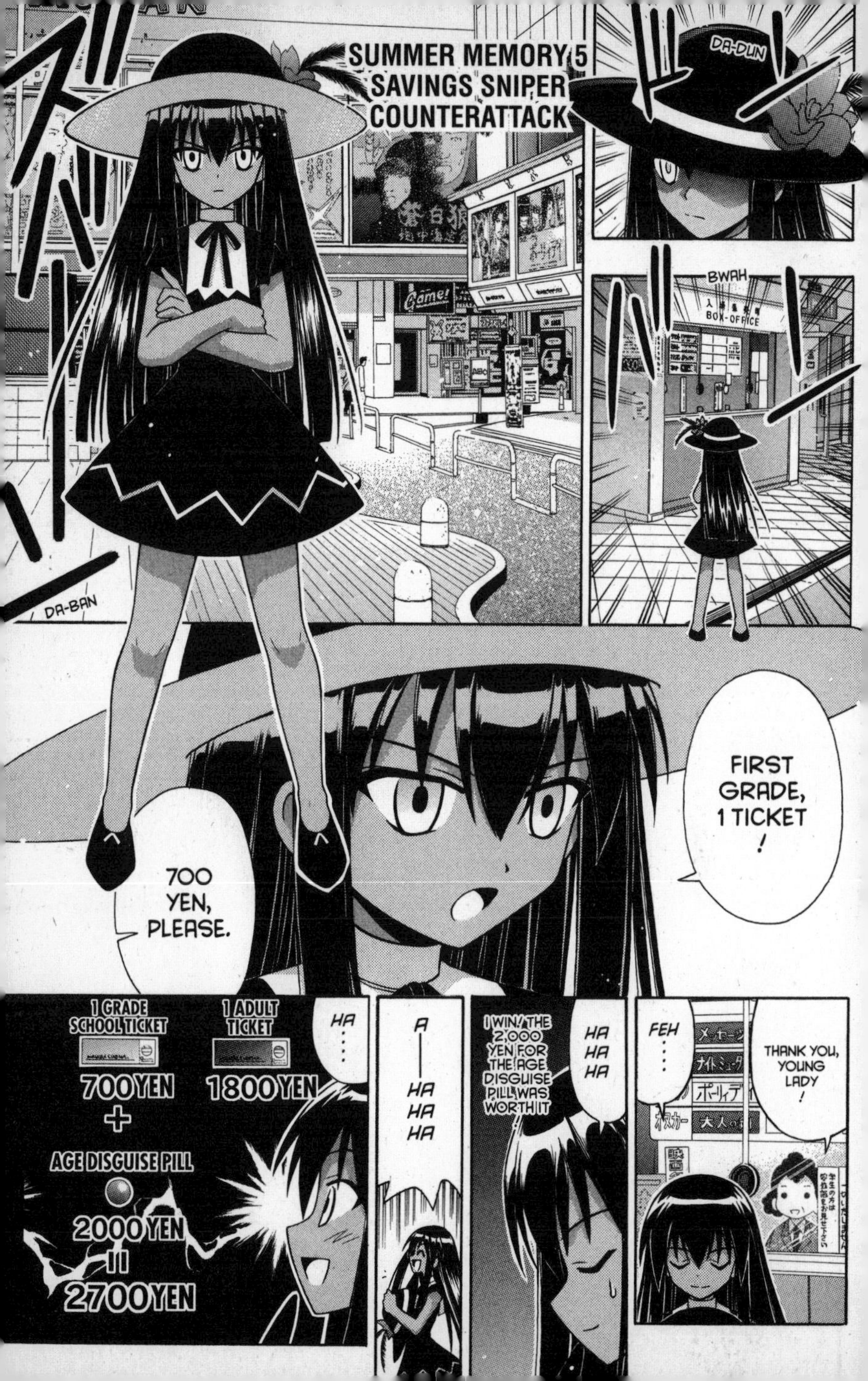
DA-DUN
BWAH
BOX-OFFICE
SUMMER MEMORY 5
SAVINGS SNIPER
COUNTERATTACK
Game!
DA-BAN
FIRST GRADE, 1 TICKET!
700 YEN, PLEASE.
THANK YOU, YOUNG LADY!
FEH...
HA HA HA
I WIN! THE 2,000 YEN FOR THE AGE DISGUISE PILL WAS WORTH IT
A—HA HA HA
HA...
1 GRADE SCHOOL TICKET
700 YEN
1 ADULT TICKET
1800 YEN
+
AGE DISGUISE PILL
2000 YEN
=
2700 YEN

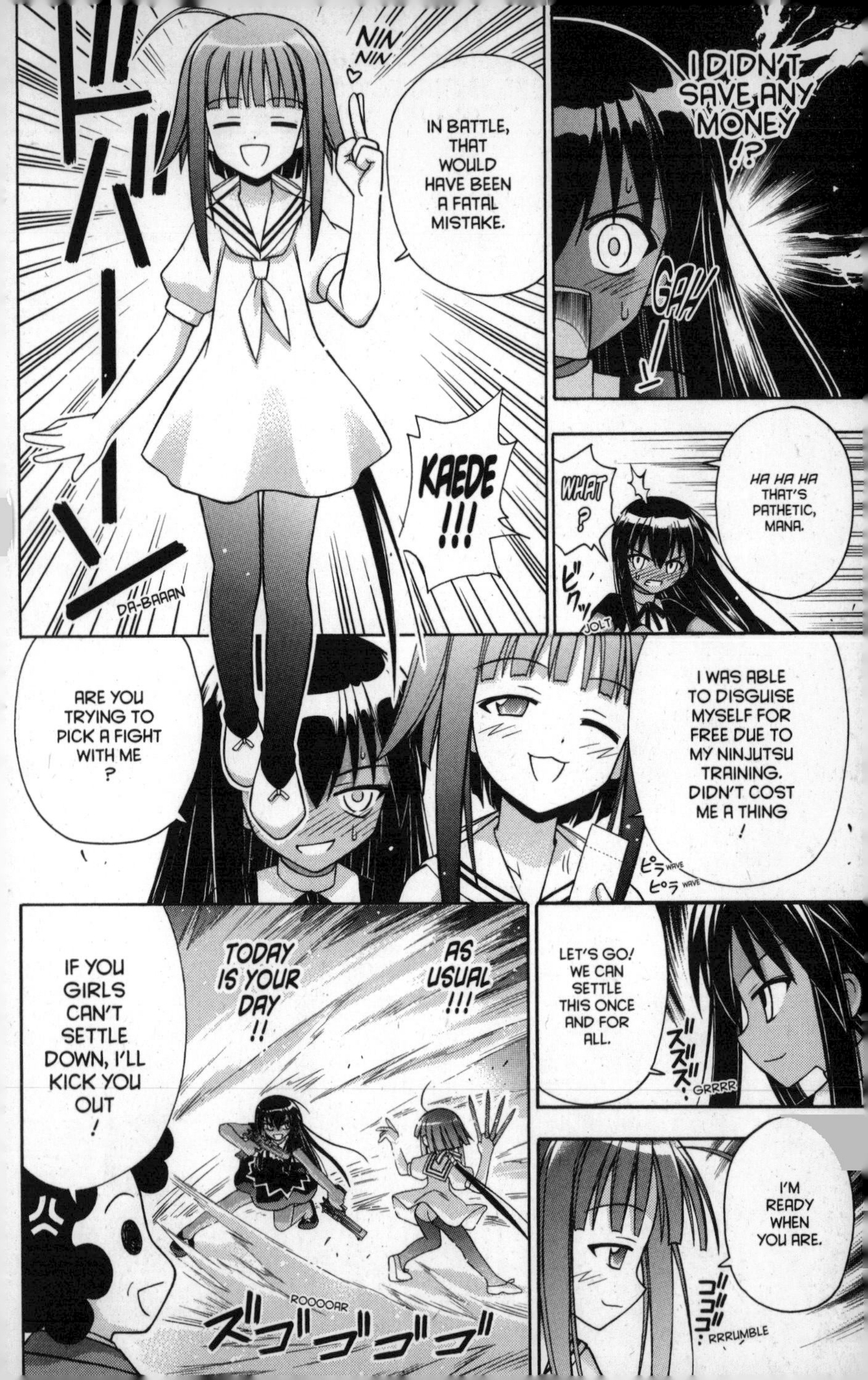
I DIDN'T SAVE ANY MONEY !?
GAH!
HA HA HA THAT'S PATHETIC, MANA.
WHAT ?
JOLT
IN BATTLE, THAT WOULD HAVE BEEN A FATAL MISTAKE.
NIN NIN ♡
KAEDE !!!
DA-BAAAN
I WAS ABLE TO DISGUISE MYSELF FOR FREE DUE TO MY NINJUTSU TRAINING. DIDN'T COST ME A THING !
ピラ WAVE ピラ WAVE
ARE YOU TRYING TO PICK A FIGHT WITH ME ?
LET'S GO! WE CAN SETTLE THIS ONCE AND FOR ALL.
GRRRR
I'M READY WHEN YOU ARE.
RRRUMBLE
AS USUAL !!!
TODAY IS YOUR DAY !!
IF YOU GIRLS CAN'T SETTLE DOWN, I'LL KICK YOU OUT !
ROOOOAR

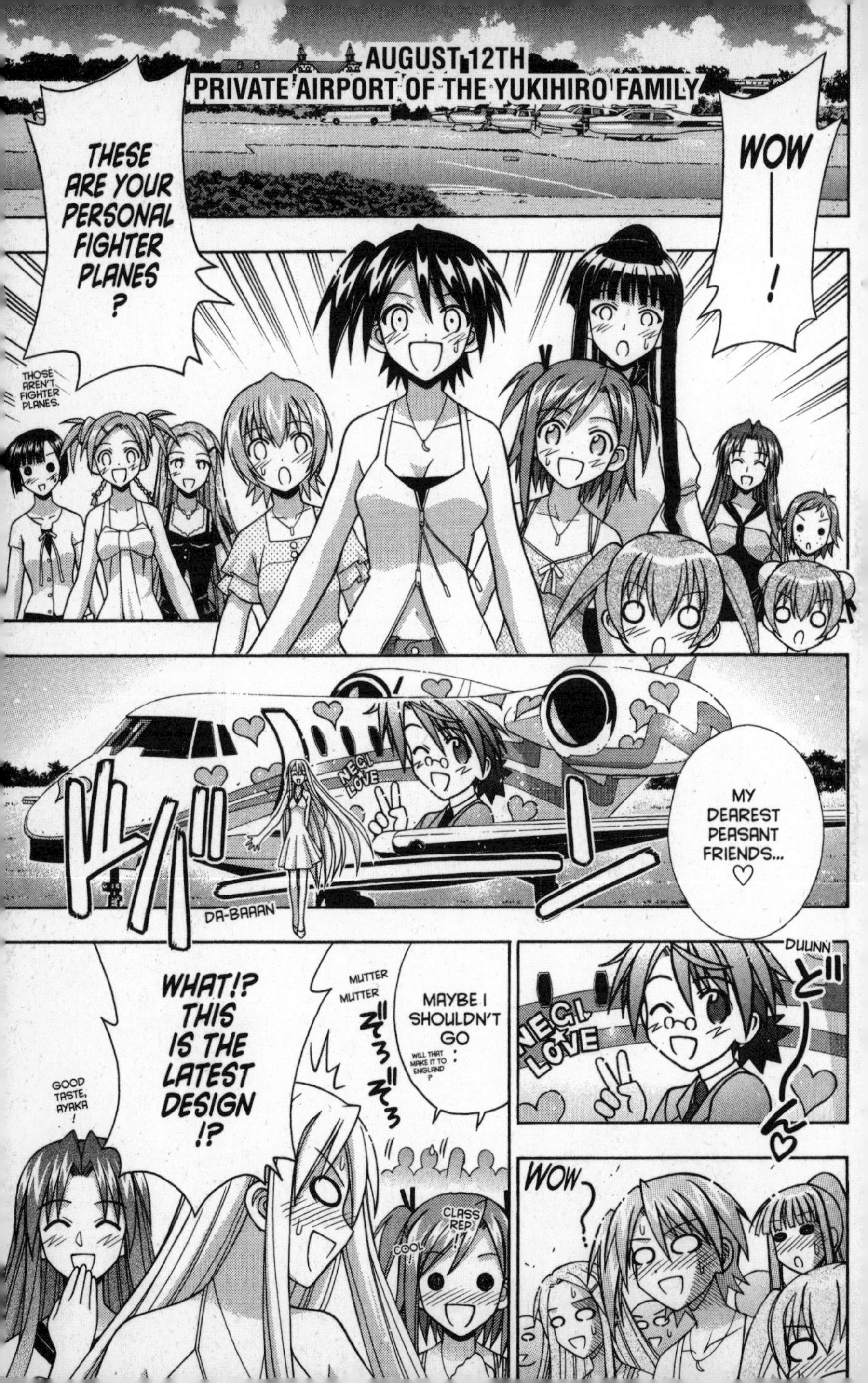
AUGUST 12TH
PRIVATE AIRPORT OF THE YUKIHIRO FAMILY
WOW—!
THESE ARE YOUR PERSONAL FIGHTER PLANES?
THOSE AREN'T FIGHTER PLANES.
MY DEAREST PEASANT FRIENDS... ♡
NEGI LOVE
DA-BAAAN
DUUNN
NEGI LOVE
WOW
MUTTER MUTTER
MAYBE I SHOULDN'T GO
WILL THAT MAKE IT TO ENGLAND?
WHAT!? THIS IS THE LATEST DESIGN!?
CLASS REP!
COOL
GOOD TASTE, AYAKA!

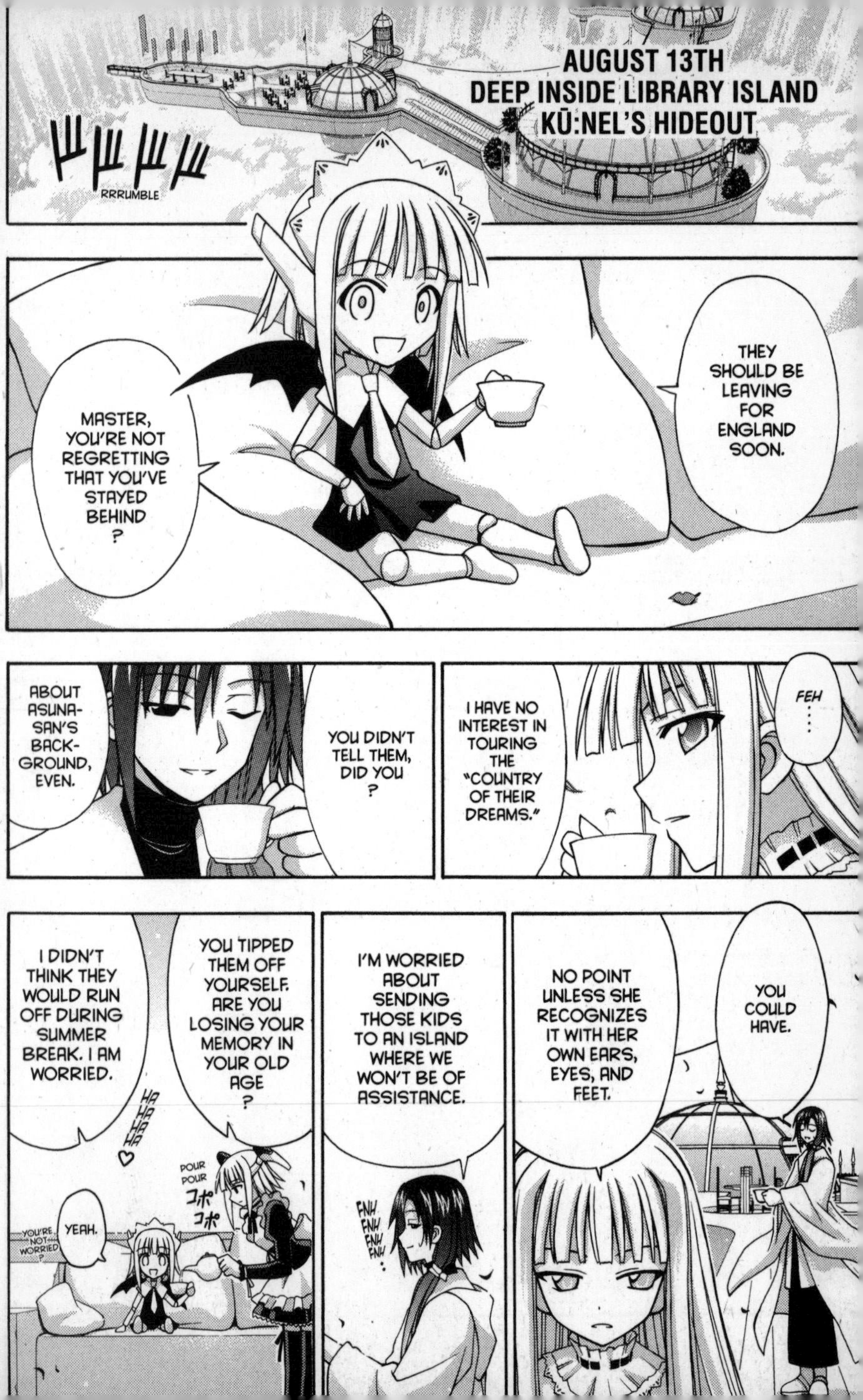
AUGUST 13TH
DEEP INSIDE LIBRARY ISLAND
KŪ:NEL'S HIDEOUT
RRRUMBLE
THEY SHOULD BE LEAVING FOR ENGLAND SOON.
MASTER, YOU'RE NOT REGRETTING THAT YOU'VE STAYED BEHIND?
FEH.....
I HAVE NO INTEREST IN TOURING THE "COUNTRY OF THEIR DREAMS."
YOU DIDN'T TELL THEM, DID YOU?
ABOUT ASUNA-SAN'S BACKGROUND, EVEN.
YOU COULD HAVE.
NO POINT UNLESS SHE RECOGNIZES IT WITH HER OWN EARS, EYES, AND FEET.
I'M WORRIED ABOUT SENDING THOSE KIDS TO AN ISLAND WHERE WE WON'T BE OF ASSISTANCE.
FNH FNH FNH FNH...
YOU TIPPED THEM OFF YOURSELF. ARE YOU LOSING YOUR MEMORY IN YOUR OLD AGE?
I DIDN'T THINK THEY WOULD RUN OFF DURING SUMMER BREAK. I AM WORRIED.
HA HA HA HA ♡
POUR POUR
コポ コポ
YEAH.
YOU'RE NOT WORRIED?

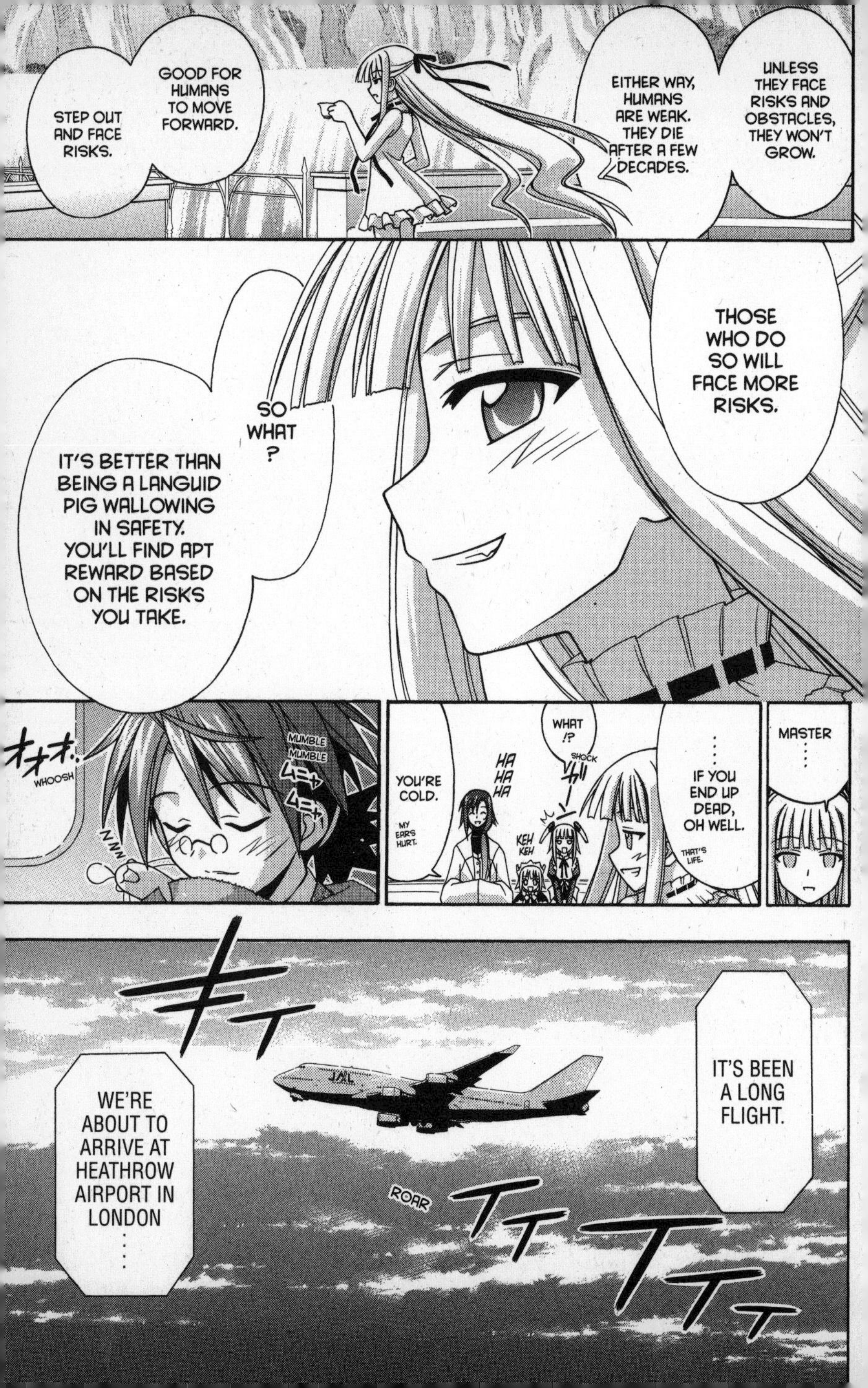
UNLESS THEY FACE RISKS AND OBSTACLES, THEY WON'T GROW.
EITHER WAY, HUMANS ARE WEAK. THEY DIE AFTER A FEW DECADES.
GOOD FOR HUMANS TO MOVE FORWARD.
STEP OUT AND FACE RISKS.
THOSE WHO DO SO WILL FACE MORE RISKS.
SO WHAT?
IT'S BETTER THAN BEING A LANGUID PIG WALLOWING IN SAFETY. YOU'LL FIND APT REWARD BASED ON THE RISKS YOU TAKE.
MASTER ....
... IF YOU END UP DEAD, OH WELL.
THAT'S LIFE.
WHAT!?
SHOCK
HA HA HA
KEH KEH
YOU'RE COLD.
MY EARS HURT.
MUMBLE MUMBLE
WHOOSH
IT'S BEEN A LONG FLIGHT.
WE'RE ABOUT TO ARRIVE AT HEATHROW AIRPORT IN LONDON ....
ROAR

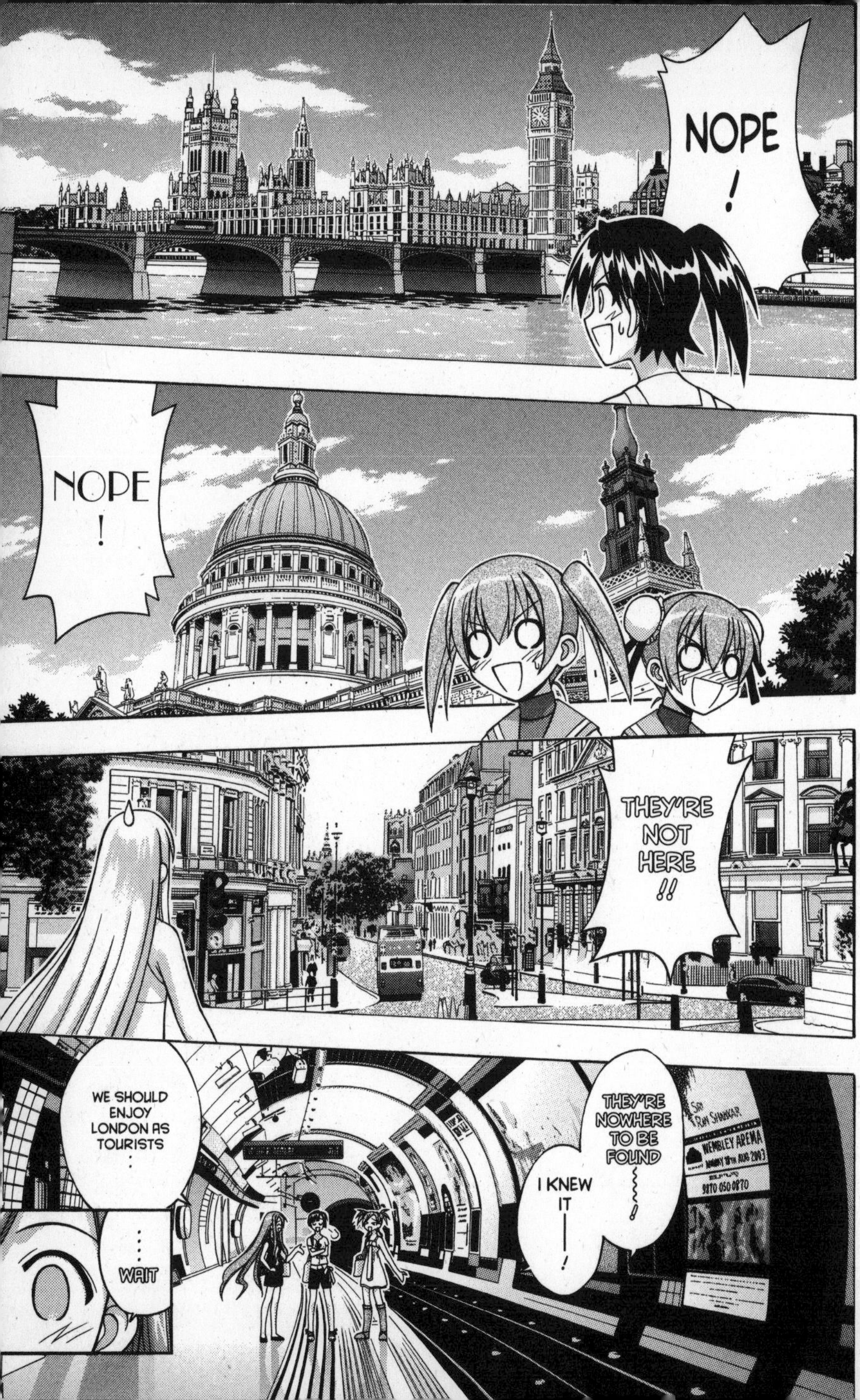
NOPE!
NOPE!
THEY'RE NOT HERE!!
THEY'RE NOWHERE TO BE FOUND~~~!
I KNEW IT——!
WEMBLEY ARENA
WE SHOULD ENJOY LONDON AS TOURISTS...
...WAIT

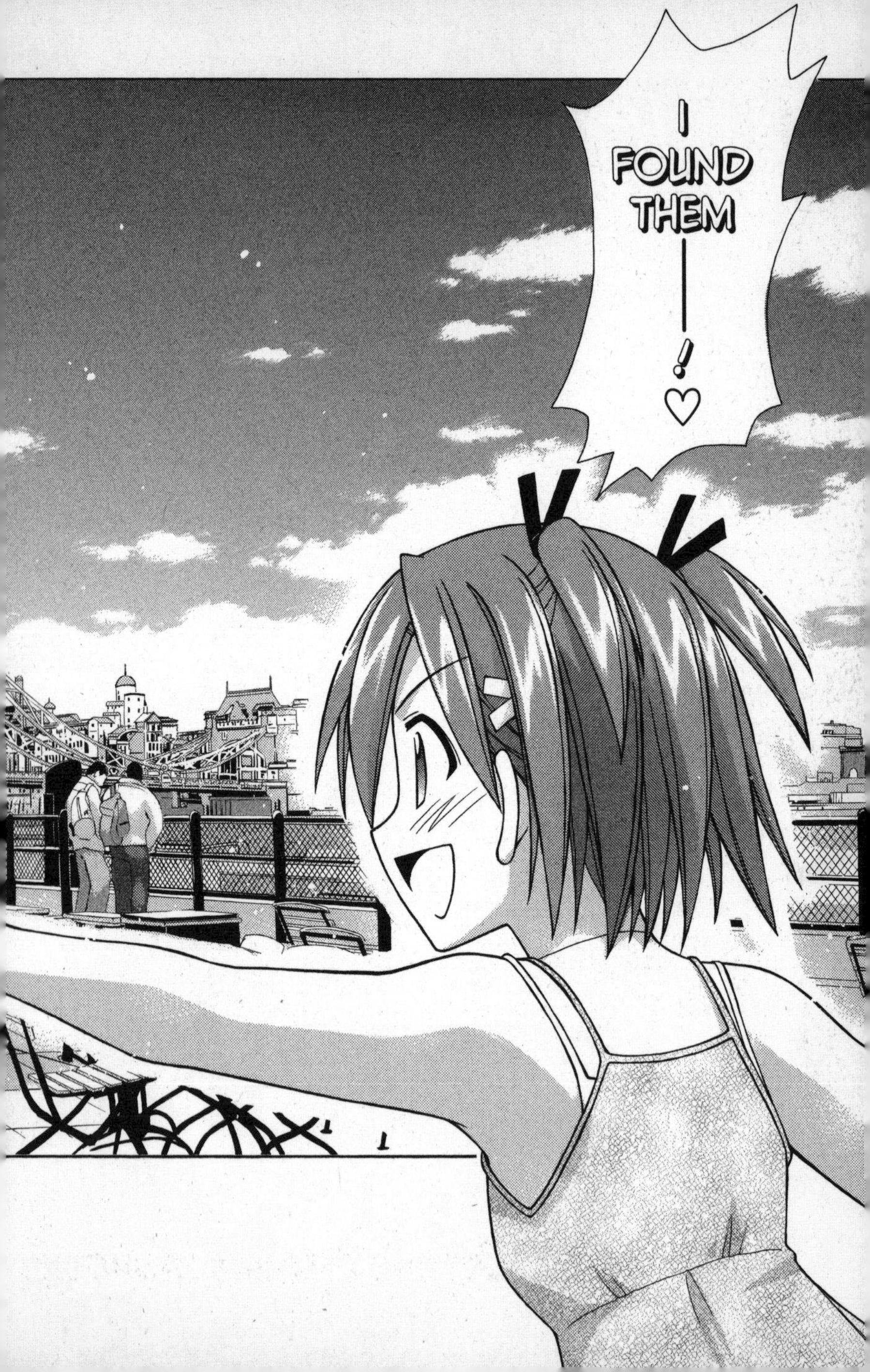
I FOUND THEM——!♡

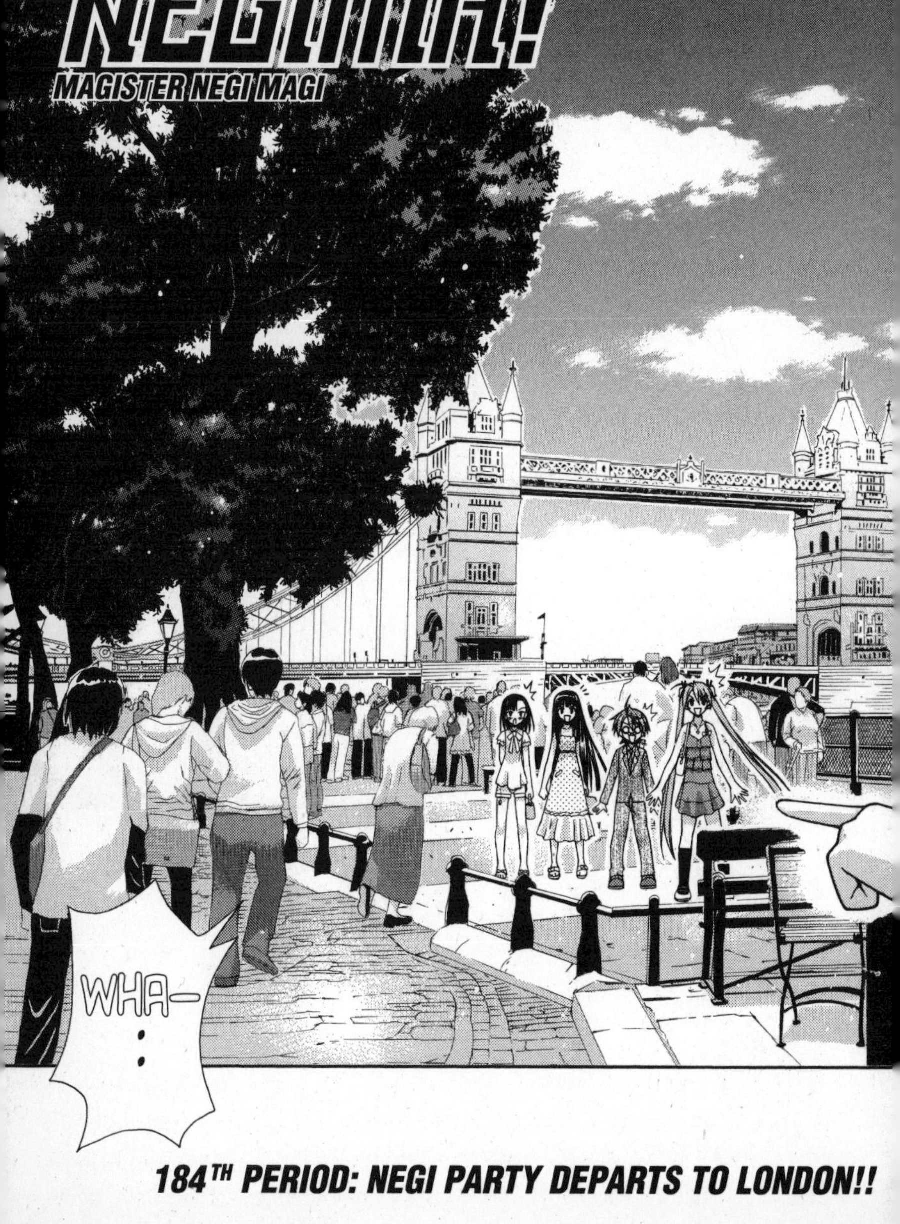
NEGIMA!
MAGISTER NEGI MAGI
WHA- . .

184TH PERIOD: NEGI PARTY DEPARTS TO LONDON!!

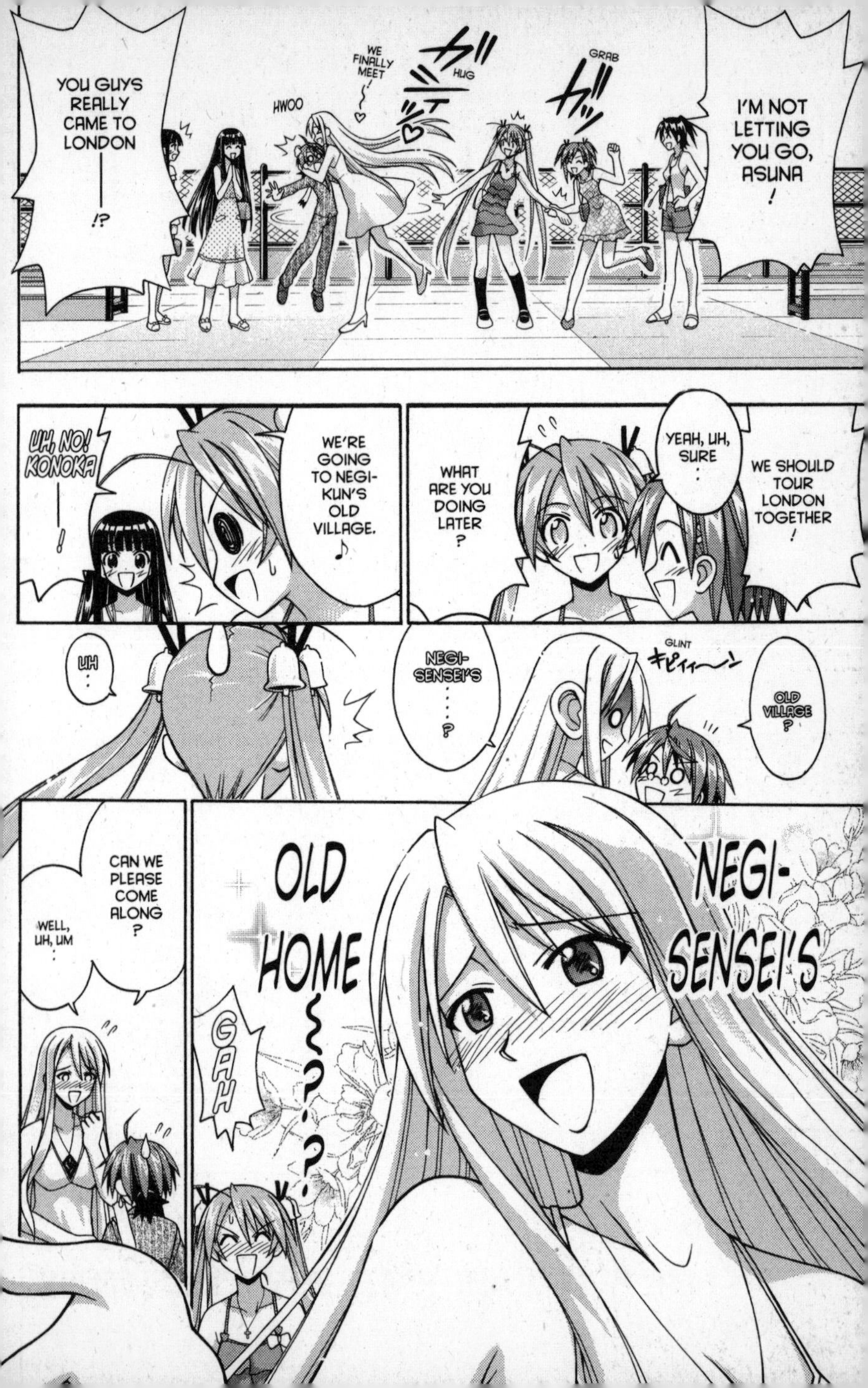
I'M NOT LETTING YOU GO, ASUNA!
GRAB
HUG
WE FINALLY MEET ~♡
HWOO
YOU GUYS REALLY CAME TO LONDON —!?
WE SHOULD TOUR LONDON TOGETHER!
YEAH, UH, SURE..
WHAT ARE YOU DOING LATER?
WE'RE GOING TO NEGI-KUN'S OLD VILLAGE. ♪
UH, NO! KONOKA —!
GLINT
OLD VILLAGE?
NEGI-SENSEI'S....?
UH..
NEGI-SENSEI'S
OLD HOME~?!?
GAH
CAN WE PLEASE COME ALONG?
WELL, UH, UM..

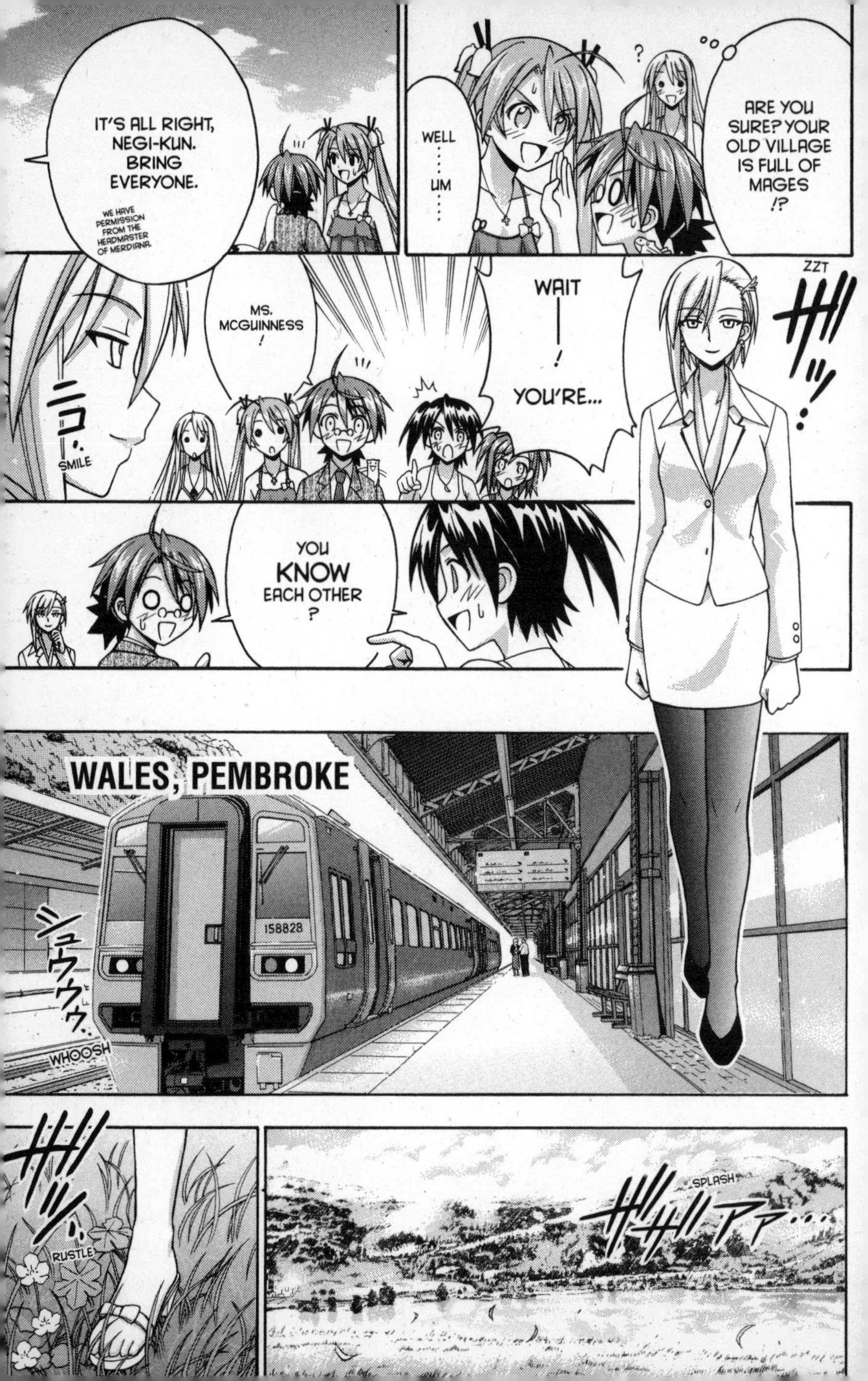
ARE YOU SURE? YOUR OLD VILLAGE IS FULL OF MAGES !?
WELL ... UM ...
IT'S ALL RIGHT, NEGI-KUN. BRING EVERYONE.
WE HAVE PERMISSION FROM THE HEADMASTER OF MERDIANA.
ザッ
ZZT
YOU'RE...
WAIT !
MS. MCGUINNESS !
ニコ
SMILE
YOU KNOW EACH OTHER ?
WALES, PEMBROKE
158828
シュウウウ
WHOOSH
SPLASH
ザッ
RUSTLE

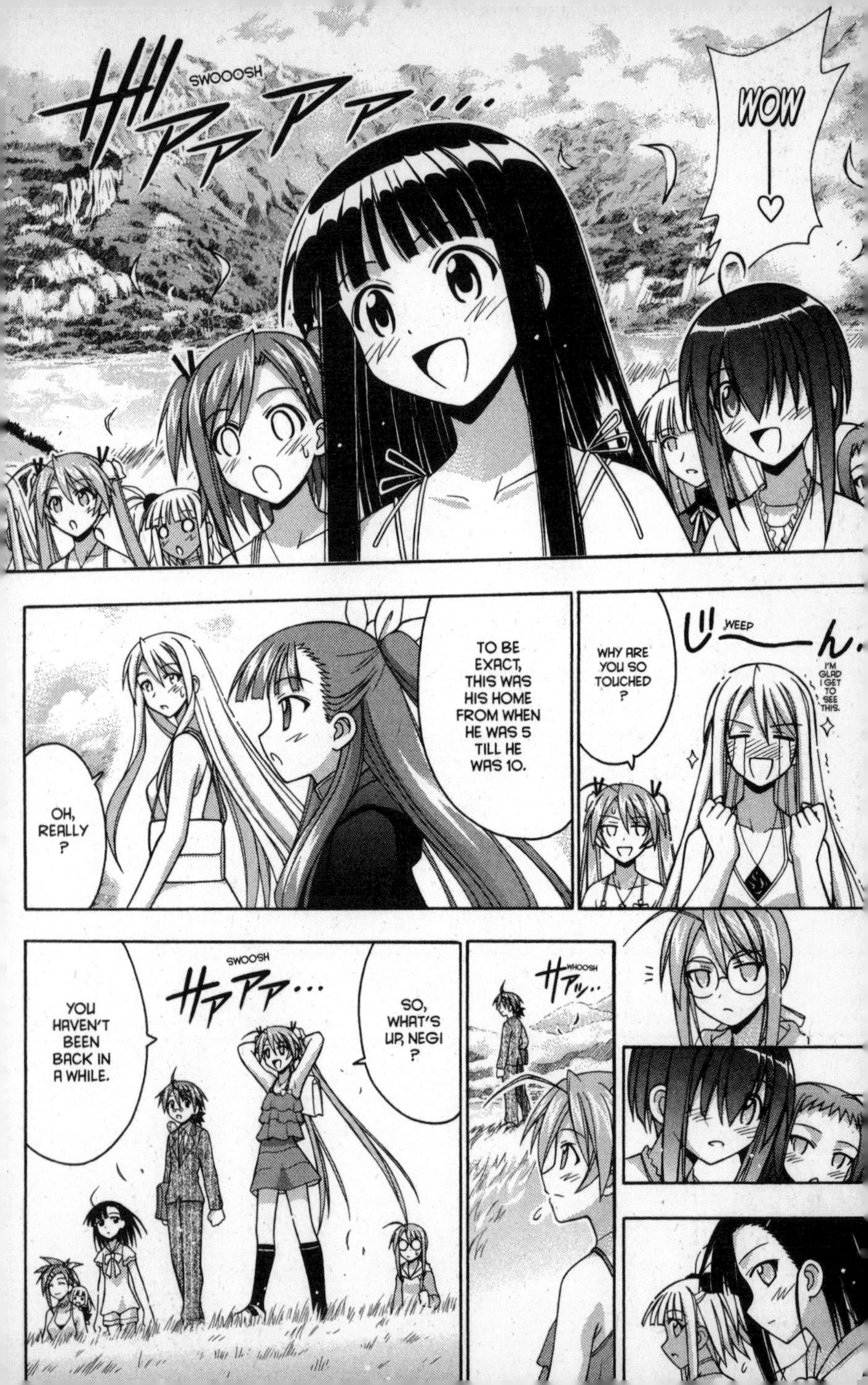
WOW
♥
SWOOOSH
WEEP
WHY ARE YOU SO TOUCHED?
I'M GLAD I GET TO SEE THIS.
TO BE EXACT, THIS WAS HIS HOME FROM WHEN HE WAS 5 TILL HE WAS 10.
OH, REALLY?
WHOOSH
SO, WHAT'S UP, NEGI?
SWOOSH
YOU HAVEN'T BEEN BACK IN A WHILE.

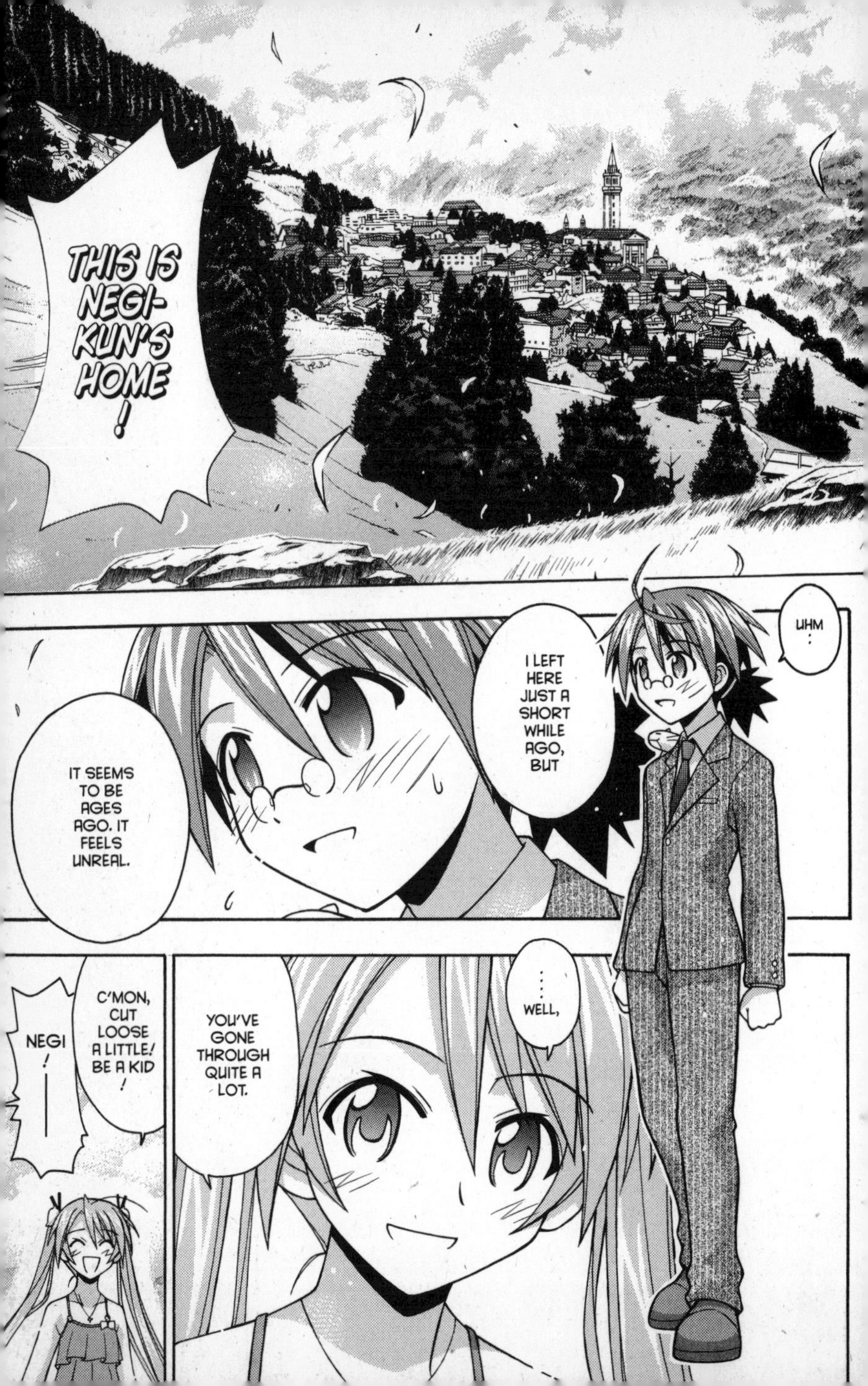
THIS IS NEGI-KUN'S HOME!
UHM...
I LEFT HERE JUST A SHORT WHILE AGO, BUT
IT SEEMS TO BE AGES AGO. IT FEELS UNREAL.
......WELL,
YOU'VE GONE THROUGH QUITE A LOT.
C'MON, CUT LOOSE A LITTLE! BE A KID!
NEGI!

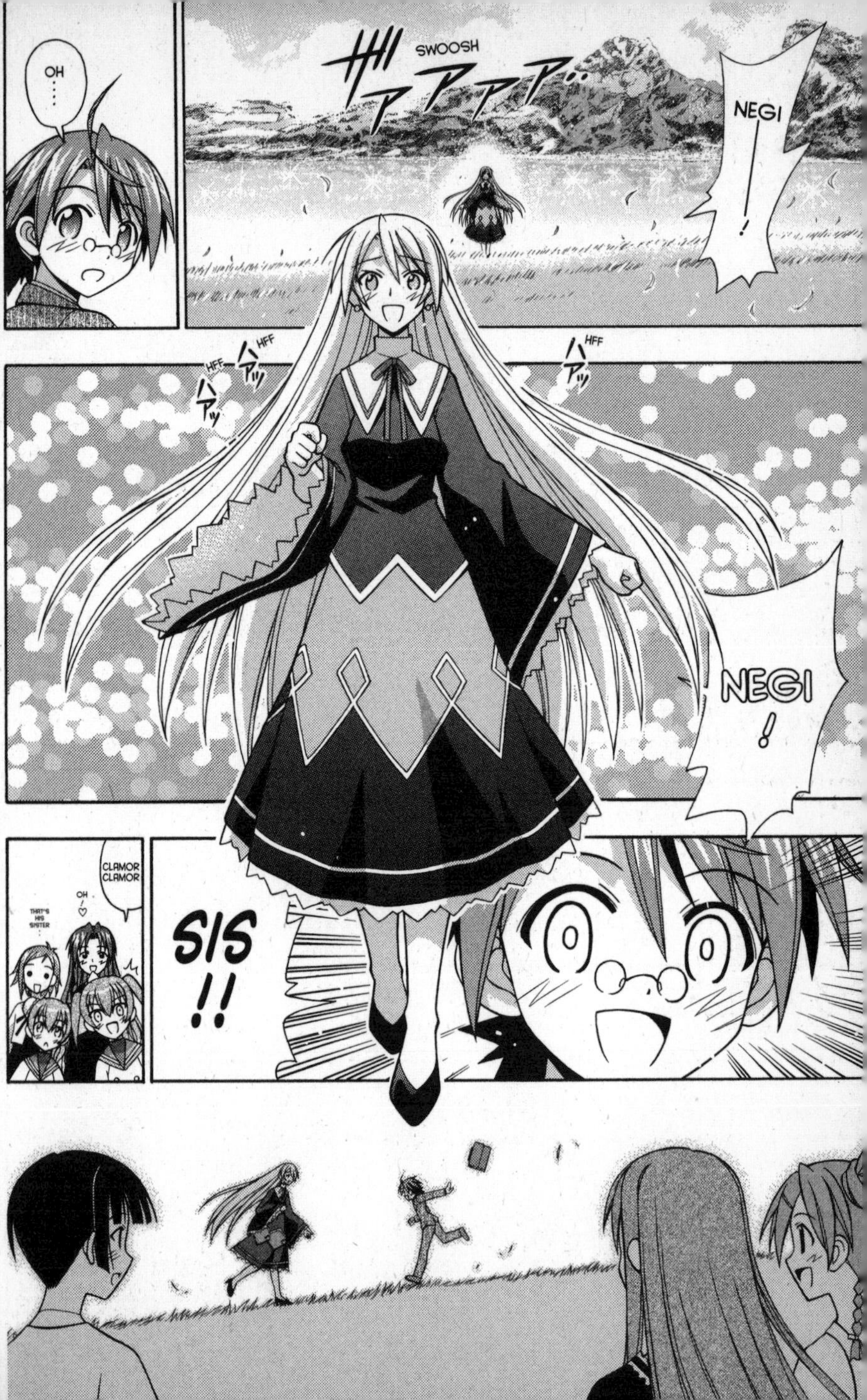
SWOOSH
NEGI—!
OH......
HFF
HFF
HFF
NEGI!
SIS!!
CLAMOR CLAMOR
OH ♡
THAT'S HIS SISTER

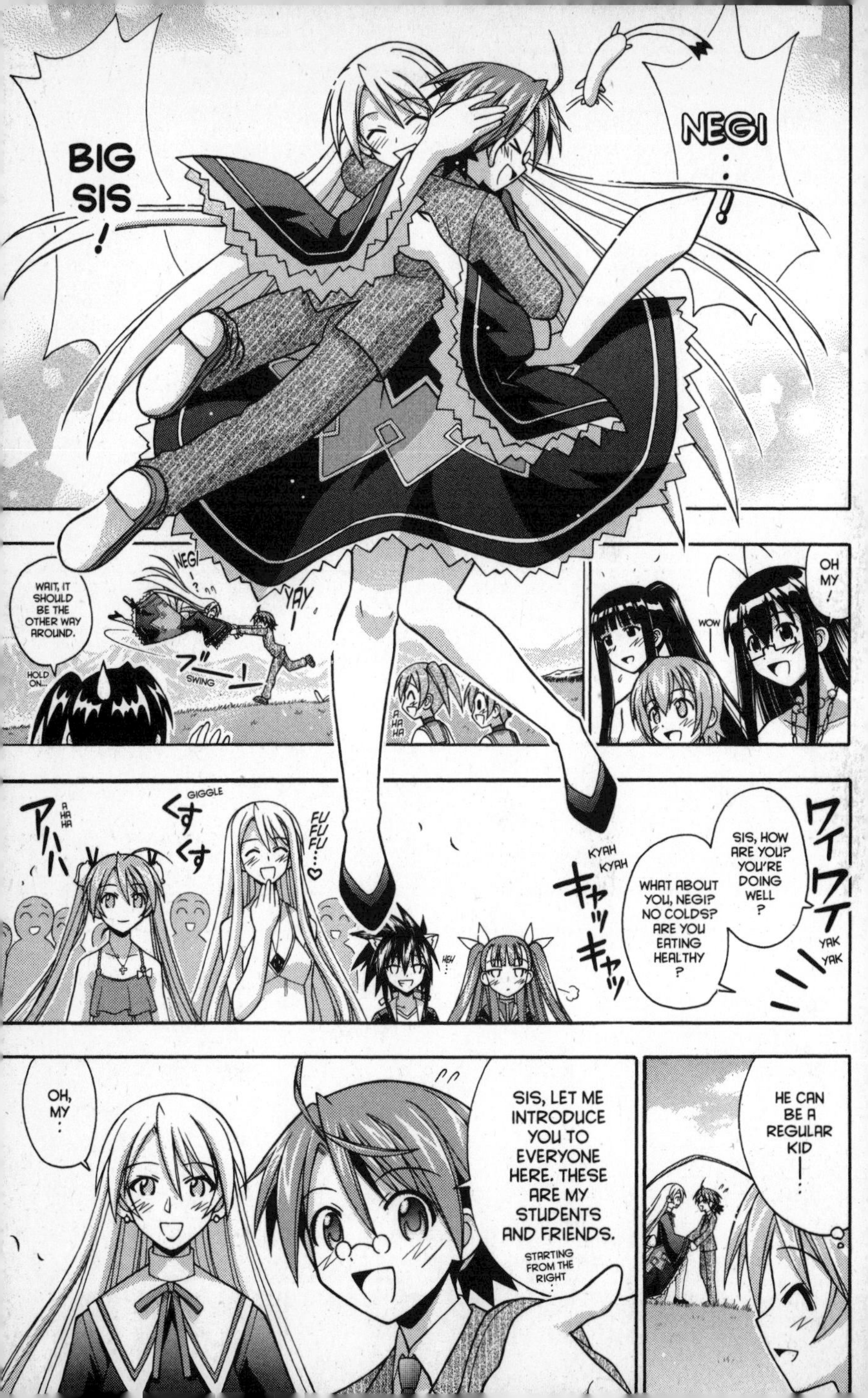
NEGI..!
BIG SIS!
OH MY!
WOW!
NEGI!?
YAY!
ブ—! SWING
WAIT, IT SHOULD BE THE OTHER WAY AROUND.
HOLD ON...
A HA HA
ワイワイ YAK YAK
SIS, HOW ARE YOU? YOU'RE DOING WELL?
WHAT ABOUT YOU, NEGI? NO COLDS? ARE YOU EATING HEALTHY?
キャッキャッ KYAH KYAH
HEH
FU FU FU...♡
くすくす GIGGLE
アハハ A HA HA
HE CAN BE A REGULAR KID...!
SIS, LET ME INTRODUCE YOU TO EVERYONE HERE. THESE ARE MY STUDENTS AND FRIENDS.
STARTING FROM THE RIGHT...
OH, MY...

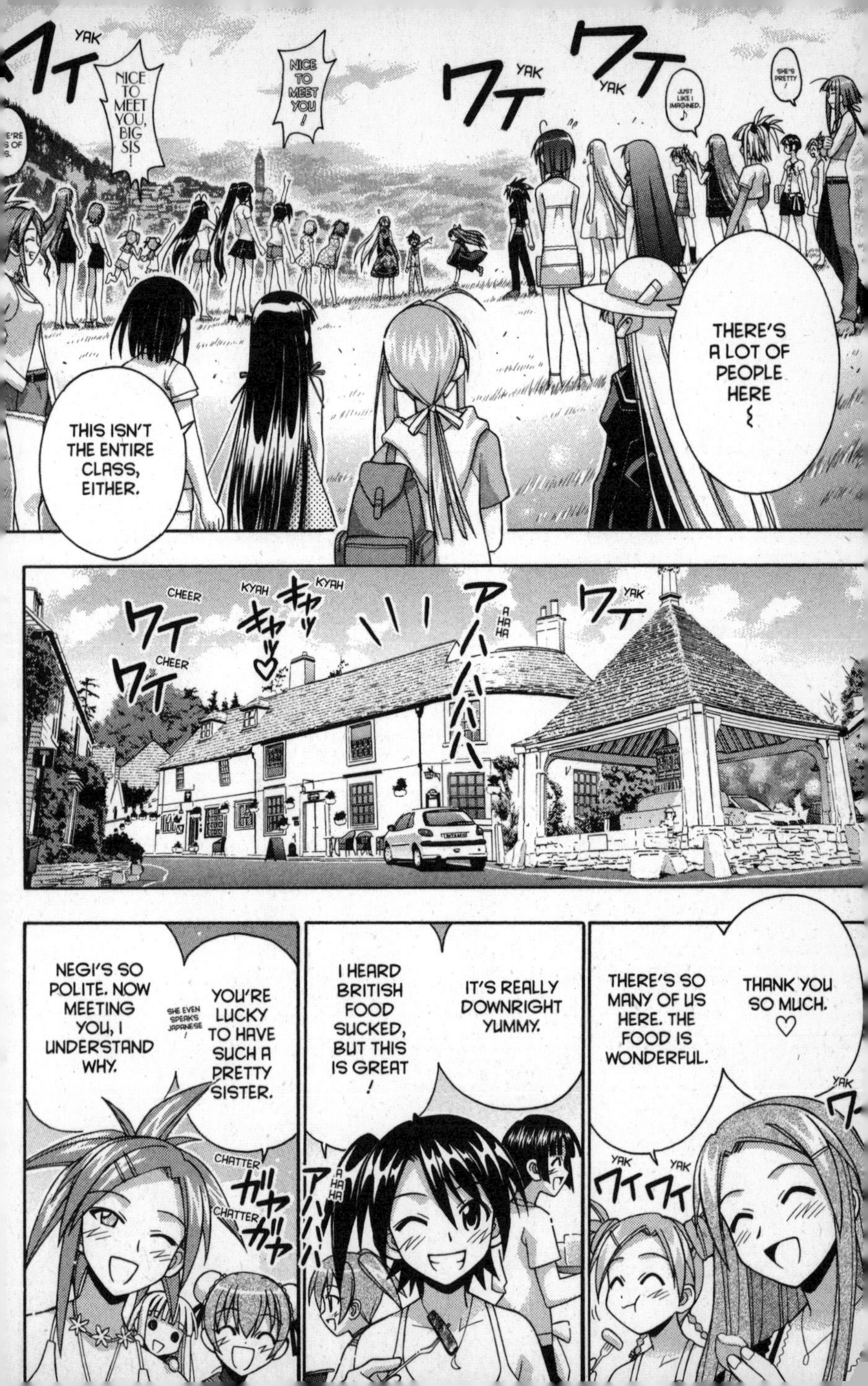
SHE'S PRETTY!
JUST LIKE I IMAGINED. ♪
YAK
YAK
YAK
NICE TO MEET YOU!
NICE TO MEET YOU, BIG SIS!
THERE'S A LOT OF PEOPLE HERE
THIS ISN'T THE ENTIRE CLASS, EITHER.
YAK
A HA HA
KYAH
KYAH
CHEER
CHEER
THANK YOU SO MUCH. ♡
THERE'S SO MANY OF US HERE. THE FOOD IS WONDERFUL.
YAK
YAK
YAK
IT'S REALLY DOWNRIGHT YUMMY.
I HEARD BRITISH FOOD SUCKED, BUT THIS IS GREAT!
A HA HA
YOU'RE LUCKY TO HAVE SUCH A PRETTY SISTER.
SHE EVEN SPEAKS JAPANESE!
NEGI'S SO POLITE. NOW MEETING YOU, I UNDERSTAND WHY.
CHATTER
CHATTER

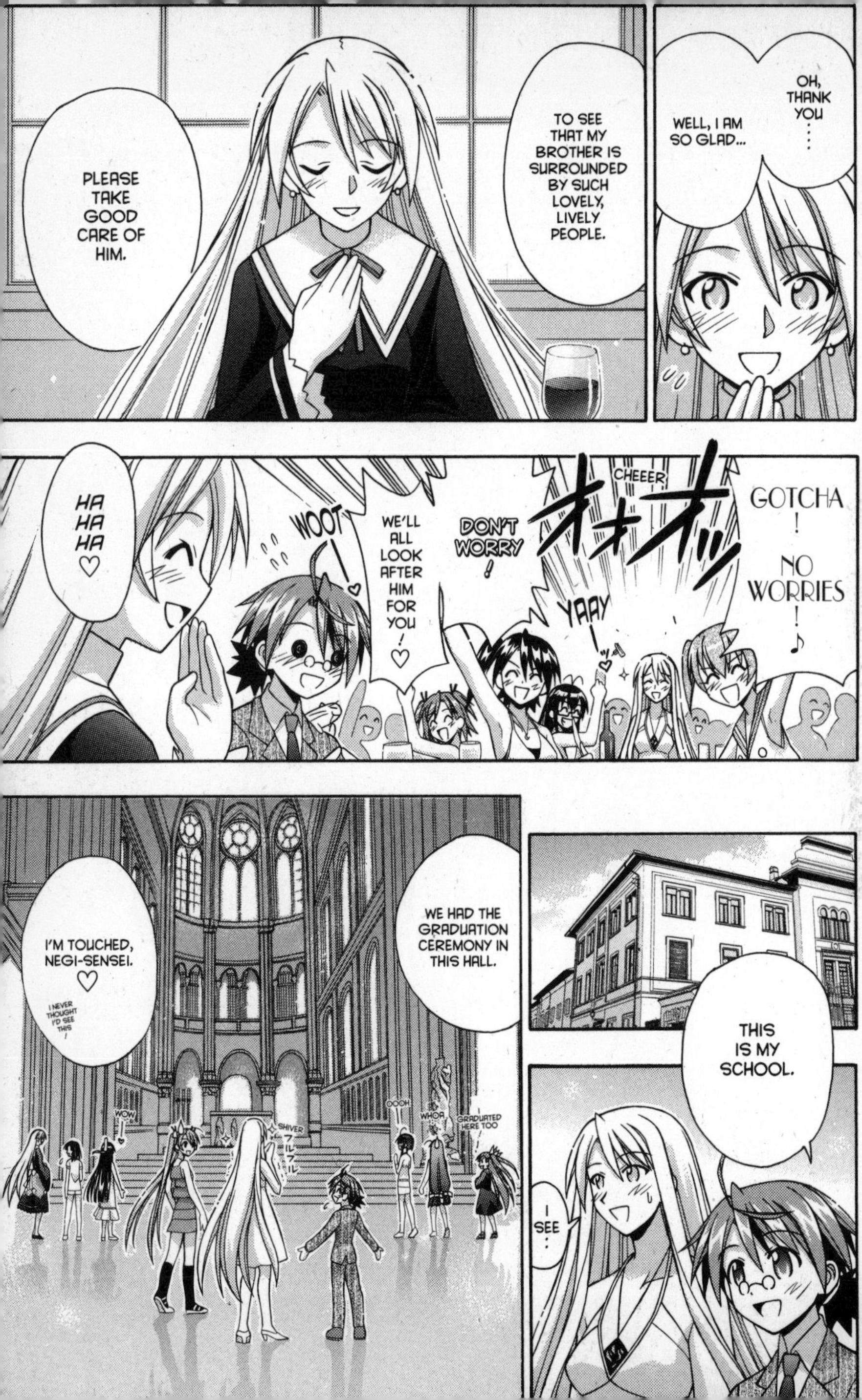

OH, THANK YOU......
WELL, I AM SO GLAD...
TO SEE THAT MY BROTHER IS SURROUNDED BY SUCH LOVELY, LIVELY PEOPLE.
PLEASE TAKE GOOD CARE OF HIM.
GOTCHA! NO WORRIES! ♪
CHEEER
YAAY!
DON'T WORRY!
WE'LL ALL LOOK AFTER HIM FOR YOU! ♡
WOOT! ♡
HA HA HA ♡
THIS IS MY SCHOOL.
I SEE...
WE HAD THE GRADUATION CEREMONY IN THIS HALL.
I'M TOUCHED, NEGI-SENSEI. ♡
I NEVER THOUGHT I'D SEE THIS!
I GRADUATED HERE TOO
WHOA
OOOH
SHIVER
WOW ♡

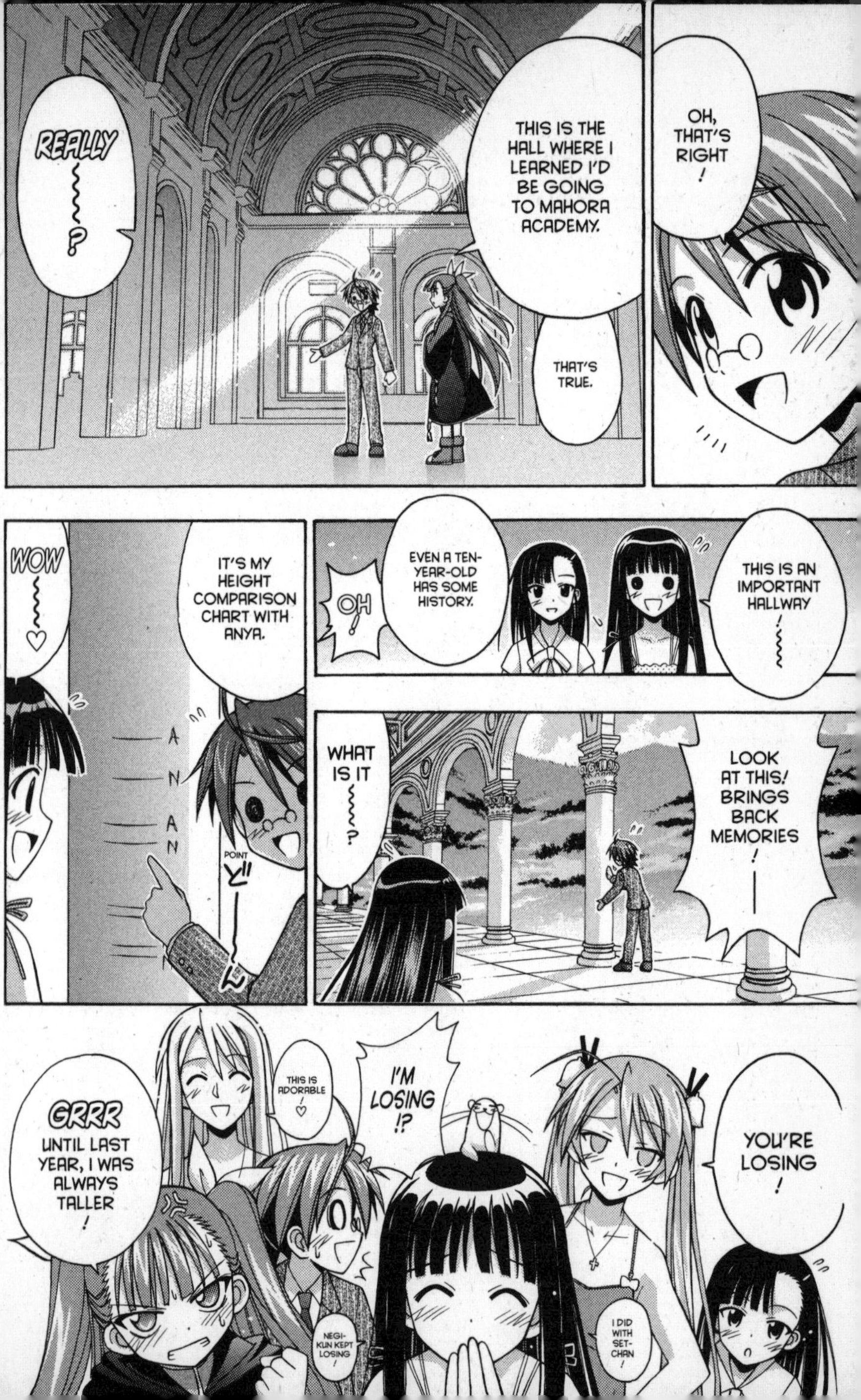
OH, THAT'S RIGHT!
THIS IS THE HALL WHERE I LEARNED I'D BE GOING TO MAHORA ACADEMY.
THAT'S TRUE.
REALLY~~~?
THIS IS AN IMPORTANT HALLWAY!~~~
EVEN A TEN-YEAR-OLD HAS SOME HISTORY.
OH!
LOOK AT THIS! BRINGS BACK MEMORIES!—
WHAT IS IT~~~?
IT'S MY HEIGHT COMPARISON CHART WITH ANYA.
POINT
WOW~~~♡
YOU'RE LOSING!
I'M LOSING!?
THIS IS ADORABLE!♡
GRRR
UNTIL LAST YEAR, I WAS ALWAYS TALLER!
I DID WITH SET-CHAN!
NEGI-KUN KEPT LOSING!

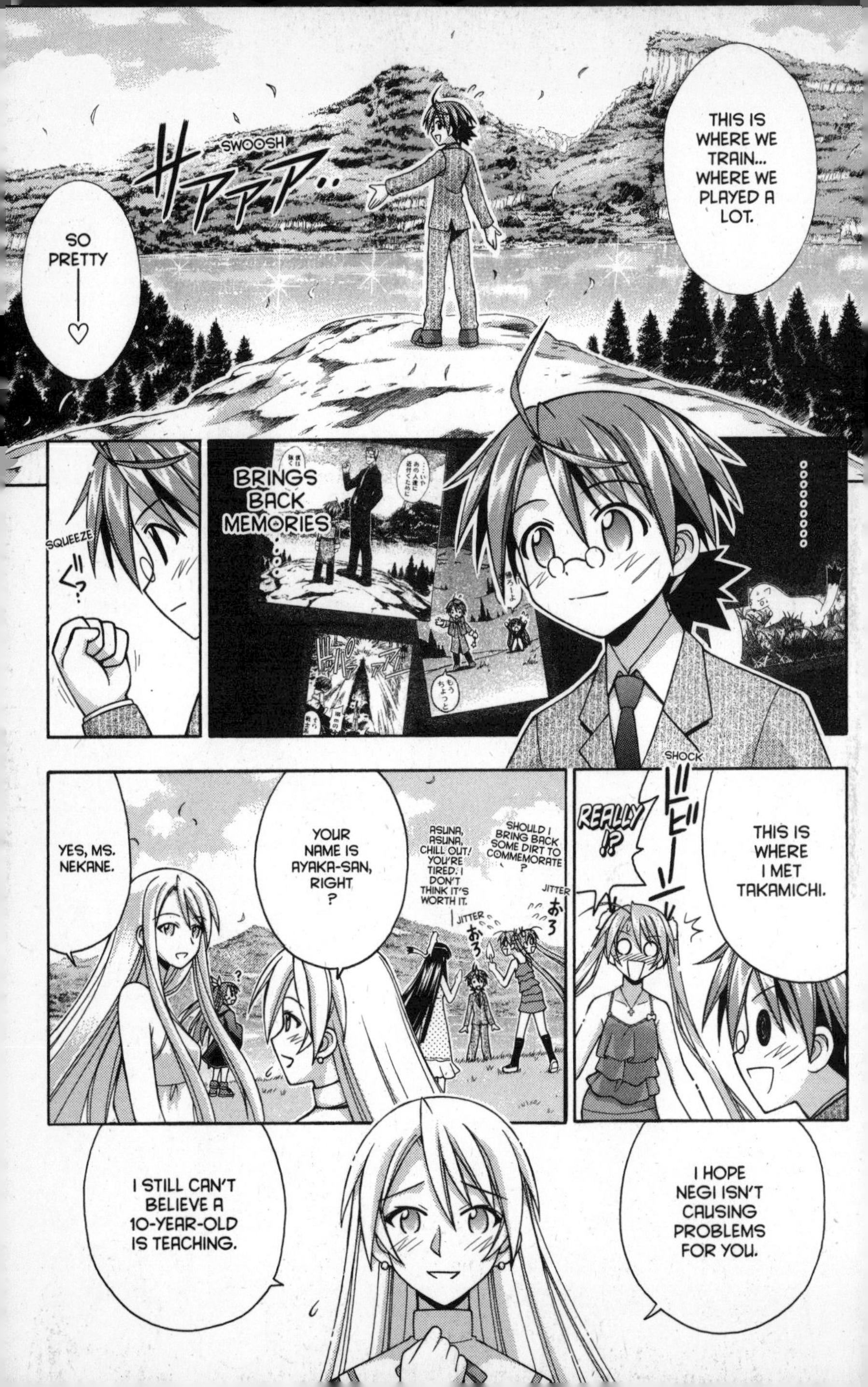
THIS IS WHERE WE TRAIN... WHERE WE PLAYED A LOT.
SWOOSH
SO PRETTY ♡
....
BRINGS BACK MEMORIES...
SQUEEZE
THIS IS WHERE I MET TAKAMICHI.
SHOCK
REALLY!?
SHOULD I BRING BACK SOME DIRT TO COMMEMORATE?
JITTER
おろ
ASUNA, ASUNA, CHILL OUT! YOU'RE TIRED. I DON'T THINK IT'S WORTH IT.
JITTER
おろ
YOUR NAME IS AYAKA-SAN, RIGHT?
YES, MS. NEKANE.
I HOPE NEGI ISN'T CAUSING PROBLEMS FOR YOU.
I STILL CAN'T BELIEVE A 10-YEAR-OLD IS TEACHING.

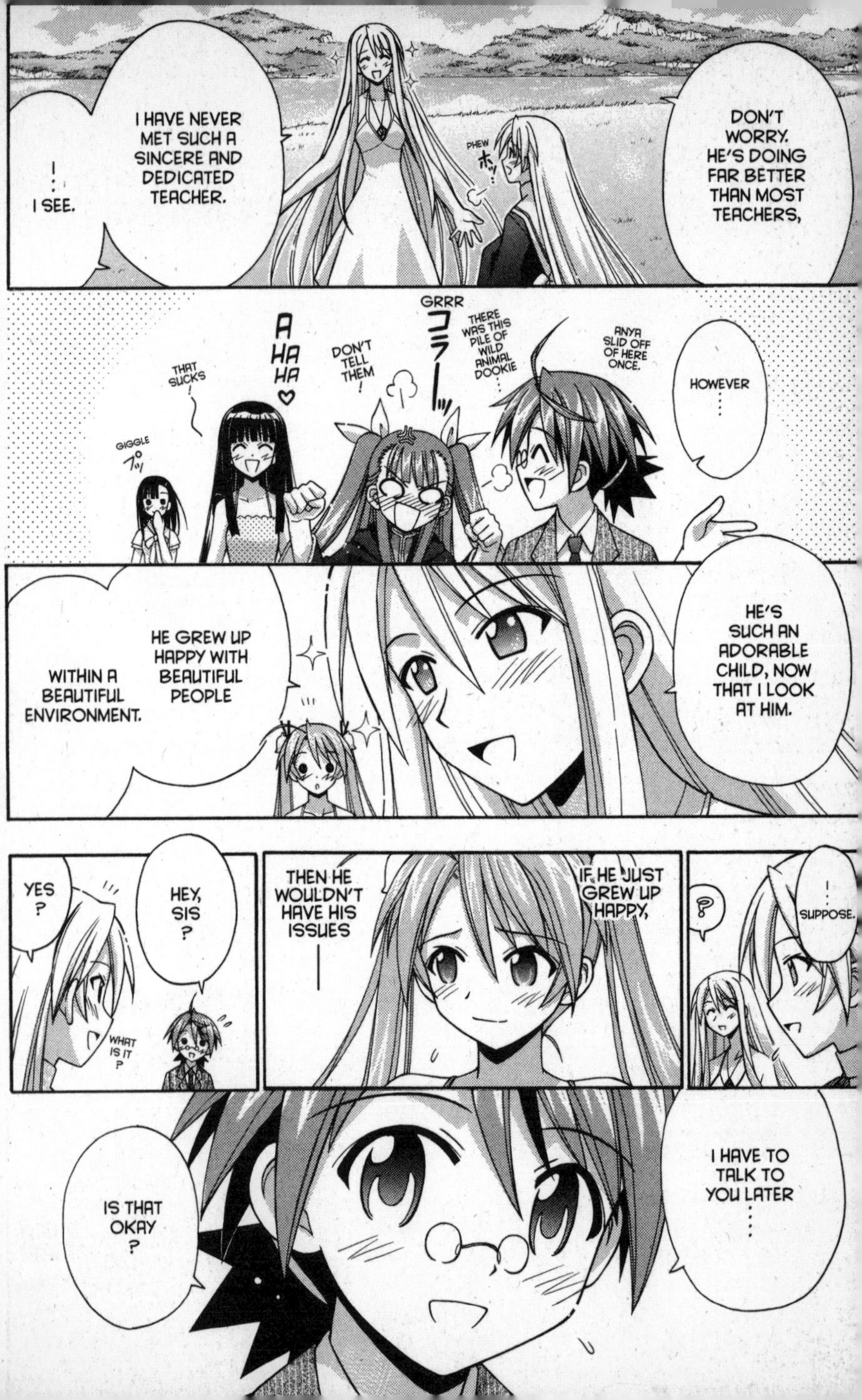
DON'T WORRY. HE'S DOING FAR BETTER THAN MOST TEACHERS,
PHEW
I HAVE NEVER MET SUCH A SINCERE AND DEDICATED TEACHER.
…! I SEE.
HOWEVER…
ANYA SLID OFF OF HERE ONCE.
THERE WAS THIS PILE OF WILD ANIMAL DOOKIE…
GRRR
DON'T TELL THEM!
AHAHAHA♡
THAT SUCKS!
GIGGLE
HE'S SUCH AN ADORABLE CHILD, NOW THAT I LOOK AT HIM.
HE GREW UP HAPPY WITH BEAUTIFUL PEOPLE
WITHIN A BEAUTIFUL ENVIRONMENT.
…I SUPPOSE.
?
IF HE JUST GREW UP HAPPY,
THEN HE WOULDN'T HAVE HIS ISSUES—
HEY, SIS?
YES?
WHAT IS IT?
I HAVE TO TALK TO YOU LATER…
IS THAT OKAY?

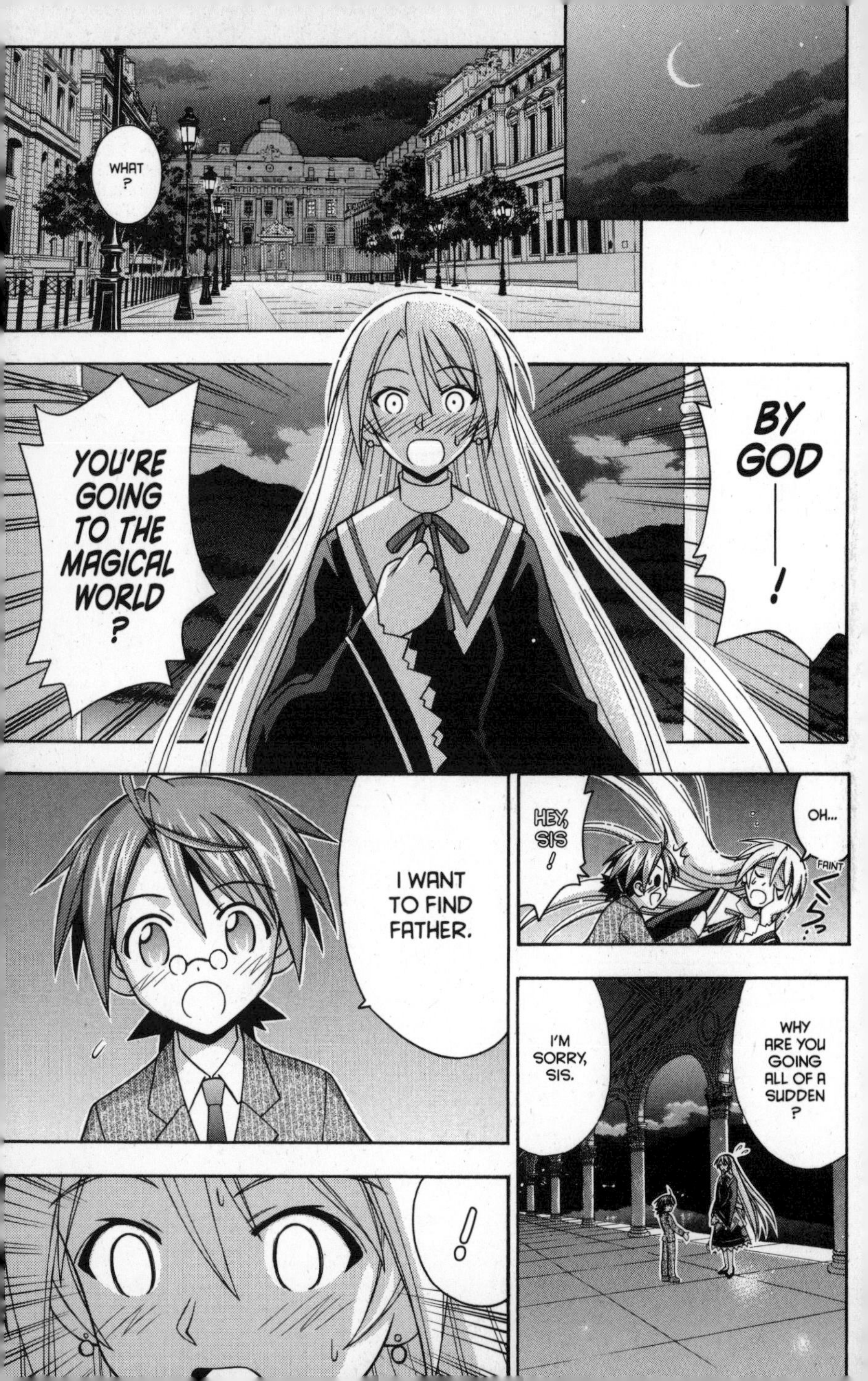
WHAT ?
BY GOD—!
YOU'RE GOING TO THE MAGICAL WORLD ?
OH...
FAINT
HEY, SIS !
WHY ARE YOU GOING ALL OF A SUDDEN ?
I'M SORRY, SIS.
I WANT TO FIND FATHER.
!

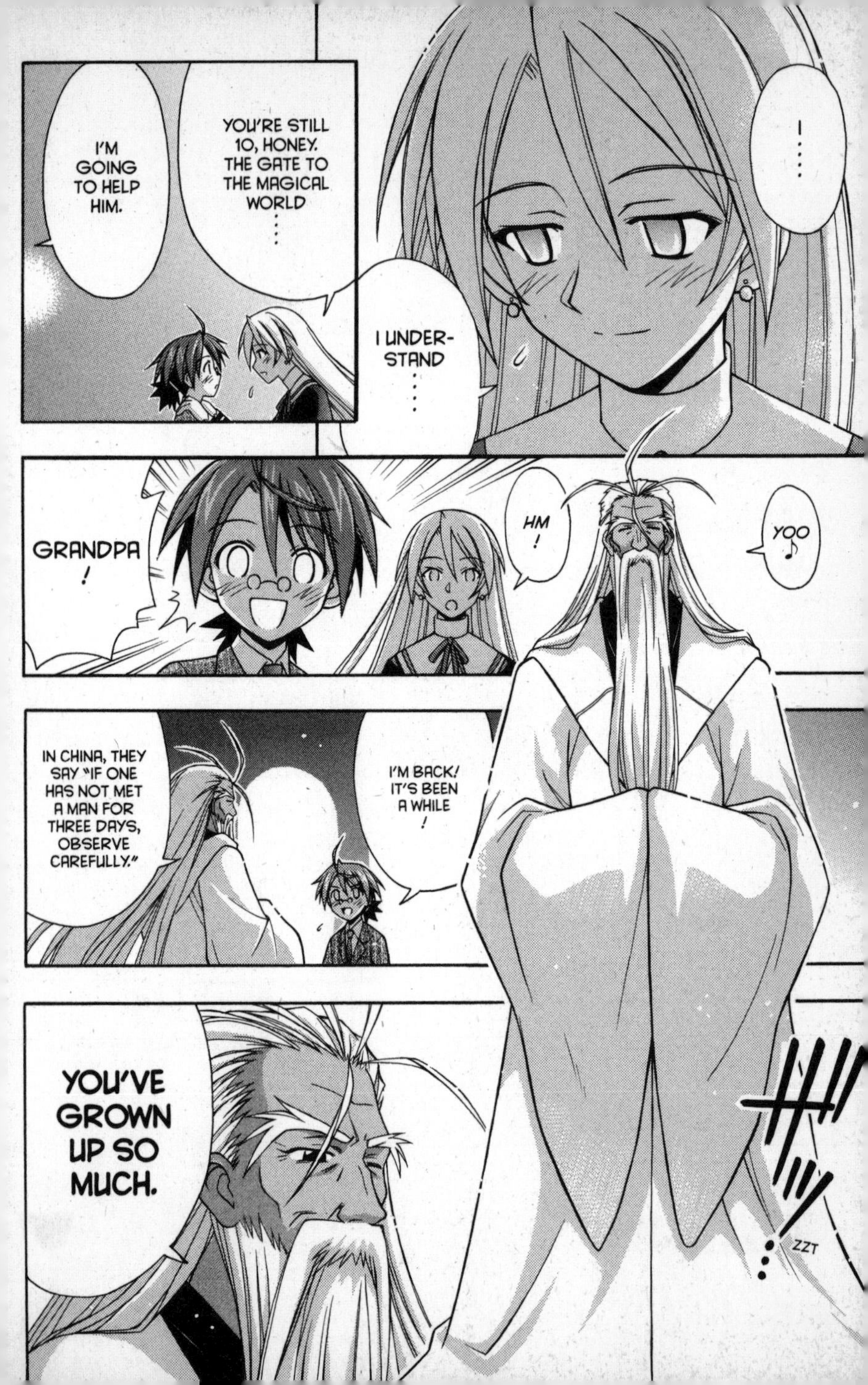
I......
I UNDER-STAND......
YOU'RE STILL 10, HONEY. THE GATE TO THE MAGICAL WORLD......
I'M GOING TO HELP HIM.
YOO♪
HM!
GRANDPA!
I'M BACK! IT'S BEEN A WHILE!
IN CHINA, THEY SAY "IF ONE HAS NOT MET A MAN FOR THREE DAYS, OBSERVE CAREFULLY."
ZZT
YOU'VE GROWN UP SO MUCH.

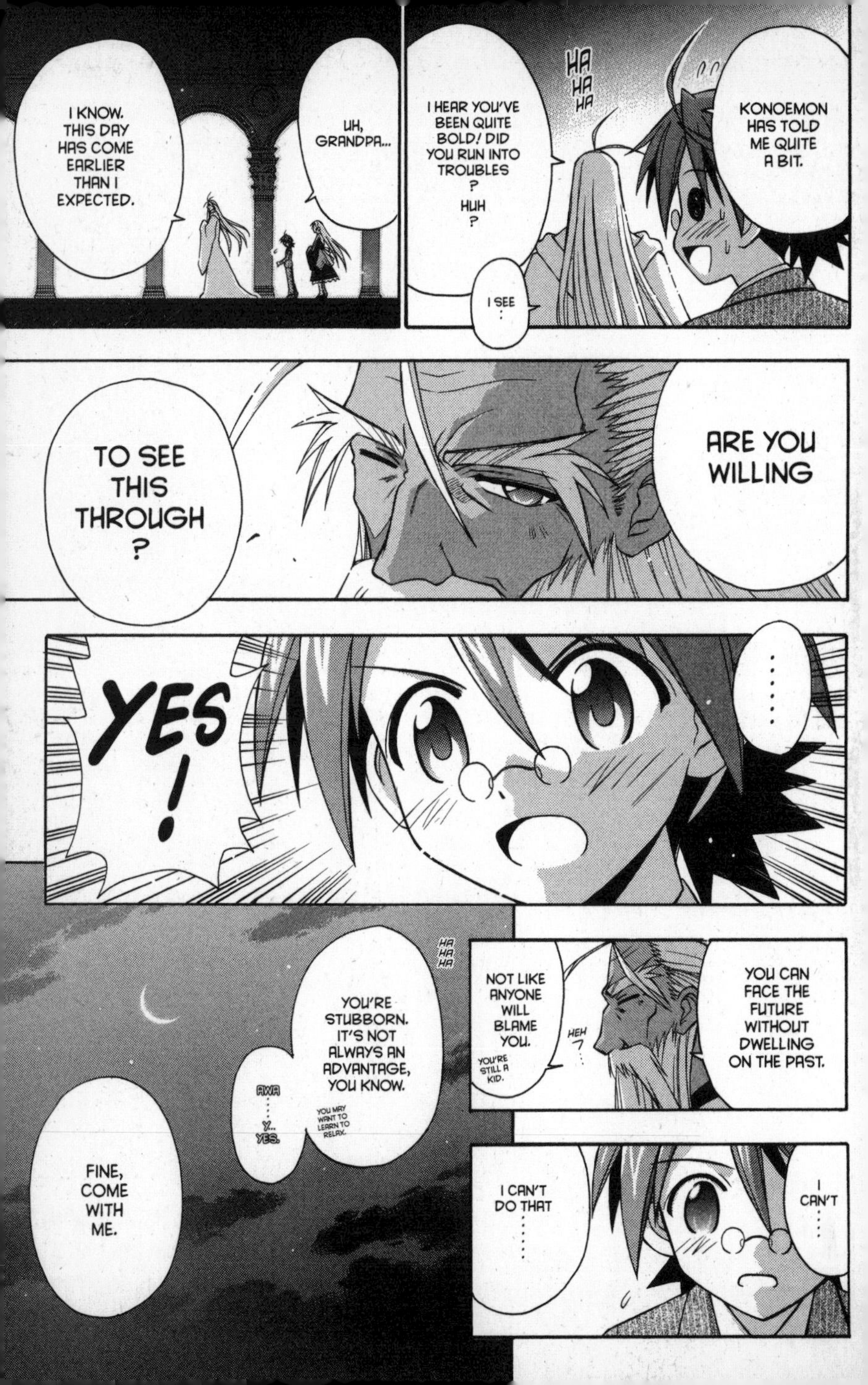
KONOEMON HAS TOLD ME QUITE A BIT.
HA HA HA
I HEAR YOU'VE BEEN QUITE BOLD! DID YOU RUN INTO TROUBLES? HUH?
I SEE...
UH, GRANDPA...
I KNOW. THIS DAY HAS COME EARLIER THAN I EXPECTED.
ARE YOU WILLING
TO SEE THIS THROUGH?
......
YES!
YOU CAN FACE THE FUTURE WITHOUT DWELLING ON THE PAST.
NOT LIKE ANYONE WILL BLAME YOU.
HEH?...
YOU'RE STILL A KID.
I CAN'T...
I CAN'T DO THAT......
HA HA HA
YOU'RE STUBBORN. IT'S NOT ALWAYS AN ADVANTAGE, YOU KNOW.
YOU MAY WANT TO LEARN TO RELAX.
AWA... Y.. YES.
FINE, COME WITH ME.

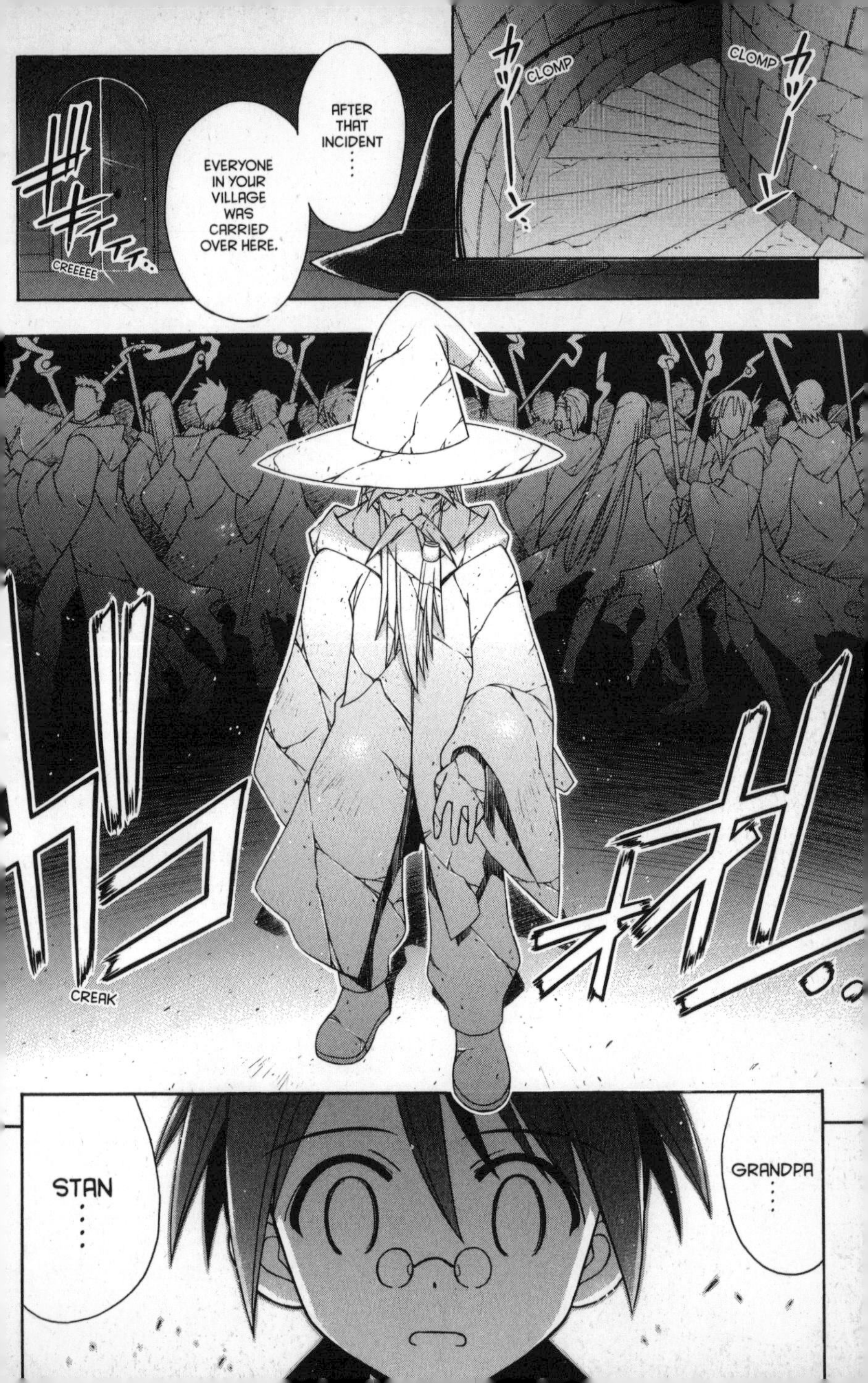
CLOMP
CLOMP
AFTER THAT INCIDENT ......
EVERYONE IN YOUR VILLAGE WAS CARRIED OVER HERE.
CREEEEE
CREAK
GRANDPA ......
STAN ......

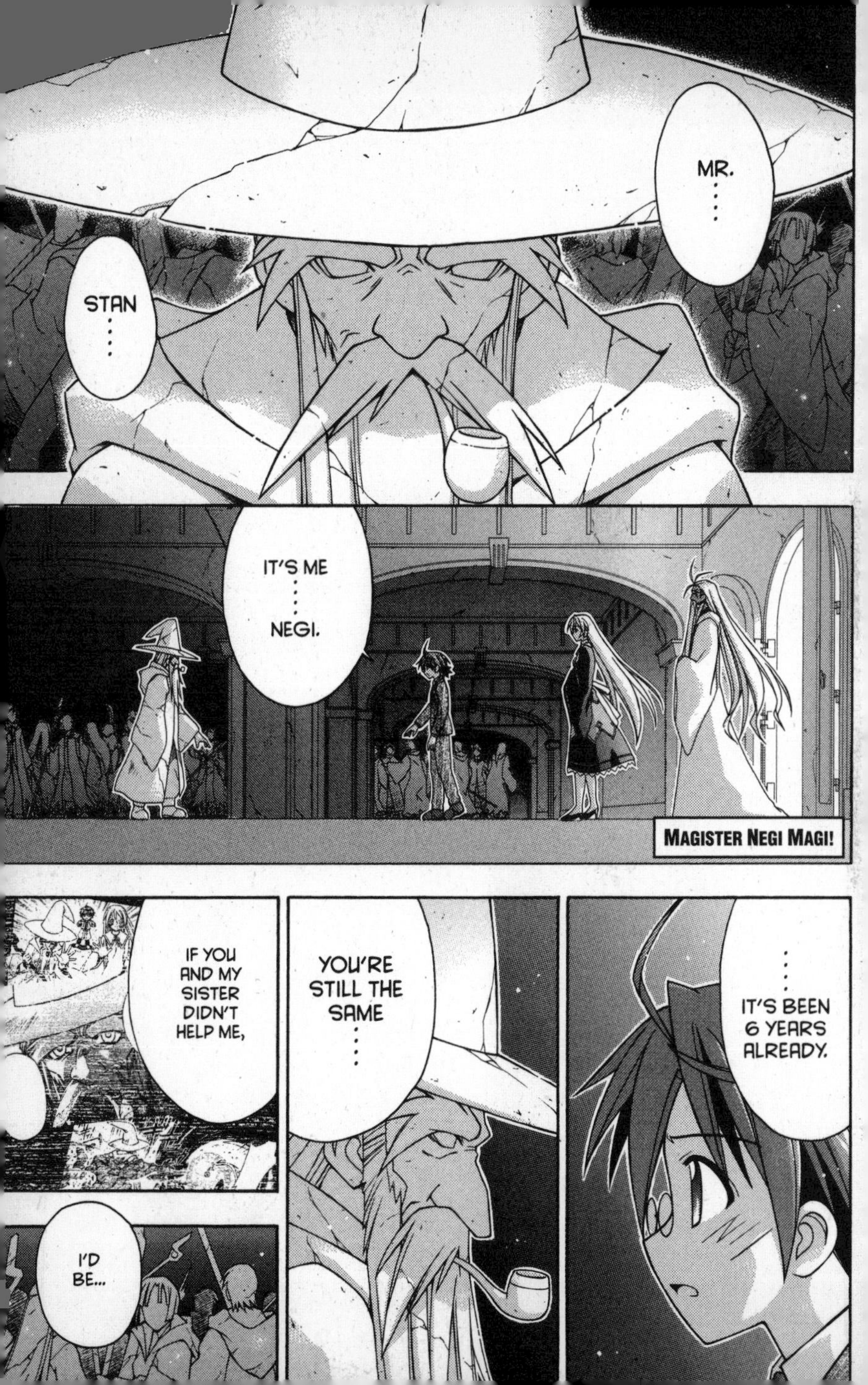
MR. ....
STAN ...
IT'S ME ... NEGI.
MAGISTER NEGI MAGI!
... IT'S BEEN 6 YEARS ALREADY.
YOU'RE STILL THE SAME ....
IF YOU AND MY SISTER DIDN'T HELP ME,
I'D BE...

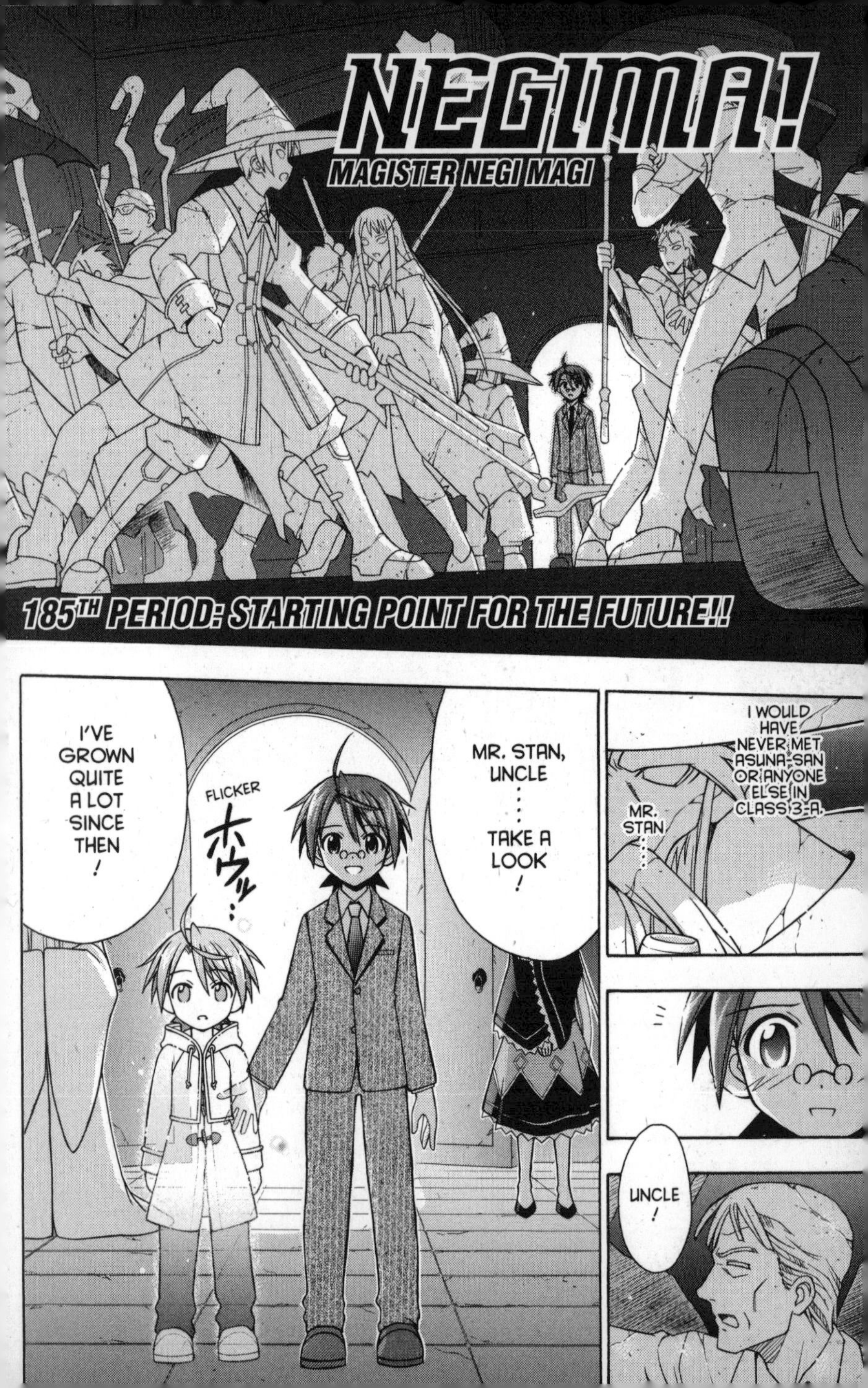
NEGIMA!
MAGISTER NEGI MAGI
185TH PERIOD: STARTING POINT FOR THE FUTURE!!
I WOULD HAVE NEVER MET ASUNA-SAN OR ANYONE ELSE IN CLASS 3-A.
MR. STAN...
UNCLE!
MR. STAN, UNCLE... TAKE A LOOK!
FLICKER
ホウッ…
I'VE GROWN QUITE A LOT SINCE THEN!

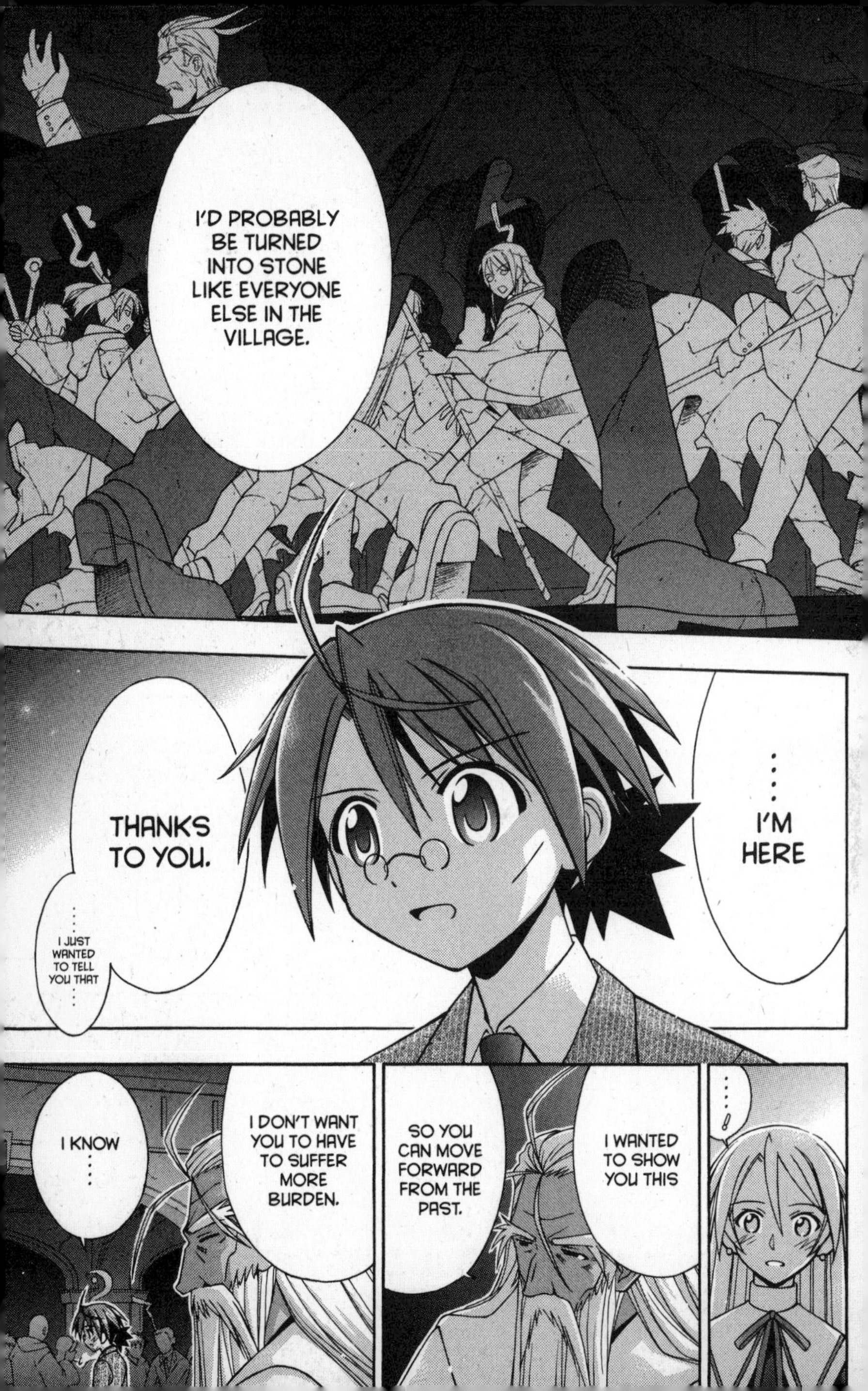
I'D PROBABLY BE TURNED INTO STONE LIKE EVERYONE ELSE IN THE VILLAGE.
...... I'M HERE
THANKS TO YOU.
...I JUST WANTED TO TELL YOU THAT...
....!
I WANTED TO SHOW YOU THIS
SO YOU CAN MOVE FORWARD FROM THE PAST.
I DON'T WANT YOU TO HAVE TO SUFFER MORE BURDEN.
I KNOW ......

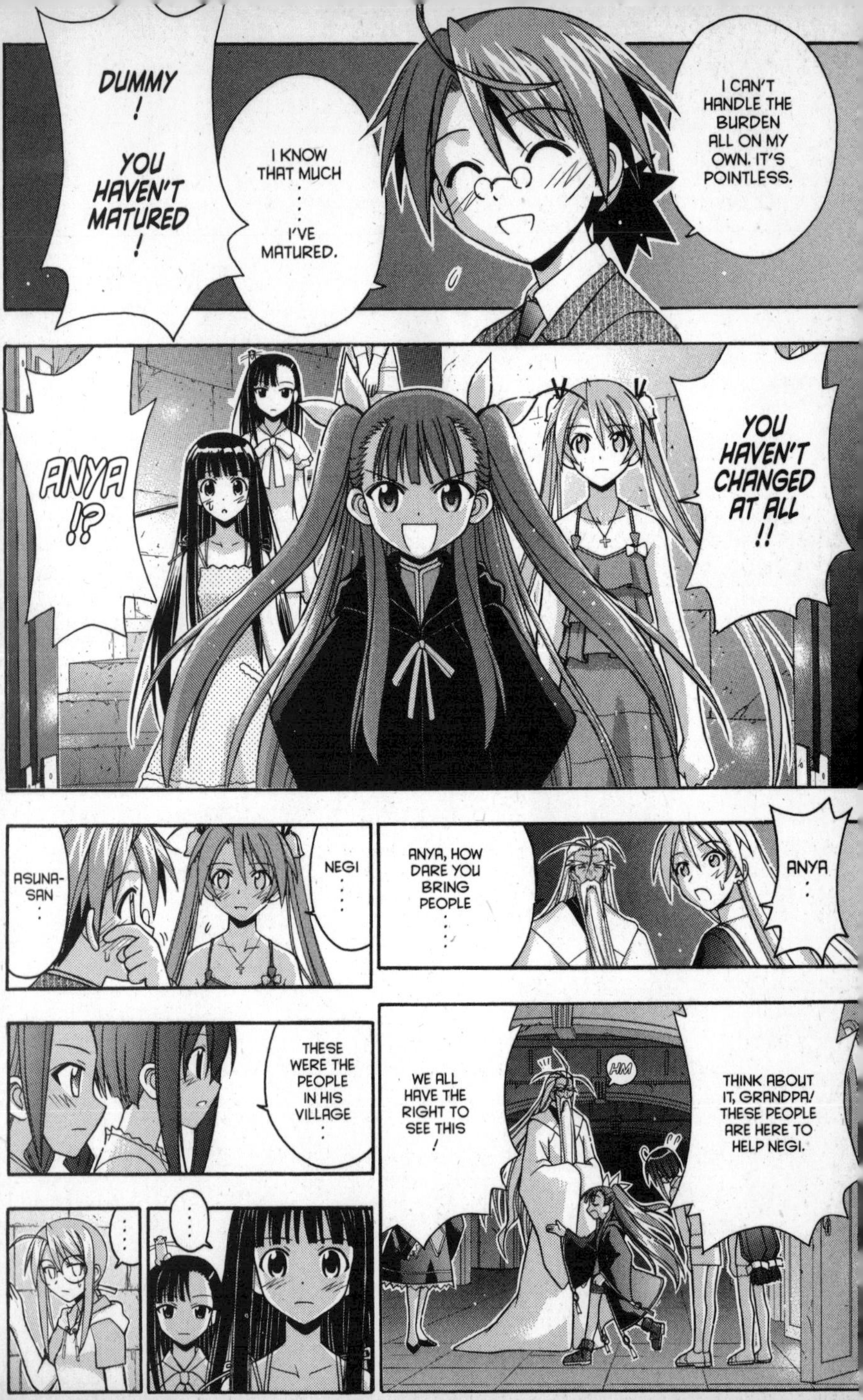
I CAN'T HANDLE THE BURDEN ALL ON MY OWN. IT'S POINTLESS.
I KNOW THAT MUCH... I'VE MATURED.
DUMMY! YOU HAVEN'T MATURED!
YOU HAVEN'T CHANGED AT ALL!!
ANYA!?
ANYA...
ANYA, HOW DARE YOU BRING PEOPLE...
NEGI...
ASUNA-SAN...
THINK ABOUT IT, GRANDPA! THESE PEOPLE ARE HERE TO HELP NEGI.
HM
WE ALL HAVE THE RIGHT TO SEE THIS!
THESE WERE THE PEOPLE IN HIS VILLAGE...
...
...

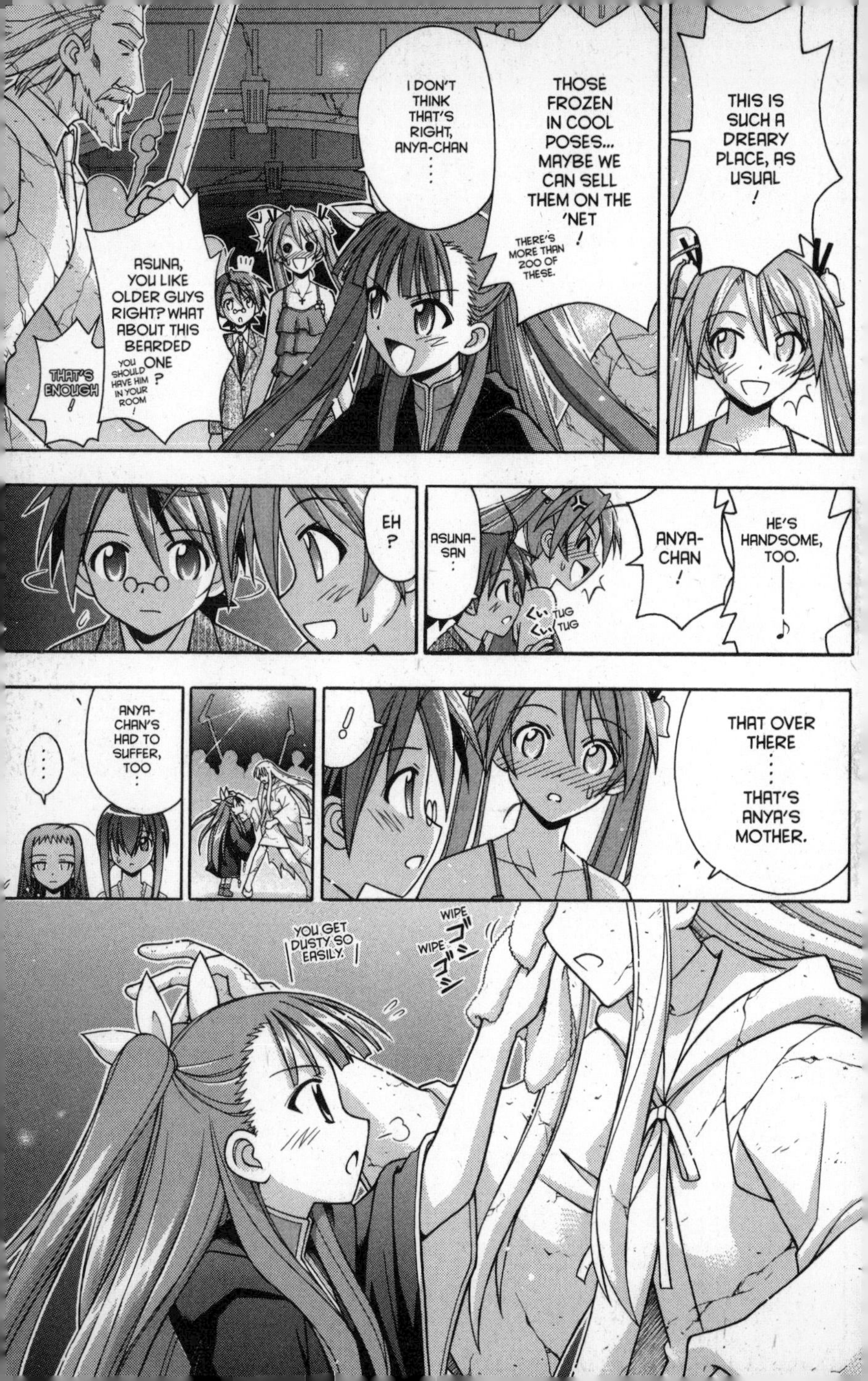
THIS IS SUCH A DREARY PLACE, AS USUAL!
THOSE FROZEN IN COOL POSES... MAYBE WE CAN SELL THEM ON THE 'NET!
THERE'S MORE THAN 200 OF THESE.
I DON'T THINK THAT'S RIGHT, ANYA-CHAN...
ASUNA, YOU LIKE OLDER GUYS RIGHT? WHAT ABOUT THIS BEARDED ONE?
YOU SHOULD HAVE HIM IN YOUR ROOM!
THAT'S ENOUGH!
HE'S HANDSOME, TOO. ♪
ANYA-CHAN!
ASUNA-SAN...
くいくい TUG TUG
EH?
THAT OVER THERE... THAT'S ANYA'S MOTHER.
!
ANYA-CHAN'S HAD TO SUFFER, TOO...
.....
WIPE ゴシ WIPE ゴシ
YOU GET DUSTY SO EASILY.

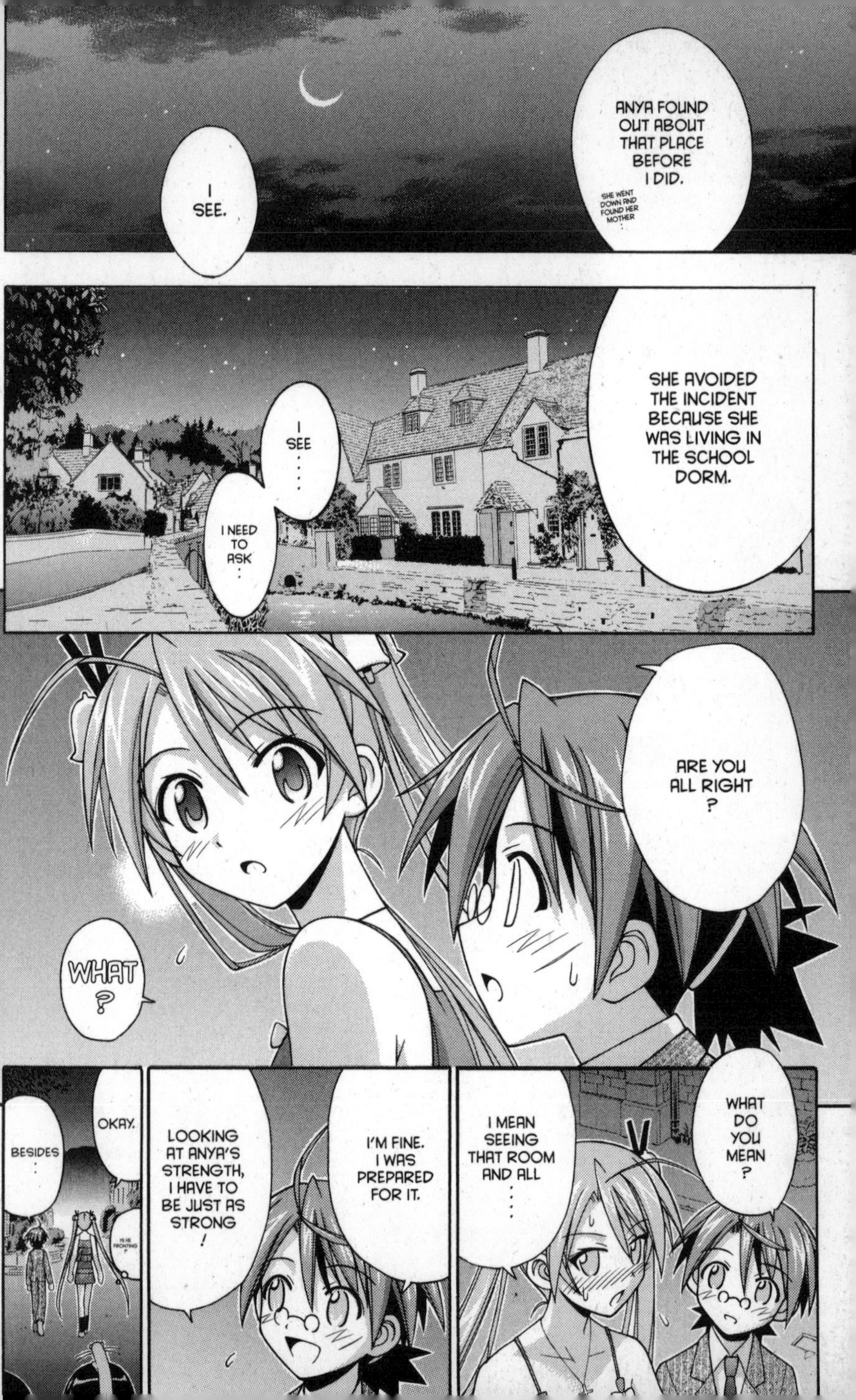
ANYA FOUND OUT ABOUT THAT PLACE BEFORE I DID.
SHE WENT DOWN AND FOUND HER MOTHER :
I SEE.
SHE AVOIDED THE INCIDENT BECAUSE SHE WAS LIVING IN THE SCHOOL DORM.
I SEE . . . .
I NEED TO ASK . .
ARE YOU ALL RIGHT ?
WHAT ?
WHAT DO YOU MEAN ?
I MEAN SEEING THAT ROOM AND ALL . . . .
I'M FINE. I WAS PREPARED FOR IT.
LOOKING AT ANYA'S STRENGTH, I HAVE TO BE JUST AS STRONG !
OKAY.
BESIDES . .
IS HE FRONTING ?

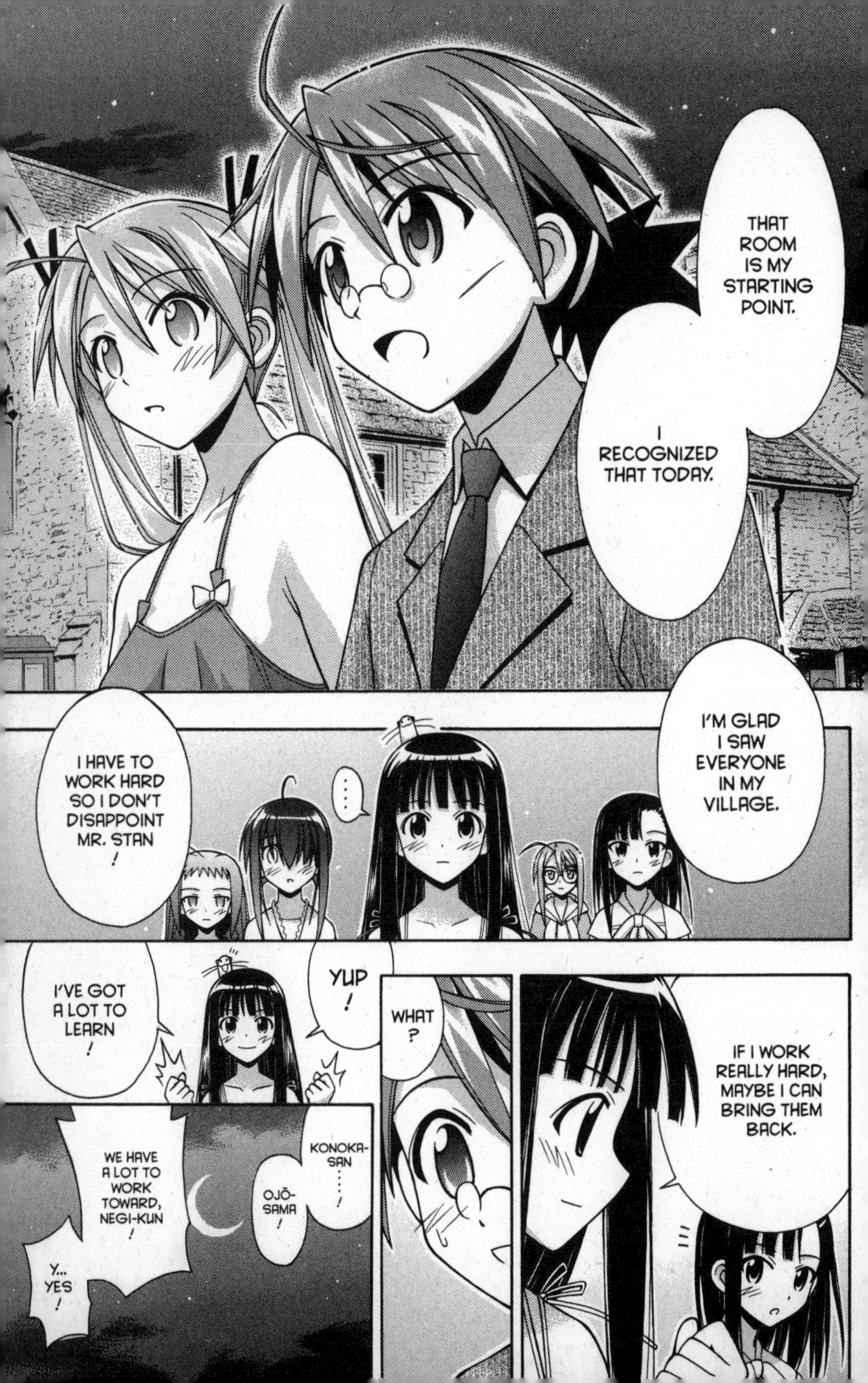
THAT ROOM IS MY STARTING POINT.
I RECOGNIZED THAT TODAY.
I'M GLAD I SAW EVERYONE IN MY VILLAGE.
...
I HAVE TO WORK HARD SO I DON'T DISAPPOINT MR. STAN!
IF I WORK REALLY HARD, MAYBE I CAN BRING THEM BACK.
WHAT?
YUP!
I'VE GOT A LOT TO LEARN!
KONOKA-SAN...!
OJŌ-SAMA!
WE HAVE A LOT TO WORK TOWARD, NEGI-KUN!
Y... YES!

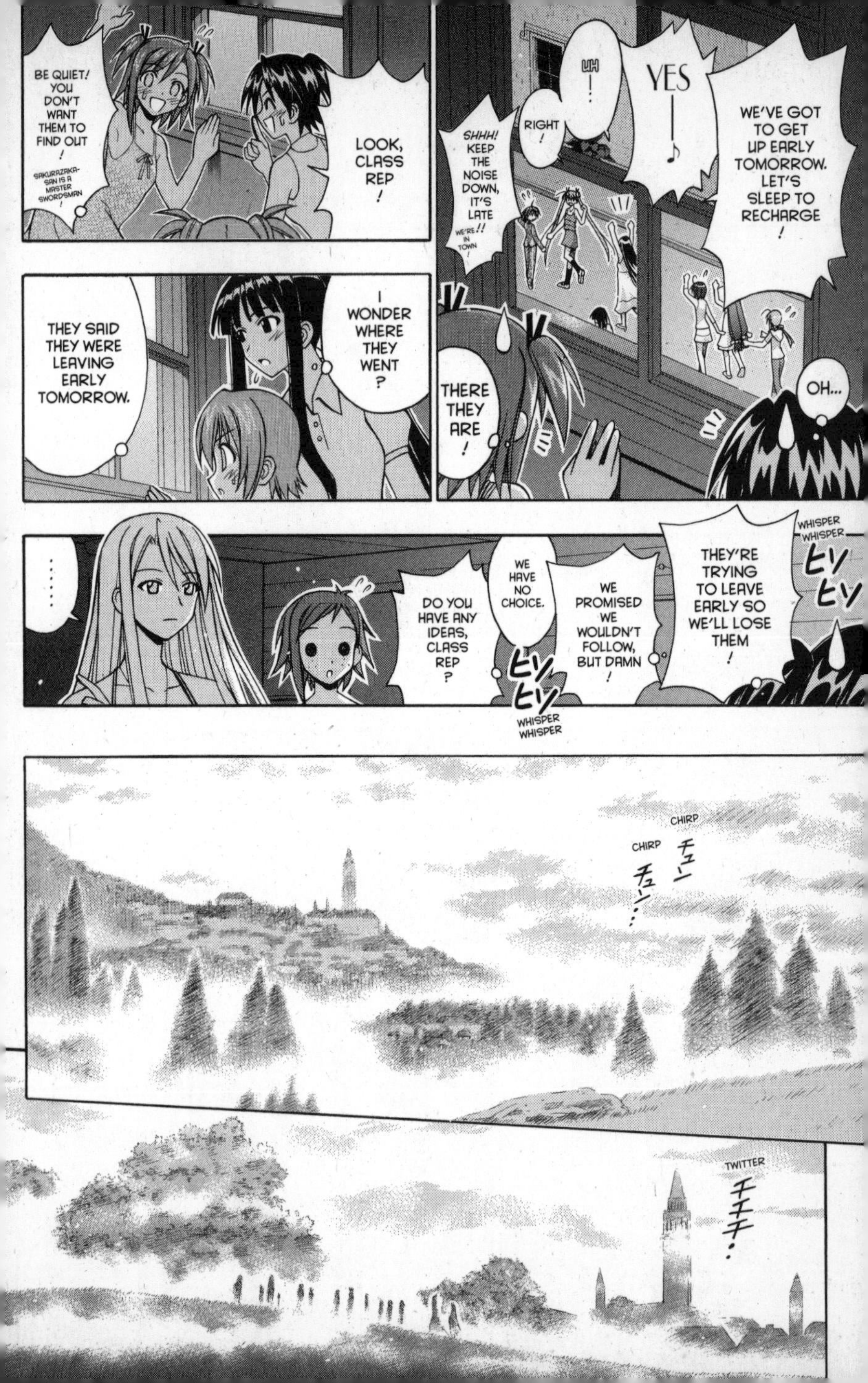
WE'VE GOT TO GET UP EARLY TOMORROW. LET'S SLEEP TO RECHARGE!
YES—♪
UH!
RIGHT!
SHHH! KEEP THE NOISE DOWN, IT'S LATE!!
WE'RE IN TOWN!
LOOK, CLASS REP!
BE QUIET! YOU DON'T WANT THEM TO FIND OUT!
SAKURAZAKA-SAN IS A MASTER SWORDSMAN!
OH...
THERE THEY ARE!
I WONDER WHERE THEY WENT?
THEY SAID THEY WERE LEAVING EARLY TOMORROW.
WHISPER WHISPER
THEY'RE TRYING TO LEAVE EARLY SO WE'LL LOSE THEM!
WE PROMISED WE WOULDN'T FOLLOW, BUT DAMN!
WE HAVE NO CHOICE.
DO YOU HAVE ANY IDEAS, CLASS REP?
WHISPER WHISPER
......
CHIRP
CHIRP
TWITTER

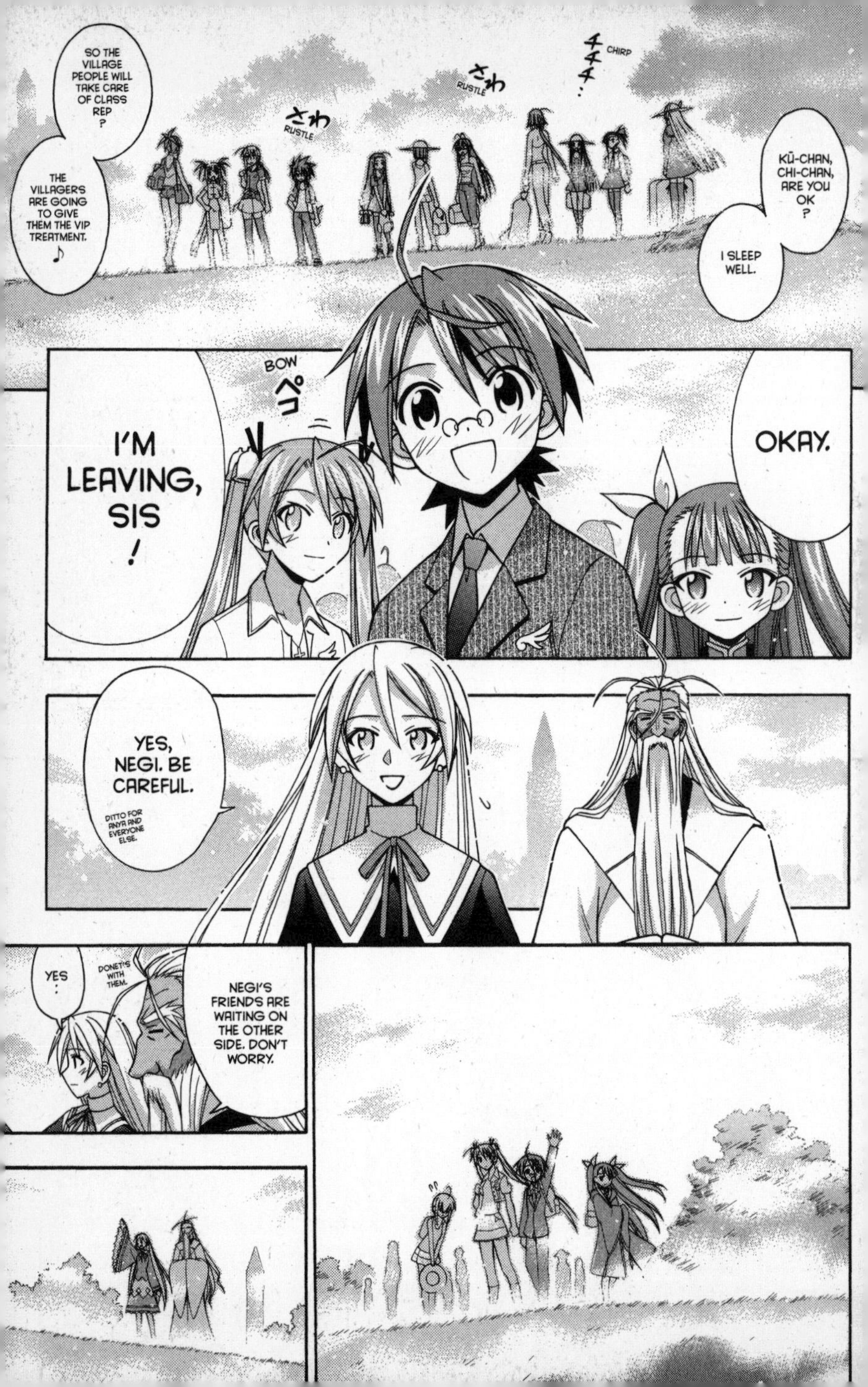
KŪ-CHAN, CHI-CHAN, ARE YOU OK?
I SLEEP WELL.
チチチ… CHIRP
さわ RUSTLE
さわ RUSTLE
SO THE VILLAGE PEOPLE WILL TAKE CARE OF CLASS REP?
THE VILLAGER'S ARE GOING TO GIVE THEM THE VIP TREATMENT. ♪
OKAY.
BOW ペコ
I'M LEAVING, SIS!
YES, NEGI. BE CAREFUL.
DITTO FOR ANYA AND EVERYONE ELSE.
NEGI'S FRIENDS ARE WAITING ON THE OTHER SIDE. DON'T WORRY.
DONET'S WITH THEM.
YES...

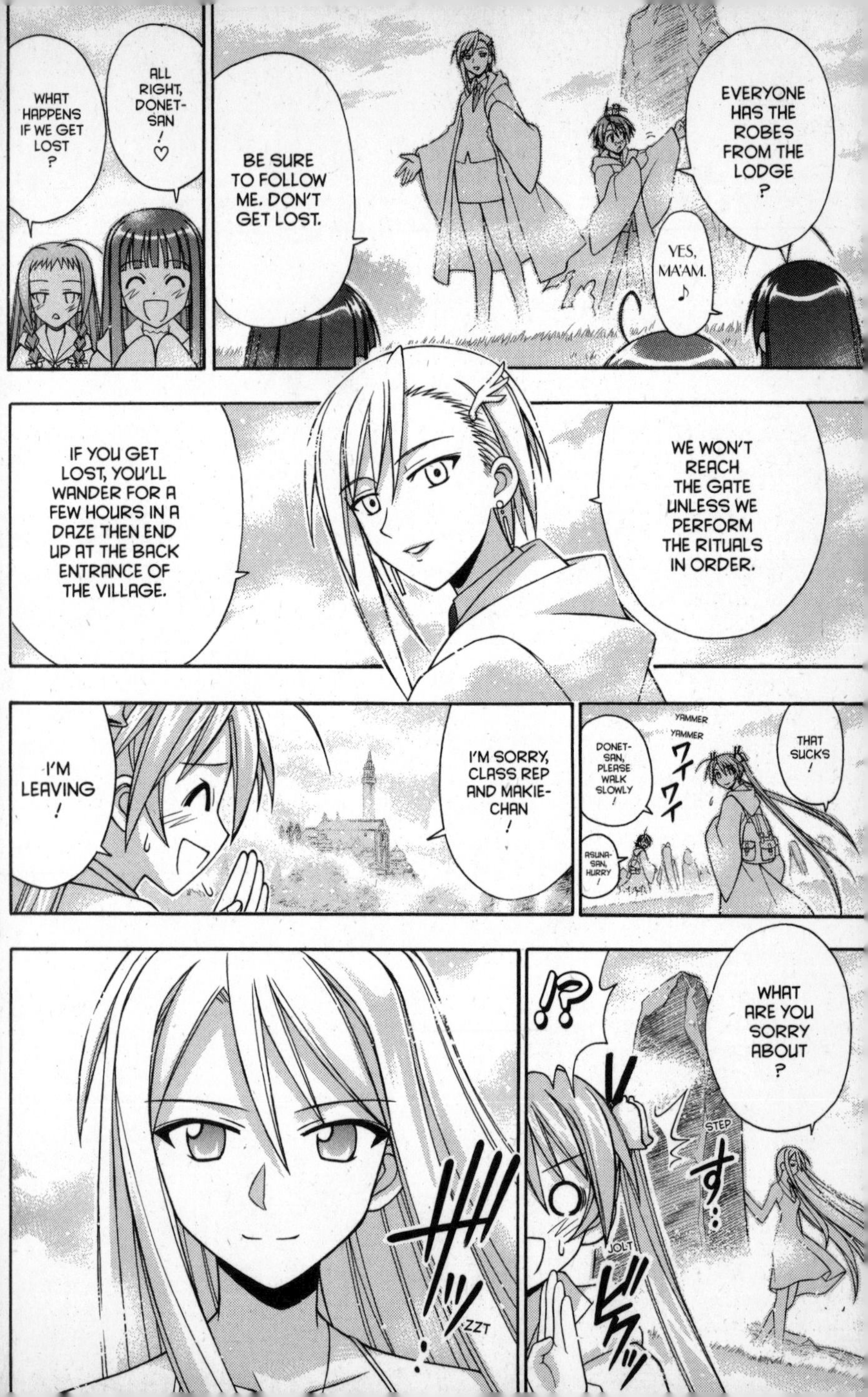
EVERYONE HAS THE ROBES FROM THE LODGE?
YES, MA'AM. ♪
BE SURE TO FOLLOW ME. DON'T GET LOST.
ALL RIGHT, DONET-SAN! ♡
WHAT HAPPENS IF WE GET LOST?
WE WON'T REACH THE GATE UNLESS WE PERFORM THE RITUALS IN ORDER.
IF YOU GET LOST, YOU'LL WANDER FOR A FEW HOURS IN A DAZE THEN END UP AT THE BACK ENTRANCE OF THE VILLAGE.
THAT SUCKS!
YAMMER YAMMER
ワイワイ
DONET-SAN, PLEASE WALK SLOWLY!
ASUNA-SAN, HURRY!
I'M SORRY, CLASS REP AND MAKIE-CHAN!
I'M LEAVING!
!?
WHAT ARE YOU SORRY ABOUT?
STEP
す…
JOLT
ZZT

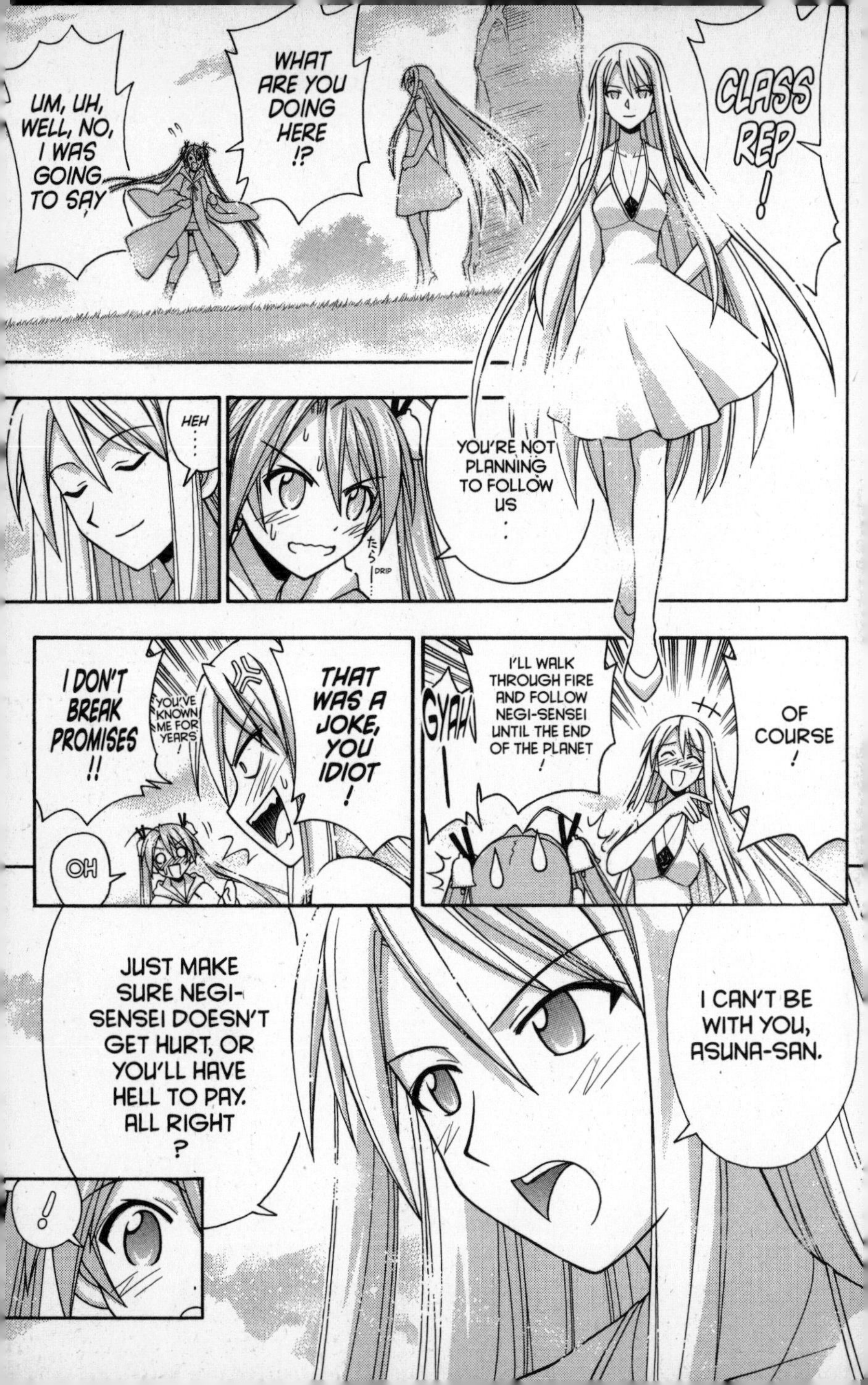
CLASS REP!
WHAT ARE YOU DOING HERE!?
UM, UH, WELL, NO, I WAS GOING TO SAY
YOU'RE NOT PLANNING TO FOLLOW US...
たら DRIP
HEH...
OF COURSE!
I'LL WALK THROUGH FIRE AND FOLLOW NEGI-SENSEI UNTIL THE END OF THE PLANET!
GYAH!
THAT WAS A JOKE, YOU IDIOT!
YOU'VE KNOWN ME FOR YEARS!
I DON'T BREAK PROMISES!!
OH
I CAN'T BE WITH YOU, ASUNA-SAN.
JUST MAKE SURE NEGI-SENSEI DOESN'T GET HURT, OR YOU'LL HAVE HELL TO PAY. ALL RIGHT?
!

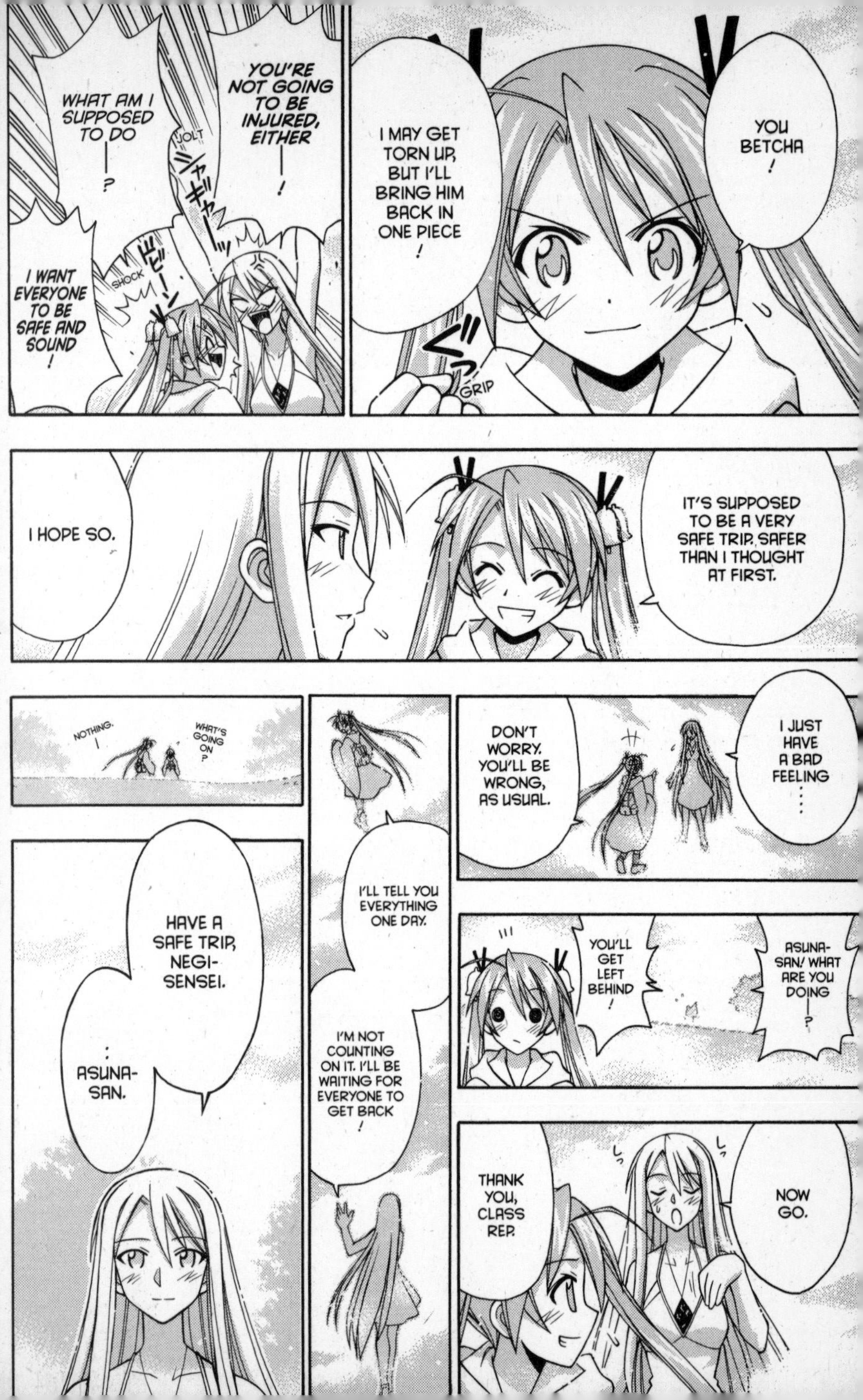
YOU BETCHA!
I MAY GET TORN UP, BUT I'LL BRING HIM BACK IN ONE PIECE!
GRIP
YOU'RE NOT GOING TO BE INJURED, EITHER!
JOLT
WHAT AM I SUPPOSED TO DO?
SHOCK
I WANT EVERYONE TO BE SAFE AND SOUND!
IT'S SUPPOSED TO BE A VERY SAFE TRIP, SAFER THAN I THOUGHT AT FIRST.
I HOPE SO.
I JUST HAVE A BAD FEELING....
DON'T WORRY. YOU'LL BE WRONG, AS USUAL.
ASUNA-SAN! WHAT ARE YOU DOING?
YOU'LL GET LEFT BEHIND!
NOW GO.
THANK YOU, CLASS REP.
WHAT'S GOING ON?
NOTHING.
I'LL TELL YOU EVERYTHING ONE DAY.
I'M NOT COUNTING ON IT. I'LL BE WAITING FOR EVERYONE TO GET BACK!
HAVE A SAFE TRIP, NEGI-SENSEI.
: ASUNA-SAN.

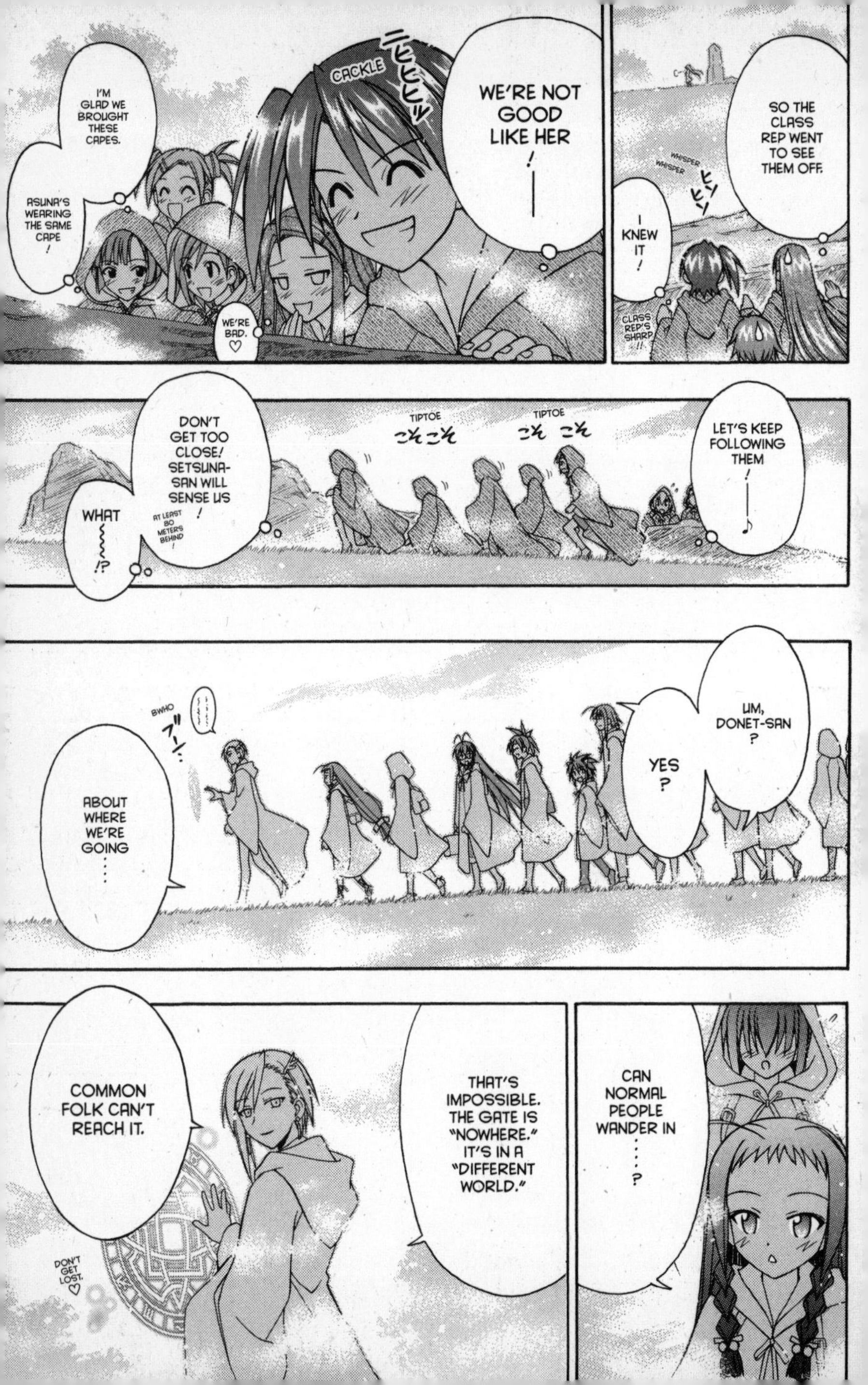
SO THE CLASS REP WENT TO SEE THEM OFF.
WHISPER WHISPER
ヒソヒソ
I KNEW IT!
CLASS REP'S SHARP!!
WE'RE NOT GOOD LIKE HER!
CACKLE
ニヒヒヒッ
I'M GLAD WE BROUGHT THESE CAPES.
ASUNA'S WEARING THE SAME CAPE!
WE'RE BAD. ♡
LET'S KEEP FOLLOWING THEM! ♪
TIPTOE
こそ こそ
TIPTOE
こそこそ
DON'T GET TOO CLOSE! SETSUNA-SAN WILL SENSE US!
AT LEAST 80 METERS BEHIND!
WHAT~~~!?
UM, DONET-SAN?
YES?
BWHO
ブーッ
ABOUT WHERE WE'RE GOING....
CAN NORMAL PEOPLE WANDER IN....?
THAT'S IMPOSSIBLE. THE GATE IS "NOWHERE." IT'S IN A "DIFFERENT WORLD."
COMMON FOLK CAN'T REACH IT.
DON'T GET LOST. ♡

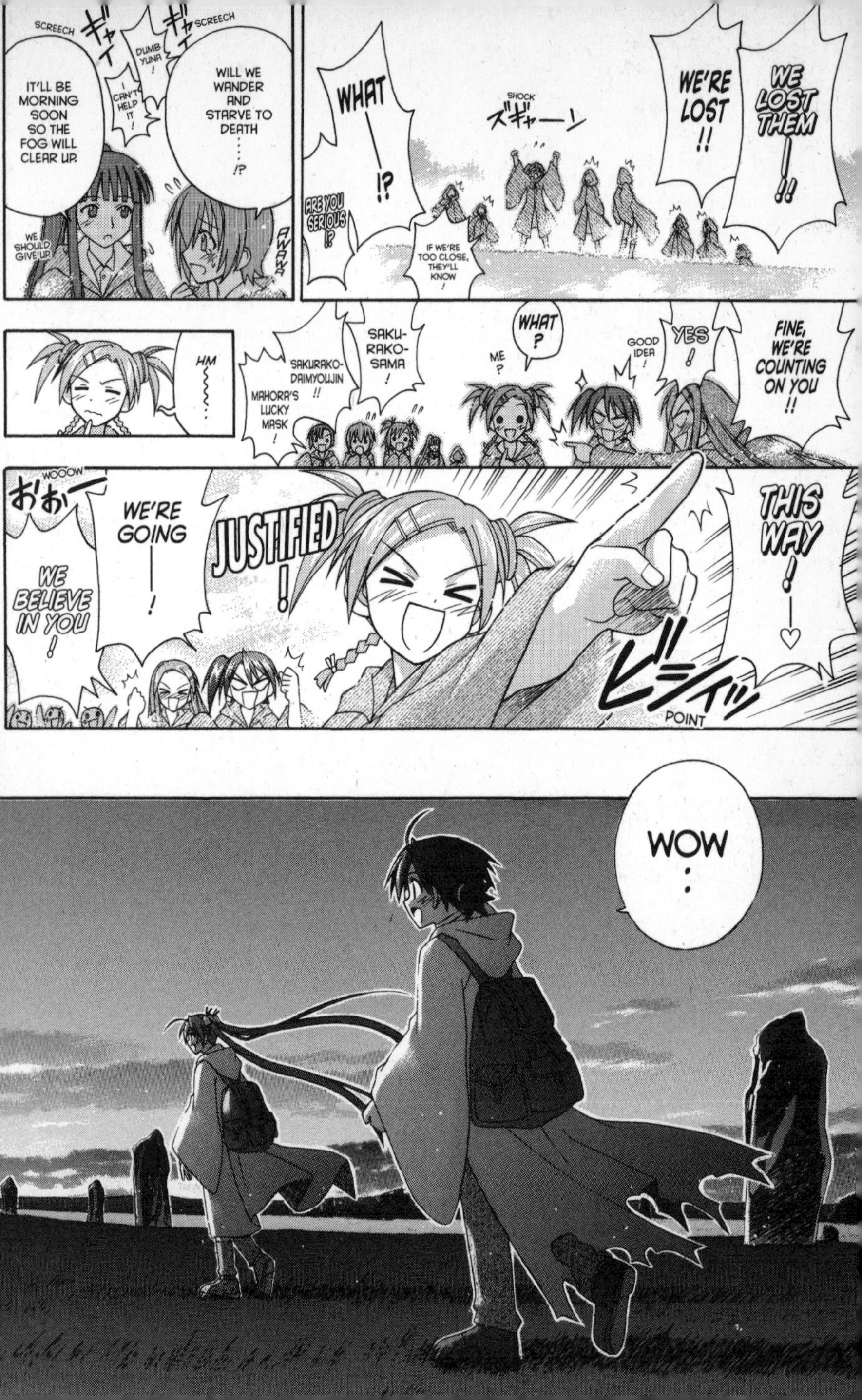
WE LOST THEM—!!
WE'RE LOST!!
SHOCK
WHAT—!?
ARE YOU SERIOUS!?
IF WE'RE TOO CLOSE, THEY'LL KNOW!
SCREECH
WILL WE WANDER AND STARVE TO DEATH.....!?
SCREECH
DUMB YUNA!
I CAN'T HELP IT!
IT'LL BE MORNING SOON SO THE FOG WILL CLEAR UP.
WE SHOULD GIVE UP.
AWAWA
FINE, WE'RE COUNTING ON YOU!!
YES!
GOOD IDEA!
WHAT?
ME?
SAKU-RAKO-SAMA!
SAKURAKO-DAIMYOUJIN!!
MAHORA'S LUCKY MASK!
HM~~~...
THIS WAY!—♥
POINT
JUSTIFIED!
WE'RE GOING—!
WOOOW
WE BELIEVE IN YOU!
WOW..

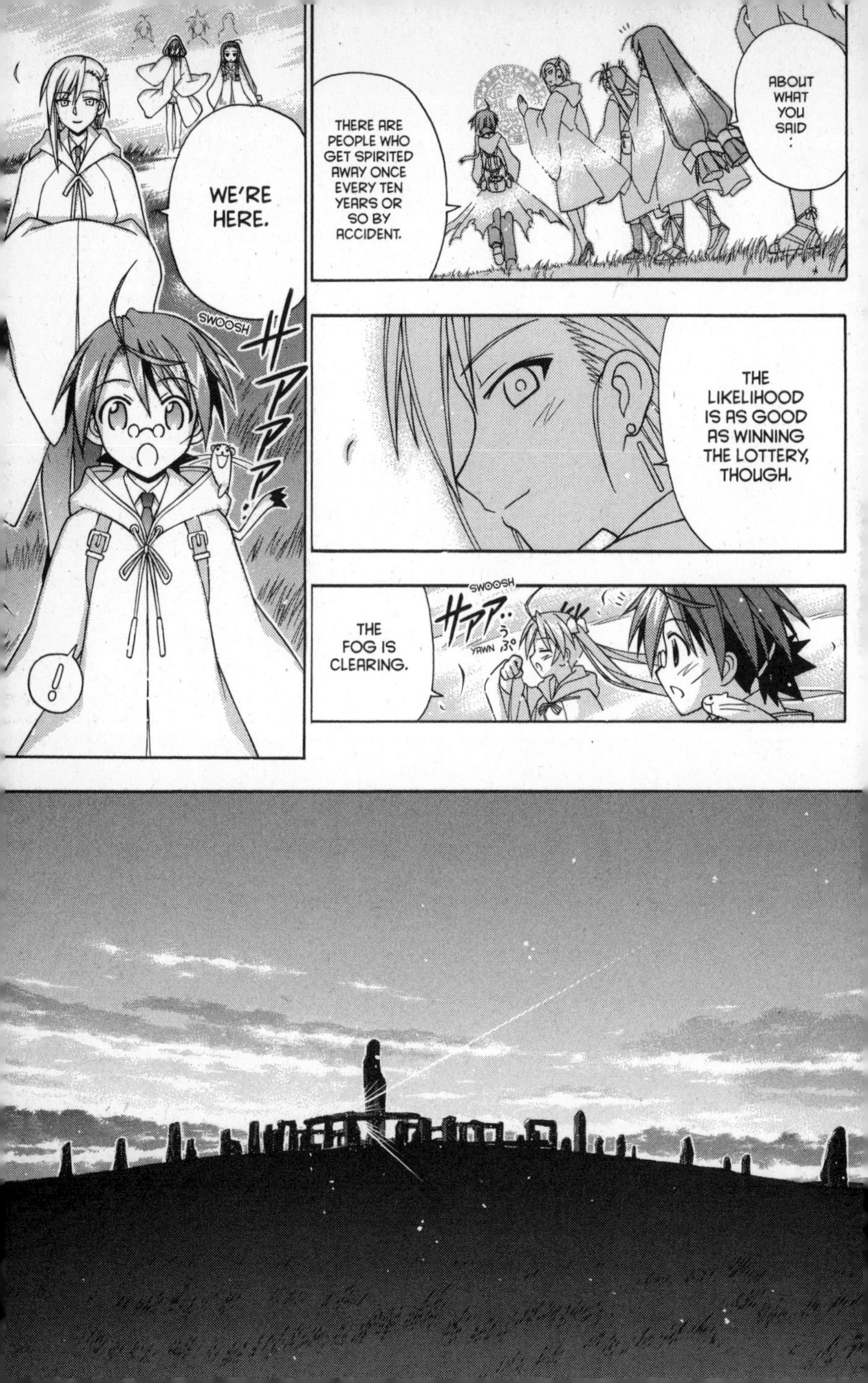
ABOUT WHAT YOU SAID:
THERE ARE PEOPLE WHO GET SPIRITED AWAY ONCE EVERY TEN YEARS OR SO BY ACCIDENT.
THE LIKELIHOOD IS AS GOOD AS WINNING THE LOTTERY, THOUGH.
SWOOSH
サアア
YAWN
ふぷ
THE FOG IS CLEARING.
WE'RE HERE.
SWOOSH
サアアア
!

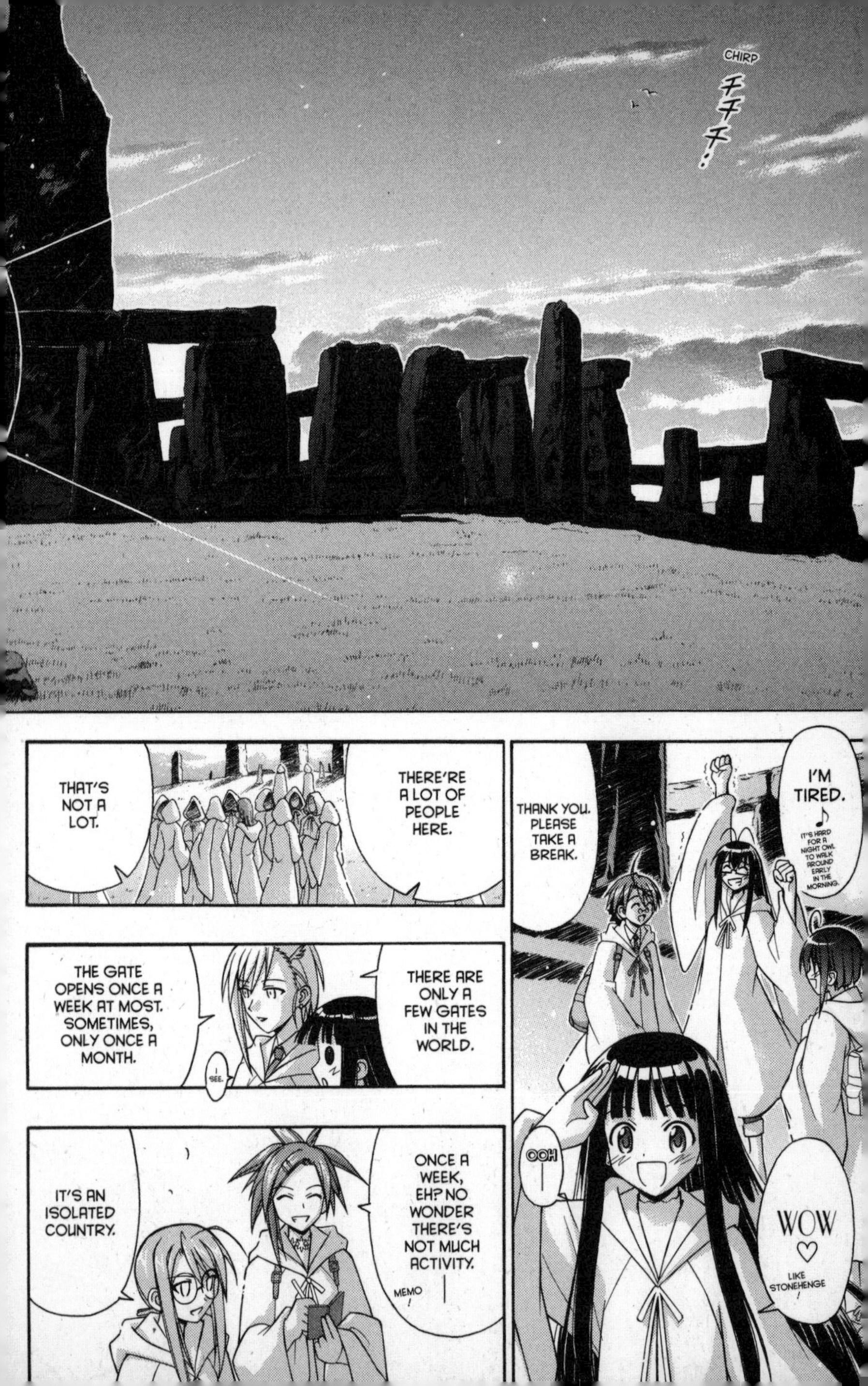
CHIRP
チチチ…
I'M TIRED. ♪
IT'S HARD FOR A NIGHT OWL TO WALK AROUND EARLY IN THE MORNING.
THANK YOU. PLEASE TAKE A BREAK.
WOW ♡
LIKE STONEHENGE!
OOH!
THERE'RE A LOT OF PEOPLE HERE.
THAT'S NOT A LOT.
THERE ARE ONLY A FEW GATES IN THE WORLD.
THE GATE OPENS ONCE A WEEK AT MOST. SOMETIMES, ONLY ONCE A MONTH.
I SEE.
ONCE A WEEK, EH? NO WONDER THERE'S NOT MUCH ACTIVITY.
MEMO!
IT'S AN ISOLATED COUNTRY.

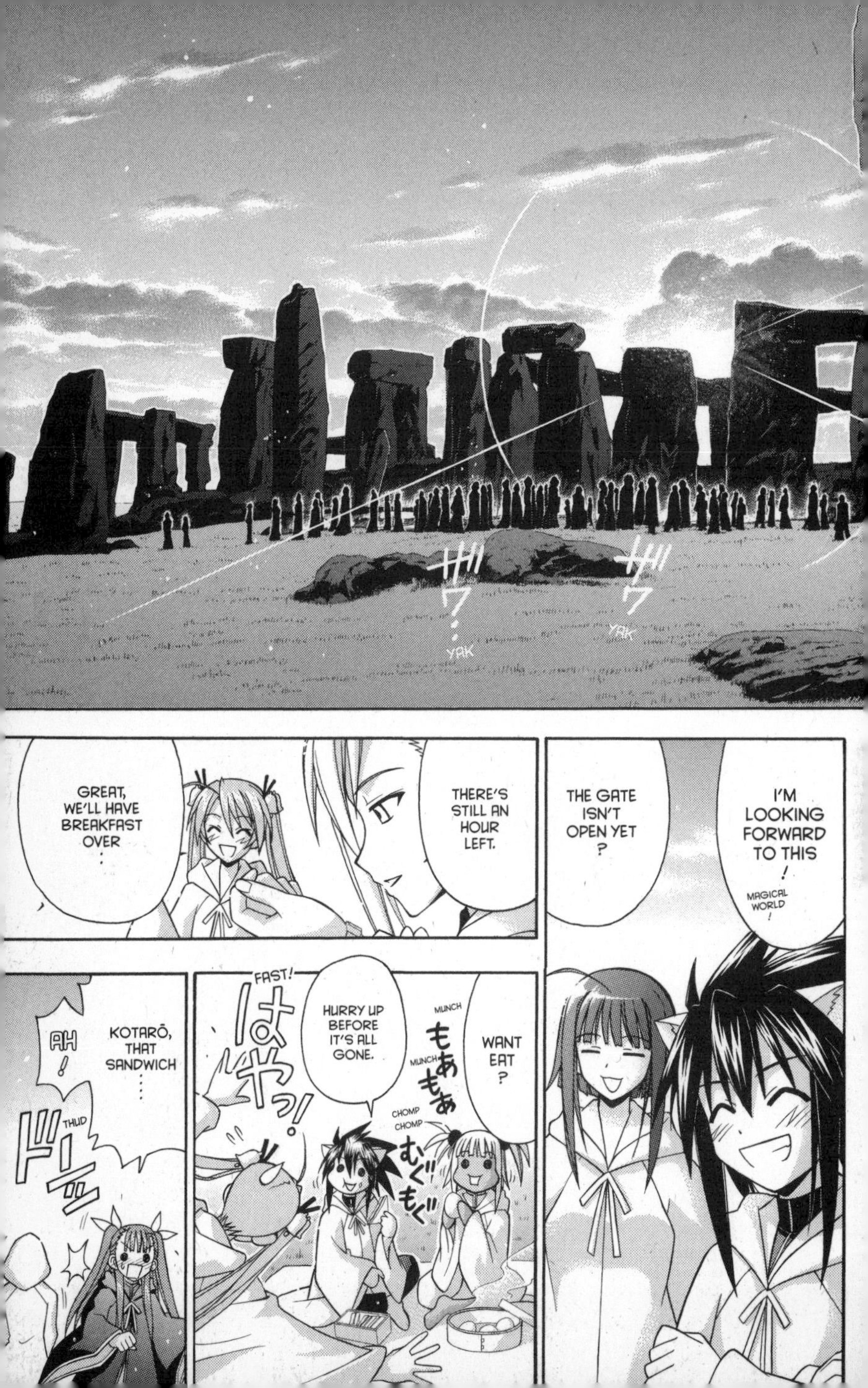
ザワ
YAK
ザワ
YAK
I'M LOOKING FORWARD TO THIS!
MAGICAL WORLD!
THE GATE ISN'T OPEN YET?
THERE'S STILL AN HOUR LEFT.
GREAT, WE'LL HAVE BREAKFAST OVER...
WANT EAT?
MUNCH
もあもあ
MUNCH
HURRY UP BEFORE IT'S ALL GONE.
FAST!
はやっ!
CHOMP CHOMP
むぐ!! もぐ
KOTARŌ, THAT SANDWICH...
AH!
THUD
ドーッ

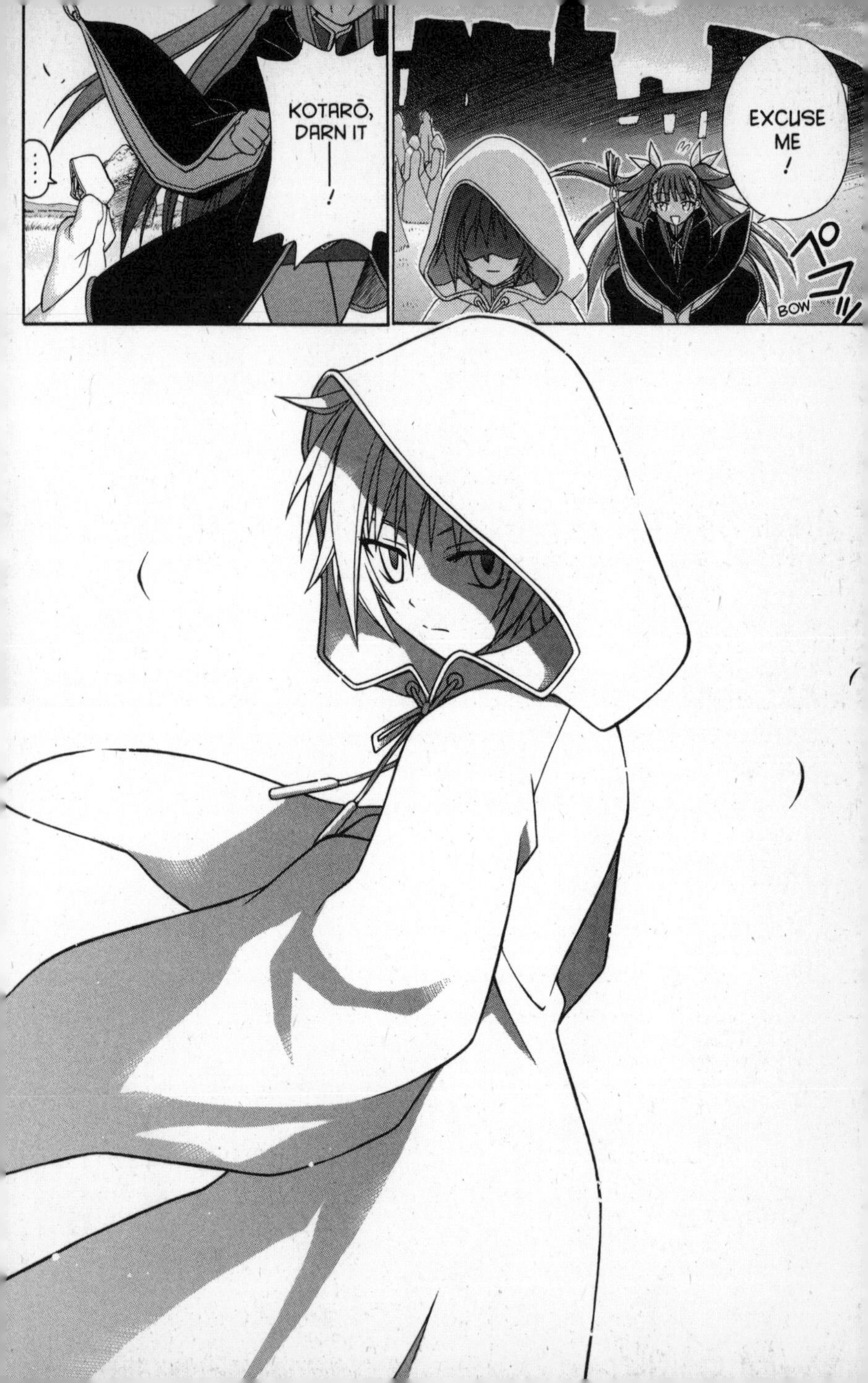
EXCUSE ME!
BOW
KOTARŌ, DARN IT—!
...

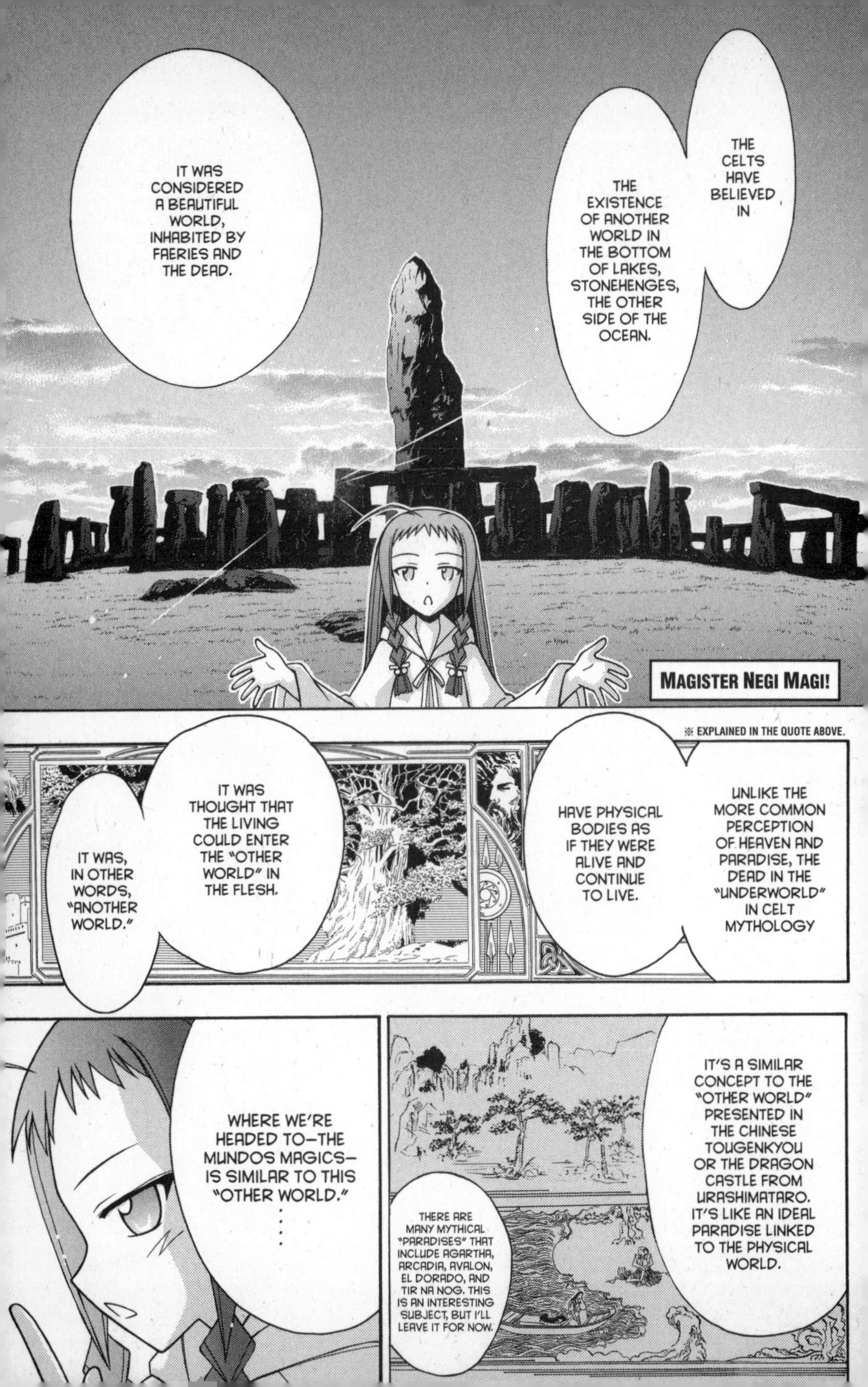
THE CELTS HAVE BELIEVED IN
THE EXISTENCE OF ANOTHER WORLD IN THE BOTTOM OF LAKES, STONEHENGES, THE OTHER SIDE OF THE OCEAN.
IT WAS CONSIDERED A BEAUTIFUL WORLD, INHABITED BY FAERIES AND THE DEAD.
MAGISTER NEGI MAGI!
※ EXPLAINED IN THE QUOTE ABOVE.
UNLIKE THE MORE COMMON PERCEPTION OF HEAVEN AND PARADISE, THE DEAD IN THE "UNDERWORLD" IN CELT MYTHOLOGY
HAVE PHYSICAL BODIES AS IF THEY WERE ALIVE AND CONTINUE TO LIVE.
IT WAS THOUGHT THAT THE LIVING COULD ENTER THE "OTHER WORLD" IN THE FLESH.
IT WAS, IN OTHER WORDS, "ANOTHER WORLD."
IT'S A SIMILAR CONCEPT TO THE "OTHER WORLD" PRESENTED IN THE CHINESE TOUGENKYOU OR THE DRAGON CASTLE FROM URASHIMATARO. IT'S LIKE AN IDEAL PARADISE LINKED TO THE PHYSICAL WORLD.
THERE ARE MANY MYTHICAL "PARADISES" THAT INCLUDE AGARTHA, ARCADIA, AVALON, EL DORADO, AND TIR NA NOG. THIS IS AN INTERESTING SUBJECT, BUT I'LL LEAVE IT FOR NOW.
WHERE WE'RE HEADED TO—THE MUNDOS MAGICS—IS SIMILAR TO THIS "OTHER WORLD."
...

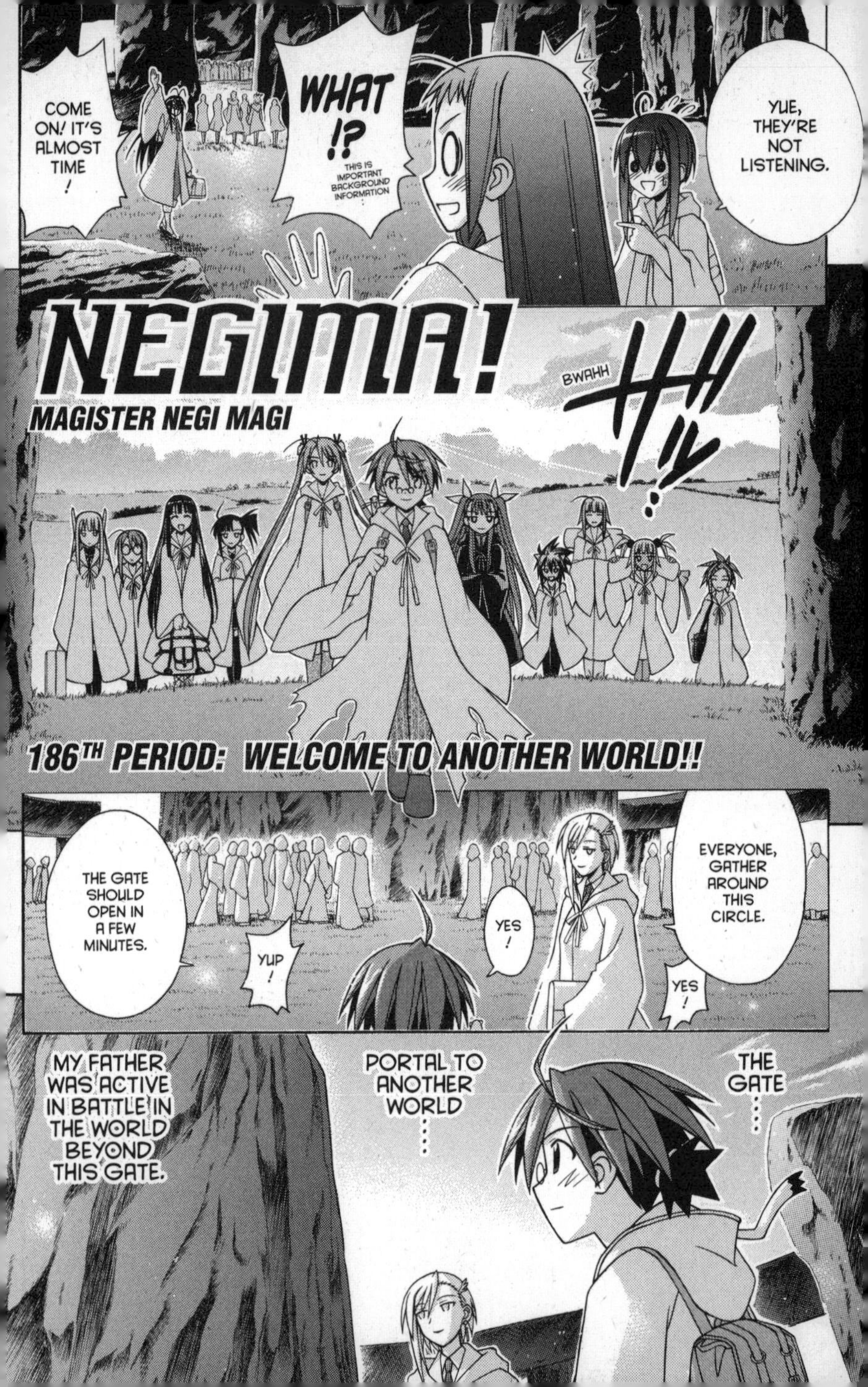
YUE, THEY'RE NOT LISTENING.
WHAT !?
THIS IS IMPORTANT BACKGROUND INFORMATION
COME ON! IT'S ALMOST TIME !
BWAHH
NEGIMA!
MAGISTER NEGI MAGI
186TH PERIOD: WELCOME TO ANOTHER WORLD!!
EVERYONE, GATHER AROUND THIS CIRCLE.
YES !
YES !
YUP !
THE GATE SHOULD OPEN IN A FEW MINUTES.
THE GATE...
PORTAL TO ANOTHER WORLD...
MY FATHER WAS ACTIVE IN BATTLE IN THE WORLD BEYOND THIS GATE.

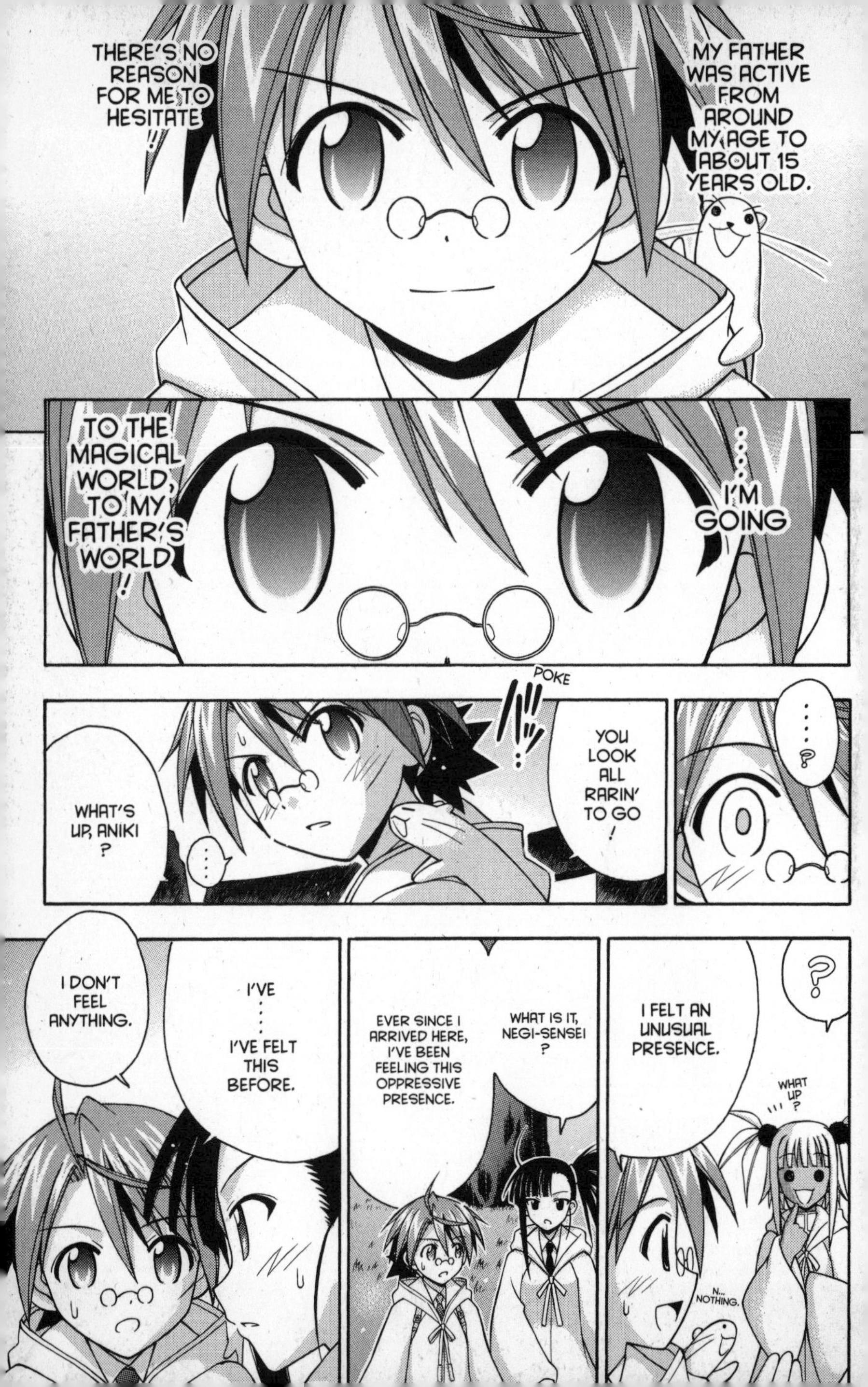
MY FATHER WAS ACTIVE FROM AROUND MY AGE TO ABOUT 15 YEARS OLD.
THERE'S NO REASON FOR ME TO HESITATE!
...I'M GOING
TO THE MAGICAL WORLD, TO MY FATHER'S WORLD!
...?
POKE
YOU LOOK ALL RARIN' TO GO!
WHAT'S UP, ANIKI?
...
?
I FELT AN UNUSUAL PRESENCE.
WHAT UP?
N... NOTHING.
WHAT IS IT, NEGI-SENSEI?
EVER SINCE I ARRIVED HERE, I'VE BEEN FEELING THIS OPPRESSIVE PRESENCE.
I'VE... I'VE FELT THIS BEFORE.
I DON'T FEEL ANYTHING.

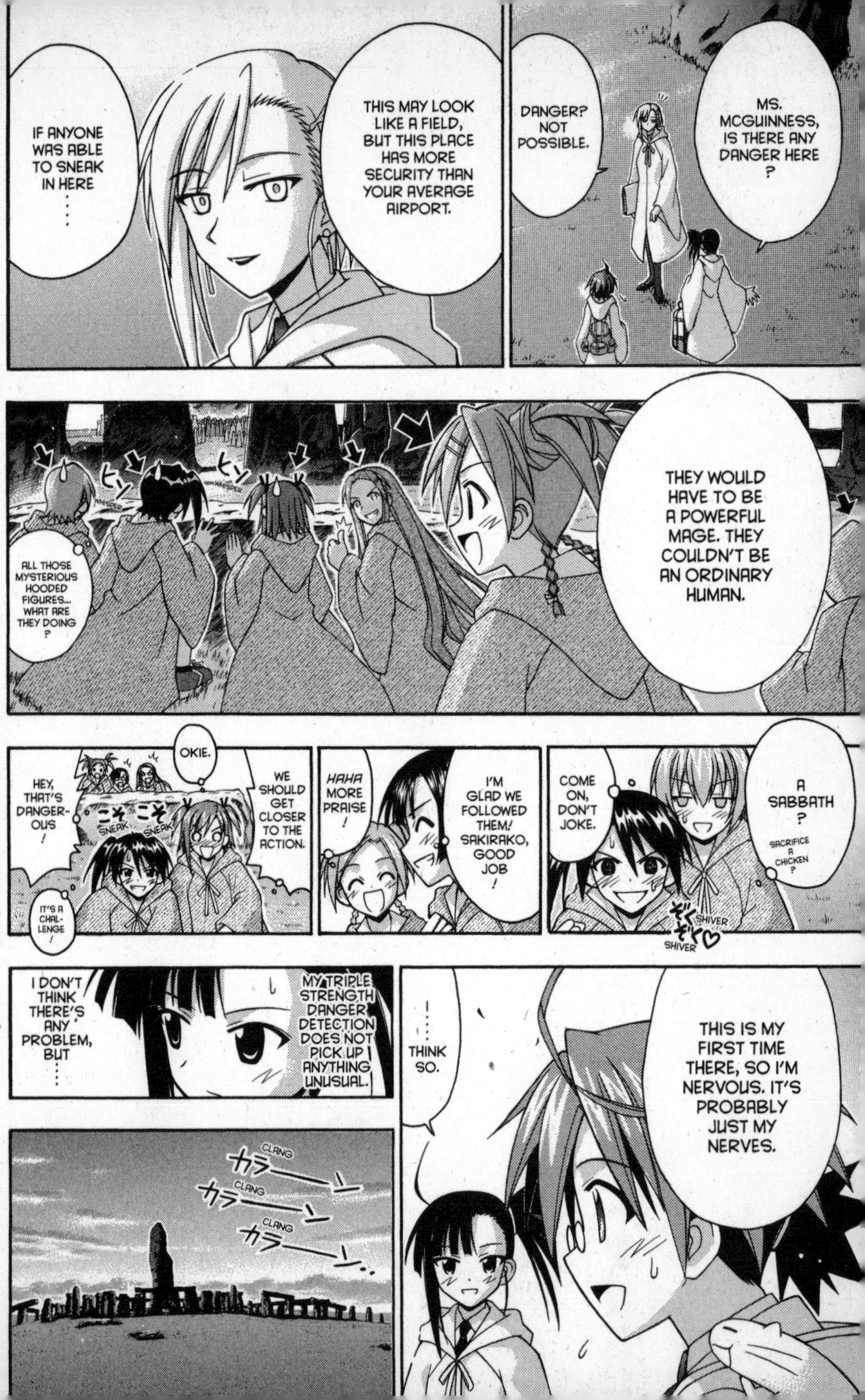
MS. MCGUINNESS, IS THERE ANY DANGER HERE?
DANGER? NOT POSSIBLE.
THIS MAY LOOK LIKE A FIELD, BUT THIS PLACE HAS MORE SECURITY THAN YOUR AVERAGE AIRPORT.
IF ANYONE WAS ABLE TO SNEAK IN HERE ...
THEY WOULD HAVE TO BE A POWERFUL MAGE. THEY COULDN'T BE AN ORDINARY HUMAN.
WHISPER
WHISPER
ALL THOSE MYSTERIOUS HOODED FIGURES... WHAT ARE THEY DOING?
A SABBATH?
SACRIFICE A CHICKEN?
COME ON, DON'T JOKE.
SHIVER
SHIVER
I'M GLAD WE FOLLOWED THEM! SAKIRAKO, GOOD JOB!
HAHA MORE PRAISE!
WE SHOULD GET CLOSER TO THE ACTION.
OKIE.
HEY, THAT'S DANGER-OUS!
SNEAK
SNEAK
IT'S A CHAL-LENGE!
THIS IS MY FIRST TIME THERE, SO I'M NERVOUS. IT'S PROBABLY JUST MY NERVES.
I ... THINK SO.
MY TRIPLE STRENGTH DANGER DETECTION DOES NOT PICK UP ANYTHING UNUSUAL.
I DON'T THINK THERE'S ANY PROBLEM, BUT ....
CLANG
CLANG
CLANG

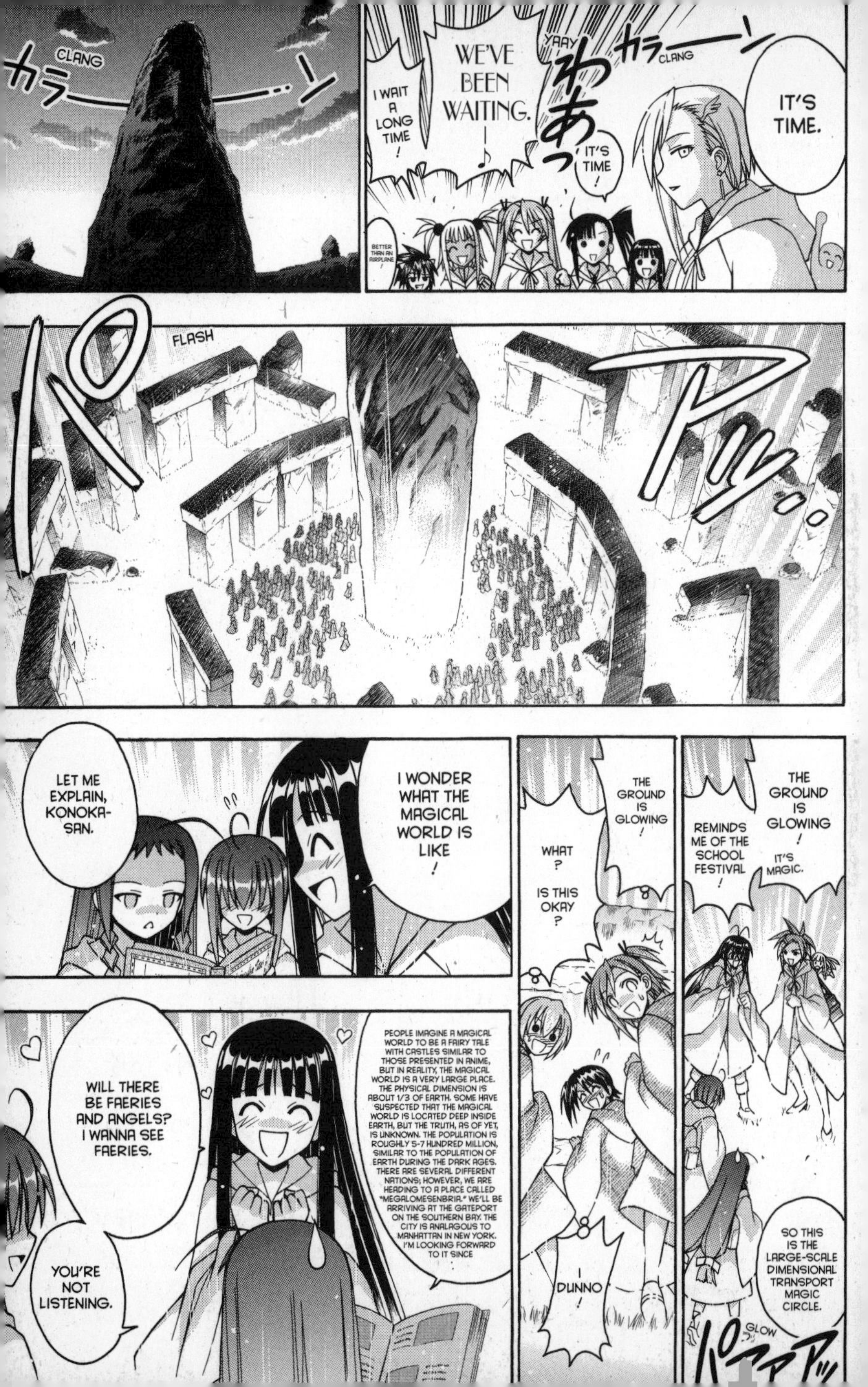
IT'S TIME.
カラーーン CLANG
わあっ YAAY
IT'S TIME!
WE'VE BEEN WAITING. ! ♪
I WAIT A LONG TIME!
BETTER THAN AN AIRPLANE!
CLANG カラーーーン
パアッ
FLASH
THE GROUND IS GLOWING!
IT'S MAGIC.
REMINDS ME OF THE SCHOOL FESTIVAL!
SO THIS IS THE LARGE-SCALE DIMENSIONAL TRANSPORT MAGIC CIRCLE.
パァァァッ GLOW
THE GROUND IS GLOWING!
WHAT? IS THIS OKAY?
I DUNNO!
I WONDER WHAT THE MAGICAL WORLD IS LIKE!
LET ME EXPLAIN, KONOKA-SAN.
PEOPLE IMAGINE A MAGICAL WORLD TO BE A FAIRY TALE WITH CASTLES SIMILAR TO THOSE PRESENTED IN ANIME, BUT IN REALITY, THE MAGICAL WORLD IS A VERY LARGE PLACE. THE PHYSICAL DIMENSION IS ABOUT 1/3 OF EARTH. SOME HAVE SUSPECTED THAT THE MAGICAL WORLD IS LOCATED DEEP INSIDE EARTH, BUT THE TRUTH, AS OF YET, IS UNKNOWN. THE POPULATION IS ROUGHLY 5-7 HUNDRED MILLION, SIMILAR TO THE POPULATION OF EARTH DURING THE DARK AGES. THERE ARE SEVERAL DIFFERENT NATIONS; HOWEVER, WE ARE HEADING TO A PLACE CALLED "MEGALOMESENBRIA." WE'LL BE ARRIVING AT THE GATEPORT ON THE SOUTHERN BAY. THE CITY IS ANALAGOUS TO MANHATTAN IN NEW YORK. I'M LOOKING FORWARD TO IT SINCE
WILL THERE BE FAERIES AND ANGELS? I WANNA SEE FAERIES.
YOU'RE NOT LISTENING.

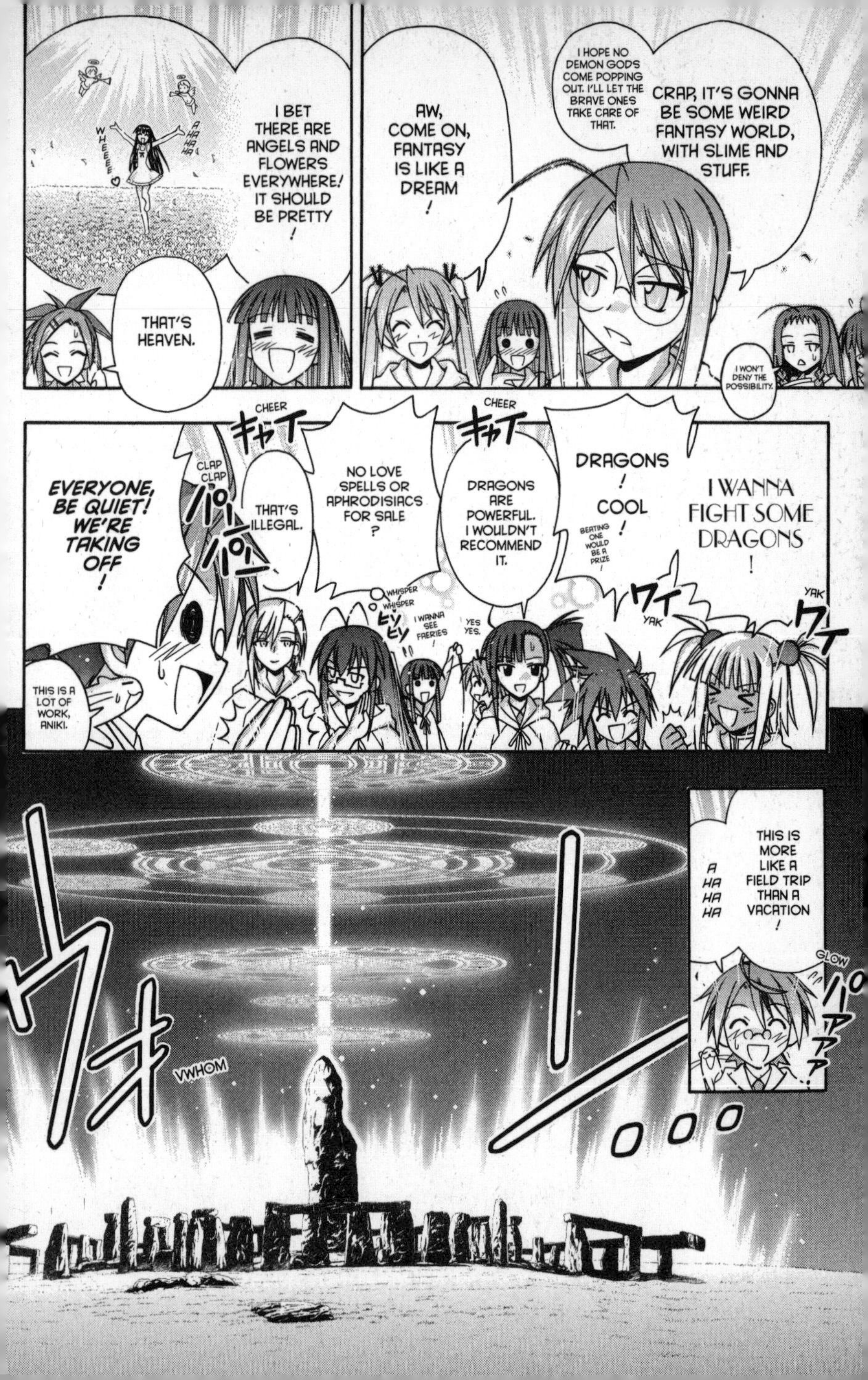
CRAP, IT'S GONNA BE SOME WEIRD FANTASY WORLD, WITH SLIME AND STUFF.
I HOPE NO DEMON GODS COME POPPING OUT. I'LL LET THE BRAVE ONES TAKE CARE OF THAT.
AW, COME ON, FANTASY IS LIKE A DREAM!
I WON'T DENY THE POSSIBILITY.
I BET THERE ARE ANGELS AND FLOWERS EVERYWHERE! IT SHOULD BE PRETTY!
A HA HA HA
WHEEEE
THAT'S HEAVEN.
I WANNA FIGHT SOME DRAGONS!
YAK
YAK
DRAGONS! COOL!
BEATING ONE WOULD BE A PRIZE!
CHEER
DRAGONS ARE POWERFUL. I WOULDN'T RECOMMEND IT.
YES YES.
I WANNA SEE FAERIES!
NO LOVE SPELLS OR APHRODISIACS FOR SALE?
WHISPER WHISPER
CHEER
THAT'S ILLEGAL.
CLAP CLAP
EVERYONE, BE QUIET! WE'RE TAKING OFF!
THIS IS A LOT OF WORK, ANIKI.
THIS IS MORE LIKE A FIELD TRIP THAN A VACATION!
A HA HA HA
GLOW
VWHOM

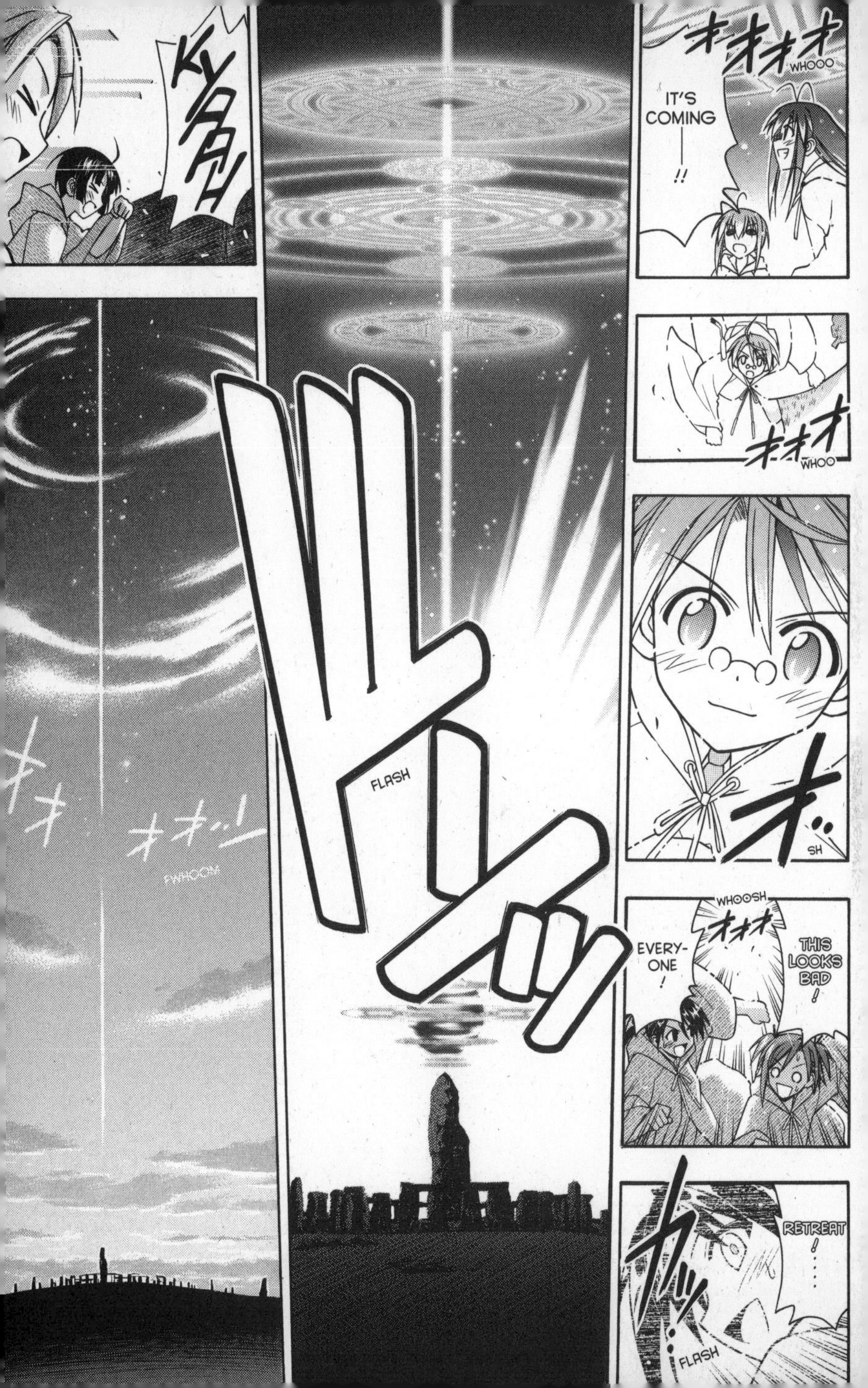
WHOOO
IT'S COMING——!!
WHOO
SH
WHOOSH
THIS LOOKS BAD!
EVERY-ONE!
RETREAT!......
FLASH
FLASH
FWHOOM

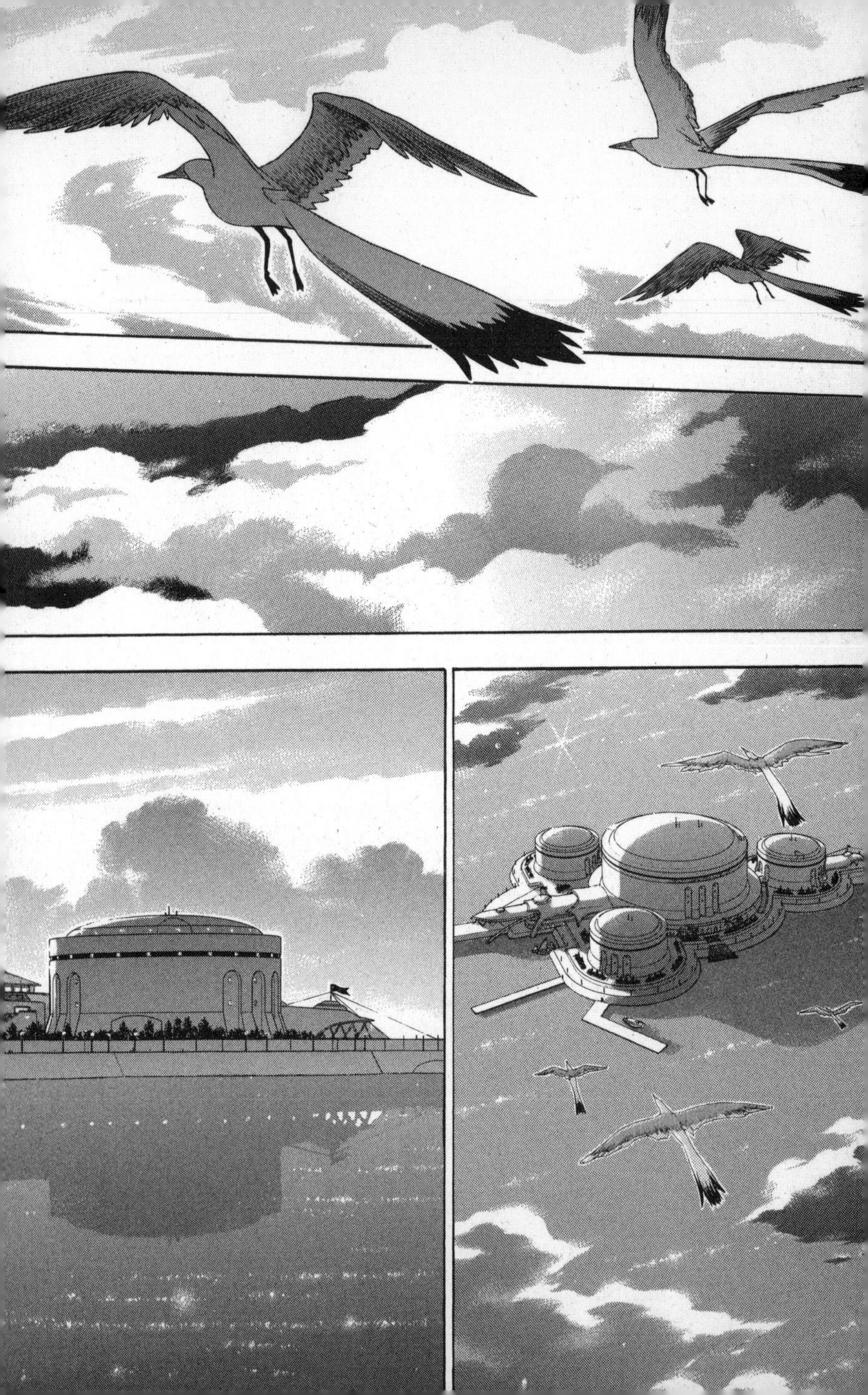

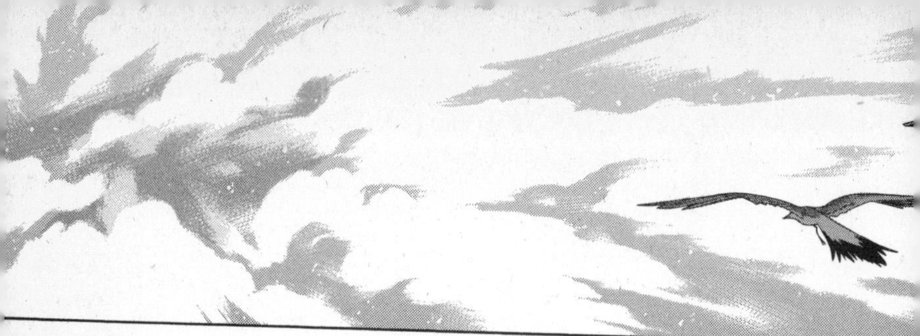

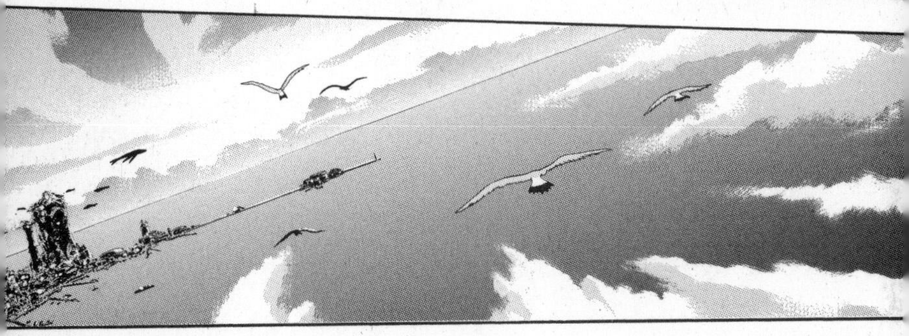

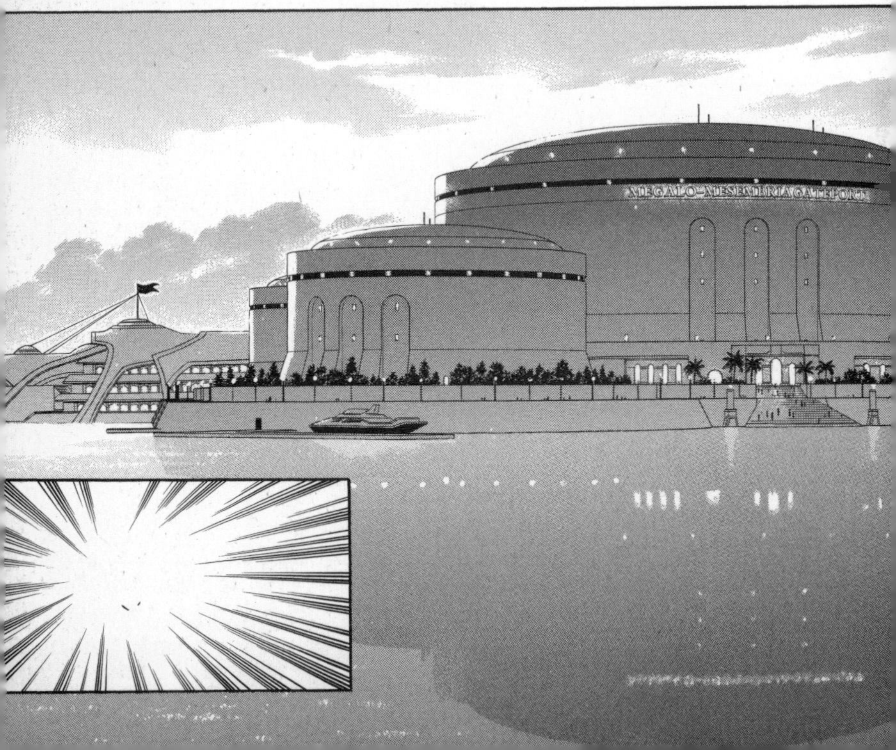
MEGALO-MESEMBRIA GATEPORT

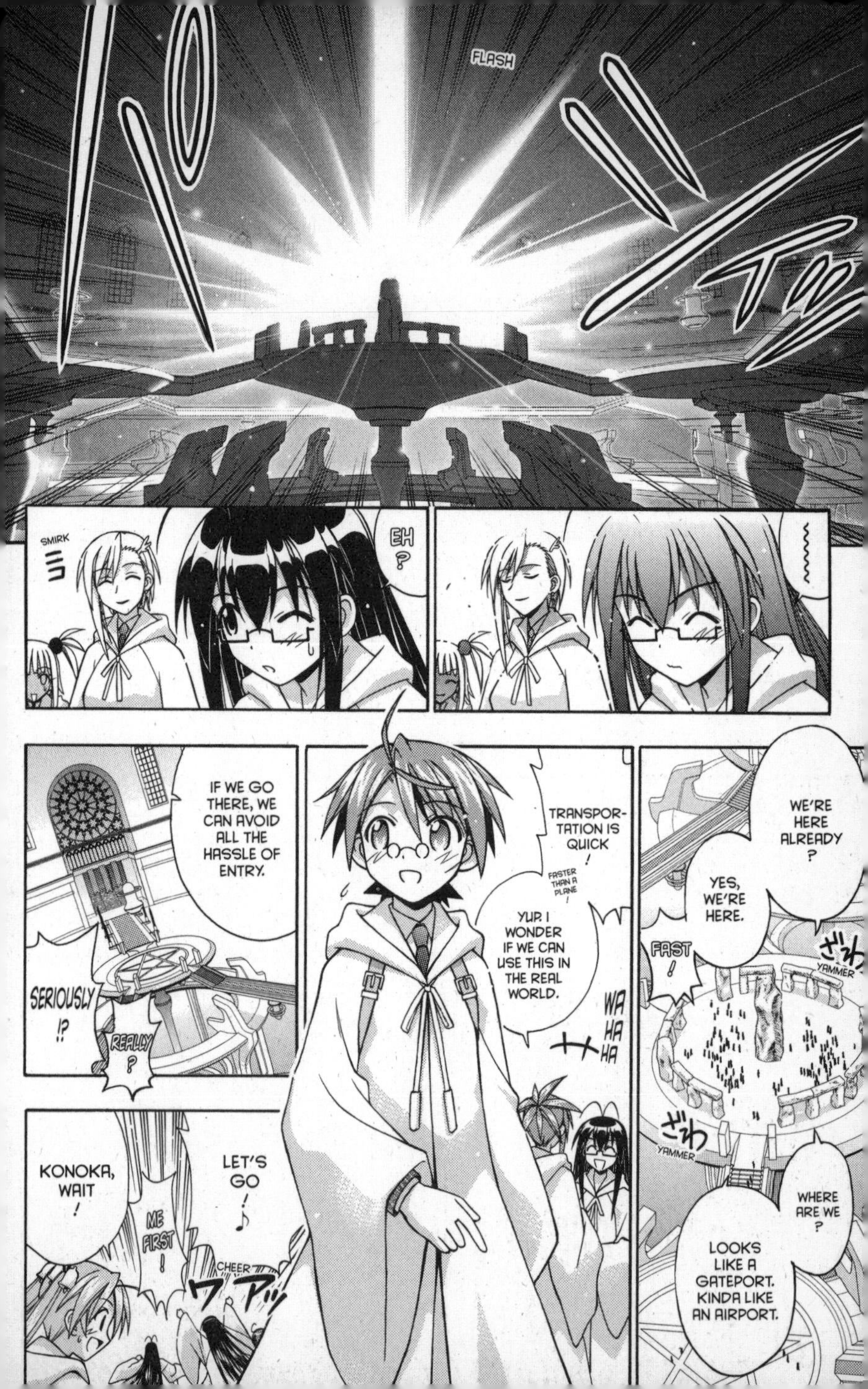
FLASH
EH?
SMIRK
WE'RE HERE ALREADY?
YES, WE'RE HERE.
FAST!
ざわ
YAMMER
ざわ
YAMMER
WHERE ARE WE?
LOOKS LIKE A GATEPORT. KINDA LIKE AN AIRPORT.
TRANSPORTATION IS QUICK!
FASTER THAN A PLANE!
YUP. I WONDER IF WE CAN USE THIS IN THE REAL WORLD.
WA HA HA
IF WE GO THERE, WE CAN AVOID ALL THE HASSLE OF ENTRY.
SERIOUSLY!?
REALLY?
LET'S GO! ♪
KONOKA, WAIT!
ME FIRST!
CHEER

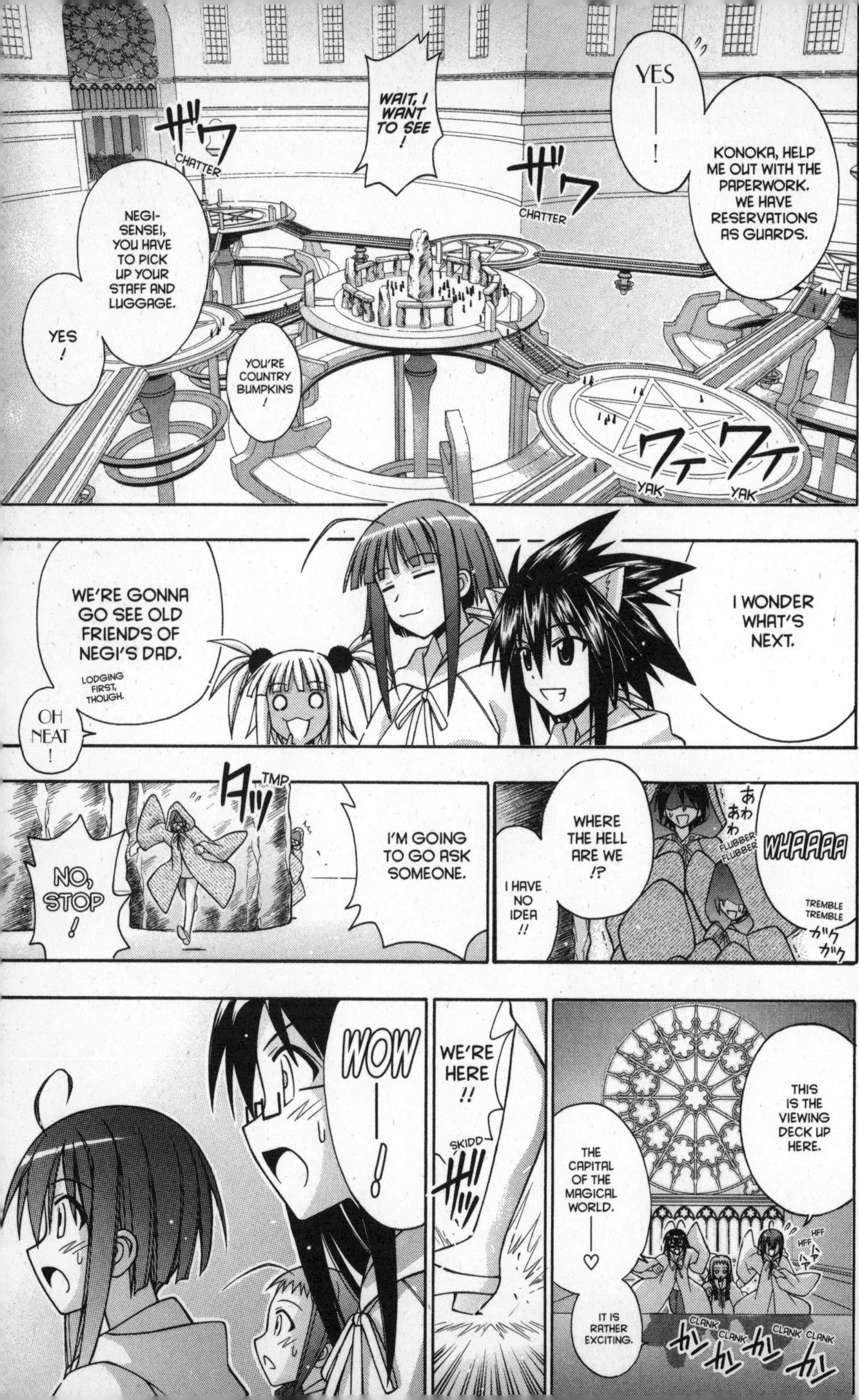
YES—!
KONOKA, HELP ME OUT WITH THE PAPERWORK. WE HAVE RESERVATIONS AS GUARDS.
CHATTER
WAIT, I WANT TO SEE!
CHATTER
NEGI-SENSEI, YOU HAVE TO PICK UP YOUR STAFF AND LUGGAGE.
YES!
YOU'RE COUNTRY BUMPKINS!
YAK YAK
I WONDER WHAT'S NEXT.
WE'RE GONNA GO SEE OLD FRIENDS OF NEGI'S DAD.
LODGING FIRST, THOUGH.
OH NEAT!
WHAAAAA
FLUBBER FLUBBER
WHERE THE HELL ARE WE!?
I HAVE NO IDEA!!
TREMBLE TREMBLE
I'M GOING TO GO ASK SOMEONE.
TMP
NO, STOP!
THIS IS THE VIEWING DECK UP HERE.
THE CAPITAL OF THE MAGICAL WORLD—♡
HFF HFF
IT IS RATHER EXCITING.
CLANK CLANK CLANK CLANK
WE'RE HERE!!
SKIDD
WOW—!

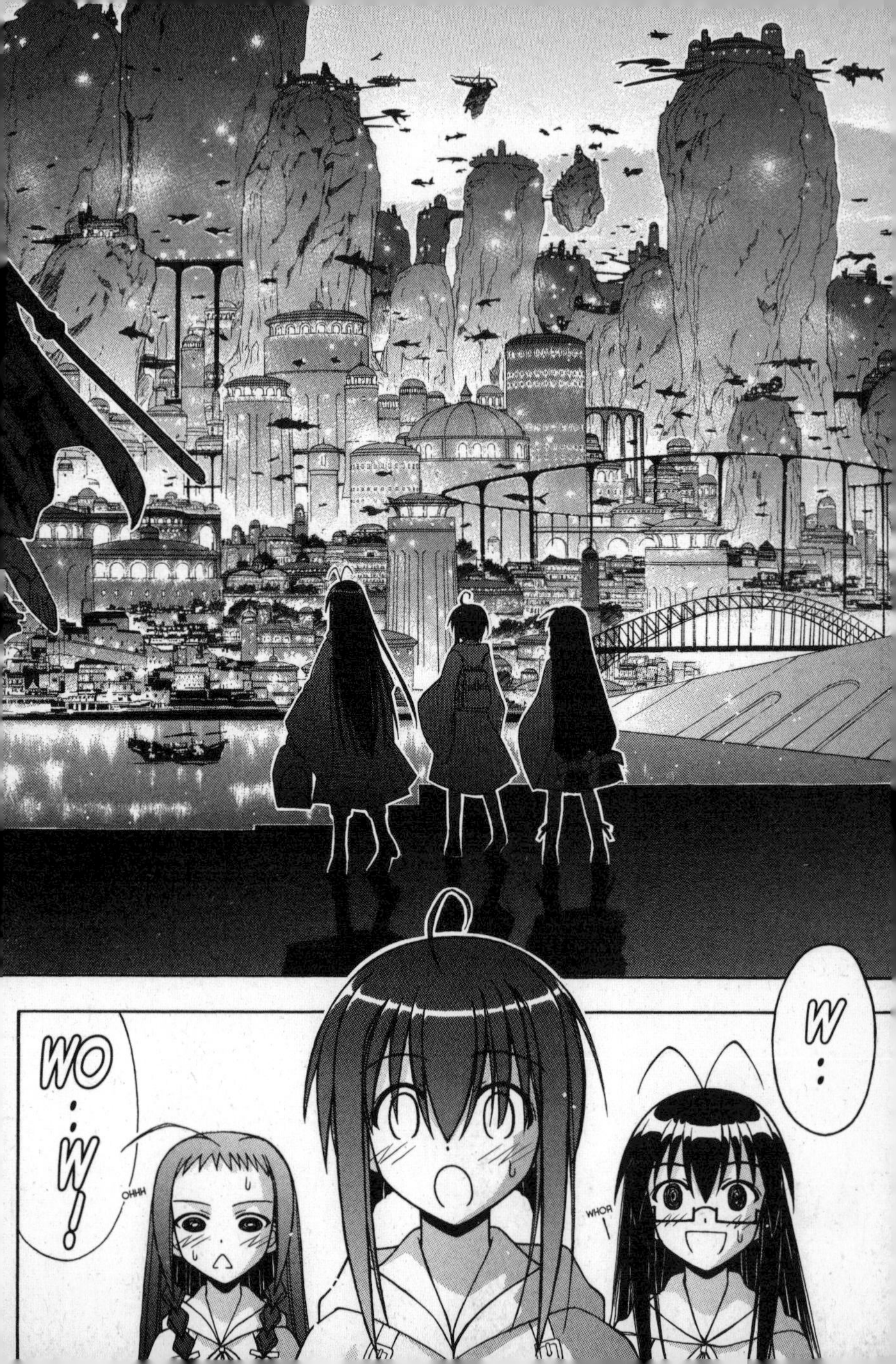
W..
WHOA
OHHH
WO...W!

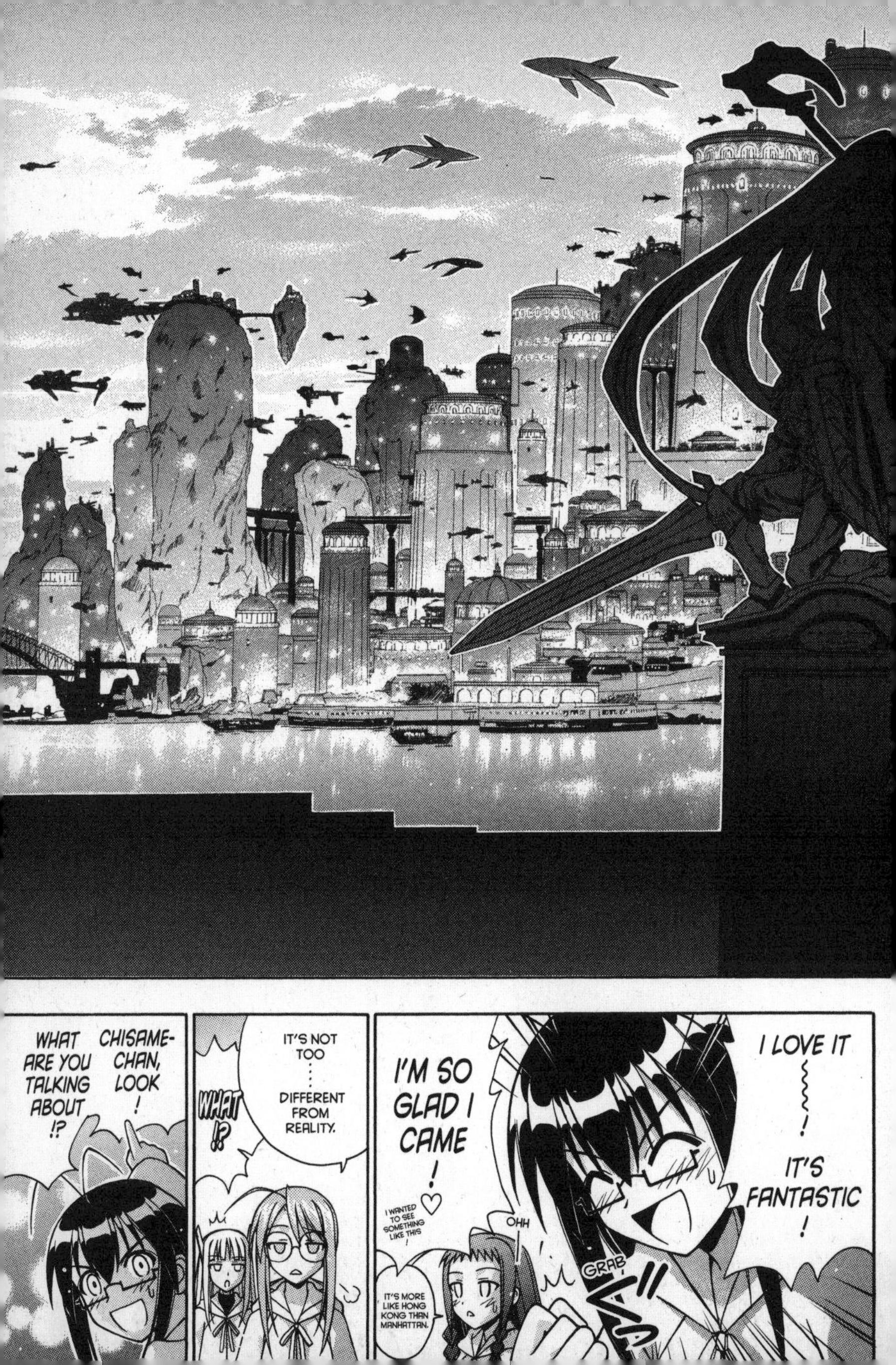
I LOVE IT ~~~!
IT'S FANTASTIC!
I'M SO GLAD I CAME!
I WANTED TO SEE SOMETHING LIKE THIS!
OHH
GRAB
IT'S MORE LIKE HONG KONG THAN MANHATTAN.
IT'S NOT TOO ... DIFFERENT FROM REALITY.
WHAT!?
CHISAME-CHAN, LOOK!
WHAT ARE YOU TALKING ABOUT!?

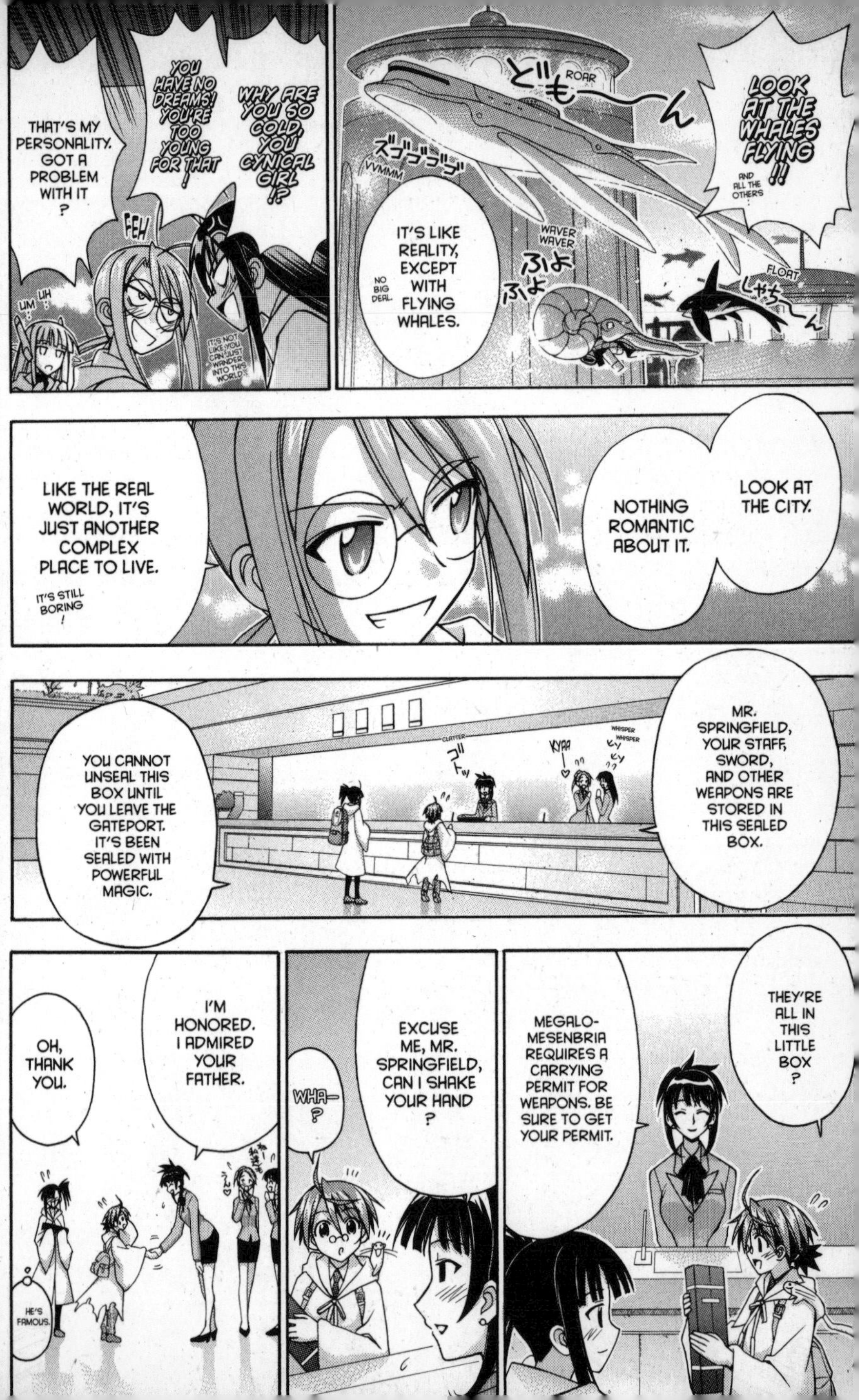
LOOK AT THE WHALES FLYING!!
AND ALL THE OTHERS
どーん
ROAR
ズゴゴゴゴ
VVMMM
IT'S LIKE REALITY, EXCEPT WITH FLYING WHALES.
NO BIG DEAL.
WAVER WAVER
ふよふよ
FLOAT
しゃちーん
WHY ARE YOU SO COLD, YOU CYNICAL GIRL!?
YOU HAVE NO DREAMS! YOU'RE TOO YOUNG FOR THAT!
THAT'S MY PERSONALITY. GOT A PROBLEM WITH IT?
FEH
IT'S NOT LIKE YOU CAN JUST WANDER INTO THIS WORLD.
UH
UM
LOOK AT THE CITY.
NOTHING ROMANTIC ABOUT IT.
LIKE THE REAL WORLD, IT'S JUST ANOTHER COMPLEX PLACE TO LIVE.
IT'S STILL BORING!
MR. SPRINGFIELD, YOUR STAFF, SWORD, AND OTHER WEAPONS ARE STORED IN THIS SEALED BOX.
WHISPER WHISPER
ヒソヒソ
KYAA
CLATTER
ゴトッ
YOU CANNOT UNSEAL THIS BOX UNTIL YOU LEAVE THE GATEPORT. IT'S BEEN SEALED WITH POWERFUL MAGIC.
THEY'RE ALL IN THIS LITTLE BOX?
MEGALO-MESENBRIA REQUIRES A CARRYING PERMIT FOR WEAPONS. BE SURE TO GET YOUR PERMIT.
EXCUSE ME, MR. SPRINGFIELD, CAN I SHAKE YOUR HAND?
WHA—?
I'M HONORED. I ADMIRED YOUR FATHER.
OH, THANK YOU.
HE'S FAMOUS.

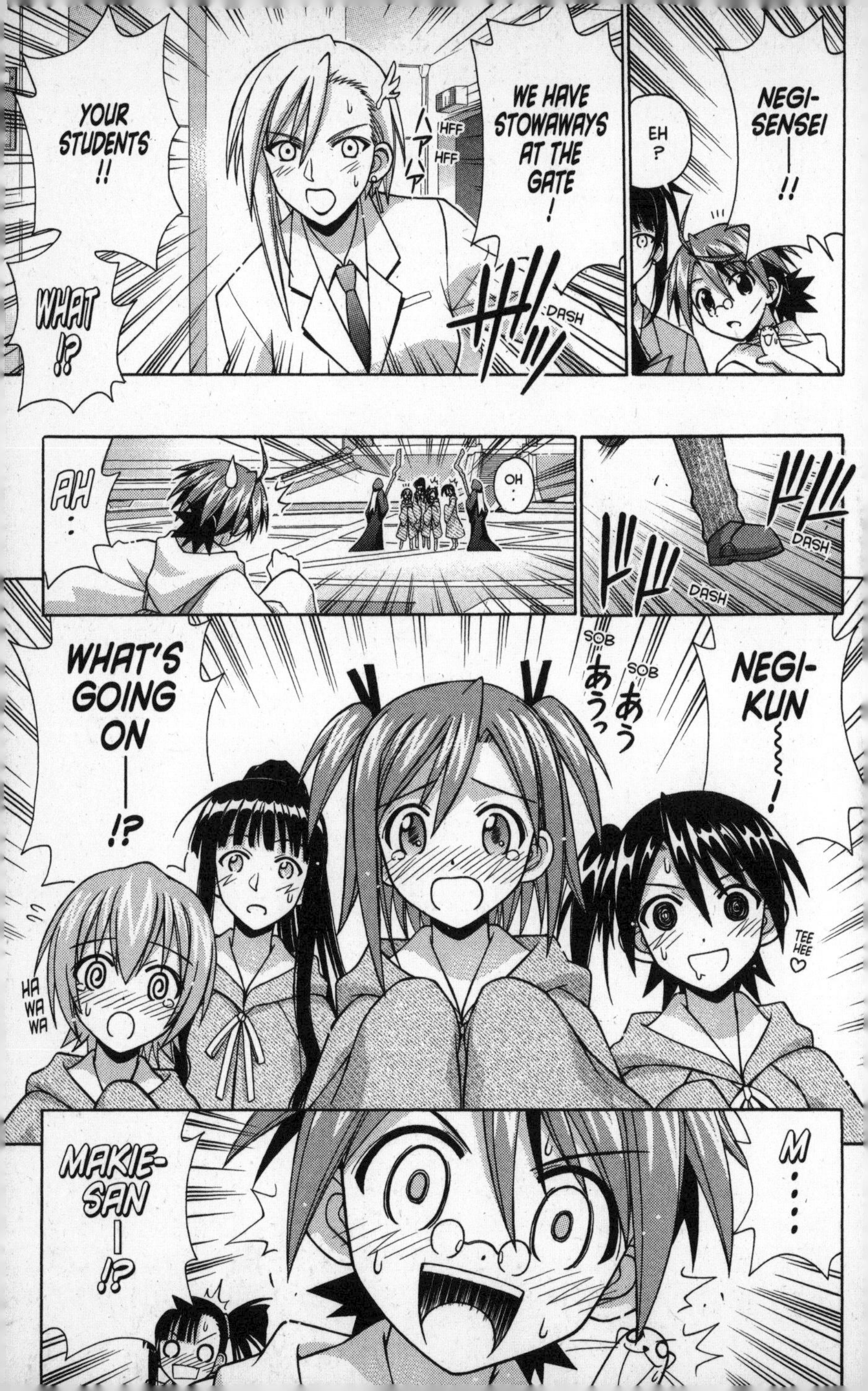
NEGI-SENSEI —— !!
EH ?
WE HAVE STOWAWAYS AT THE GATE !
ハアハア
HFF HFF
DASH
YOUR STUDENTS !!
WHAT !?
DASH
DASH
OH . .
AH . .
NEGI-KUN ~~~ !
あう SOB
あうっ SOB
TEE HEE ♡
WHAT'S GOING ON —— !?
HA WA WA
M . . . .
MAKIE-SAN — !?

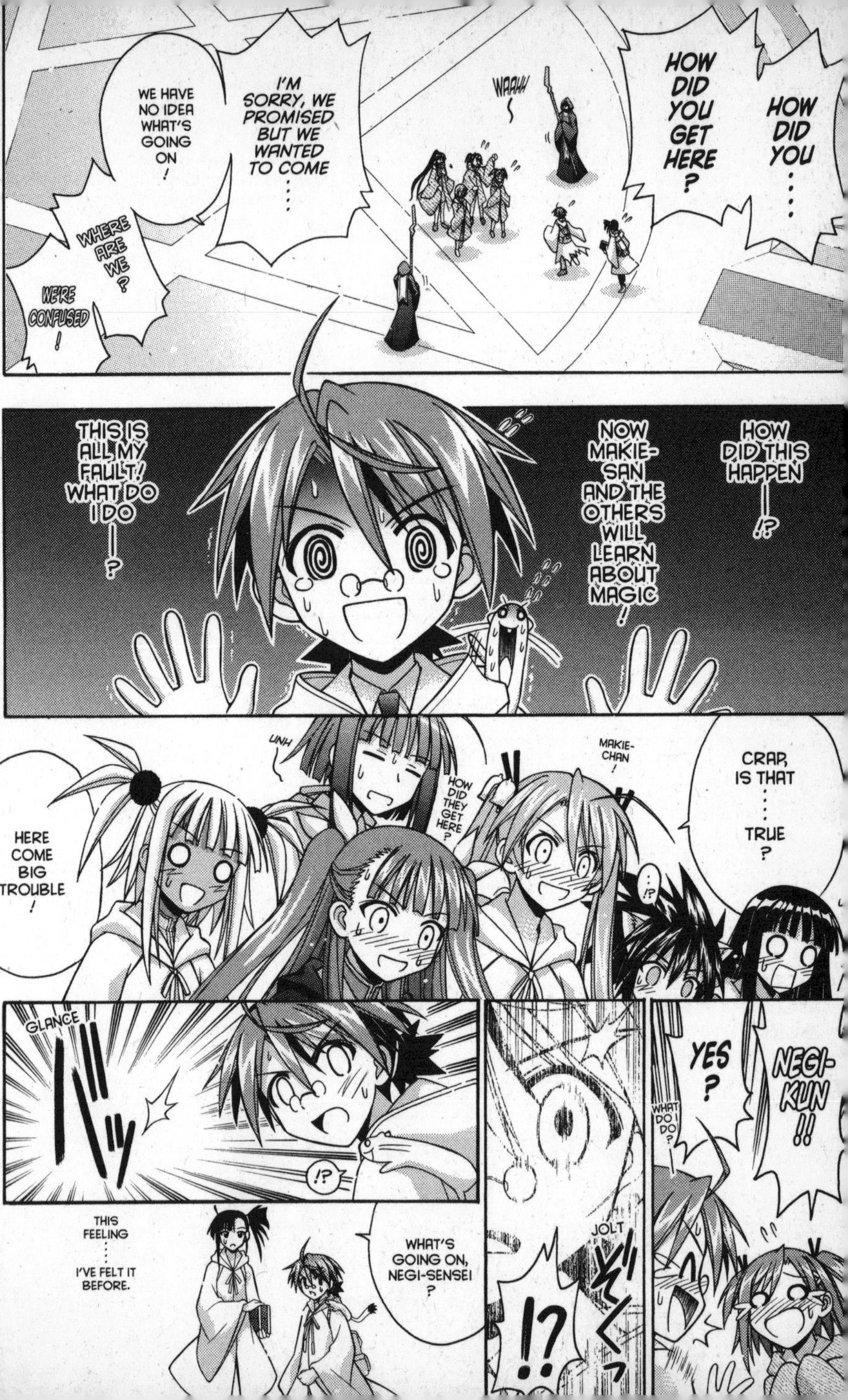
HOW DID YOU......
HOW DID YOU GET HERE?
WAAHH~
I'M SORRY, WE PROMISED BUT WE WANTED TO COME......
WE HAVE NO IDEA WHAT'S GOING ON!
WHERE ARE WE?
WE'RE CONFUSED!
HOW DID THIS HAPPEN—!?
NOW MAKIE-SAN AND THE OTHERS WILL LEARN ABOUT MAGIC!
THIS IS ALL MY FAULT! WHAT DO I DO—?
CRAP, IS THAT......TRUE?
MAKIE-CHAN!
...!?
HOW DID THEY GET HERE?
UNH~
HERE COME BIG TROUBLE!
NEGI-KUN!!
YES?
WHAT DO I DO?!
JOLT
!?
GLANCE
!?
WHAT'S GOING ON, NEGI-SENSEI?
THIS FEELING...... I'VE FELT IT BEFORE.

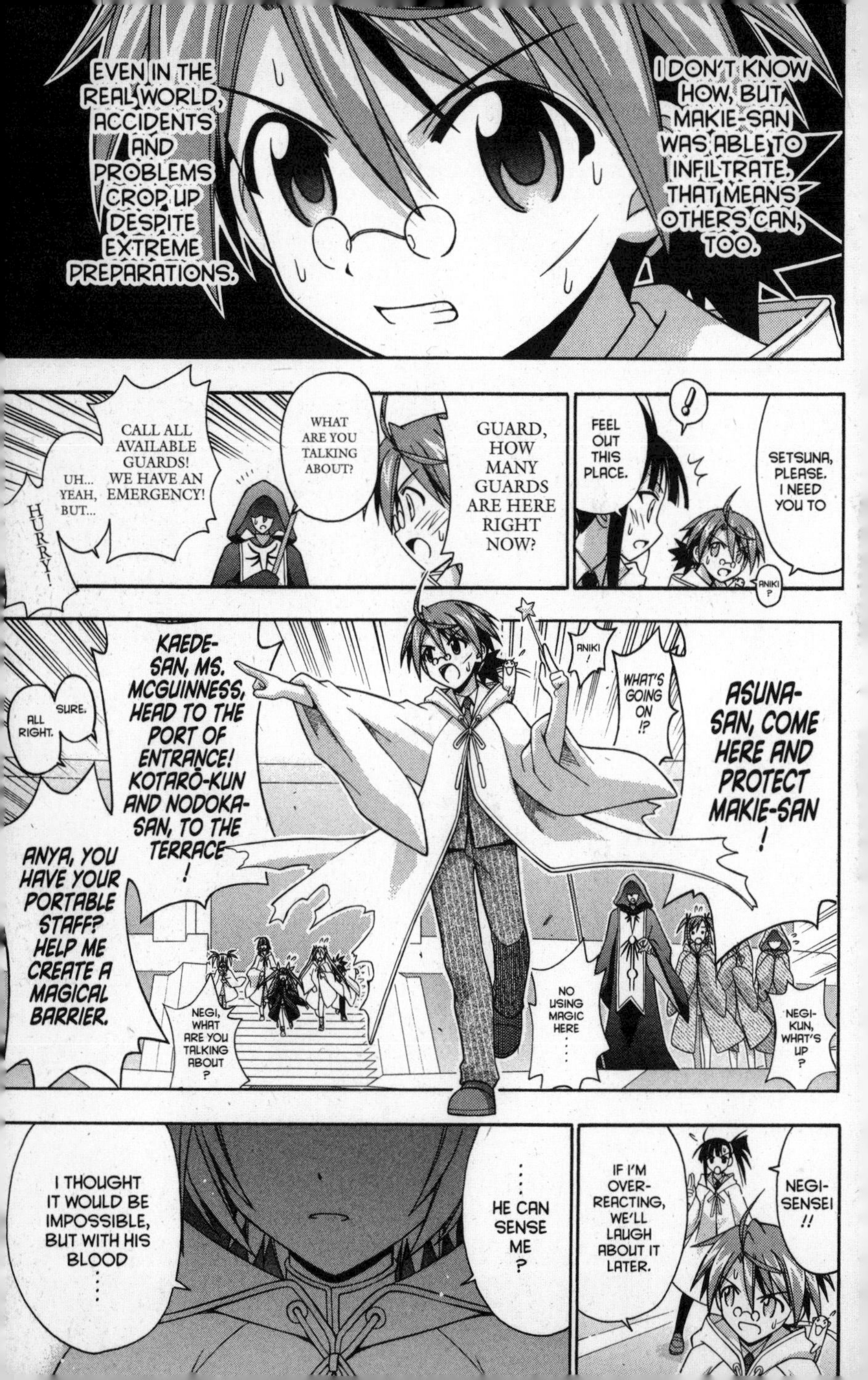
I DON'T KNOW HOW, BUT MAKIE-SAN WAS ABLE TO INFILTRATE. THAT MEANS OTHERS CAN, TOO.
EVEN IN THE REAL WORLD, ACCIDENTS AND PROBLEMS CROP UP DESPITE EXTREME PREPARATIONS.
SETSUNA, PLEASE. I NEED YOU TO
!
FEEL OUT THIS PLACE.
ANIKI ?
GUARD, HOW MANY GUARDS ARE HERE RIGHT NOW?
WHAT ARE YOU TALKING ABOUT?
CALL ALL AVAILABLE GUARDS! WE HAVE AN EMERGENCY!
UH... YEAH, BUT...
HURRY!
ASUNA-SAN, COME HERE AND PROTECT MAKIE-SAN!
WHAT'S GOING ON !?
ANIKI !
KAEDE-SAN, MS. MCGUINNESS, HEAD TO THE PORT OF ENTRANCE! KOTARO-KUN AND NODOKA-SAN, TO THE TERRACE!
SURE.
ALL RIGHT.
NEGI-KUN, WHAT'S UP ?
NO USING MAGIC HERE....
ANYA, YOU HAVE YOUR PORTABLE STAFF? HELP ME CREATE A MAGICAL BARRIER.
NEGI, WHAT ARE YOU TALKING ABOUT ?
NEGI-SENSEI !!
IF I'M OVER-REACTING, WE'LL LAUGH ABOUT IT LATER.
....HE CAN SENSE ME ?
I THOUGHT IT WOULD BE IMPOSSIBLE, BUT WITH HIS BLOOD....

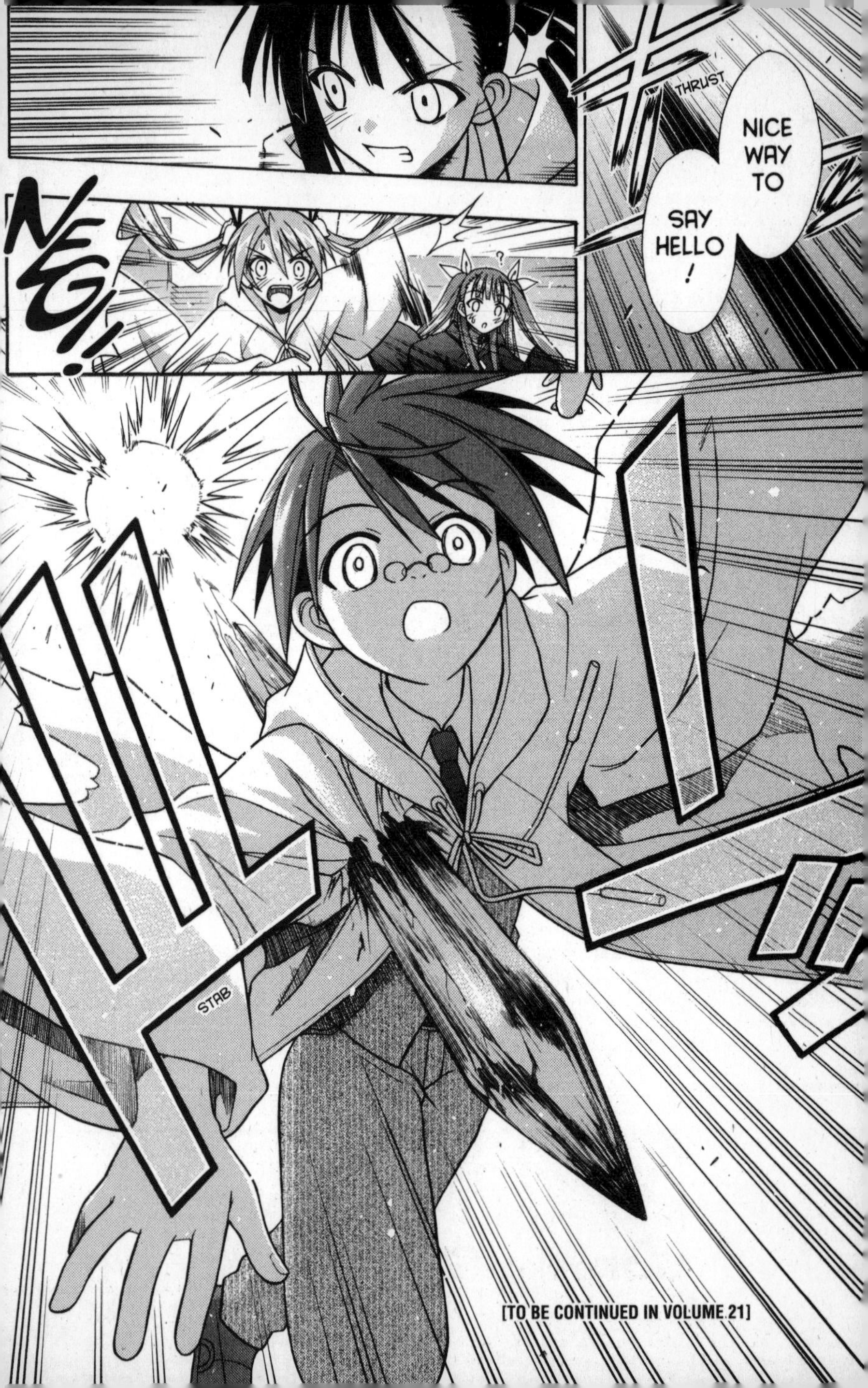
THRUST
NICE WAY TO SAY HELLO!
NEGI!!
?
STAB

[TO BE CONTINUED IN VOLUME 21]

-STAFF-

Ken Akamatsu
Takashi Takemoto
Kenichi Nakamura
Masaki Ohyama
Keiichi Yamashita
Tadashi Maki
Tohru Mitsuhashi

Thanks to
Ran Ayanaga
Sophie Thomas

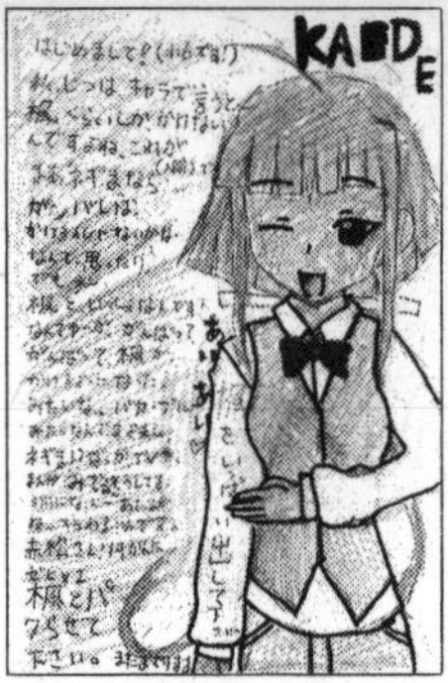
KAEDE

▲ THE WINK IS ADORABLE

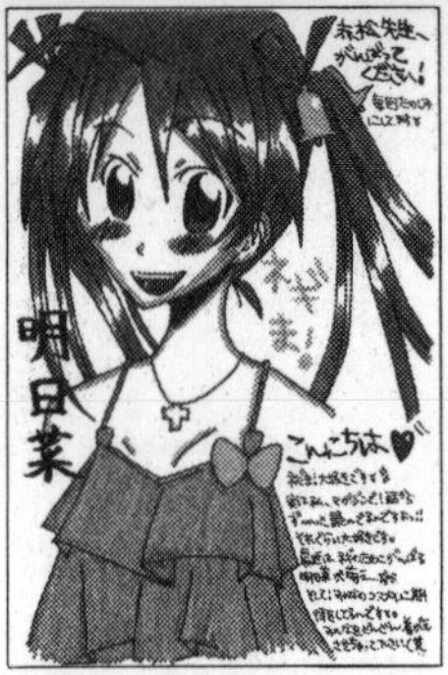

▲ A HEALTHY-LOOKING ASUNA

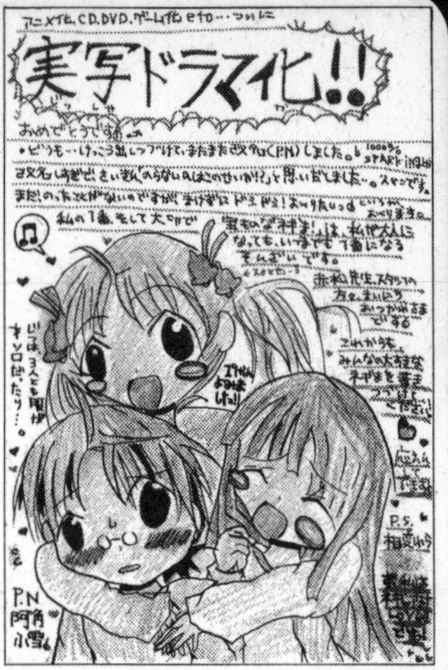
実写ドラマイ化!!

▲ SO ADORABLE!

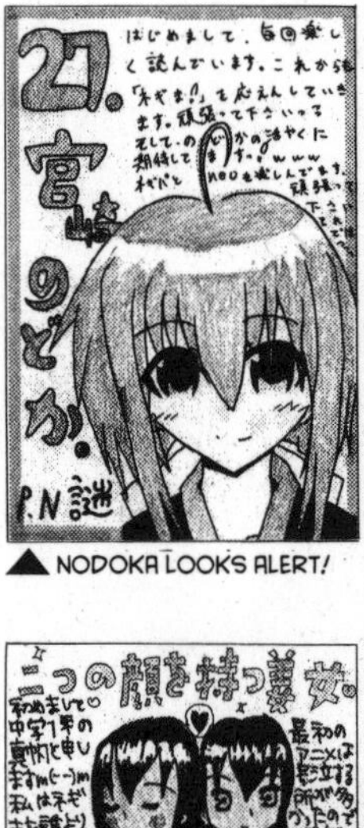

▲ NODOKA LOOKS ALERT!

NEGIMA!
FAN ART CORNER

EVERYONE, THANKS FOR YOUR LETTERS AND ILLUSTRATIONS AS ALWAYS. ☆ WE'VE BEEN GETTING MORE ASUNA ILLUSTRATIONS LATELY. I WONDER WHY? NOW, LET'S GET STARTED WITH TODAY'S ILLUSTRATIONS. PLEASE SEND YOUR CONTRIBUTIONS TO THE EDITORIAL OFFICES OF KODANSHA COMICS. ☆

TEXT BY ASSISTANT MAX

▼ SEXY NODOKA!

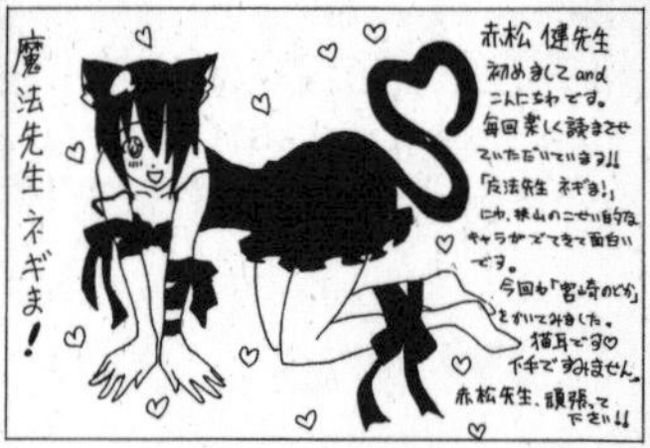
魔法先生ネギま!

▼ CUTE MANA!

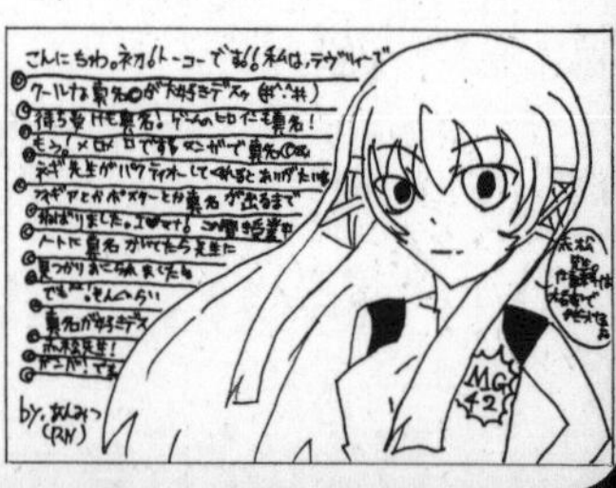

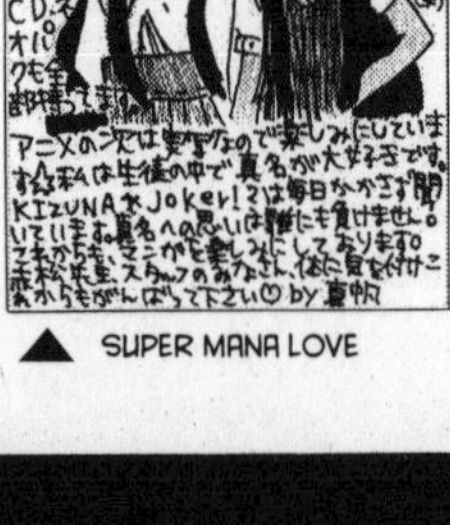
二つの顔を持つ美女。

▲ SUPER MANA LOVE

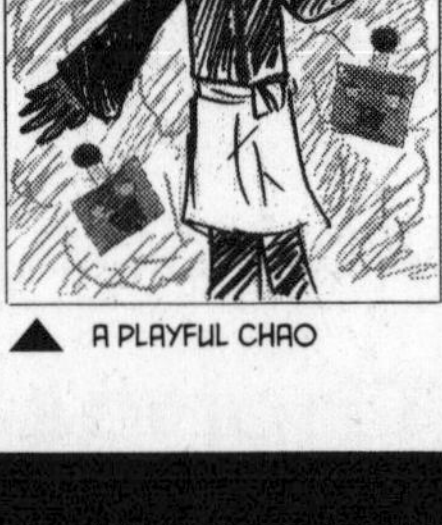
赤松先生
ガンバですよ〜。

▲ A PLAYFUL CHAO

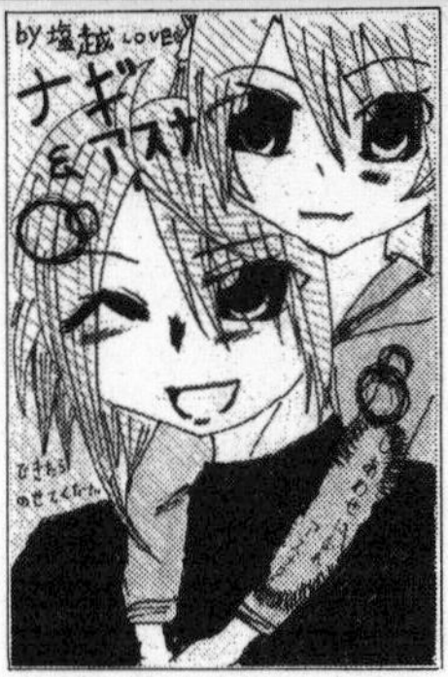
by 塩越 LOVE
ナギ と アスナ

▲ LOOKS HAPPY ☆☆

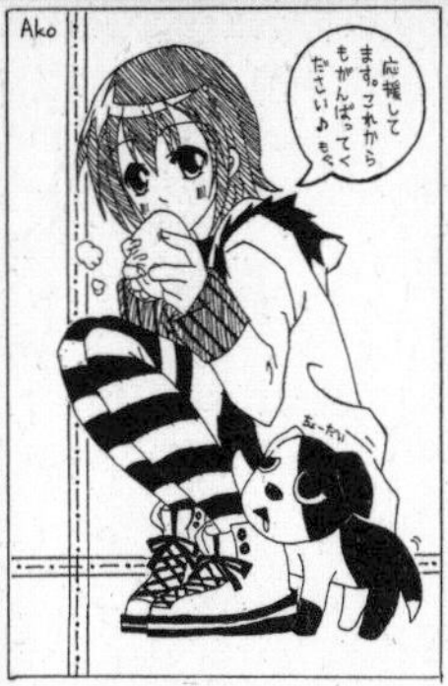
Ako
応援してます。これからもがんばってください♪

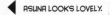

▲ THE STEAMED PORK BUNS LOOK WARM!

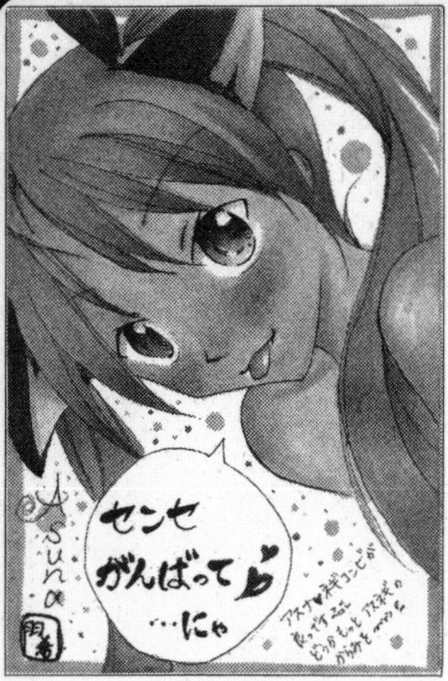
センセ
がんばって
…にゃ

◀ ASUNA LOOKS LOVELY.

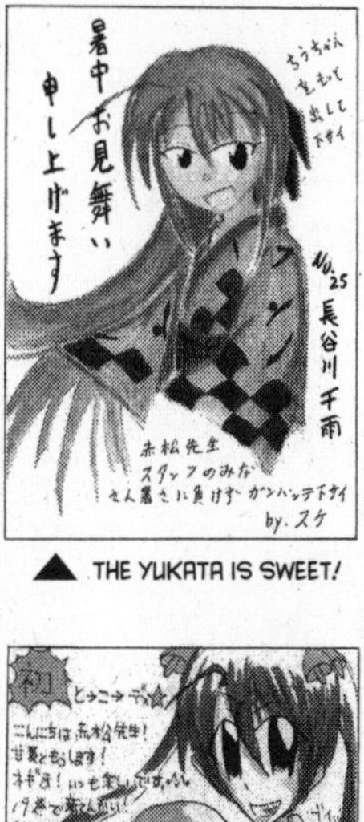
暑中お見舞い申し上げます
No.25
長谷川千雨
赤松先生
スタッフのみなさん暑さに負けずガンバッテ下サイ by.スケ

▲ THE YUKATA IS SWEET!

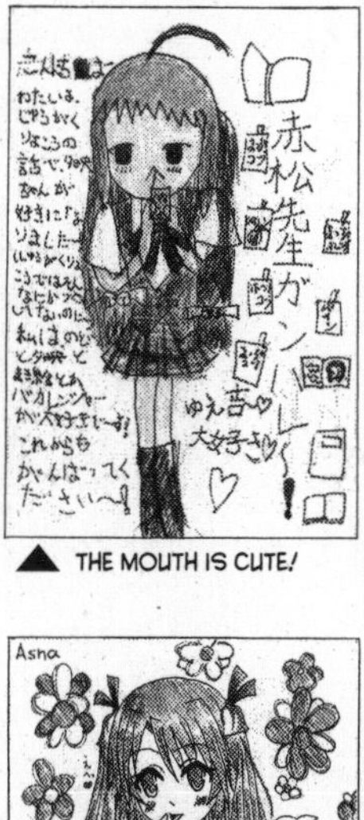
赤松先生ガンバレ!
ゆえ吉♡大好き
これからもがんばってくださ〜い

▲ THE MOUTH IS CUTE!

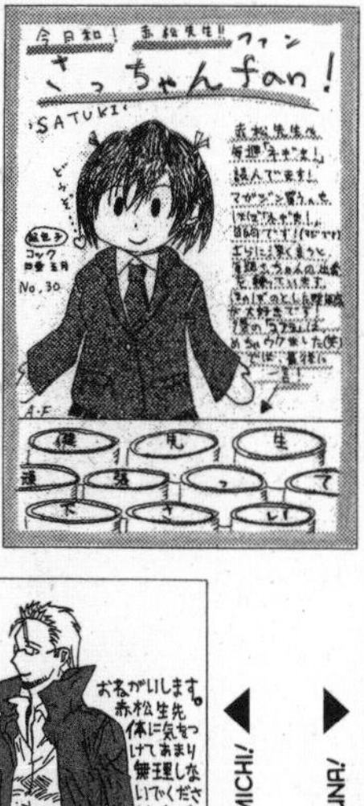
赤松先生!! ファン
さっちゃんfan!
SATUKI
No.30

▶ A SAT-CHAN FAN!

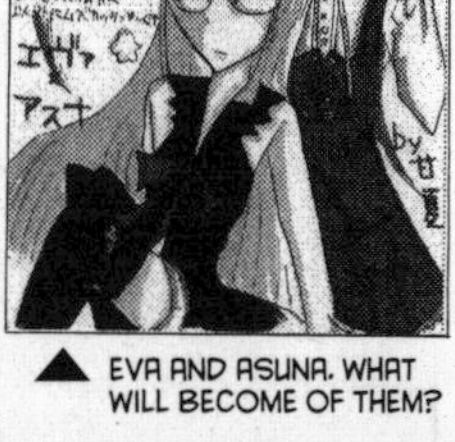
こんにちは 赤松先生!
エヴァ
アスナ
by 甘夏

▲ EVA AND ASUNA. WHAT WILL BECOME OF THEM?

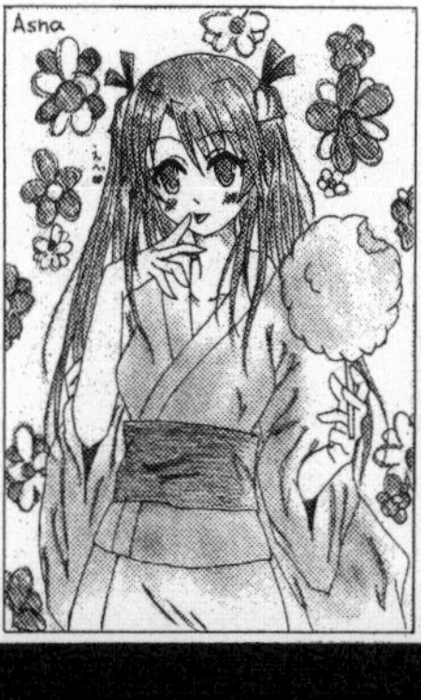
Asna

▶ GOOFY ASUNA!

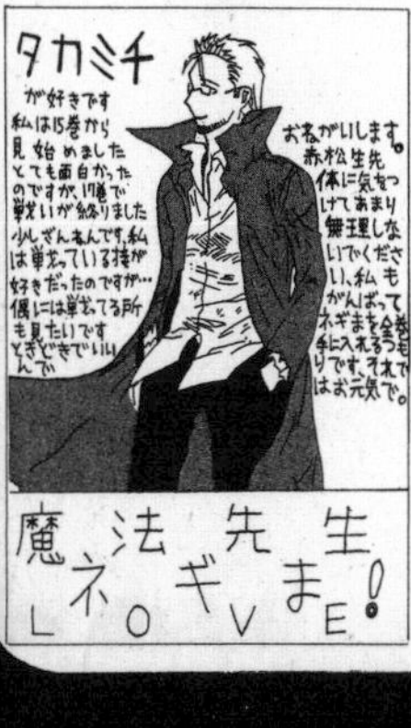
タカミチ
が好きです
私は15巻から見始めました
とても面白かったのですが、17巻で戦いが終りました
お願いします。
赤松先生
体に気をつけてあまり無理しないでください。私もがんばってネギまを全部手に入れるつもりです。それではお元気で。
魔法先生ネギま!
LOVE

◀ COOL TAKAMICHI!

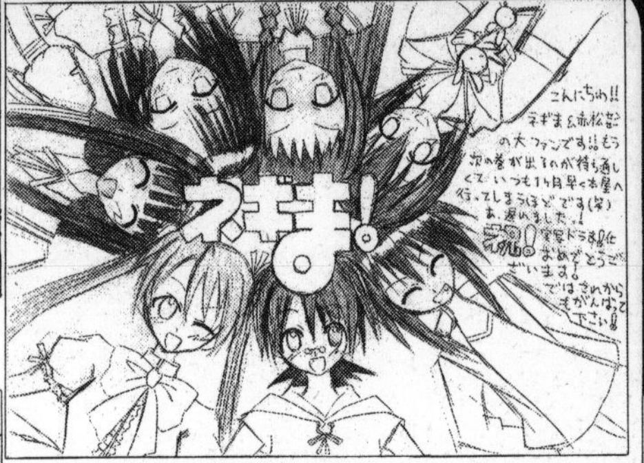
ネギま!
こんにちゎ!! ネギま&赤松先生の大ファンです!! もう次の巻が出るのが待ち遠しくて いつも1ヶ月早く本屋へ行ってしまうほどです(笑)
祝! 実写ドラマ化 おめでとうございます。
では これからもがんばって下さい!!

▲ WHAT A GOOD FEELING! ★★★

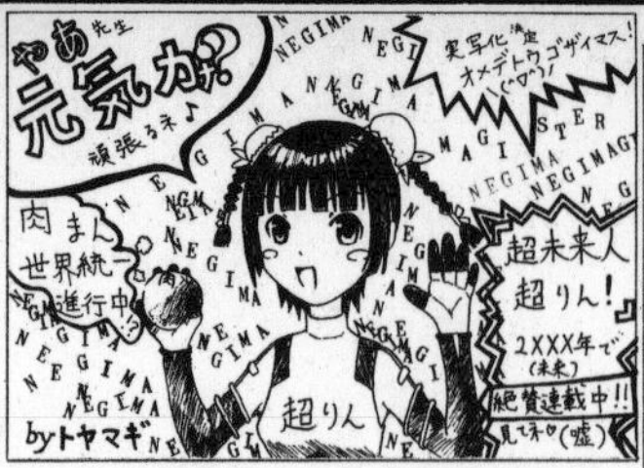
やあ 先生 元気カ??
頑張るネ♪
実写化決定 オメデトウゴザイマス!
肉まん 世界統一 進行中!
『超未来人 超りん!』
2XXX年で(未来) 絶賛連載中!!
見てネ☆(嘘)
超りん
byトヤマギ
NEGIMA MAGISTER NEGIMA

▲ WHAT A SWEET CHAO. (LAUGH)

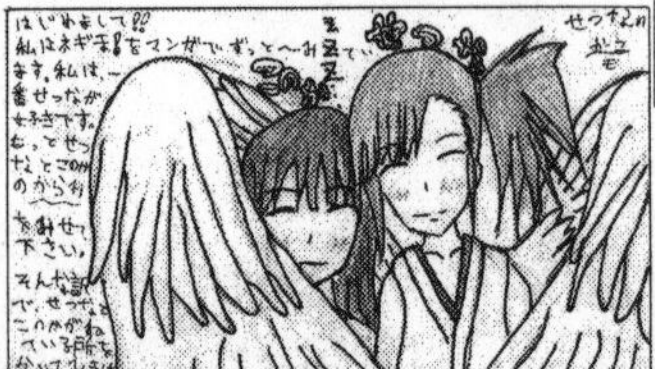
はじめまして!!

◀ THEY LOOK LIKE FRIENDS.

▼ I WAS WAITING FOR THIS. (LAUGH)

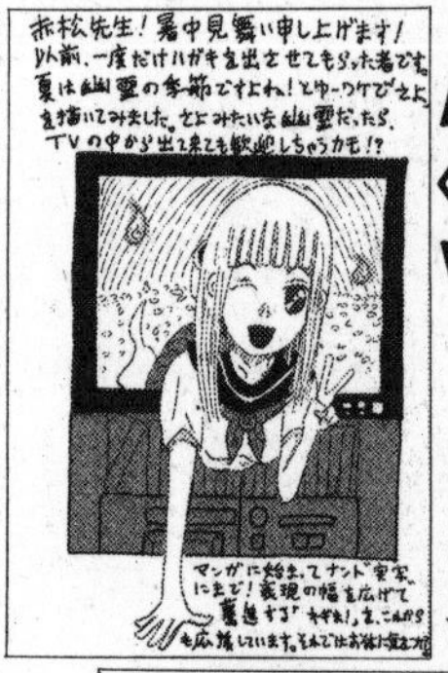
赤松先生! 暑中見舞い申し上げます!
以前、一度だけハガキを出させてもらった者です。
夏は幽霊の季節ですよね! とゆーワケでさよちゃん描いてみました。
さよみたいな幽霊だったら、TVの中から出て来ても歓迎しちゃうカモ!?

▼ YES, IT'S HARD. (LAUGHS)

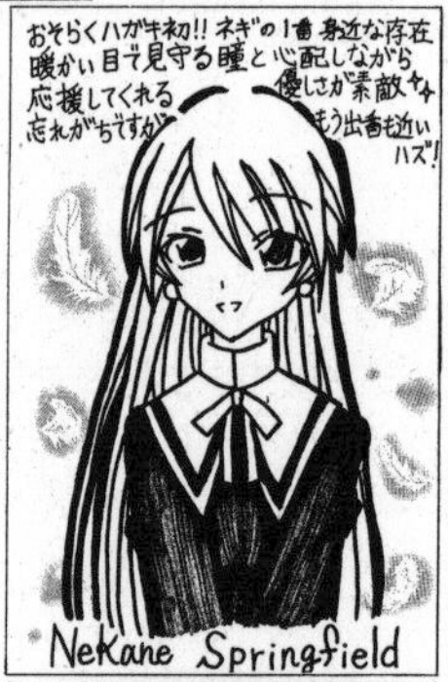
おそらくハガキ初!! ネギの1番身近な存在
暖かい目で見守る瞳と 心配しながら
応援してくれる 優しさが素敵☆
忘れがちですが もう出番も近いハズ!
Nekane Springfield

◀ IT'S A LITTLE OFF. (LAUGH)

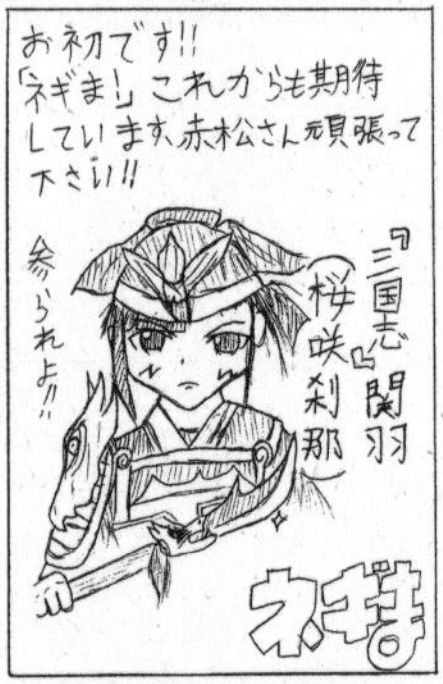
お初です!!
「ネギま!」これからも期待しています、赤松さん頑張って下さい!!
『三国志』関羽
桜咲刹那
参られよ!!
ネギま

SHE LOOKS NERVOUS. ▼

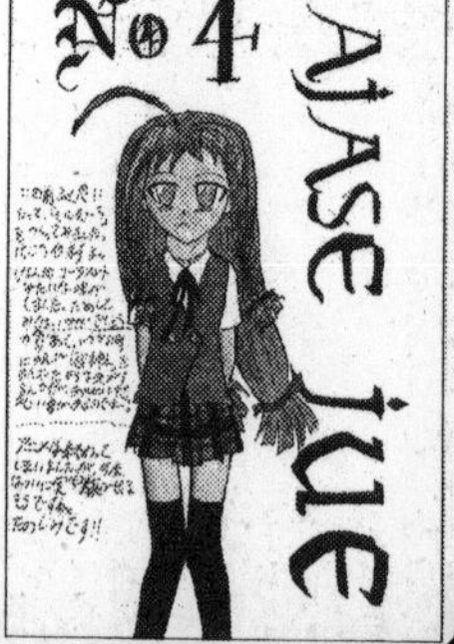
No 4
AYASE YUE

◀ YUNA IS LOOKING WELL!

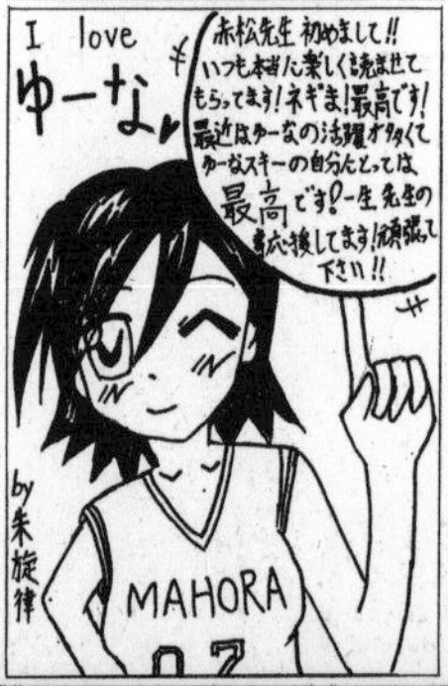
I love ゆーな
赤松先生 初めまして!! いつも本当に楽しく読ませてもらってます! ネギま! 最高です! 最近はゆーなの活躍が多くて ゆーなスキーの自分にとっては最高です!! 一生先生の応援してます! 頑張って下さい!!
by 朱旋律
MAHORA
07

◀ NICE AND RELAXED!

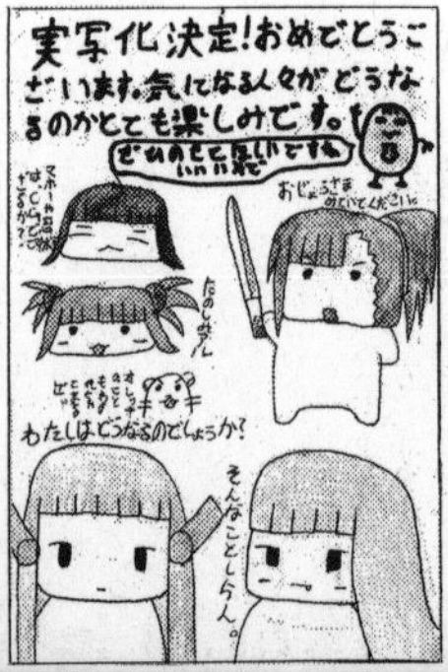
実写化決定! おめでとうございます。気になる人々がどうなるのかとても楽しみです。
わたしはどうなるのでしょうか?
そんなことしらん。

NEGI MA!

今回の
FEATURED CHARACTER
EVANGELINE A. K. MCDOWELL RANKING

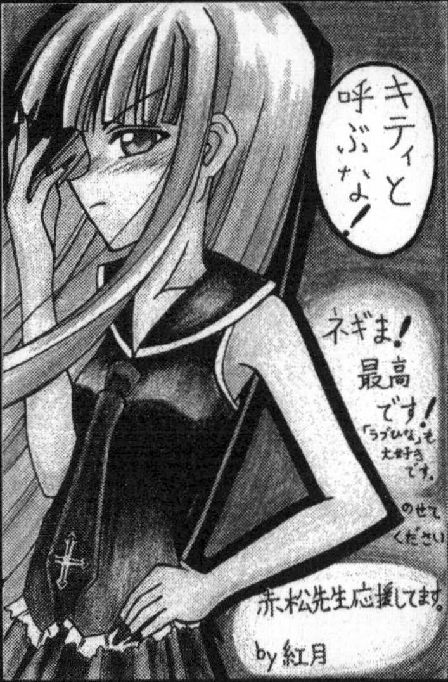
キティと呼ぶな!
ネギま!最高です!
「ラブひな」も大好きです。
のせてください
赤松先生応援してます。
by 紅月

第1位 ▶ EVA'S ATTITUDE SHOWS THROUGH HERE! (BY AKAMATSU)

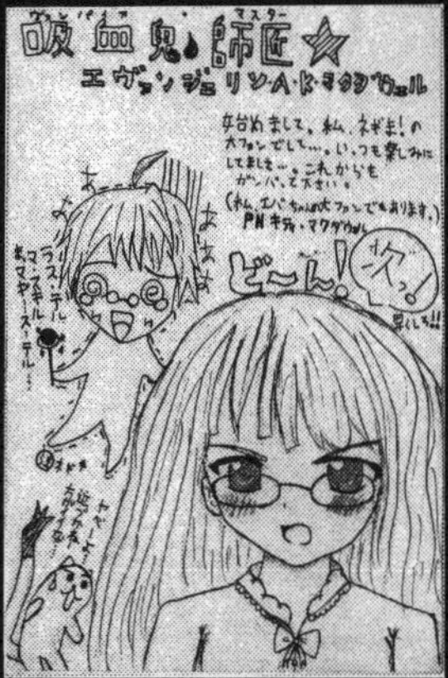
吸血鬼・師匠☆
エヴァンジェリン・A・K・マクダウェル
ど~ん!

第2位 ▲ EVA IS POPULAR WITH GLASSES!

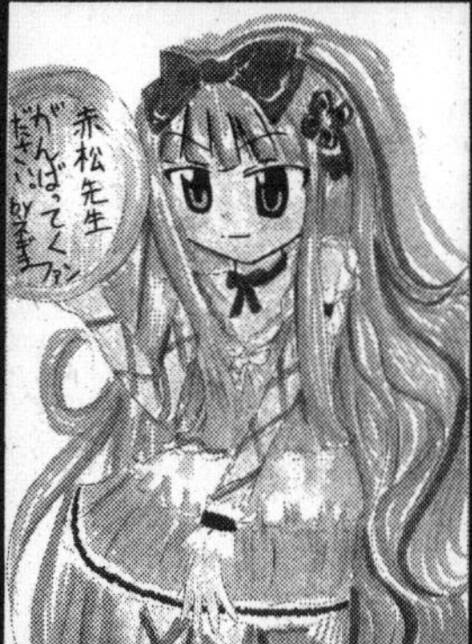
赤松先生がんばってください by ネギまファン

第3位 ▶ EVA'S A GOTHIC LOLITA FAN. THE BIG RIBBON IS CUTE.

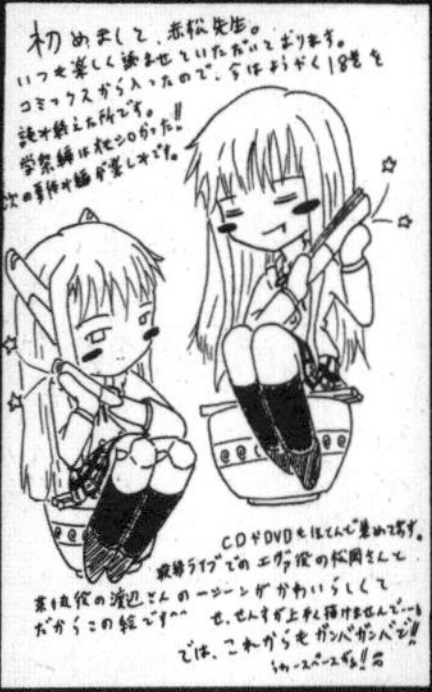
初めまして、赤松先生。

第5位 ▶ FOCUS ON THE VOICE ACTRESS—INTERESTING! THIS IS A PREFACE.

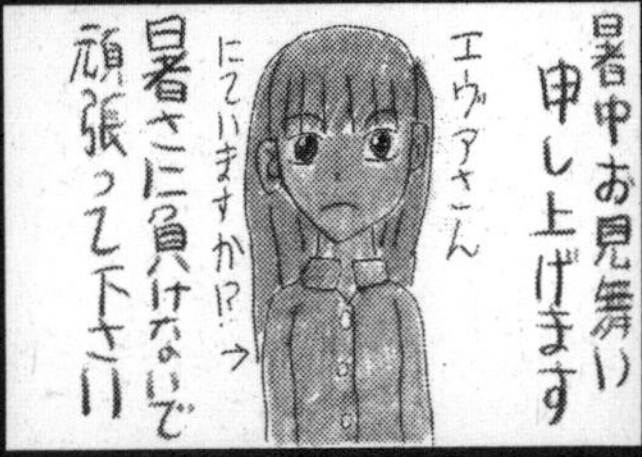
暑中お見舞い申し上げます
エヴァさん
にていますか!?→
暑さに負けないで頑張って下さい

第6位 ▲ SHE LOOKS LIKE KONOKA...

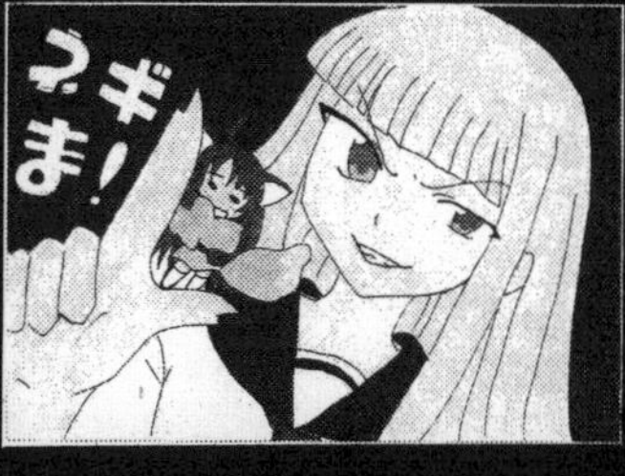
ネギま!

第4位 ▶ FOXY NEGI IS CUTE!

MAGISTER NEGI MAGI

ITINERARY FOR BRITAIN

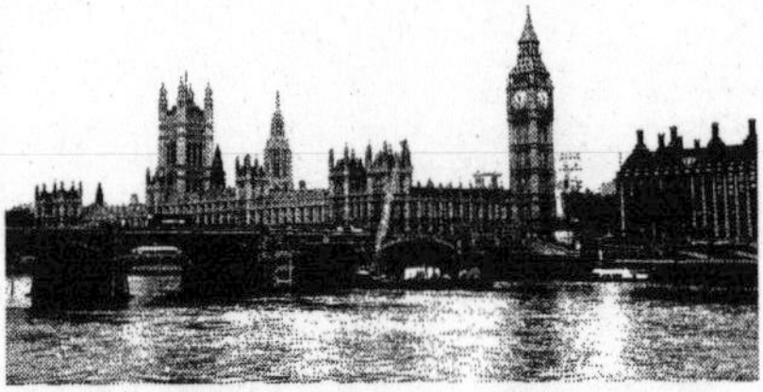

THE VIEW FROM BA LONDON EYE. THE OFFICIAL NAME IS WESTMINSTER CASTLE, WHICH INCLUDES THE BRITISH PARLIAMENT BUILDING. A FIRE IN 1834 DESTROYED THE BUILDING EXCEPT FOR THE WESTMINSTER HALL. IT WAS REBUILT IN 1860. THE TOWER ON THE LEFT IS VICTORIA TOWER. THE TOWER ON THE RIGHT IS BIG BEN.

THE NEO-GOTHIC BUILDING ALONG THE THAMES RIVER IN LONDON IS THE BRITISH PARLIAMENT BUILDING. ALONG WITH BIG BEN, IT IS ONE OF THE MOST RECOGNIZABLE BUILDINGS IN LONDON. THE HOUSE OF BRITISH PARLIAMENT, CREATED IN 1295 BY EDWARD I, IS STILL ACTIVE. ON THE FLOOR OF THE HOUSE, THERE ARE TWO LINES THAT ARE SEPARATED BY A WIDTH SLIGHTLY WIDER THAN THE SWORD. THESE LINES ARE CALLED THE SWORDLINE. DURING QUESTIONING, NO ONE IS ALLOWED TO CROSS THIS LINE—TO AVOID BLOODSHED DURING DEBATES. MODERN PARLIAMENTARY GOVERNMENT WAS ESTABLISHED IN BRITAIN AND SPREAD INTERNATIONALLY AFTER THE PURITANICAL REVOLUTION.

THE LONDON SUBWAY SYSTEM IS KNOWN COLLOQUIALLY AS THE TUBE. THE CENTRAL MODE OF TRANSPORTATION IN LONDON, IT IS EXPANSIVE AND TRAVELS IN VARIOUS DIRECTIONS. UNLIKE IN TOKYO'S SYSTEM, THERE IS NO CENTRAL LONDON STATION. BRITAIN IS THE BIRTHPLACE OF THE RAILROAD, AND INITIALLY, RAILROADS WERE NOT BUILT IN IN URBAN AREAS. AS A RESULT, MANY OF THE STATIONS ARE BUILT OUTSIDE OF THE CITY. SO LONDON-BOUND TRAINS CAN STOP AT VARIOUS STATIONS, SUCH AS VICTORIA, WATERLOO, PADDINGTON, AND KING'S CROSS. THE SUBWAYS CONNECT THESE VARIOUS TERMINALS TOGETHER TO HELP SMOOTH OUT TRAFFIC IN LONDON.

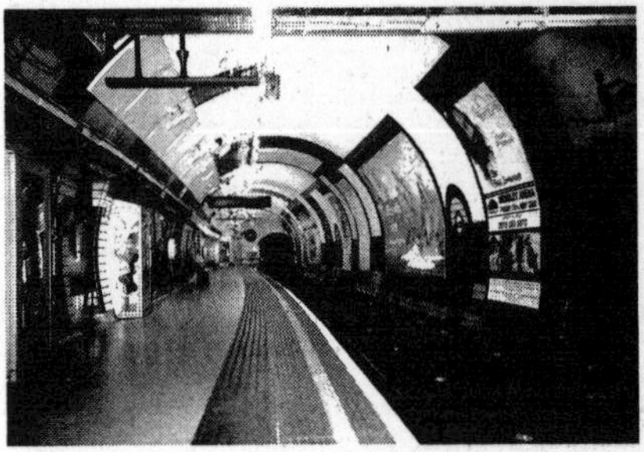

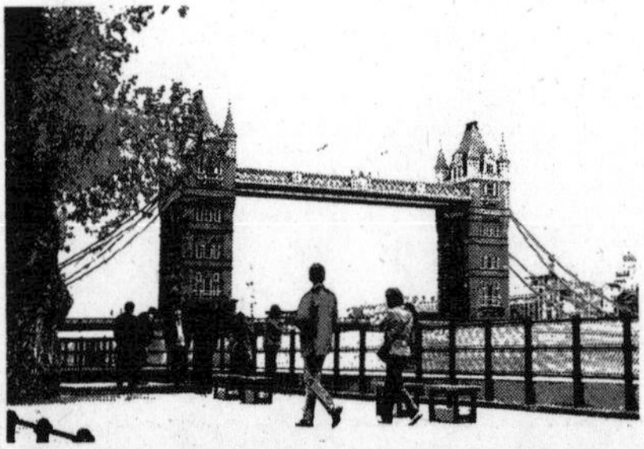

VIEW OF THE TOWER BRIDGE FROM THE BACK OF THE LONDON TOWER. IT IS ONE OF LONDON'S MOST POPULAR TOURIST SPOTS, DUE TO ITS PROXIMITY TO THE TOWER OF LONDON. THE BRIDGE CONNECTING THE TWO TOWERS IS LINED WITH GLASS. THE CITY OF LONDON CAN EASILY BE VIEWED FROM THE BRIDGE. THE ENGINE THAT OPERATES THE BASCULE BRIDGE IS VIEWABLE BY THE PUBLIC.

ONE OF LONDON'S FAMOUS BRIDGES, THE TOWER BRIDGE. IT IS NEAR THE LONDON TOWER, WHICH USED TO BE THE RESIDENCE FOR WILLIAM THE CONQUERER. IT WAS CONSTRUCTED DURING THE LATTER HALF OF THE 19TH CENTURY, BEGINNING IN 1886 AND COMPLETED IN 1898. COMMERCIAL EXPANSION DURING THE 19TH CENTURY NECESSITATED THE CONNECTION OF THE NORTH AND SOUTH SIDES OF THE THAMES RIVER. DUE TO THE LARGE SIZE OF THE SHIPS TRAVELING THE RIVER, A BASCULE BRIDGE WAS BUILT SO THE TRAFFIC ALONG THE RIVER WOULD NOT BE BLOCKED. HOWEVER, LARGE SHIPS NO LONGER TRAVEL ALONG THE THAMES RIVER. AS A RESULT, THE BASCULE BRIDGE IS NO LONGER SEEN IN ACTION. HOWEVER, THE BASCULE BRIDGE IS STILL COMPLETELY FUNCTIONAL.

CASTLE COMBE IN COTSWOLD IS ONE OF THE MOST BEAUTIFUL VILLAGES IN ENGLAND. THE SCENERY IS BREATHTAKING, AND THE BUILDINGS IN THE CITY HAVE BEEN PRESERVED AS HISTORICAL LANDMARKS. TRAFFIC CAN BE HEAVY, HOWEVER, SINCE VISITORS FLOCK TO THIS VILLAGE ON WEEKENDS. THE VILLAGE WAS ONCE KNOWN FOR ITS WOOL INDUSTRY; A LARGE MARKET WAS HELD IN THE CENTER OF THE VILLAGE KNOWN AS MARKET CROSS. THE VILLAGE IS CURRENTLY RATHER SMALL—ONLY ABOUT 1/5 OF A MILE WIDE. THE ARISTOCRATIC MANOR NEAR THE VILLAGE HAS BEEN CONVERTED INTO A HOTEL. SURROUNDED BY IDYLLIC FARMS, THE SCENERY SHOWS US WHAT PRE-MODERN EUROPE MIGHT HAVE LOOKED LIKE.

THERE ARE SEVERAL WAYS TO PRONOUNCE "CASTLE COMBE," BUT TAXI DRIVERS WILL KNOW WHERE YOU NEED TO GO. THE MARKET HALL IN THE MIDDLE OF MARKET CROSS WAS BUILT DURING THE 14TH CENTURY.

THE PLATFORM FOR THE STATION AT FISHGUARD HARBOR. THE BUILDING ACROSS FROM THE EXIT IS THE LOBBY FOR THE FERRY. THERE ARE ONLY TWO PASSENGER TRAINS, ONE AT MIDNIGHT AND ONE AT NOON. AS A RESULT, THERE IS NO TICKET OFFICE. TICKETS ARE PURCHASED FROM TRAIN ATTENDANTS.

FISHGUARD, LOCATED ON THE SOUTHEAST CORNER OF PEMBROKE, WALES. A FERRY THAT TRAVELS TO IRELAND DEPARTS FROM THE HARBOR NEAR FISHGUARD HARBOR TRAIN STATION.

WHILE THE TRAIN STATION IS AN IMPORTANT ONE IN TERMS OF TRAFFIC, NOT MANY TRAINS STOP AT THIS STATION. AS A RESULT, THE STATION IS VERY QUAINT. OCCASIONALLY, SEA BIRDS WILL OPEN THE AUTOMATIC DOORS TO THE STATION AND ENTER THE STATION LOBBY. PEMBROKE IS A NATIONAL PARK FROM THE HARBOR TO THE NEARBY HILLS. THE PARK IS ABOUT 620 SQUARE KILOMETERS IN SIZE. THE BEACH, SWAMP, AND FOREST WITHIN THE PARK ARE ALL VERY SCENIC.

THE STONES USED IN THE FAMOUS STONEHENGE ORIGINATE FROM PRESELI HILLS IN PEMBROKE. THE PRESELI HILLS ARE 125 MILES FROM STONEHENGE. PEMBROKE MUST HAVE BEEN AN IMPORTANT AREA, EVEN IN ANCIENT TIMES, FOR THE STONES TO BE CARRIED OVER SUCH A DISTANCE. BEAUTIFUL NATURAL DOLMENS REMAIN IN THE NATIONAL PARK IN PEMBROKE. WALES AND PEMBROKE ARE HOME TO THE MYSTERIOUS CULTURE THAT LEFT THE GIGANTIC STONE MONUMENTS.

THE BEAUTIFUL DOLMENS IN THE NATIONAL PARK AT PEMBROKE ARE KNOWN AS PENTRE IFAN. THE STONE IS CALLED BLUESTONE, THE SAME STONE USED FOR THE FAMOUS STONEHENGE. PENTRE IFAN WAS A STONE ROOM THAT REPRESENTED REBIRTH AND THE WOMB.

DIRECTIONS TO FISHGUARD

2 HOURS AND 16 MINUTES FROM CARDIFF CENTRAL TO FISHGUARD CENTRAL ON THE ARRIVA TRAINS WALES.

3-D BACKGROUNDS EXPLANATION CORNER
THIS VOLUME HAS VARIOUS BACKGROUNDS, FROM JAPANESE-STYLE ROOMS TO THE MAGICAL WORLD.

● SCENE NAME: JAPANESE ROOM
POLYGON COUNT: 24,175

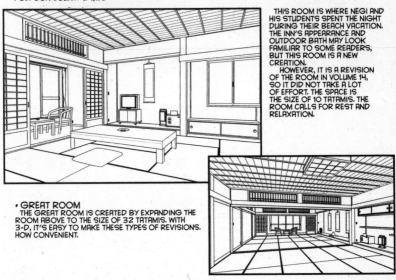

THIS ROOM IS WHERE NEGI AND HIS STUDENTS SPENT THE NIGHT DURING THEIR BEACH VACATION. THE INN'S APPEARANCE AND OUTDOOR BATH MAY LOOK FAMILIAR TO SOME READERS, BUT THIS ROOM IS A NEW CREATION.

HOWEVER, IT IS A REVISION OF THE ROOM IN VOLUME 14, SO IT DID NOT TAKE A LOT OF EFFORT. THE SPACE IS THE SIZE OF 10 TATAMIS. THE ROOM CALLS FOR REST AND RELAXATION.

● GREAT ROOM
THE GREAT ROOM IS CREATED BY EXPANDING THE ROOM ABOVE TO THE SIZE OF 32 TATAMIS. WITH 3-D, IT'S EASY TO MAKE THESE TYPES OF REVISIONS. HOW CONVENIENT.

● SCENE NAME: CATACOMB AT THE SCHOOL
POLYGON COUNT: 38,582

THIS IS THE BASEMENT WHERE THE STONE REMAINS OF THE VILLAGERS ARE STORED. THE EXISTENCE OF THIS ROOM IS ONLY KNOWN TO A FEW PEOPLE. GENERALLY, IT IS PROTECTED BY A MAGICAL BARRIER AGAINST INTRUDERS. ORIGINALLY, THE REQUEST WAS TO CREATE A CATACOMB-LIKE ROOM. HOWEVER, THE END RESULT IS MORE REMINISCENT OF A TEMPLE.

THE CREATION OF THIS ROOM WAS SIMPLE BECAUSE IT INVOLVED COPYING AND ROTATING ONE SECTION AND PUTTING THEM TOGETHER.

● CIRCULAR STAIRCASE
WE'LL KEEP THIS A SECRET. IN ONE FRAME, THE STAIRS WIND CLOCKWISE, AND IN ANOTHER FRAME, THE STAIRS WIND COUNTERCLOCKWISE. MAYBE THE MAGICAL BARRIER CREATES A TWIST IN THE PHYSICAL DIMENSION. (LAUGHS)

• SCENE NAME: GATEPORT EXTERIOR
POLYGON COUNT: 28,168

THIS IS THE GIGANTIC, CIRCULAR BUILDING INSIDE THE MAGICAL METROPOLIS OF MEGALOMESENBRIA. THIS GATEPORT CONNECTS IMPORTANT PLACES INSIDE THE MAGICAL WORLD. THIS GATEPORT ALSO CONNECTS THE MAGICAL WORLD TO THE HUMAN WORLD. MANY PEOPLE TRAVEL THROUGH THIS GATEPORT, AND THE GATEPORT IS ENORMOUS ENOUGH THAT IT CAN BE CONSIDERED A CITY BY ITSELF. THE CIRCULAR AREA AND THE BASE ARE IN 3-D, THE REST IS DRAWN BY HAND. THE BUILDING SHOWN HERE IS THE DRAWING BEFORE IT WAS REVISED, SO SOME DIFFERENCES CAN BE SEEN FROM THE FINAL VERSION.

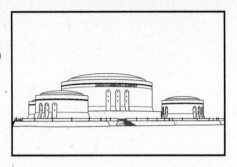

• SCENE NAME: IMMIGRATION GATE
POLYGON COUNT: 971,088

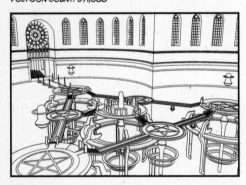

THIS IS THE INTERIOR OF THE GATEPORT. THE GATES ARE THE CIRCULAR LANDINGS SURROUNDING THE CENTRAL STONE. EACH LANDING CONNECTS TO A DIFFERENT LOCATION. THERE USED TO BE A WAY TO CHECK THE IDENTITY OF THE PEOPLE PASSING THROUGH THE PENTAGRAMS AS WELL AS THEIR DESTINATIONS, BUT FATE WAS ABLE TO CANCEL OUT THAT FUNCTION. THIS AREA IS LARGER THAN THE EXTERIOR BUILDING SURROUNDING IT. AS A RESULT, IT IS PRESUMED THAT SOME TYPE OF DIMENSIONAL ALTERING MAGIC WAS USED IN ITS CREATION. HOWEVER, THE DETAILS ARE NOT KNOWN AT THIS TIME.

• SCENE NAME: MAGIC TOWERS
POLYGON COUNT: 971,088

THIS IS THE VIEW OF THE CITY AS SEEN FROM THE GATEPORT. THERE ARE VARIOUS-SIZE BUILDINGS FILLING THE CITYSCAPE. CIRCULAR BUILDINGS ARE EASY TO CREATE IN 3-D. AFTER THE TOWERS WERE COMPLETED, THE ROCKY MOUNTAIN AND DETAILS WERE DRAWN BY HAND. THE PICTURE SHOWN IS THE SCENE BEFORE THE FINAL REVISION. AS A RESULT, THERE ARE FLOATING TOWERS. (^_^;)

THERE ARE 8 TYPES OF FLOATING TOWERS. THE TOWERS ARE TAKEN FROM THE TOWERS IN EVA'S GETAWAY.

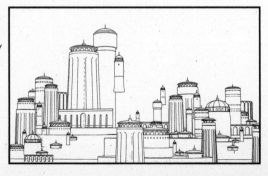

魔法先生 ネギま!
MAGISTER NEGI MAGI

赤松 健
SHONEN MAGAZINE COMICS
KEN AKAMATSU

20

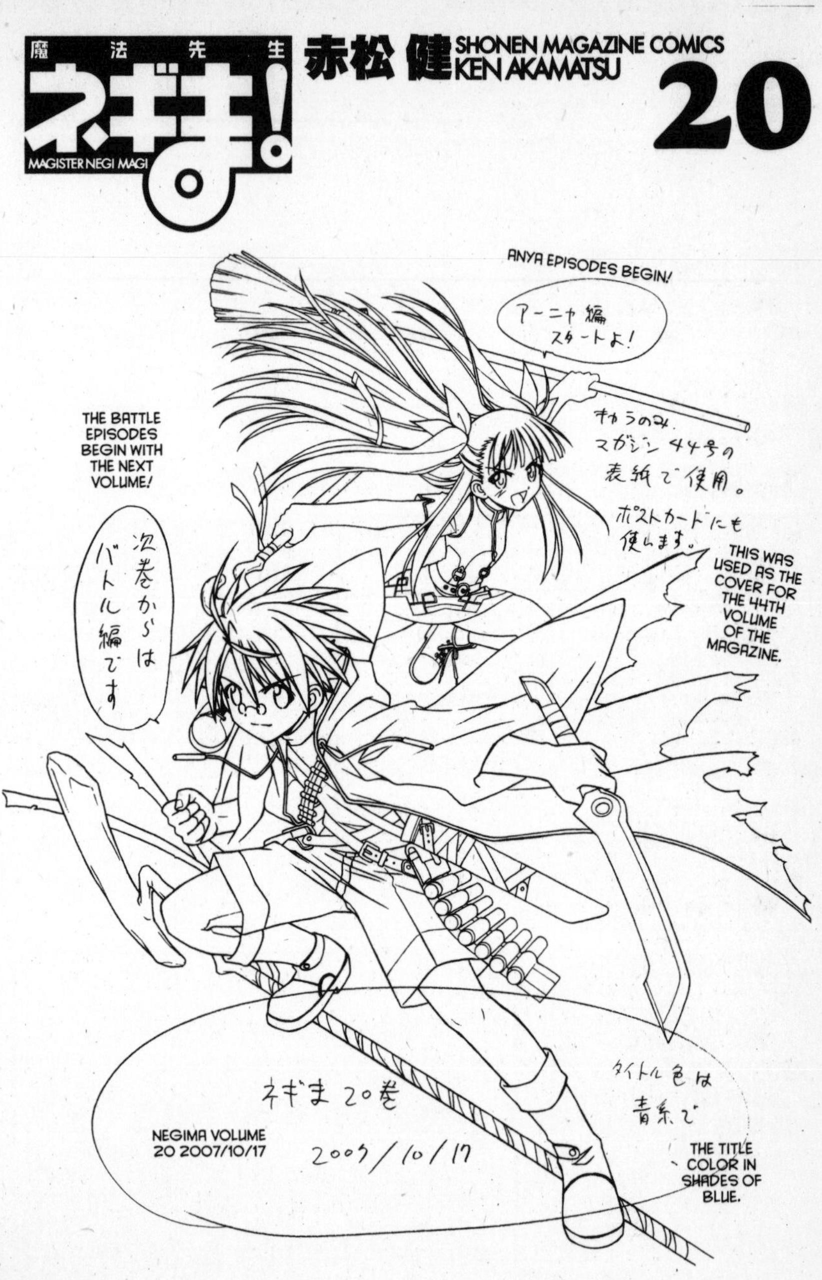
ANYA EPISODES BEGIN!
アーニャ編スタートよ!
キャラのみ. マガジン44号の表紙で使用。
ポストカードにも使います。
THIS WAS USED AS THE COVER FOR THE 44TH VOLUME OF THE MAGAZINE.
THE BATTLE EPISODES BEGIN WITH THE NEXT VOLUME!
次巻からはバトル編です
ネギま20巻
2007/10/17
NEGIMA VOLUME 20 2007/10/17
タイトル色は青系で
THE TITLE COLOR IN SHADES OF BLUE.

キャラ解説
CHARACTER PROFILE

⑰ 椎名 桜子
⑰ SAKURAKO SHIINA

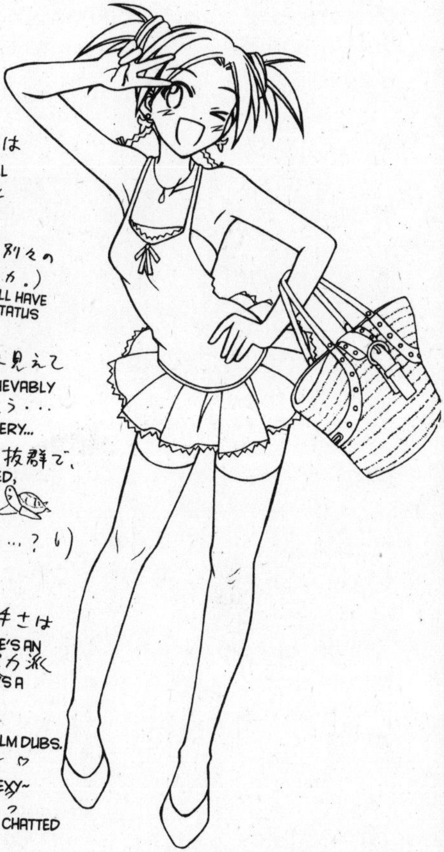

もしパクティオーしたら、桜子の能力は
IF SAKURAKO RECEIVES A PACTIO FROM NEGI, SHE'LL
「マスターのLUCK値（幸運度）アップ」と
RECEIVE AN INCREDIBLE NEW POWER: SHE'LL BE THE
すでに決まっています。（チア3名はそれぞれ別々のステータスUP能力。）
MASTER OF LUCK!
(THE 3 CHEERLEADERS WILL HAVE DIFFERENT, INCREASED STATUS ABILITIES.)

この巻でも、あふれる強運がかいま見えていますが。（笑） 宝クジ買ったらスゴそう…
IN THIS VOLUME, HER LUCK BECOMES ALMOST UNBELIEVABLY GOOD (LAUGHS). IF SHE DECIDES TO PLAY THE LOTTERY...
チアガールなだけあってプロポーション抜群で、いつも笑顔を絶やしません。
WATCH OUT! SHE'S A CHEERLEADER, AND AS EXPECTED, SHE'S ALWAYS CHEERFUL...AND HAS A GREAT BODY!
（口をとじてることってあるんでしょうか…？）
(DOES SHE EVER CLOSE HER MOUTH?)

アニメCVは大前茜さん。絵の上手さはプロ級 吹き替えの出演も多い実力派なのです。（へ～）
THE VOICE ACTRESS FOR THE ANIME IS AKANE OOMAE. SHE'S AN EXCELLENT ARTIST—SHE COULD BE A PROFESSIONAL. SHE'S A TALENTED LADY WHO DOES A LOT OF VOICE-OVERS FOR FILM DUBS. (WOW)
ドラマ版は香山碧さん。セクシ～♡
AOI KAYAMA IS THE ACTRESS FOR THE DRAMA. SHE'S SEXY~
え…リネージュガールだったんですか？？ ネットゲームの話すればよかったな。
I DIDN'T KNOW SHE WAS A LINEGE GIRL. I SHOULD HAVE CHATTED ABOUT ONLINE GAMING WITH HER!

赤松
AKAMATSU

次の21巻はすごいですよ～!!
VOLUME 21 WILL BE EXCITING!!

Translation Notes

Japanese is a tricky language for most Westerners, and translation is often more an art than a science. For your edification and reading pleasure, here are notes on some of the places where we could have gone in a different direction or where a Japanese cultural reference is used.

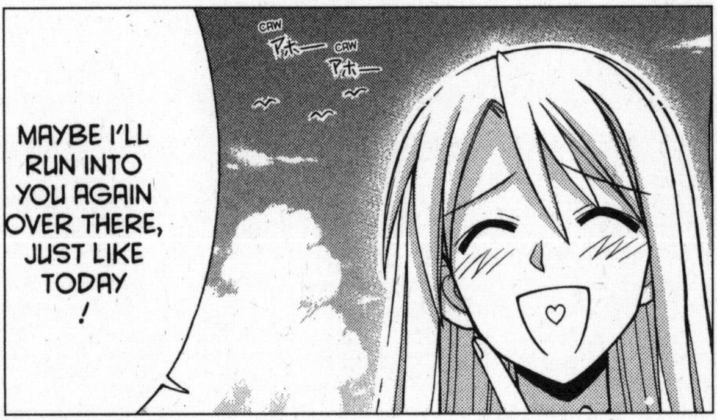
CAW
アホー
CAW
アホー
MAYBE I'LL RUN INTO YOU AGAIN OVER THERE, JUST LIKE TODAY!

Caw, page 11

The original Japanese says Ahō, which is a sound effect for a bird cawing as well as the word dummy in Japanese. In this case, it's a play on words.

Bourgeois, page 12

Bourgeois means "middle class." The word can also be used as a slight to describe something ordinary and commonplace.

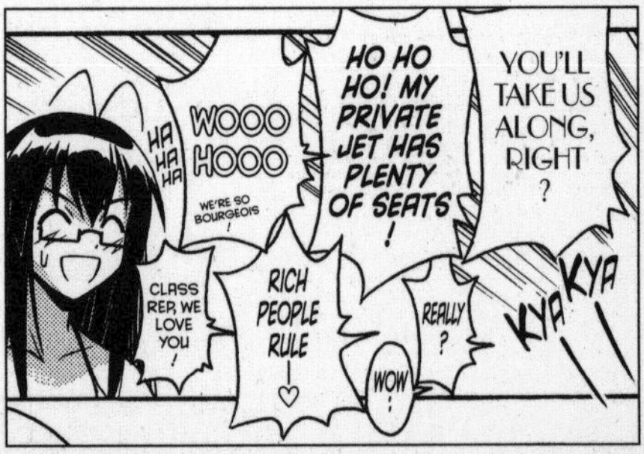
YOU'LL TAKE US ALONG, RIGHT?
HO HO HO! MY PRIVATE JET HAS PLENTY OF SEATS!
WOOO HOOO
HA HA HA
WE'RE SO BOURGEOIS!
KYA KYA
REALLY?
RICH PEOPLE RULE ♡
WOW!
CLASS REP, WE LOVE YOU!

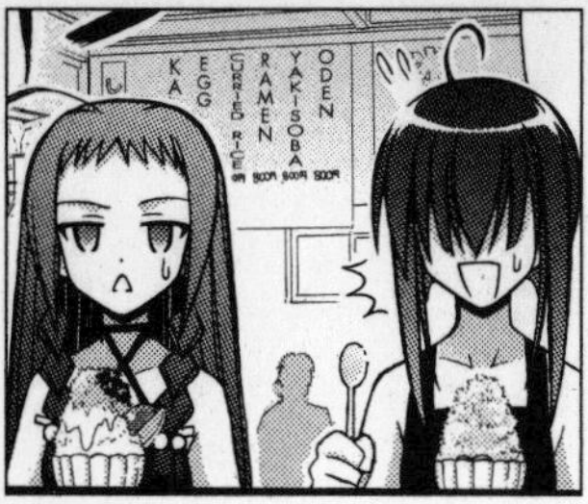
ODEN
YAKISOBA
RAMEN
CURRIED RICE
EGG
KA

Oden, page 15

Oden is a Japanese dish commonly available and consumed during the winter. Ingredients vary by home and region, but the basic ingredients consist of boiled eggs, various vegetables, and konjac jelly simmered in a light, fish and soy sauce-based broth.

Mount Osore, page 95

Mount Osore is located in Aomori Prefecture. Osore means "fear" in Japanese, and Mount Osore was considered the gateway to the underworld in Japanese mythology. The area is famous for the blind mediums who deliver messages from the dead called *itako.*

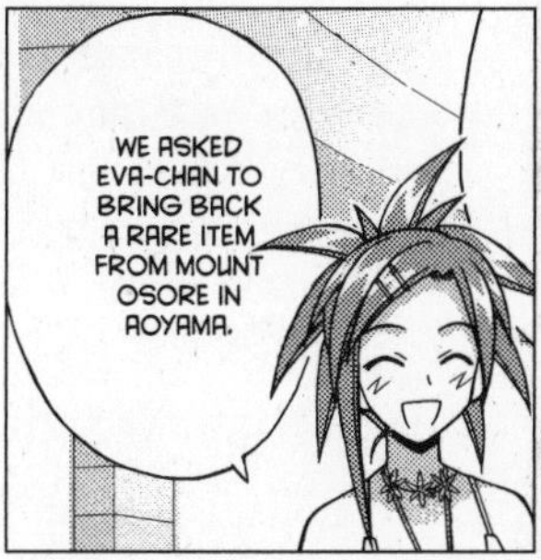
WE ASKED EVA-CHAN TO BRING BACK A RARE ITEM FROM MOUNT OSORE IN AOYAMA.

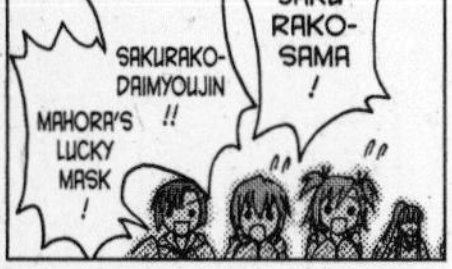
SAKU-RAKO-SAMA!
SAKURAKO-DAIMYOUJIN!!
MAHORA'S LUCKY MASK!

Daimyoujin, page 138

Daimyoujin, also spelled Daimyojin, is a title for Shinto demigods.

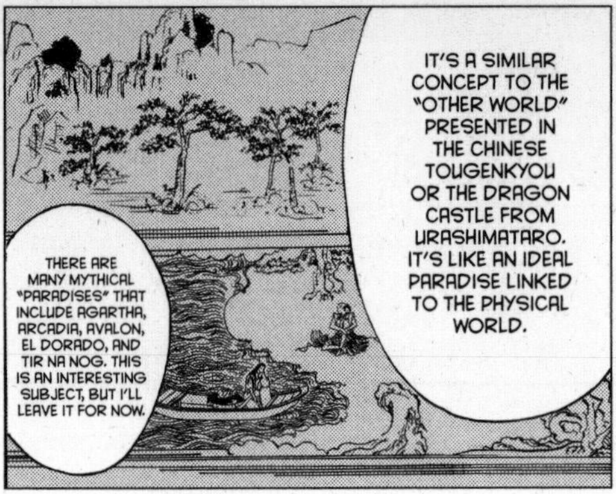
IT'S A SIMILAR CONCEPT TO THE "OTHER WORLD" PRESENTED IN THE CHINESE TOUGENKYOU OR THE DRAGON CASTLE FROM URASHIMATARO. IT'S LIKE AN IDEAL PARADISE LINKED TO THE PHYSICAL WORLD.
THERE ARE MANY MYTHICAL "PARADISES" THAT INCLUDE AGARTHA, ARCADIA, AVALON, EL DORADO, AND TIR NA NOG. THIS IS AN INTERESTING SUBJECT, BUT I'LL LEAVE IT FOR NOW.

Urashimataro, page 143

Urashimataro is the name of a hero of a Japanese fairy tale. He's a young fisherman who, when he saves a turtle, discovers that it's actually a magical being who whisks him away to an underwater paradise. Urashimataro spends three heavenly days there, but when he returns home, he is distressed to find out that a hundred years have passed in the human world.

Agartha, Arcadia, Avalon, El Dorado, Tir Na Nog, page 143

These are names of legendary cities taken from several world folklore traditions. Agartha is located in the Earth's core. Arcadia is the name for a utopian ideal of a pastoral paradise. Avalon and Tir Na Nog come from the folklore from the British Isles. El Dorado is the legendary "City of Gold" that Spanish conquistadors searched for in South America.

Tatami count, page 168

Japanese room sizes are often described by the number of tatamis (straw mats) that fit into the room.

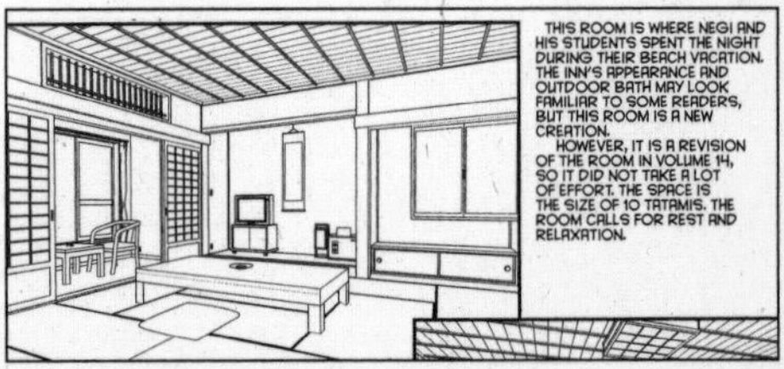
THIS ROOM IS WHERE NEGI AND HIS STUDENTS SPENT THE NIGHT DURING THEIR BEACH VACATION. THE INN'S APPEARANCE AND OUTDOOR BATH MAY LOOK FAMILIAR TO SOME READERS, BUT THIS ROOM IS A NEW CREATION.
HOWEVER, IT IS A REVISION OF THE ROOM IN VOLUME 14, SO IT DID NOT TAKE A LOT OF EFFORT. THE SPACE IS THE SIZE OF 10 TATAMIS. THE ROOM CALLS FOR REST AND RELAXATION.

About the Creator

Negima! is only Ken Akamatsu's third manga, although he started working in the field in 1994 with *AI Ga Tomaranai* (released in the United States with the title *A.I. Love You*). Like all of Akamatsu's work to date, it was published in Kodansha's *Shonen Magazine*. *AI Ga Tomaranai* ran for five years before concluding in 1999. In 1998, however, Akamatsu began the work that would make him one of the most popular manga artists in Japan: *Love Hina*. *Love Hina* ran for four years, and before its conclusion in 2002, it would cause Akamatsu to be granted the prestigious Manga of the Year award from Kodansha, as well as going on to become one of the best-selling manga in the United States.

Preview of *Negima!* Volume 21

We're pleased to present you with a preview of volume 21. Please check our website (www.delreymanga.com) to see when this volume will be available in English. For now you'll have to make do with Japanese!

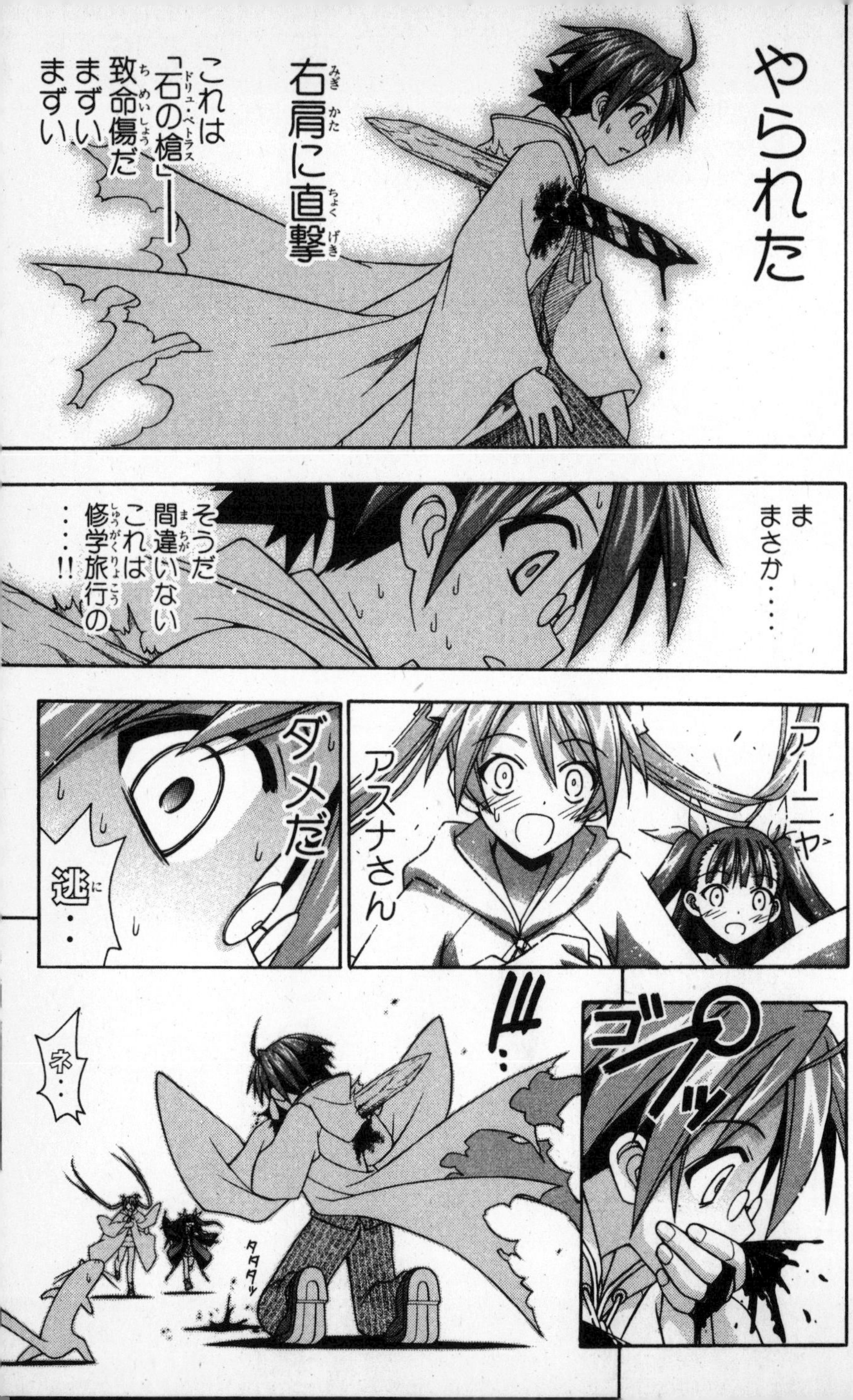

やられた
右肩に直撃
これは「石の槍」──
致命傷だ
まずい
まずい
ま
まさか・・・・
そうだ
間違いない
これは
修学旅行の
・・・・!!
アーニャ
アスナさん
ダメだ
逃・・
ゴパッ
ネ・・・
タタタッ

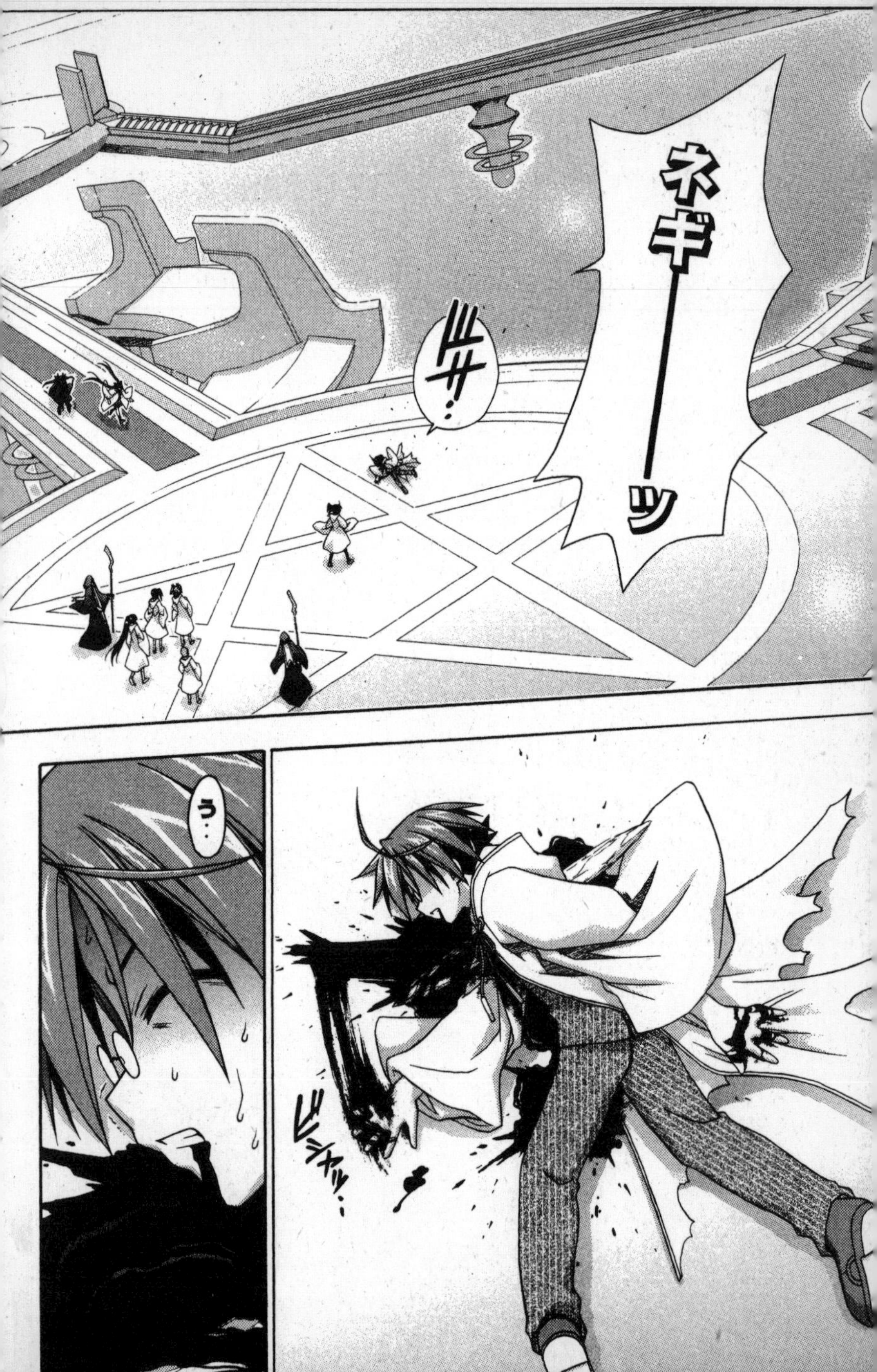
ネギーーッ
ザザ!
ビシャッ…
う…

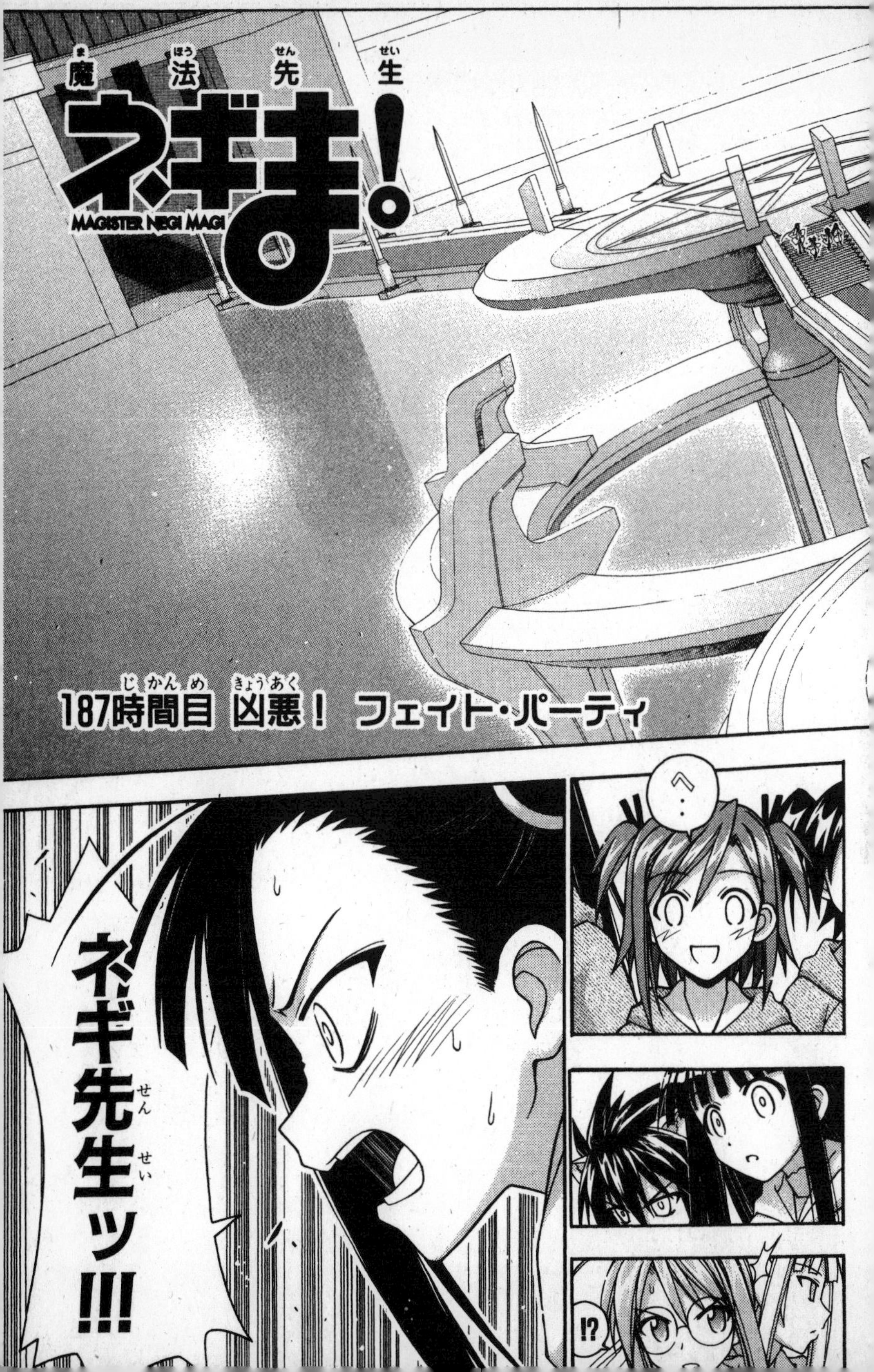
魔法先生
ネギま!
MAGISTER NEGI MAGI
187時間目 凶悪! フェイト・パーティ
へ…
!?
ネギ先生ッ!!!

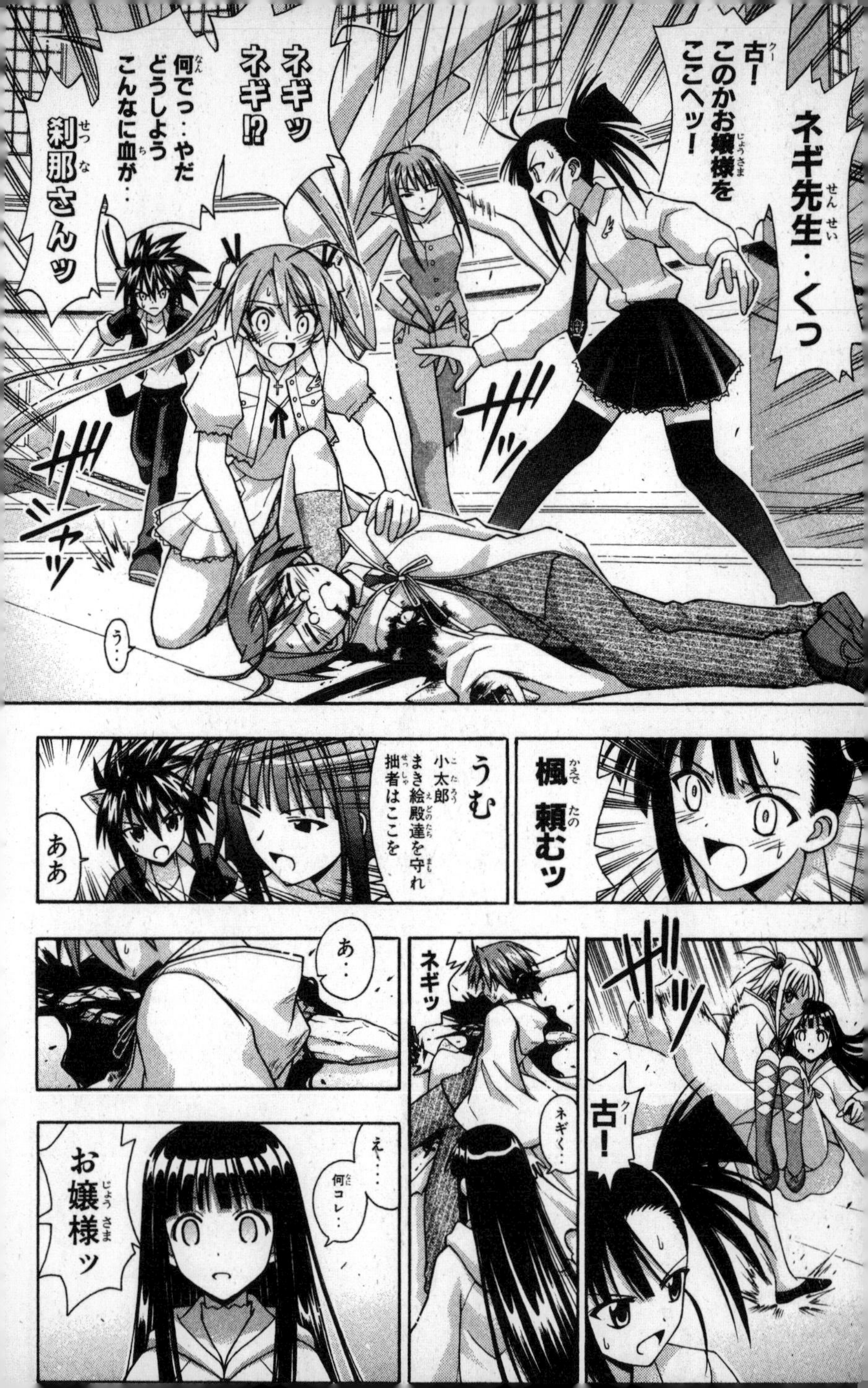
ネギ先生・・くっ
古！ このかお嬢様を ここへッ！
ネギッ ネギ!?
何でっ・・やだ どうしよう こんなに血が・・
刹那さんッ
ザザッ
ザザッ
シャッ
う・・
楓 頼むッ
うむ
小太郎 まき絵殿達を守れ 拙者はここを
ああ
ザザッ
古！
ネギッ
ネギく・・・
あ・・
え・・・・
何コレ・・
お嬢様ッ

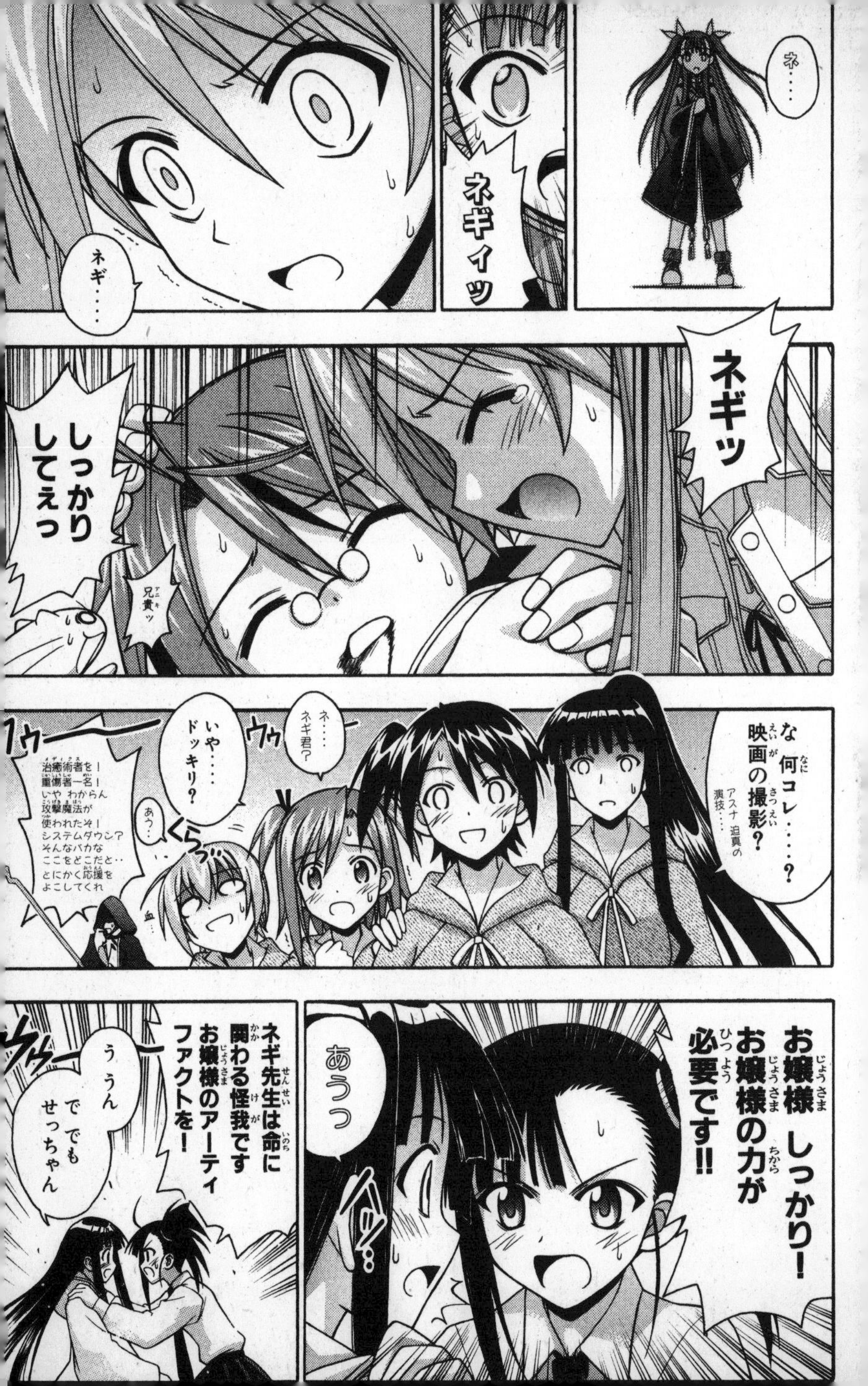
ネ・・・・
ネギイッ
ネギ・・・・・
ネギッ
しっかりしてえっ
兄貴ッ
な 何コレ・・・・・？
映画の撮影？
アスナ 迫真の演技・・・・
ネ・・・・ネギ君？
いや・・・・ドッキリ？
あう・・・
くらっ
血・・・
ウゥーー
治癒術者を！重傷者一名！いや わからん 攻撃魔法が使われたぞ！システムダウン？ そんなバカな ここをどこだと・・とにかく応援をよこしてくれ
ウゥーー
お嬢様 しっかり！お嬢様の力が必要です!!
あうっ
ネギ先生は命に関わる怪我です お嬢様のアーティファクトを！
う うん で でも せっちゃん

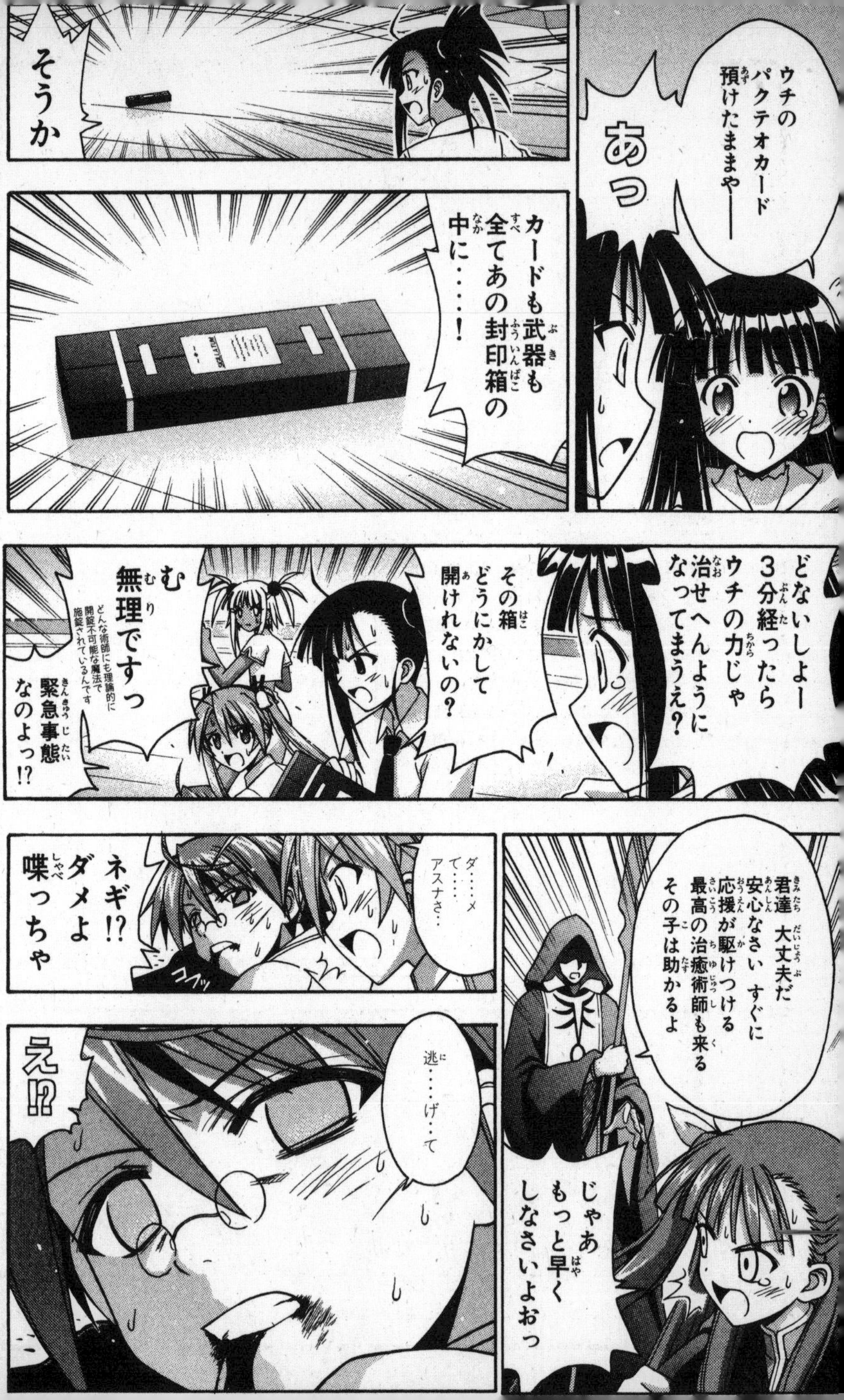
あっ
ウチのパクテオカード預けたままや――
そうか
カードも武器も全てあの封印箱の中に・・・・!
どないしよー3分経ったらウチの力じゃ治せへんようになってまうえ？
その箱どうにかして開けれないの？
む
無理ですっ
どんな術師にも理論的に開錠不可能な魔法で施錠されているんです
緊急事態なのよっ!?
君達 大丈夫だ 安心なさい すぐに応援が駆けつける 最高の治癒術師も来る その子は助かるよ
じゃあもっと早くしなさいよおっ
ダ・・・・メ て・・・・ アスナさ・・・
ネギ!? ダメよ喋っちゃ
コフッ
逃・・・・げ・・・て
え!?

STORY BY SURT LIM
ART BY HIROFUMI SUGIMOTO

A DEL REY MANGA ORIGINAL

Exploring the woods, young Kasumi encounters an ancient tree god, who bestows upon her the power of invisibility. Together with classmates who have had similar experiences, Kasumi forms the Magic Play Club, dedicated to using their powers for good while avoiding sinister forces that would exploit them.

Special extras in each volume! Read them all!

STORY BY KIO SHIMOKU
ART BY KOUME KEITO

FROM THE PAGES OF *GENSHIKEN*!

The Genshiken gang have long obsessed over a manga called *Kujibiki Unbalance,* the story of an average boy who becomes class president at a ritzy academy. Now *Kujibiki Unbalance* is a real-life manga for every fan's enjoyment!

• The eagerly awaited spin-off to the bestselling *Genshiken* series!

Special extras in each volume! Read them all!

VISIT WWW.DELREYMANGA.COM TO:
• Read sample pages
• View release date calendars for upcoming volumes
• Sign up for Del Rey's free manga e-newsletter
• Find out the latest about new Del Rey Manga series

RATING OT AGES 16+

DEL REY MANGA デルレイ
The Otaku's Choice.™
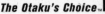

BY YUKO OSADA

SEE THE WORLD WITH ME!

Kakashi is a small-town boy with a big dream: to travel around the world. He's so determined to leave his little island home behind that he stows away onboard a marvelous zeppelin—one that just happens to be loaded with treasure and a gang of ruthless criminals!

Special extras in each volume! Read them all!

VISIT WWW.DELREYMANGA.COM TO:

- Read sample pages
- View release date calendars for upcoming volumes
- Sign up for Del Rey's free manga e-newsletter
- Find out the latest about new Del Rey Manga series

RATING | T AGES 13+

DEL REY MANGA デルレイ

The Otaku's Choice™

TOMARE!

[STOP!]

You're going the wrong way!

Manga is a completely different
type of reading experience.

To start at the *beginning,*
go to the *end!*

That's right! Authentic manga is read the traditional Japanese way—
from right to left, exactly the *opposite* of how American books are
read. It's easy to follow: Just go to the other end of the book, and read
each page—and each panel—from right side to left side, starting at
the top right. Now you're experiencing manga as it was meant to be.